EVERYDAY

BIBLICAL

LITERACY

The Essential Guide to Biblical
Allusions in Art, Literature, and Life

J. STEPHEN LANG

WRITER'S DIGEST BOOKS

www.writersdigest.com
Cincinnati, Ohio

11 10 09 08 07 5 4 3 2 1

Distributed in Canada by Fraser Direct
100 Armstrong Avenue
Georgetown, ON, Canada L7G 5S4
Tel: (905) 877-4411

Distributed in the U.K. and Europe by David & Charles
Brunel House, Newton Abbot, Devon, TQ12 4PU, England
Tel: (+44) 1626 323200, Fax: (+44) 1626 323319
E-mail: postmaster@davidandcharles.co.uk

Distributed in Australia by Capricorn Link
P.O. Box 704, Windsor, NSW 2756 Australia
Tel: (02) 4577-3555

Library of Congress Cataloging-in-Publication Data

Lang, J. Stephen.
  Everyday biblical literacy / J. Stephen Lang.
    p. cm.
  Includes index.
  ISBN-13: 978-1-58297-460-6 (hardcover : alk. paper)
  ISBN-10: 1-58297-460-8
  1. Bible--Dictionaries. I. Title.
  BS440.L36 2007
  220.3--dc22
                         2006034946

Editor: Amy Schell
Additional editorial assistance by: Rachel McDonald
Cover designed by: Grace Ring
Interior designed by: Grace Ring and Claudean Wheeler

CONTENTS

Foreword

In our culture, you can't get away from the Bible, even if you wanted to. Its ideas, phrases, people, and events are so embedded in our lives that even people who have never opened a Bible have some biblical images in their minds, without even knowing it. The 2006 remake of the horror film *The Omen* featured the sinister number 666 in the ads (as did the original movie of 1976). The number is found in one place in the Bible, the Book of Revelation, yet the songs, films, books, and TV shows that refer to the 666 and the evil "Beast" and Antichrist associated with the number are countless. In everyday speech, we refer to someone as being "old as Methuselah," of being a "Judas," of a man brawny as Samson or a woman wicked as Jezebel, of a "doubting Thomas." We talk of someone who doesn't "suffer fools gladly," of a dependable person who is the "salt of the earth," of doing a "labor of love," "practicing what you preach," "going the extra mile," and "risking our necks"—just a handful of phrases from the Bible.

Pop singer Bryan Adams recorded the song "Please Forgive Me (I Know Not What I Do)," echoing a statement of Jesus on the cross: "Father, forgive them; for they know not what they do." Years earlier, Billy Joel sang of "Keeping the Faith," probably not aware that the phrase (and idea) was from the New Testament, as is the related phrase "fight the good fight." Politicians for centuries have been warning of an "Armageddon," a site mentioned in Revelation as the scene of the ultimate battle between good and evil. Men (in the pre-feminist era, anyway) referred to women as "the weaker vessel," borrowing a phrase from the New Testament. Sometimes the borrowing isn't quite correct—for example, we all know the phrase "money is the root of all evil," but the actual words of the Bible are "the love of money is the root of all evil." Some words and images get twisted for the sake of advertising—for example, "fruit of the womb" (referring to someone's first-born child) somehow morphed into the brand name Fruit of the Loom. The British owe their familiar phrase "God save the king" (immortalized in their national anthem) to the Bible. A radio personality referred to Anna Nicole Smith as an "Abishag," which at least a few listeners knew referred to a young attractive woman who was brought in to "warm the bones" of King David in his old age—in other words, young babe and old codger sharing a bed.

So far we've mentioned only the more lighthearted cultural references to the Bible. Some are more serious—lethally so, in fact. Jews trace their ancestry to the patriarch Abraham in the Book of Genesis, believing this gives them the right to inhabit the nation of Israel. Arab Muslims also see themselves as descendants of Abraham (or *Ibrahim*, in the Koran), and believe *they* are his true heirs. They believe the Bible is incorrect when it says the land passed on to Abraham's son Isaac—rather, it passed to his other son, Ishmael, their ancestor. Obviously this dispute over which people have the right to the land is in the news every day—a long and very violent feud hinging on whether a story in the Book of Genesis is correct or not. Understanding a little about Abraham and his two sons can help us get a handle on the violence in the Middle East and elsewhere.

Understanding the Bible can also help you appreciate movies, literature, art, and music more. If you see a painting titled *The Transfiguration* (and there are thousands of them), you can appreciate the picture better if you know that the Transfiguration is an important scene in the Bible, where Jesus meets the long-dead Moses and Elijah. You can understand Christmas (and composer George Frideric Handel) better if you know just what the word *Messiah* means. You can appreciate a movie like *Raiders of the Lost Ark* better if you know a little more about the real ark in the Bible. You can learn why movies showing Jesus' crucifixion generate so much controversy if you know a little about the Jewish high priest Caiaphas (a rather rotten character, by the way). You can understand the mindset of Saddam Hussein if you know a little about the ancient Babylonian empire (something Saddam hoped to re-create). You can even look up Peter and learn why the thousands of jokes about someone dying and going to heaven always mention St. Peter standing at the gates.

The aim of this book is to give you a painless, entertaining education in the people, places, ideas, events, and phrases of the Bible. The entries are arranged alphabetically, and if you can't find what you're looking for in the alphabetical listing, the helpful cross references should steer you right. Some people—Jesus and Moses, for example—are so important that it takes several entries to cover them. Some people who are connected—brothers Cain and Abel, for example—are covered in the same entry. You can use the book as a reference tool, but you'll probably get more of your money's worth if you make it into a well-thumbed "browse book," something you keep at hand because you're always tempted to pick it up, open it at random, and read for pleasure. Useful information, useless information—it's all good.

PEOPLE, PLACES, AND THINGS

Aaron

The man with the twelve stones

Aaron has two claims to fame: the brother and right-hand man of Moses and also Israel's first high priest (and ancestor of its later priests). When God appeared to Moses in the burning bush and told him he would lead the Hebrews out of Egypt, Moses lamented that he was slow of speech, but God told him that his brother Aaron would be his "mouth" (meaning "spokesman"). Aaron (who was three years older) was at Moses' side during his many confrontations with Egypt's Pharaoh in the Book of Exodus. The staff Aaron carried was miraculously turned into a serpent, and when Egyptian magicians duplicated the miracle, Aaron's serpent devoured theirs (Exodus 7). Aaron was also at Moses' side when God sent the ten plagues on the Egyptians. Despite all the good things he did, Aaron was guilty of caving in to the Israelites' demand for an idol to worship while Moses was with God on Mount Sinai. It was Aaron who made the infamous golden calf, which Moses destroyed (Exodus 32). At one point both Aaron and their sister Miriam were guilty of sibling rivalry, and they angered God by their jealousy of Moses (Numbers 12). Both Moses and Aaron died before the Israelites entered the promised land of Canaan.

Aaron was made Israel's first high priest, and his priestly garb, including the "breastplate" with twelve stones (each one inscribed with the name of one of the tribes of Israel) is described in detail in Exodus 28, along with the priest's robe, turban, and sash. The stones symbolized that when the priest entered the the tabernacle of the congregation, he would bear the names of the sons of Israel over his heart.

Aaron may have been a worthy man, but his two worthless sons, Nadab and Abihu, were both destroyed by God for offering "strange fire," something Bible scholars still don't fully understand (Leviticus 10). As a result of their untimely deaths, Israel's priesthood was passed on not through Nadab and Abihu, but through Aaron's younger son, Eleazar.

Aaron stands in the shadow of his more impressive brother, Moses, who is called a "prophet" of God. The Israelites generally held prophets in higher esteem than priests (on the assumption that prophets were speaking the words God told them to speak). But in the centuries between the Old and New Testaments, when there were no prophets, the priests—the "sons of Aaron"—became more important. Many times the Old Testament speaks of "Moses and Aaron" in the same verse, so both were considered important figures. However, when the Romans destroyed the Jewish temple in the year 70 A.D., the priesthood ended forever, and descent from Aaron ceased to mean anything. The New Testament's Letter to the Hebrews states that no human priests like Aaron are needed because Jesus Christ, in heaven, is the high priest forever. Luke 1 mentions that Elizabeth, the mother of the prophet John the Baptist, was a descendant of Aaron.

Aaron is an important character in art and literature, often seen at Moses' side or, as in the infamous episode of the golden calf, leading the Israelites in idol worship while the angry Moses comes down from Mount Sinai bearing the Ten Commandments. In many artworks, Aaron is shown in the priestly garments described in the Bible. Many old Bibles, on the opening page of the Old Testament, showed both Moses and Aaron, symbolizing Israel's prophets and priests. Composer Arnold Schoenberg wrote an opera, *Moses und Aron*, which included the golden calf incident. Films about the Exodus, such as the famous 1956 epic *The Ten Commandments*, usually give Aaron a very minor role compared to Moses.

Numbers 17 says that Aaron's rod miraculously bloomed and produced almonds. Several blooming garden plants are known by the name "Aaron's rod." The name "Aaron's beard" is also given to several garden plants, following Psalm 133, which refers to precious oil running down Aaron's beard.

The *Aaronic benediction* is a blessing found in Numbers 6:24-26, and often quoted by both Jews and Christians: "The Lord bless you and keep you; the Lord make his face to shine upon you, and be gracious to you; the Lord lift up his countenance upon you, and give you peace." Many pastors use it in concluding a worship service.

Muslims honor Aaron—*Harun*—as one of the prophets.

Abaddon
Oh, hell

In the Book of Revelation, Abaddon is name of the angel of the bottomless pit—hell, that is (Revelation 9:11). In John Milton's poem *Paradise Lost*, he gives the name Abaddon to the pit itself. In his epic poem *The Messiah*, the German poet Friedrich Klopstock created a character named Abaddona, an angel who only half willingly follows Satan in his rebellion against God, and who lingers at the cross hoping for forgiveness.

Revelation also calls Abaddon by the name Apollyon, and in John Bunyan's *The Pilgrim's Progress*, Apollyon is a fierce demon. In the days of French emperor Napoleon, many of his enemies claimed his real name was N'Apollione and that he was the evil Apollyon of the Book of Revelation.

Abigail
Desperate housewife

Abigail was one of the wives of David, and the story of how they met is told in 1 Samuel 25. David and his men were living an outlaw existence in the wilderness. They asked for hospitality from a rich sheepherder named Nabal, but he behaved abominably to them. Abigail packed up mutton, bread, and wine and made her way to David, apologizing for her surly husband being a fool—after all, as she pointed out, "fool" is what Nabal means in Hebrew. The next day, while Nabal was nursing a hangover, Abigail told him what she had done. He was so chagrined that he died ten days later. David was so impressed with Abigail that he made her his wife.

Because Abigail introduced herself to David as "your servant," Abigail became a stock name in literature for any servant woman. The fact that she was described as "beautiful and intelligent" has also kept the name viable for girls, with Gail or Gale being variants of the full name.

Abishag

Platonic warmth

According to 1 Kings 1, when Israel's King David grew old, he could not keep warm. A beautiful young woman, Abishag, was brought in as a sort of "bed-warmer"—but with no sex involved (1 Kings 1). The name Abishag passed into the language as referring to a woman who marries a much older man, presumably with no sex involved. Catherine Howard, the fifth wife of England's King Henry VIII, was only a teenager when she married the ailing, middle-aged king, and people referred to her as "the king's Abishag." (Catherine found pleasure elsewhere—and got beheaded.)

After David's death, when his son Solomon became king, Abishag found herself caught up in palace politics. David's son Adonijah asked if he could have Abishag as a wife. Solomon saw this as a signal that Adonijah intended to make himself king in Solomon's place (which was true). Solomon had him killed.

Abner

Such violent times to live in

Abner was the cousin of Israel's king Saul and also commander of his armies. He brought the boy David to Saul after David killed the giant Goliath. Later, however, he accompanied Saul in his homicidal pursuit of David. After Saul's death, Abner had Saul's son Ish-bosheth made king of Israel. However, Ish-bosheth and Abner quarreled over possession of Saul's concubine, and Abner went over to David's side. Abner was later slain by Joab for having killed Joab's brother. The murder was treacherous, for Joab approached Abner in a friendly way, then stabbed him in the belly.

Abner, being short and pleasant-sounding, was a fairly common name for men, until the hillbilly comic strip "Li'l Abner" gave the name a "hick" connotation.

Abraham (Abram, Ibrahim)

Father of the (feuding) faithful

Abraham is considered the physical and spiritual ancestor of the Jews—and, as *Ibrahim*, of Muslims also. His story begins in Genesis 12. God calls him from the pagan city of Ur (the region that would later be called Babylonia and is today Iraq) to live in Canaan and become the father of a great nation. By leaving his homeland, Abraham would give up the worship of many gods and their idols and serve only the one true God.

God's promise of descendants seems to go unfulfilled, for Abraham's beloved wife Sarah remains childless. In desperation, Sarah gives her maid Hagar to Abraham as a concubine, and she bears Abraham the son Ishmael (whom the Arabs call *Ismail* and consider their ancestor). But this isn't the son God had promised. In the form of three visitors, God pays a call on Abraham and promises that in a while he will return, and this time, Sarah will be pregnant. Sarah overhears and laughs, and God hears her. The prophecy proves true, and Sarah bears Abraham the son Isaac (whose name means "laughter"). When this birth occurred, Sarah was ninety and Abraham one hundred. (The three visitors are sometimes called the "Old Testament Trinity." SEE PAGE 370.)

Abraham Receives God's Promise of a Son
GENESIS. CHAPTER 18, VERSES 1-10.

The three visitors also inform Abraham they are on their way to wicked Sodom to see if it is as bad as its reputation. If so, it will be destroyed. There is a famous "bargaining" session, in which Abraham asks God if he will destroy Sodom if there are a certain number of righteous people in it. As it turns out, there aren't very many righteous people there at all, only Abraham's nephew Lot, who flees the doomed city with his wife and two daughters. (Lot's wife is the one who looks back and turns into a pillar of salt.)

The practice of circumcision among the Jews is attributed to Abraham. In Genesis 17, God tells him to circumcise each male child when it is eight days old.

(Presumably, Abraham himself and all the adult males in his household had to be circumcised as well.) Several of the nations around Israel practiced circumcision, but Abraham and his descendants saw it as having a spiritual significance, a reminder that God had made a lasting covenant with Abraham.

One of the key events in Abraham's story is the near sacrifice of his beloved son Isaac. (SEE PAGE 157 for that fascinating (and frightening) incident.)

Abraham underwent a name change, as ordered by God. His original name was Abram, meaning "exalted father," but God changed it to Abraham, "father of a multitude" (Genesis 17:5). He also changed his wife's name from Sarai (unknown meaning) to Sarah, meaning "princess."

One important incident in Abraham's saga was his meeting with the priest-king Melchizedek. (SEE PAGE 240 for more about him.)

Although the nation Israel took its name from the alternate name for Jacob, Abraham's grandson, the people of Israel saw themselves as "Abraham's seed." They were the "children of Abraham" not only in the physical sense, but also spiritually, worshipping the one God who gave Abraham the land of Canaan to possess. Centuries after Abraham died, the Book of Exodus records the plight of the Hebrew slaves in Egypt: "God heard their groaning, and God remembered his covenant with Abraham, with Isaac, and with Jacob" (Exodus 2:24). When God revealed himself to Moses in the burning bush, he said, "I am the God of thy father, the God of Abraham, the God of Isaac, and the God of Jacob" (Exodus 3:6). Given all the gods in the ancient world, Moses had to be told that this God in the burning bush was the God that had made a covenant with his ancestor Abraham. Isaiah the prophet has God speaking of "the seed of Abraham, my friend" (Isaiah 41:8). Many prayers in the Old Testament are addressed to the "God of Abraham, Isaac, and Jacob."

In the New Testament period, Abraham was still held in high regard, which is why Matthew's genealogy traces Jesus all the way back to Abraham, showing that Jesus was a genuine descendant of the Jews' ancestor. However, Jesus and the apostles had a different attitude about being descended from Abraham: they held him in high regard, but they did not believe that being his physical descendants was enough, spiritually speaking. In fact, Jesus jarred his listeners by telling them that he himself existed before Abraham did (John 8:58). In many of his epistles, Paul, the apostle to the Gentiles (non-Jews), drove the point home again and again: having faith like Abraham's was what counted, not being his biological descendants. For Paul, Abraham was the great role model of trusting in God:

"Abraham believed God, and it was accounted to him for righteousness" (Galatians 3:6). The same thought is found in the Letter to James: "Abraham believed God, and it was credited to him as righteousness: and he was called the Friend of God" (James 2:23). No other person in the Bible is called "God's friend." Abraham is mentioned seventy times in the New Testament, more than any other Old Testament character except for Moses.

In one of his parables, Jesus referred to a man dying and being taken to "Abraham's bosom" (Luke 16:22). Jews had come to believe that Abraham was, of course, in heaven, and going to heaven meant being near the great man of faith. The expression "Abraham's bosom" became a synonym for heaven, and it is found in many hymns, notably the old spiritual "Rock-a My Soul in the Bosom of Abraham."

Jews still honor Abraham (called the *hanif*, the "rightly guided one"), and among devout Muslims, *Ibrahim* is a common name for a male child. The name has been less common among Christians, possibly because some Christians see it as a "Jewish name." (The name got a new lease on life after a U.S. president bore the name.) Based on the Koran, Ibrahim is regarded as the first true Muslim, and Muslims believe that Ibrahim and his son Ismail (Ishmael) built the famous Ka'ba shrine in Mecca, Saudi Arabia. Muhammad taught that his religion, Islam, was really only a continuation of the religion of Ibrahim—a religion the Jews had distorted. For Muhammad, the true followers of Ibrahim were Muslims, not Jews. The long, violent history of Jew versus Muslim is rooted in the two groups both claiming descent from Abraham, and claiming rights to the land that came to be called Israel. In Muslim legend, the ram that Abraham found after his near-sacrifice of Isaac is one of the ten animals in heaven. Muslims also believe that the highest heaven, the seventh, is ruled by Ibrahim.

Abraham is an admirable character in many ways, but aside from the near sacrifice of his son Isaac, his story has not appealed much to artists and authors. Few movies have dealt with him, although the popular 1966 film *The Bible … In the Beginning*, told his tale from its beginning in Genesis 12 through the sacrifice of Isaac in Genesis 22, including the story of Sodom and Gomorrah. Artists have depicted Abraham in many paintings, the favorite being the near sacrifice of Isaac.

Mormon founder Joseph Smith published a brief (and very strange) Book of Abraham, which he claimed was written by Abraham himself and later hidden in "the catacombs" of Egypt.

The ancient city of Hebron in Israel is the location of the cave that, tradition says, is the burial place of Abraham and Sarah.

Absalom, Amnon, and Tamar

The disaster of the blended family

Israel's king David may have been a "man after God's own heart" (1 Samuel 13:14), but he wasn't perfect, and he certainly was not successful in keeping his large brood of children in line. It was inevitable that a household of brothers and sisters by different mothers would have some problems. David's oldest son Amnon would probably have been heir to the throne—if he had lived. But he began lusting after his beautiful and virtuous half-sister, Tamar. A roguish friend of Amnon had a plan: play sick and ask Tamar to comfort him. She did, even doing some baking for him, but then he sprung the trap: "Come lie with me, my sister" (2 Samuel 13:11). She wouldn't do so willingly, so he raped her, then his lust turned immediately to hate: "Arise, be gone!" In the eyes of the ancient world, Tamar was "damaged goods," even though it was all Amnon's fault.

But Tamar had someone watching out for her—not her father, but her full brother, Absalom. He took Tamar into his own home and took his time hatching a plot to avenge her rape. He and some friends got Amnon drunk and murdered him. By law, Absalom could have been executed for this, but David showed mercy and sent him into exile for three years.

Absalom repaid his father's mercy by plotting to take the throne himself. He was David's favorite son, handsome and charismatic. The Bible says that when his thick mane of hair was cut, the clippings weighed five pounds (2 Samuel 14:26). Living in exile, he gathered around him everyone who had some kind of grievance against the government (that is, against his father, the king). Ahitophel, a former counselor of David, went over to Absalom's side and helped him plot to take over the throne. At one point, David and the court had to flee Jerusalem. Absalom showed his contempt for his father in a crudely unforgettable way: He pitched a tent on the roof of the palace and had sex with David's concubines, with people watching (2 Samuel 16:20-23).

But David still had some loyal subjects. The faithful warrior Joab found Absalom in a wonderful pose: as he was riding his mule, he passed under a tree and got his head caught in the branches, while the mule walked on. Joab was elated: the king's treasonous son was dangling in the air. Joab killed him with three spears through the heart.

If he expected the king's gratitude, he did not get it. He may have saved David's life, but David went into deep mourning, with his famous lament found in 2 Samuel 18:33, NIV: "O my son Absalom! My son, my son Absalom! If only I had died instead of you—O Absalom, my son, my son!" Joab gave the king a harsh scolding, reminding him that he had saved his life by killing Absalom. Absalom's was not the only death: Ahitophel, the counselor who had deserted David for Absalom, committed suicide by hanging, one of the few suicides mentioned in the Bible.

Rape, murder, treason, suicide—David's family seemed to be fulfilling the prophecy of Nathan, who told David that because of his adultery with Bathsheba (and murder of her husband), the sword would never depart from David's house (2 Samuel 12:10).

This seems like a sordid story, and it definitely is. In the ancient world, where men of wealth had children by various wives and concubines, it probably wasn't rare for half-siblings to be having sex (willingly or not) and plotting against each other. The whole trashy saga is a good argument against polygamy. The Bible is to be commended for showing the great King David's family "warts and all."

One of the great works of English literature based on this part of David's life is *Absalom and Achitophel*, a long poem by John Dryden, published in 1681. The story of David and Absalom had parallels to the contemporary story of King Charles II and the threat of a rebellion by the young duke of Monmouth, one of his illegitimate sons. Dryden's political satire retold the biblical story in such a way that people knew he was referring to recent events, not just the events in the Bible.

American novelist William Faulkner titled one of his novels *Absalom, Absalom!*, borrowing it from David's lament in 2 Samuel 18:33. The story takes place in the Civil War South, but the plot is loosely based on the story of David and Absalom. Italian composer Domenico Cimarosa wrote a 1782 oratorio about Absalom.

The 1985 film *King David* depicted some of the incidents of the Absalom saga, though it omitted the actual rape of Tamar.

Acts
Luke's amazing sequel

The Book of Acts follows the four Gospels in the New Testament and continues the story of Jesus' apostles. It was written by Luke, author of the third Gospel. Luke was a traveling companion of the apostle Paul, and some of the late sections of Acts are known as the "we passages" because Luke narrates in the first person, letting readers know he was an eyewitness of the events he is telling. Acts opens with Jesus' ascension into heaven, followed by the story of Pentecost, when the apostles were filled with the Holy Spirit and began preaching and healing with great power. As Jesus predicted, the apostles are persecuted, with some thrown in prison and one (James) executed. The book tells of the stoning of the saintly Stephen in Jerusalem and the apostle Peter converting the Roman soldier Cornelius. Much of the book is devoted to the apostle Paul, a zealous Jew who persecuted Christians, then was dramatically converted to Christianity himself. The later chapters of Acts tell of Paul's missionary travels, involving preaching, persecution (including scourging and several attempts to kill him), encounters with magicians and pagan philosophers, a riot in Jerusalem, and Paul being taking to Rome for trial, a journey that involved a shipwreck. At the end of the book, Paul is witnessing to the faith in Rome, where he is under house arrest.

Acts is one of the most interesting books in the Bible, full of dramatic stories, and without it we would be in the dark about the history of the early Christians. Luke addressed the book to a certain Theophilus, who may have been an actual person, but since the name means "one who loves God," Luke may have intended the book for anyone who loves God. As in his Gospel, Luke was writing primarily for Gentile (non-Jewish) readers.

Incidentally, although the book is often called "the Acts of the Apostles," its original title in Greek was simply *Praxeis*, "acts" or "deeds." Several of the important people in the book, such as Stephen, were not apostles.

In the 1500s, English composer Christopher Tye set much of the Book of Acts to music in his *Acts of the Apostles*. The Book of Acts formed part of the subject matter of the 1981 TV mini-series A.D.

Adam and Eve

Humankind, square one

It won't surprise you that the Hebrew word *adam* means simply "man" or "humankind." The first man in the Bible (and the world) was not only an individual, but also the representative and prototype of the entire human race. When Adam disobeyed God and was driven out of Eden, the whole human race was being represented—that is, every person disobeys God, which is why life on earth is so difficult. Presumably if the two had not disobeyed, they would have lived forever in Eden.

Made from the dust of the ground, the man came to life when God breathed his spirit into him. He had the company of the animals, but there was no suitable companion for him, so God put him into a deep sleep, took one of his ribs, and fashioned for him Eve, the first woman. The two live in the garden of Eden, where they are told to tend the garden, and where they have everything they need. They may eat from any tree in the garden, except for the tree of knowledge of good and evil. If they eat its fruit, God says, they will die. The two are "naked and unashamed"—temporarily, anyway.

The Fall of Man
GENESIS. CHAPTER 3, VERSES 1-6.

The crafty snake (or serpent, depending on the translation) tells Eve that they will not die if they eat the forbidden fruit—rather, they will become like gods themselves. Eve eats the fruit, then gives some to Adam—and suddenly they are ashamed of being naked, so they cover themselves with fig leaves. They hide themselves from God, who asks them why they ate the fruit of the tree. Adam has an excuse: the woman gave him the fruit. Eve has an excuse also: the snake tempted her. God curses the snake and says it will crawl on its belly and be trampled on by human beings. Eve is cursed with the pain of childbirth and being dominated by her husband. Adam is cursed with having to labor for his food. God clothes the two in animal skins and drives them out of the garden, placing a flaming sword at the gate so they can never return. The couple's disobedience is often called the Fall of Man, or simply the Fall. Their disobedience is also called "original sin," with "original" meaning "from the origin." The idea that the original sin was sex isn't true; although it is true that Adam and Eve don't produce any children until after they leave the garden.

Eve bears the first son, Cain, then Abel, and Cain murders Abel out of jealousy. Then Eve bears Seth. Adam lives to the ripe age of 930 years, fathering many other sons and daughters before his death.

Their familiar story is found in Genesis 1-4. Oddly, the first couple on earth is barely mentioned again in the Old Testament. One passing mention is the beginning of

1 Chronicles, which traces King David's family tree all the way back to Adam. But in the New Testament, Adam is mentioned several times, notably in Paul's letters, where the disobedient Adam is contrasted with the obedient Jesus Christ, who is a "second Adam," resisting temptation and giving people eternal life while the first Adam brought them death (1 Corinthians 15:21-22). Thanks to Paul, Christians have often spoken of "the old Adam" or "the offending Adam," contrasting him with Christ.

Genesis 1:27 says that mankind was made "in the image of God." Theologians have been debating for centuries over just what the "image" means. It definitely doesn't refer to the physical body, but probably refers to man having a personality something like God's.

Theologians have also argued about just why God allowed Adam and Eve to disobey—and why he made one tree in Eden off-limits. One obvious reason: he gave human beings free will, including the power to disobey and do evil. Adam and Eve failed the test. They ate the fruit because the snake told them it would make them "like gods"—but instead it destroyed the bliss they had.

Genesis does not actually say that the snake in the garden was Satan, but by the time of Jesus, most Jews believed that Satan had assumed the form of a snake in order to lead Adam and Eve into sinning.

While the Bible's story of Adam and Eve is short, a huge body of legend has grown up around them. In Jewish legend, Adam's first wife was Lilith, who abandoned him and became an evil spirit. In Arabic legend, Lilith bore all the other evil spirits with the devil. Some people have thought that only the Jews were descended from Adam and that the other people of the world were descended from "pre-Adamite" humans.

Various religious sects have called themselves Adamites, who generally have been nudists. In fact, nudists in general point to Genesis and claim that it was God's intention for people to live naked. In the Bahai religion, Adam is the first of a line of prophets that also includes Moses and Jesus (but also Krishna, Buddha, and other figures from different religions).

Adam and Eve have fascinated authors throughout the centuries, the most famous being English poet John Milton, whose great epic poem *Paradise Lost* shows man's fall into sin, coupled with the story of how Satan and his demon followers were thrown out of heaven. On the lighter side, Mark Twain's *Diary of Adam and Eve* is intended for laughs. Twain's *Letters from the Earth* tells the story of the temptation from the viewpoint of Satan. Poet Archibald MacLeish wrote *Songs for Eve*, claiming that the fall of man was a fall *up*, not down, since man became independent. His play *Nobodaddy* retells the story of Adam, Eve, Cain, and Abel. Southern author Roark Bradford published *Ol' Man Adam an' His Chillun*, retelling Old Testament stories in the dialect of black slaves. The stories were the basis of the popular play and film *The Green Pastures*.

Artists have loved to depict Adam and Eve in Eden, partly because it gives them an excuse to paint nude bodies, but also because they can get creative with depicting the serpent and the tree of knowledge. Since the snake was cursed to crawl on its belly after it tempted Adam and Eve, artists have sometimes depicted the snake as a reptile walking upright. The serpent painted by Michelangelo on the Sistine Chapel ceiling has a humanlike torso ending in a serpentine tail. Thanks to Michelangelo, the image of Adam on the Sistine ceiling is one of the most famous art images in the world. Adam is nude, young, and beardless, and he stretches one hand toward the muscular, gray-bearded God, with their index fingers not quite touching.

Adam and Eve have seldom been depicted in motion pictures (the nudity creating an obvious obstacle), though the story was well handled in the 1966 film *The Bible ... In the Beginning*. Numerous films and TV comedies have done spoofing versions of the story, of course. Composer Franz Joseph Haydn's oratorio *The Creation* is based on Genesis and on *Paradise Lost*.

Adam's name appears in many popular phrases, such as "old as Adam," "wouldn't know him from Adam," "Adam's ale" (water), "Adam's profession" (gardening), etc. Incidentally, Genesis does *not* say that the forbidden fruit in Eden was an apple. We don't know what kind of fruit it was, although in Muslim legends the fruit was a fig—or banana.

The island of Sri Lanka (Ceylon) has a high mountain called Adam's Peak, and on the summit is a large impression said to be the footprint of Adam, according to Muslims, although Hindus say it is the footprint of their god Shiva, and Buddhists say it is the print of Buddha. All three religions regard the place as sacred, although Christians and Jews do not.

Ahab

Bad government personified

If you read 1 and 2 Kings in the Bible, you get the impression that most of the kings were pretty rotten characters. Some, however, stand out for being more rotten than the rest, and one of these was Ahab, who "did evil in the sight of the Lord, more than all who were before him" (1 Kings 16:30, NIV). Ahab's wife was Jezebel (SEE PAGE 180), who was a devotee of the god Baal and who hoped to supplant the worship of Israel's God. Ahab went along with her idolatry, but both king and queen met their match in the prophet Elijah, who went to Ahab to predict a drought of many years as punishment for Ahab's wickedness (1 Kings 17:1). Ahab called Elijah "the troubler of Israel," but Elijah replied that Ahab was the real troubler, since he didn't live according to God's laws. Elijah and the pagan prophets faced off in a showdown on Mount Carmel (1 Kings 18), in which Elijah and his God won the day, and the pagan prophets were all killed. Following this, the drought ended, and Elijah, charged by the Spirit, outran the chariot of Ahab back to the capital.

In our pluralistic, multi-cultural society, we may cut Ahab and Jezebel some slack, figuring that if they wanted to worship Baal, fine. But Ahab and his wife didn't seem to have much respect for private property. You might say they had a very broad concept of "eminent domain." Ahab wanted to purchase a vineyard near his palace, but its owner, Naboth, refused to sell his ancestral land. Ahab went into a deep sulk. Jezebel taunted him, "Just who's in charge here anyway?" She devised a plot: two rogues accused Naboth of blaspheming God and plotting treason against the king. He was stoned to death, and Ahab took his land. When Ahab went to survey his new acquisition, Elijah met him and foretold doom for Ahab and his family (1 Kings 21). Elijah shared the feeling of all other Israelites that kings were not tyrants and could not do whatever they wished, including the seizing of private property. Elijah went into detail about the deaths that would occur: Jezebel would be eaten by dogs. Ahab had enough fear of the prophet that he repented—for a while—so God relented—for a while. But Elijah's predictions did come true in time (SEE PAGE 180).

During his twenty-two-year reign, Ahab was at war with Syria. He decided to join forces with Jehoshaphat, the king of Judah. Before setting out for battle, Jehoshophat suggested they consult a prophet of God. Ahab's court prophets were all "yes men," so whatever Ahab decided to do, they agreed with. But the prophet Micaiah was a true-blue prophet, and Jehoshaphat asked that he be summoned. At first Micaiah said to Ahab, "Go forth into battle." Ahab sensed sarcasm, so he insisted Micaiah speak the truth. Micaiah predicted—correctly—that Ahab would not come back alive. For speaking the truth, Ahab had him thrown in prison and put on bread and water rations. In the battle that followed, Ahab was killed by an arrow. When his chariot with his body returned to the capital, the dogs licked up his blood, as Elijah had prophesied.

Ahab and Jezebel had some equally wicked children. One was the next king of Israel, Ahazaiah, and another was their daughter, Athaliah, who married the king of Judah and eventually ruled there herself (SEE PAGE 38). In the course of time, all of Ahab's idol-worshipping family were exterminated by Jehu (SEE PAGE 169).

There were plenty of bad kings in the Old Testament period, but Ahab symbolized the rottenness of them all—idol-worshipping, tyrannical, etc.

Needless to say, Ahab has not been a name anyone wished to bestow on a child. However, in Herman Melville's novel *Moby-Dick*, the maniacal captain of the whaling ship is named Ahab, and he is probably more famous than the biblical king for whom he is named.

Amen
The biblical "Yes!"

The Hebrew word *amen* simply means "so be it" or "yes, indeed." Jews and Christians have used the word as the Bible uses it, as a way of ending a prayer. Jesus prefaced some of his sayings with "Amen, amen, I say to you ..." which most English versions have as "Truly, truly, I say to you ..." In churches with an informal style of worship, people sometimes shout "Amen!" when they agree with something in the pastor's sermon.

Amos
Sheep farmer with a social conscience

The Book of Amos is third among the twelve so-called Minor Prophets in the Old Testament ("minor" because their books are briefer than the "major" prophets). Amos is considered the "prophet of justice" because he spoke out boldly against the rich taking advantage of the poor. His brief book has several often-quoted phrases, such as "they sell the righteous for silver, and the poor for a pair of shoes" (Amos 2:6, NIV) and "let justice roll down like waters, and righteousness like an ever-flowing stream" (Amos 5:24). He spoke out against those who "that pant after the dust of the earth on the head of the poor and turn aside the way of the meek" (Amos 2:7). Amos, like many other prophets, spoke out against people paying lip service to their religion while having no love for their fellow man, and in his book, God says, "I despise your feasts and take no delight in your solemn assemblies" (Amos 5:21). He speaks out against those "at ease in Zion," thinking they are spiritually and physically secure when doom awaits them because of their injustice and contempt for the poor. Though he was only a sheep farmer, he was courageous enough to stand up to the priest Amaziah. Amos predicted, correctly, that the kingdom of Israel would be conquered and its people scattered (Amos 7:11). But like other prophets, his warnings were tempered with a call to repentance: "Seek good and not evil, that you may live" (Amos 5:14). The Eastern Orthodox churches observe June 15 as the feast of the Holy Prophet Amos.

Ananias and Sapphira
Lethal transaction

One of the most disturbing stories in the Bible is found in Acts 5, which tells of Ananias and Sapphira, a married couple in Jerusalem. The two became Christians, and they sold some land and donated the money to the apostles—but kept part of it for themselves. Peter, the chief apostle, scolded Ananias for lying about the money and saying it was the full price for the property. Ananias dropped stone dead at Peter's words. Later, Sapphira came to Peter (not knowing her husband had died) and also lied about the amount of the money. Peter told her of her husband's fate, and she too dropped stone dead. "And great fear came upon all the church, and upon as many as heard these things" (Acts 5:11).

The story strikes many readers as cruel, even though Acts does not say that Peter caused the two deaths, or that God did. Presumably Ananias and Sapphira died of shame, although their deaths were interpreted as a warning against trying to lie to God—or the apostles. The sin was not in keeping some of the money for themselves, but in trying to appear more generous than they really were—in other words, they were serious hypocrites.

The death of the two has been frequently depicted in artworks, partly because it sends the message that people should not think that they can get away with lying to God—or to the church authorities.

Andrew

From Jewish fisherman to golf ...

The apostle Andrew stands in the shadow of his more famous brother, Simon Peter. But in fact, Andrew (a fisherman, like Peter) was the first disciple Jesus called to follow him. He must have been a religious fellow because he had earlier been a disciple of Jesus' kinsman, John the Baptist. He brought some curious Greeks to meet with Jesus, but otherwise we know little about him, except he was apparently not part of the "inner circle" of the disciples that included Peter, James, and John.

Although not terribly important in the Bible, Andrew is claimed as a patron saint of three different countries: Greece, Russia, and Scotland. An old tradition does connect him with missionary activity in Greece, and he was supposedly crucified there on an X-shaped cross, which explains why that form of cross is known as the "St. Andrew's cross." Why Russia claims him as patron saint is a puzzle. An old tradition in Scotland says that his relics were brought there in the fourth century, and the town of St. Andrews (now famous for its golf course) is named for him. For many years the head of the Scottish church was headquartered at St. Andrews. The Scottish national flag is a white St. Andrew's cross on a blue field, which later became part of the United Kingdom's national flag, the "Union Jack."

Centuries ago, Andrew's preserved head was taken from Constantinople to Rome, where the Vatican kept it. It was returned—after five hundred years—by Pope Paul VI in 1964. The Catholic churches and Eastern Orthodox churches observe November 30 as the Feast of St. Andrew The Apostle. Along with his brother Peter, Andrew has been considered the patron saint of fishermen.

angels

Mostly wingless

Our word angel comes from the Greek *angelos* which simply means "messenger." In the Old Testament, the word is *malakh*, which means (surprise!) "messenger." Either word can refer to a human messenger, so you have to judge by the context whether a particular "angel" is human or divine. Apparently, some of the angels in the Bible appeared so human that they went mostly unnoticed by the humans they visited. In the Book of Judges, the military leader Gideon talks with an angel and does not know it until the angel sets a rock on fire (Judges 6). Later in Judges, however, Samson's parents are quite aware that an angel has visited them: "Then the woman came and told her husband, saying, A man of God came unto me, and his countenance was like the countenance of an angel of God, very terrible: but I asked him not whence he was, neither told he me his name" (Judges 13:6). Later the same angel makes a striking exit: "It came to pass, when the flame went up toward heaven from off the altar, that the angel of the Lord ascended in the flame of the altar. And Manoah and his wife looked on it, and fell on their faces to the ground" (Judges 13:20).

Two things important to remember: the angels encountered in the Bible are always *adult* figures, nothing like the adorable child moppets you're used to seeing on greeting cards. The other thing is that they are not mentioned as having wings, except for the beings called cherubim and seraphim (SEE PAGES 66, 334). The angels in the Bible are nameless, with the exception of Michael, referred to as an "archangel" (meaning "ruling angel") and Gabriel, who is connected with the story of Mary and the virgin birth.

Although the Old Testament says nothing about bad angels who rebelled against God, people certainly believed it in the New Testament period, as seen in 2 Peter 2:4: "God did not spare angels who sinned, but sent them to hell." The early Christians believed that Satan and the demons had once been good angels, but rebelled against the rule of God. The Book of Revelation says that at the end of time, Michael and the good angels will finally defeat Satan and the wicked angels (Revelation 12:9).

Throughout the Bible, God is frequently referred to as "the Lord of Hosts"— "hosts" meaning "armies." The assumption was that though he was all-powerful, he still had entire armies of beings to do his bidding. Angels are God's court, also his soldiers and servants. Angels are mentioned frequently in the New Testament: announcing Jesus' conception to Mary, announcing his birth to the shepherds, ministering to Jesus following his temptation, etc. According to Matthew's Gospel, an angel rolled away the stone from Jesus' tomb. In the Book of Acts, an angel delivers the apostle Peter from prison. The most "angelic" book in the Bible is Revelation, which mentions them more than seventy times. In fact, the book opens with the statement that it was delivered to the author, John, by an angel. Revelation also depicts four "living creatures" with six wings and "full of eyes around and within"

(Revelation 4:8). The four praise God continually around his throne. The Letter to the Hebrews, however, contains these words: "Be not forgetful to entertain strangers, for thereby some have entertained angels unawares" (Hebrews 13:2). The early Christians recalled that God's angels could sometimes be walking about in human guise.

Despite the fact that angels in the Bible aren't described as winged, they are almost always shown that way in art. Apparently the idea was that messengers from God had to be capable of flight, plus the wings help distinguish the angels from the humans in any picture. Some artists took the wings a step further and showed angels in robes made of feathers. While they are almost always depicted as male (and in the Bible, always referred to as male), they are almost always beardless and young-looking. In a time when most men wore beards, making angels beardless was probably a way of making them appear otherworldly. The rich robes worn by many angels in paintings are probably rooted in the idea that they are members of God's "court" and must be dressed appropriately. Michelangelo, one of the greatest artists ever, broke from the usual and showed his angels wingless. In the Renaissance period, child angels became popular in art, which was probably a sign that Christians no longer seemed to take angels seriously. The adorable child angels are nothing like the beings encountered in the Bible. Incidentally, these child angels are technically called *putti* (plural of *putto*, "little boy"). Pieter Bruegel was one of the many artists who painted *The Fall of the Rebel Angels*, showing the transformation of the beautiful divine beings into loathsome demons as they fall from heaven.

In some of the apostle Paul's letters, he refers to certain types of heavenly beings: "principalities," "powers," "thrones," and "dominions" (Romans 8:38, Ephesians 3:10, Colossians 1:16). Later writers assumed these were "orders" of angels that had certain functions assigned to them. An author in the Middle Ages using the pen name Dionysius wrote a book called *The Celestial Hierarchy*, going into great detail about these "ranks" of angels and what their specific duties were. The book had much more influence on Christian thinking about angels than the Bible itself did.

Angels figure in too many works of literature to list here. Probably the best known is John Milton's *Paradise Lost*, which tells of the war in heaven that led to the good angels casting out the rebel angels, who were under the leadership of Satan. The angels in Milton's poem are powerful beings—good, but somewhat intimidating, which is true of the angels in the Bible.

In films, angels don't necessarily have wings, but they do tend to be non-threatening, perhaps best exemplified by the sweet but goofy Clarence in *It's a Wonderful Life*. Television angels have been comic figures as well, but the 1980s series *Highway to Heaven* and the 1990s series *Touched by an Angel* put more emphasis on angels as God's helpers on earth.

Annunciation
Gabriel at the door

According to Luke's Gospel, the angel Gabriel appeared to the virgin Mary in Nazareth and told her she would bear the "Son of the Most High" and "of his kingdom there will be no end." Mary, who was engaged to marry Joseph, asked how this could be, since she had not "known" (had sexual relations with) a man. Gabriel told her that "the power of the Most High will overshadow you" (Luke 1:35)—something Christians have referred to as the "virgin birth." Gabriel also told Mary that her aged cousin Elizabeth had conceived a child—so two miraculous births were on the way.

This episode is much of what lies behind the Catholic and Orthodox churches' reverence for Mary, since Gabriel tells her she has "found favor with God." Even Protestants would agree that the woman chosen to bear God's Son would have to be very special in some way—although Protestants are not willing to call her "Mother of God" and "Queen of Heaven," as Catholics do.

The Annunciation
LUKE. CHAPTER I, VERSES 28-33.

The episode is known as the Annunciation (meaning "announcing") and has been the subject of countless paintings, most of them making no attempt at showing what a woman in first-century Palestine would have actually looked like. (Most artists had no idea, but chose to represent her as a woman of their own time and place.) Painting the angel Gabriel—sometimes without wings, but more often with them—seems to stir artists' creative juices. Fra Angelico's *Annunciation* in

Florence, Italy, is probably one of the most reproduced paintings in the world, especially on Christmas cards. In movies about the life of Jesus, the presence of Gabriel has often been "off-camera," with the film showing Mary engaged in conversation with an unseen presence, leaving Gabriel to the viewer's imagination.

Catholic and Orthodox Christians celebrate the Feast of the Annunciation on March 25—which is exactly nine months before Christmas day. For several centuries, Europe considered March 25, not January 1, to be the beginning of the year. The day was often called Lady Day, in honor of "Our Lady," Mary. The town of Nazareth in Israel has a Church of the Annunciation, supposedly built on the site where Mary received her angelic visitor.

Antichrist

One wicked being, or several?

The actual word "antichrist" is found only in two of John's epistles (1 John 2:18, 2 John 1:7). John uses it not to refer to one specific individual but to anyone opposing the work of Christ, and there are "many" already in the world, John says. The word "antichrist" could mean both "opponent of Christ" or "false Christ." Paul did not use the word "antichrist" but did speak of a "son of perdition" or (in some modern versions) "man of lawlessness" which is clearly the same thing (2 Thessalonians 2:3). Jesus himself warned his disciples that "false Christs" would arise (Mark 13:22). The Book of Revelation speaks of the "Beast" symbolized by the number 666 (SEE PAGE 342), and presumably this is also an antichrist, or perhaps the final one who will cause a great persecution against religion. There are a million ways of trying to interpret all the Bible's passages about the Antichrist, Beast, 666, etc., which is why Christians for centuries have loved to speculate about just who, or what, the antichrist is, or will be. It's probable a safe assumption that the early Christians believed there would be many antichrists, but that there would be a final one at the end of time who would make the others seem small by comparison. In the 1500s, the Protestants generally agreed that the Antichrist was the Catholic pope. Most tyrants and dictators in the past two thousand years have been identified as Antichrist—Napoleon, Kaiser Wilhelm, Stalin, Hitler, etc.

Interestingly, the 1976 movie *The Omen* was originally supposed to be titled *The Antichrist*, which is the movie's subject. It began the genre of apocalyptic horror movies dealing with the coming of the Antichrist to earth. The German philosopher Friedrich Nietzsche, a minister's son who despised Christianity, referred to himself as the Antichrist and wrote a book with that title.

The Antichrist has intrigued writers more than it has artists, but there are paintings of the Antichrist and his false miracles in the cathedral of Orvieto, Italy. The Renaissance artist Luca Signorelli made the Antichrist part of his frescoes showing the Last Judgment, heaven, and hell.

Antioch
Gospel Central for the Gentiles

Antioch in Syria was the third-largest city in the Roman Empire, with a population of about a half-million in the New Testament period. Like any large city, it was very cosmopolitan, with a huge mix of religions and beliefs. Its citizens were proud of it, calling the city "Antioch the Golden." Christianity was preached there very soon after the time of Jesus, and it was in Antioch that the term "Christians" was first used (Acts 11:19-26). The Christian community there sent Paul and his companion apostles out on three missionary journeys, and the city is an important locale in the Book of Acts. In a sense it was "home base" for the missionaries preaching to Gentiles, as Jerusalem was base for the preaching to the Jews. An old tradition says that Luke, author of Acts and the Gospel of Luke, was a native of Antioch.

Because of its importance in the New Testament, the name Antioch has been used for numerous churches, and also for several cities in the U.S.

Anti-Semitism
Almost as old as history

In the ancient world, tolerance and inclusiveness were not highly valued, and it was assumed people preferred their own customs and beliefs to those of others, with no apology. Whether the Jews were singled out for persecution more than any other group is debatable, but it is definitely true that in ancient times the Jews stood out for their custom of making no pictures or statues of their one God, having only one temple dedicated to him, and also for having their males circumcised. Even in foreign lands that allowed them to prosper and rise to high office, Jews could suffer persecution, seen most vividly in the Book of Esther, where there is a threat of all the Jews in the Persian Empire being exterminated. The Book of Daniel shows high-ranking Jews condemned to death because they would not engage in pagan worship.

In the New Testament period, the Romans who ruled the Jews mocked their customs (no idols, circumcision, the Sabbath day off, etc.) but did extend certain privileges to the Jews (their men were not crucified nude, for example). The Greeks in the Roman Empire also mocked Jewish customs and the stories of their God—which was ironic, considering what a bunch of temperamental, promiscuous rogues the Greek and Roman gods were. (One forgotten element of anti-Semitism is that the early Christians were mocked by many Greeks and Romans because of the value they placed on the Old Testament. Snobbish pagans dismissed both Jews and Christians and their "vulgar" writings.) When some of the later Roman emperors demanded to be worshipped as gods, both Jews and Christians refused and suffered the consequences.

As time passed, more people converted to Christianity, so that in many regions Christians were in the majority. A new situation arose: Christian intolerance of Jews. Anti-Semitism in the Middle Ages and later is often blamed on the Gospels' accounts of Jesus' trial and crucifixion, with the Jewish priests charging him with blasphemy and handing him over to Pilate, the Roman governor, for execution. Pilate was reluctant to grant the death penalty, but the priests' minions provoked the crowd to yell for Jesus' crucifixion, and when Pilate publicly washed his hands of the matter, the crowd called out, "His blood be on us and on our children!" (Matthew 27:25). Most Jews believe that the Gospels whitewashed Pilate and unfairly placed the blame on the Jews, and that Christians have persecuted Jews because of the words of Matthew 27:25. However, Mark's Gospel states bluntly that when Pilate ordered Jesus crucified, he was "wishing to satisfy the crowd"—a cynical politician giving the public what it wanted, in other words. The cruel episode of the Roman soldiers pressing a crown of thorns on Jesus' head and mocking him as "king" shows that the Gospels didn't put all the blame on the Jews. In short, the Gospels show clearly that both the Romans and the Jewish leaders were to blame for the death of Jesus. Still, Christian persecution of Jews over the centuries is inexcusable.

Apocalypse

(see Revelation)

the Apocrypha, Old Testament

Loading the canon

One huge question about the Bible: Who decided what was included and excluded? Devout people would say, "God did." On the human level, certain books were included because over time they impressed many people as *inspired* by God himself. The books that were considered inspired were known as the canon, a word meaning "standard" or "rule." These books were thought of as "sacred Scripture" or "holy Scripture."

For the Jews, the first books they consider inspired are the five books of Moses: Genesis, Exodus, Leviticus, Numbers, Deuteronomy. These are called the Torah, the Pentateuch, or the Law. The second group of books to be accepted as inspired are called the Prophets: Joshua, Judges, 1 Samuel, 2 Samuel, 1 Kings, 2 Kings, Isaiah, Jeremiah, Ezekiel, and the twelve Minor Prophets. We know that at the time Jesus lived, Jews spoke of the Law and the Prophets as books given to them by God. All the books of the Law and Prophets are still accepted as canon by all Jews and all Christians.

The disagreement comes with the third group of books, called the Writings. These include Psalms, which is easily accepted as inspired. Others are Proverbs, Ecclesiastes, the Song of Solomon, Job, 1 and 2 Chronicles, Ezra, Nehemiah, Esther, Lamentations, and Daniel. The Jews were slower in accepting these as inspired, especially Ecclesiastes, but finally all were. Like the Law and Prophets, all the Writings are considered "holy Scripture" by Jews and Christians. To Christians, they are the "Old Testament," while several specifically Christian books are called the "New Testament." Jews do not accept the New Testament; what Christians call "the Old Testament" is called simply "the Bible" by Jews.

Some widely read books did not make it onto the Jews' list: 1 and 2 Maccabees, Tobit, Judith, Wisdom of Solomon, Ecclesiasticus (not the same as Ecclesiastes),

Baruch, and additions to Esther and Daniel. None of these books is quoted in the New Testament, which is a sign that the Jews in Jesus' day may have read the books but did not regard them the same way as the Law, Prophets, and Writings. The books just mentioned are known collectively as the *Apocrypha*, which means "hidden things." All were written in the period between the Old and New Testaments.

Around the year 400, the Christian scholar Jerome was working on his great translation into Latin. Jerome learned that the Jewish rabbis had chosen not to include the Apocrypha in their Bibles. He and other Christian scholars agreed that if the Jews did not consider these books sacred, neither should Christians. But the Apocrypha had been around a long time, and Jerome was pressured to include it in his Latin Bible, which was called the Vulgate. So between 400 and 1500, almost all Christian Bibles included the Apocrypha.

In the 1500s, the leaders of the Protestant Reformation remembered Jerome's doubts about the Apocrypha. Most of the Protestant leaders said it was all right to read the Apocrypha, but that the books were not on the same level as the other books in the Bible. In 1546 the Catholics reacted by issuing a decree that, yes, definitely, the Apocrypha was a part of sacred Scripture. (In fact, the council that issued the decree said that anyone that disagreed would go to hell.)

So today most Protestant Bibles do not include the Apocrypha, and all Catholic Bibles do. The Eastern Orthodox churches went their own direction and in 1672 accepted four books of the Apocrypha—Wisdom, Ecclesiasticus, Tobit, and Judith—as Scripture. So in Christianity there are three different canons—Catholic (the longest), Protestant (the shortest), and Orthodox (in-between).

Of the books of the Apocrypha, the most interesting are Wisdom and Ecclesiasticus, which are very similar to the Book of Proverbs. Also, 1 and 2 Maccabees are interesting because they tell a lot about Jewish history in between the Old and New Testaments.

Because of their doubtful status, the books of the Apocrypha have never had as much influence on artists, writers, and theologians as the other books of the Bible have. The heroine of the Book of Judith, who beheads an invading general and helps save her people, has been featured in many paintings and several films. From the Book of Tobit, the character Tobias, who is guided by the angel Raphael, has often been painted walking with the angel, his dog tagging along (the only mention of a pet dog in the Bible, incidentally). Although the Apocrypha was included in the original King James Version, few of its phrases have entered the language, although the line, "The souls of the righteous are in the hands of God" from the Book of Wisdom is fairly familiar and has been used in funeral services.

Apocryphon of the New Testament
Filling in the Gospels' gaps?

The New Testament has four Gospels, one Acts of the Apostles, and one Apocalypse (Revelation), but there were dozens of other Gospels, Acts, and Apocalypses that didn't make it into the Bible. Most of them were attributed to the apostles (Peter, Thomas) or other figures in the Gospels (Nicodemus). Many of them mingled authentic parts of the four Gospels together with new material, sometimes providing extra details about the boyhood of Jesus, the life of Mary before she married, the life of Pontius Pilate, etc. It's conceivable that some of these books might include facts, but mostly they are "historical fiction," padding the Gospels with imaginative material, not always very inspiring. Some of the Gospels were produced by the Gnostics, a sect that had some Christian elements but also beliefs totally at odds with the four Gospels in the Bible.

Some of the stories in these books were so widely read that many Christians accepted them as true. For example, a book called the Protoevangelium of James claimed that Joseph was a much older man than Mary and had been previously married, so that the "brothers" of Jesus mentioned in the Gospels were Joseph's children, but not Mary's. This is the reason that most paintings show Joseph as much older than Mary, when in fact the Bible says nothing at all about his age. Some of the writings stated that Pilate's wife—who is unnamed in the New Testament—was named Claudia, which might possibly be true, and in several films about Jesus, the name Claudia is used.

The Bible's Apocalypse—the Book of Revelation—was written by the apostle John. There were many other Apocalypses, most of them claiming to be written by some notable person in the Bible, such as Peter, Moses, Isaiah, etc. Most of them claim to be revelations of future events, as does the one in the Bible.

There were also many "Acts of" certain people, including the apostles but also Pontius Pilate. They answer the question, "What happened to these people once the Bible's Book of Acts ended?" Most of them depict the apostle working miracles and traveling to some distant land, for example, the apostle Thomas taking the Gospel to faraway India. There may be some bits of truth in these writings, mingled with lots of imagination.

The early Christians were actually rather picky about accepting any writings as "the real thing"—a good thing, since if they hadn't been so finicky, the New Testament would probably be thousands of pages long. The head of one church lost his post because he had written an "Acts of Paul" that was mostly the work of his own imagination. Though he defended himself by saying he wrote it to inspire people, the verdict was that people wanted their stories of the apostle to be truth, not fiction.

apostles

Sent men

In the New Testament, Jesus' twelve closest followers were referred to as both disciples (meaning "followers" or "learners") and apostles (meaning "those sent out" or "messengers" or "representatives"). After the traitor Judas committed suicide, the eleven remaining disciples/apostles chose a replacement, Matthias. Acts 1:21-22 indicate that the Twelve, including Matthias, were men who had followed Jesus from the time of his baptism to his ascension into heaven.

The apostles are often referred to simply as "the Twelve," but there were more than twelve eventually, because Paul, Barnabas, and others who were not part of the original twelve are referred to as apostles. The original twelve had all seen the risen Jesus, and so had Paul, in his famous Damascus road vision (SEE PAGE 84). The Book of Acts is often called Acts of the Apostles because its main characters are apostles. All were sent to proclaim the Gospel to the world, at first to their fellow Jews, but later to the Gentiles (non-Jews), and the most famous apostle, Paul, called himself the "apostle to the Gentiles." Several of Paul's epistles begin with the greeting, "From Paul, an apostle of Jesus Christ"—ditto for the two epistles of Peter.

Christians have honored the memory of the apostles, naming many churches, schools, and cities in their honor. Most of the books of the New Testament were written by the apostles. The Catholic and Orthodox churches have special feast days for the first twelve apostles, and also for Paul, Barnabas, and Matthias. Many large churches contain statues or stained-glass windows depicting the twelve apostles. In a way, this is ironic, since some of the twelve apostles are such minor characters in the Bible that we know almost nothing about them. Legends exist about all of them, usually stories of them traveling to a far country, preaching the Gospel, and being martyred in a horrible way. Some of the legends may be based on fact.

Composer Edward Elgar wrote an oratorio *The Apostles* and a sequel, *The Kingdom*, and Richard Wagner composed *The Love Feast of the Apostles*. Artist Albrecht Durer's drawing *Study of an Apostle's Hands* is the basis of the many "Praying Hands" pictures many Christians have in their homes.

Luke's Gospel is the only one to refer to a larger group of disciples, seventy in all (or seventy-two, in some old versions of the Gospel). These were sent out in

Jesus Dispatches the Twelve Apostles
Matthew. Chapter 10, Verses 5-10, 16.

twos by Jesus to go ahead of him in the villages and towns, preparing the way spiritually. Apparently some of them had power to cast out demons (Luke 10:1-20).

One of the oldest Christian creeds is known as the Apostles' Creed, and it is probably recited by millions of Christians on any given Sunday. An old legend says it was literally composed by the twelve apostles, with each one contributing a section of the creed. It was almost certainly written after the deaths of the actual apostles, but it is "theirs" in the sense that it does sum up the beliefs of the earliest Christians.

Many Christian denominations use the word "apostolic" in their name, meaning that they seem themselves as being based on the faith of the apostles of the New Testament. The Catholic, Orthodox, and Episcopal churches believe in "apostolic succession," the idea that their bishops were ordained in a line going back to the apostles themselves. The Christian theologians who wrote in the generation after the apostles were known as the Apostolic Fathers, since some of them had known the apostles personally.

Beginning in the 1400s in Europe, silversmiths began making sets of "apostle spoons," thirteen in all, each handle having the name and small figurine of Jesus and the twelve apostles. They were frequently given by godparents to the family of a newly baptized infant. The general rule was that a wealthy person would give an entire set, while the less affluent might only give one spoon. The spoon representing Jesus was known as the "Master spoon" and was usually larger than the others. Sometimes Paul was included, making a set of fourteen in all. The spoons were considered precious heirlooms, and today are considered highly desirable by antique collectors.

The Apostle Islands lie in Lake Superior off Wisconsin. Early missionaries named the islands, thinking there are twelve of them, but there are actually twenty-two.

Over the years, various groups have referred to themselves as "apostles," most famously the "Cambridge Apostles," which began in 1820 with twelve Cambridge students who rather modestly considered themselves the smartest people on campus. The group still exists as a kind of club, mixing debate and socializing.

Arabs
The pre-Muhammad kind

Arabs are mentioned several times in the Bible, with the name generally referring to peoples living in the desert region east and south of the land of Israel. In fact, the Hebrew word we translate as "Arabs" meant simply "desert dwellers." They were thought of as descendants of Abraham's son Ishmael, or of Jacob's brother Esau—so, loosely, they were kin to the Israelites, but quarrelsome kin, more often fighting than not. The Book of Nehemiah shows them opposing the work of the Jews in rebuilding the city of Jerusalem—a kind of preview of centuries of hostility between Arab and Jew. However, the Arabs of biblical times were not Muslims yet—it was several centuries after the time of Jesus that Muhammad began the new religion of Islam, to which all the Arabs converted.

Aramaic
Language of the Lord

Thanks to the Mel Gibson film *The Passion of the Christ*, many people for the first time heard words in Aramaic. It was the language of Jesus and his disciples, the common language of Jews in that period. Aramaic originally was the language of ancient Syria, but it spread to many areas, and by the time of Jesus had replaced Hebrew as the language used by most Jews, although the two languages have some similarities. (Language scholars say the two are similar in roughly the same way that modern-day Spanish and Italian are similar.) Many Jews in the region of Judea (centered in Jerusalem) still spoke Hebrew, which is why some of them looked down on the Aramaic-speaking Jews of Galilee, such as Jesus and his disciples.

Most Jews in Jesus' time did not read the Old Testament in the original Hebrew, but in Aramaic translations called Targums. Though the Gospels were written in Greek, on a few occasions they give the actual Aramaic words used by Jesus—with their Greek translations. When Jesus was crucified, a plaque placed over his head had the inscription "Jesus of Nazareth, King of the Jews"—written in Aramaic, Greek, and Latin, so that anyone passing by would understand it.

Gibson's movie was probably incorrect in having Pontius Pilate speak to the Jews in Latin, since they would not have understood a word of it. More likely, they spoke to each other in Greek, the international language that was used throughout the Roman Empire.

Some of the very late parts of the Old Testament (parts of Daniel, Ezra, and Jeremiah) were written in Aramaic instead of Hebrew. The Assyrian, Babylonian, and Persian empires all used Aramaic as their second language. Aramaic was the most common language of the Middle East until the new religion of Islam (beginning around 650) spread its own common language, Arabic.

In the popular 1977 movie, *Oh, God!*, God (played by George Burns) was asked to translate something written in Aramaic—which he was able to do, of course.

the ark of the covenant
Don't touch!

Unless you are a religion professor (or, at least, a dedicated reader of the Old Testament), you might never have heard of the ark of the covenant if it hadn't been for the 1981 Steven Spielberg movie *Raiders of the Lost Ark*, in which professor-adventurer Indiana Jones tries to find the ark in Egypt before the Nazis do. While the movie was pure fiction, the ark wasn't. It was built in the time of Moses to the specifications in Exodus 25:10-22, and the ark in the film followed those specifications. The ark was a wooden chest covered with gold, with a solid gold lid (the "mercy seat") and two winged creatures facing each other, their wings touching. The ark was so sacred it wasn't supposed to be touched, and it was carried on two poles by the rings on its corners. The Israelites didn't worship the ark, but it did symbolize the presence of God. It was at the center of the tabernacle, the large tent that was Israel's center of worship until a temple was built to house it.

The ark was involved in some miracles, such as crossing the Jordan River on dry land (Joshua 3) and the famous "tumbling down" of the walls of Jericho, in which the priests marched around the city's walls carrying the ark (Joshua 6). The warlike Philistines captured the ark and put it in the temple of their god Dagon, but they found the Dagon idol on its face with its hands and head broken off (1 Samuel 5). It also caused a plague among them, so they wised up and returned the sacred object to the Israelites. Since the ark had a kind "charm," it was taken into battle by Saul and David (1 Samuel 14:18, 2 Samuel 11:11).

King David had the ark brought to Jerusalem, and at one point it seemed to be falling off a wagon, and when a man named Uzzah touched it to try to steady it, he was struck dead (2 Samuel 6:3-8). David was so ecstatic about having the ark in his capital city that he stripped off his shirt and "danced before the Lord with all his might" (2 Samuel 6:14). David's son Solomon built the awesome temple that had the ark in its central sanctuary, the Holy of Holies, where only the high priest of Israel could actually see it (1 Kings 8:3-9). It is likely that the ark was taken out of the Holy of Holies and paraded around on holy days. The ark was not just a hollow chest; inside were the stone tablets with the Ten Commandments. At one time it also held a gold jar of manna, the miraculous food the Israelites ate while in the wilderness.

The winged creatures on the lid of the ark were known as *cherubim*. Several times the Old Testament speaks of "the Lord that dwells between the cherubim" (1 Samuel 4:4, Psalm 99:1). Since the Israelites did not make statues or idols of God, the ark was the closest they had to a "place" for God, and they seemed to imagine that he invisibly existed on top of the ark, between the outstretched wings of the cherubim—even though they also knew he was too big to be contained anywhere.

The ark is, as the movie title said, "lost." One of the great mysteries of the Bible is that it says so much about the ark, yet doesn't say when or how it was taken from the temple. The best guess is that the Babylonians took it when they burned the temple in 586 b.c., but what became of it after that is a mystery. They must have regarded it as irreplaceable, because when a new temple was built years later, they did not construct another ark. One old tradition, found in the Apocrypha, is that the prophet Jeremiah hid it in a cave. That legend is ironic, since Jeremiah prophesied a time when the ark would no longer be significant in worship (Jeremiah 3:16). The idea, or at least the name, of the ark didn't vanish, however, because every Jewish synagogue has a chest or closet called the "ark," which holds the scrolls of the Torah. The Orthodox Church of Ethiopia also has an ark in each of its churches.

The Bible's last mention of the ark is in Revelation 11, where the temple in heaven has the ark, accompanied by lightning, thunder, hail, and an earthquake.

The movie *Raiders of the Lost Ark* showed spirits (or demons?) emerging from the ark when the Nazi captors dared to open it, killing them all. This was silly (and a good excuse for special effects), but it does have a loose connection to the story of Uzzah dying when he dared to touch the ark.

The ark played a role in another popular film, the 1951 *David and Bathsheba*, where studio craftsmen constructed an ark to the exact specifications in Exodus, making it from acacia wood and covering it with real gold, as Exodus says.

Armageddon
Global showdown

Revelation 16 tells of a great battle at the end of time, the final face-off between God and the demon-led kings of the earth. The battle will take place at Armageddon (Revelation 16:16). The site takes its name from Megiddo, the scene of several fateful battles in the Old Testament. People have used the name Armageddon to refer to any decisive battle or conflict. When Theodore Roosevelt ran for president as a Progressive in 1912, he proclaimed that "We stand at Armageddon and we battle for the Lord!"—a typical case of political overstatement. During World War I, several battles were fought in the vicinity of Megiddo, so many people thought of this war as the Armageddon of Revelation. It may be that the Book of Revelation intended the name to be symbolic, and did not refer to the literal site of Megiddo.

Artemis
Goddess pep rally

The virgin goddess Artemis was widely worshipped by the Greeks and others, and the Book of Acts records a confrontation between Christian missionaries and the devotees of Artemis. This occurred in Ephesus, a city where a famous temple to Artemis existed, so beautiful that it was considered one of the Seven Wonders of the World. The Artemis that was worshipped in Ephesus was not the chaste, slim, young maiden-goddess of Greece, but a kind of "fertility mother," her statue covered all over with breasts. Local craftsmen made little silver shrines that visitors to Ephesus would buy. One craftsman, Demetrius, stirred up a riot against the Christian missionaries, fearing the new religion would lead people away from Artemis (and ruin his trade, of course). He led the Artemis devotees to the local amphitheatre, where the mob of thousands joined in a two-hour chant of "Great is Artemis of the Ephesians!" (Acts 19:34). (The King James Version is incorrect in using the name "Diana" for the goddess. Most versions have the correct name "Artemis.") The town clerk had to literally read them the riot act to break up the fanatical crowd.

Ascension
No place to go but up

What happened to Jesus after he came back from the dead? According to Luke's Gospel and the Book of Acts, forty days after the resurrection, he was with his disciples, then "as they were looking on, he was lifted up, and a cloud took him out of their sight" (Acts 1:9). The event is mentioned many other times in the New Testament, which refers to his being "gone into heaven" (1 Peter 3:22), "received into glory" (1 Timothy 3:16), and "passed through the heavens" (Hebrews 4:14). In the episode of the saintly Stephen being stoned to death, Stephen claimed he could see into heaven, where Jesus was at "the right hand of God" (Acts 7:56).

This event, called the Ascension, has been a key belief held by Christians since the earliest times. The old Apostles Creed, for example, states that Jesus "ascended into heaven," and most of the creeds use very similar wording. In times past, the period between the Ascension and Pentecost was called Expectation Week, because the disciples waited for the sending of the Holy Spirit.

The Ascension of Christ
Acts. Chapter 1, Verses 9-11.

Many churches celebrate the Feast of the Ascension forty days after Easter. The name Church of the Ascension is used by many local churches, and there is an Ascension Island in the north Atlantic. Israel has a Chapel of the Ascension, which supposedly is on the spot where Jesus ascended, but no one is certain about this. Composer Carl Philipp Emanuel Bach wrote an oratorio, *Resurrection and Ascension of Jesus*.

Ashtoreth
Baal's better half

Most religions have some kind of goddess who is the consort of the chief god. In the case of the Canaanites, Ashtoreth was consort of the fertility god Baal (see page 41). As with Baal, the rituals involved in her worship often involved promiscuous sex with the "shrine prostitutes," both male and female. The prophets of Israel constantly preached to the people that they should worship only Israel's God, not Baal or Ashtoreth. The wise King Solomon, who had built the beautiful temple to God in Jerusalem, later allowed his foreign wives to lead him into worshipping their gods, including Ashtoreth.

A similar goddess was named Asherah, Baal's mother, not wife. Apparently a sacred pole was used in her worship, and some of the Israelite kings got into trouble by setting up Asherah poles. The saintly king Josiah took it on himself to finally rid the land of Asherah worship (2 Kings 23).

Asia

Not as big as you thought

The name Asia occurs several times in the Bible, but in those days it did not refer to the whole continent. Rather, it was the area that today we call Turkey. The Romans gave the name Asia to a province in that area. The Book of Revelation was addressed to "the seven churches that are in Asia" (1:4). The Book of Acts shows that the early Christian missionaries like Paul spread the new faith in Asia, where most of the people were Greek-speaking pagans.

Assyria

Evil empire

With its great city of Nineveh, Assyria was a mighty empire—and mighty cruel also. Roughly occupying the area that is Iraq today, Assyria under its king Tiglath-Pileser III invaded Israel more than once, at one point forcing the king to send the treasures of God's temple as tribute (2 Kings 16). In 722 B.C., the Assyrian king Shalmaneser V conquered the northern kingdom of Israel and deported the people (who became the ten "lost tribes"—SEE PAGE 221). The Assyrians settled their own people and foreigners in Israel, and these inter-married with the remaining Israelites. Their descendants were the ancestors of the Samaritans, hated by Jews in the New Testament period. An old tradition says that Assyria was founded by Nimrod, the "mighty hunter" mentioned in Genesis 10.

Assyria inevitably attacked the southern kingdom, Judah. The mighty king Sennacherib sent 185,000 soldiers, but 2 Kings 19 states that the Lord's angel killed them. (The English poet Lord Byron commemorated this event in his poem "The Destruction of Sennacherib.") Sennacherib got his punishment for besieging Jerusalem: while in the temple of his god Nisroch, his own sons assassinated him. In time Assyria was absorbed into another oppressive empire, Babylonia.

God's prophets, particularly Isaiah, frequently denounced Assyria's cruelty. The Book of Nahum is one long rant against Assyria's cruelty and a prophecy of its doom. The Assyrians were notorious for raping the women of the conquered, and beheading, impaling, or skinning alive the men. The ones who were merely deported or made into slaves considered themselves lucky.

Both the Assyrian and Babylonian empires were centered in the area called Mesopotamia—meaning "between the rivers" (the Tigris and Euphrates). The area roughly corresponds to modern-day Iraq. Until archaeologists began poking around Iraq in the 1800s, the information about Assyria in the Bible was almost all that the world knew about the mighty Assyrian empire.

Athaliah

Queen of mean, second generation

King Ahab and his wicked wife Jezebel (SEE PAGES 15, 180) are some of the worst villains in the Bible, so it's no surprise that their daughter inherited all their bad genes. Her name was Athaliah, and she married Jehoram, king of Judah. Athaliah loved power (as her parents did), and after both her son and husband died, she ruled Judah herself. Not wanting any rivals, she killed forty-two princes of the royal family. (In the words of the King James Version, she "destroyed all the seed royal.") As often happens in the Bible, God sees to it that a child escapes massacre (as with Moses and Jesus), and the prince Joash is hidden away in the temple, under the care of the priest Jehoiada and his wife. Athaliah reigned six years, but in her seventh year, Jehoiada arranged for Joash's coronation. The sounds of the crowd drew Athaliah to the temple, where the people's shout of "Long live the king!" was met by her cry of "Treason! Treason!" The crowd dragged her out and killed her with a sword (2 Kings 11:1-16). Apparently she had inherited from her parents not only the hunger for power, but also the tendency to die violently.

The great French dramatist Jean Racine's last tragedy, written in 1691, was *Athalie*, based on the story of the wicked queen and Joash. George Frideric Handel wrote an oratorio about her, and Felix Mendelssohn wrote some fine music to accompany Racine's tragedy.

Athens

Snubbing the babbler

Athens, Greece was one of the intellectual and cultural centers of the ancient world, but its one appearance in the Bible makes its citizens appear to be cynical snobs. Acts 17 tells of the Christian missionary Paul's visit to Athens, where the statues of the Greek gods—things we consider works of art today—really vexed him. (Since Jews did not make images of their one God, most Jews found statues—"idols"—extremely offensive.) Nonetheless, he was a man with a mission, so he preached the Gospel first to the Jews in their synagogue there, then debated with the Epicurean and Stoic philosophers, who referred to him as a "babbler" (17:18). But the people were willing to give him a listen, since, according to Acts, the Athenians spent their time "in nothing except telling or hearing something new." (We would call them "intellectually trendy.") The locals took Paul to the local forum, the Areopagus ("hill of Ares," Ares being the god of war) to present his message. Paul noted that he had seen an altar devoted "To the Unknown God," and he told the Athenians that this "Unknown God" was the one he served, and the only god in the universe. (Archaeologists tell us that such altars to "unknown gods" were common in ancient Greece.) As a kind of "hook" to his audience, Paul quoted from two Greek poets, Epimenides and Arastus. The snooty Athenians were not impressed, although Acts mentions at least two converts in the city.

One of the converts mentioned was a man called Dionysius the Areopagite, which indicates he had some connection with the Areopagus. In the Middle Ages, several books supposedly by Dionysius were widely read, including *The Celestial Hierarchy*, which described the nine types of angels and their duties. The books were actually written much later than the lifetime of the real Dionysius, but whoever wrote them had a powerful influence on Christian beliefs about angels.

Paul spoke to the Athenians at the Areopagus, which in some older translations is "Mars Hill." (Mars was the Roman equivalent to the Greek god of war, Ares.) For some reason Mars Hill has been used often as a name for churches, and there is also a Mars Hill College. In Christian tradition, the episode is an example of faith encountering intellectual resistance and mockery. In one of his epistles, Paul stated (correctly) that the gospel he preached was considered "folly" by most of the Greeks. Part of Pope John Paul II's 2001 Great Jubilee pilgrimage to the Holy Land included visiting the Areopagus. He regarded Paul's sermon there as a metaphor for the church in the modern world.

American author John Steinbeck titled one of his novels *To a God Unknown*, borrowing the phrase from the altar Paul saw in Athens. English poet Alfred Noyes titled his spiritual autobiography *The Unknown God*.

Baal

Lord, but not the right one

Baal (pronounced like "bail") is the most-mentioned god in the Bible, not counting Israel's God. He was also the most serious rival to God, since the Israelites were always tempted to worship this fertility god of the Canaanites. His actual name was *Hadad*, but he was almost always addressed as *Baal*, a title meaning "master" or "lord" (just as the Israelites used their Hebrew word for "lord" when referring to God). Baal was typical of fertility gods of that region: his "worship" often involved people having sex with either male or female "shrine prostitutes"—or to be brutally honest, "worship" was just a good excuse for wild, abandoned sex with either gender, supposedly because such acts made the land, crops, and livestock more fertile. This appalled the Israelites, as did the occasional human sacrifice offered to Baal (Jeremiah 19:5). Also, the Canaanites bowed down to Baal idols, while the Israelites believed any kind of idol worship was wrong. Baal priests often cut themselves with knives to make blood flow, in the belief this would make Baal send rain.

With Baal worship being so sexual in nature, Israel's prophets referred to the people "whoring" after Baal and other gods. This was true in a spiritual sense also: God was Israel's true lord and master, so worshipping Baal meant Israel was being unfaithful. Many Israelites also worshipped Baal's female counterpart, the goddess Ashtoreth.

Baal was not the Canaanites' chief god. That was El, Baal's father, but Baal was more widely worshipped than El.

King Ahab of Israel married Jezebel, a foreign woman totally devoted to Baal worship—and to stamping out the worship of Israel's God. (See pages 180 and 106 for more about her and her nemesis, the great prophet Elijah.)

In the 1930s, archaeologists in Syria unearthed parts of *The Poem of Baal*, an epic. It is dated around 1400 b.c. or earlier. In the poem, Baal triumphs over Yam, the god of the sea, and Mot, the god of death. Baal also mates numerous times with a cow, which is the kind of mythological crudeness that the Israelites found so distasteful.

In one of history's odd little quirks, the depraved Roman emperor Elagabalus tried to impose Baal worship on the empire around the year 220—which is not surprising, considering he was descended from priests of Baal. Most Romans were outraged by this mandatory worship of a god imported from the Middle East. On the other hand, some Romans chose to identify Baal with their chief god, Jupiter, just as many Greeks identified Baal with Zeus.

Baal's name lives on in the ancient town of Baalbek in Lebanon. And one of the most renowned military leaders of ancient times was the famous Hannibal, whose name meant "favor of Baal."

Babel

Can you hear me now?

By a pure coincidence, the name Babel and our word "babble" are pronounced alike, which fits nicely, since Babel was the site where God caused human beings to begin speaking different languages, so they could not understand each other. The name Babel actually means "gate of God" in Hebrew. Genesis 10 says it was one of the cities founded by Nimrod, who was the "mighty hunter before the Lord." Genesis 11 says that "the whole earth had one language and the same words." They chose a site "in the land of Shinar" and decided to build a tower "with its top in the heavens," and "let us make a name for ourselves." God looked down on the tower and viewed it as a symbol of human arrogance. So he "confused their tongues" so they could not understand each other, and they stopped building the tower and scattered over the earth. This occurred at Babel, so the unfinished tower became known as "the tower of Babel." The point of the story was not just to show what human pride can lead to, but also to explain why human beings speak different languages. In a sense, human beings were repeating the mistake of Adam and Eve—trying to be like gods. They were as unsuccessful as Adam and Eve were.

The musical play *Godspell* opens with an episode of people talking *at* (not *to*) each other, called "Tower of Babble." The tower of Babel episode was featured in the 1966 film *The Bible ... In the Beginning*, which depicted Nimrod as the architect of the ill-fated

The Tower of Babel
GENESIS. CHAPTER 11, VERSES 1-9.

tower. The tower has been painted by many artists, notably Pieter Bruegel the Elder, who based it on the Babylonian spiral towers known as ziggurats. Belgian composer Cesar Franck wrote an oratorio *The Tower of Babel*, as did Russian composer Anton Rubinstein. You occasionally still hear the word "Babel" applied to any state of confusion, and a "tower of Babel" to mean any visionary scheme that had no chance of succeeding.

Babylon
Saddam Hussein's role model

Babylon was one of the great empires of the ancient world, one that did a great deal of harm to Israel. It is first mentioned in 2 Kings 20, where Hezekiah, the ailing king of Judah, receives gifts from the king of Babylon. Rather foolishly, Hezekiah shows the Babylonian visitors all his treasures. The prophet Isaiah tells Hezekiah that some day the Babylonians will carry off those same treasures. A few generations later, it came to pass. The most famous Babylonian king, Nebuchadnezzar (SEE PAGE 253), besieged Jerusalem and carried off the king, installing a puppet king. A few years later he completely destroyed the temple and carried off its treasures, sending most of the population into exile in Babylon (2 Kings 24-25). The king of Judah, Zedekiah, saw his sons slaughtered in front of him, then was blinded and taken in chains to Babylon. (This was the type of cruelty the Babylonians were notorious for.) Judah's chief priests were executed. One of the most famous Psalms in the Bible, Psalm 137, begins "By the waters of

Babylon, we sat down and wept, when we remembered Zion." (Zion was another name for Jerusalem.) The Psalm laments the exile and looks forward to a time when Babylon itself would be conquered, with the dashing of Babylonian babies against the rocks.

What the Psalm hoped for came to pass. The Babylonians were conquered by the Persians. Being more tolerant, the Persians allowed the Jewish exiles to return home and rebuild their temple. Many of the younger Jews, who had no memory of Judah, chose to stay in Babylon, which they found tolerable with the Persians in power. The Greek conqueror Alexander the Great conquered the Babylonians and in 323 B.C. he died in the palace built by Nebuchadnezzar.

Naturally, the Jews hated the Babylonians for all they had done. They associated the name Babylon with oppression, tyranny, and idolatry. By the time of Jesus, the main city of Babylon was practically empty, and the new oppressive empire was Rome. In speaking of Rome, some of the early Christian writers used the name "Babylon" as a kind of code, so the apostle Peter addressed his first epistle from "Babylon," meaning he was writing from Rome (1 Peter 5:13). The Book of Revelation uses the name Babylon many times, referring to an evil and oppressive power that persecutes people of faith. The author may have been thinking of Rome, but he may have intended "Babylon" to mean any tyrannical, immoral government that persecutes innocent people. Revelation depicts the eventual fall of the evil empire: "Babylon is fallen, is fallen, that great city, because she made all nations drink of the wine of the wrath of her fornication" (Revelation 14:8, NIV). Thanks to the Book of Revelation, people through the centuries used "Babylon" to mean any kind of wicked, decadent place. Practically every large city on earth has been referred to as a "Babylon" at one time or another. Some people take delight in thinking of their locale as a Babylon—for example, the Babylon Nightclub in the 1983 movie *Scarface*. In the classic 1916 silent movie *Intolerance*, the fall of Babylon is depicted as a tragedy, with the Babylonians depicted as kind and tolerant and the conquering Persians as narrow and intolerant—which was the opposite of reality.

Babylon has been the setting for many musical works, including Guiseppe Verdi's opera *Nabucco*, George Frideric Handel's oratorio *Belshazzar*, and Ludwig Spohr's oratorio *The Fall of Babylon*.

One person in our time who seriously hoped to create a new Babylonian empire was a man named Saddam Hussein. He failed.

the Babylonian Captivity
Punished by the pagans

The mighty king Nebuchadnezzar of Babylon sacked Jerusalem and destroyed the Jews' temple in 586 B.C. Most of the Jews were carried to exile in Babylon, a period known as the Babylonian Captivity. Some Jews, among them the prophet Jeremiah, went to live in Egypt. In 539 B.C., the Persians conquered Babylon and allowed the Jews to return to their homeland and rebuild their temple. Probably more remained than returned, for the younger ones had no memory of the land their parents thought of as home. The Jews saw the Babylonian Captivity as punishment for their many sins, and the ones who returned home dedicated themselves to keeping the Law of Moses seriously to avoid another national disaster. But on the positive side, the Captivity taught the Jews a valuable spiritual lesson: they could serve and worship God away from their homeland. The old idea of God being tied to the locale of Israel gave way to the idea of God as being everywhere.

The Book of Ezekiel was written by a prophet who lived among the exiles in Babylon.

In the Middle Ages, the home of the popes was for several decades moved from Rome to Avignon in southern France. Some refer to these years as the Babylonian Captivity of the papacy. In the 1500s, Martin Luther referred to the popes' corruption of their office as the Babylonian Captivity (meaning that he saw the popes of his era as just as immoral and unspiritual as the ancient Babylonians were).

Mormons believe that prior to the Babylonians' conquest of Judah, some faithful Jews fled and eventually settled in the Americas.

Balaam
An ass with vision

In the Book of Numbers, Balak, the king of Moab, sent the prophet Balaam to put a curse on the Israelites as they passed by on their way to Canaan. The ass Balaam rode veered off the path three times, and Balaam beat the beast unmercifully, until it finally spoke to him and asked why it was being beaten. Then Balaam's eyes were opened and he saw that the Lord's angel was barring their way. Balaam continued on his way, but instead of cursing the Israelites, he pronounced blessing on them. The story is found in Numbers 22-23.

In Muslim legend, Balaam's donkey is one of the ten animals allowed to enter heaven.

baptism
Drowning to live

In the Bible, baptism is a sign of repentance, of putting aside one's sins and following a new way of life. Jews did not generally baptize other Jews, but when a non-Jew wished to formally embrace the Jews' religion, he had to undergo baptism. The most famous baptizer in the Bible is John the Baptist, who broke tradition by telling his fellow Jews to repent and be baptized. John baptized his kinsman Jesus, which theologically presents a problem, for Christians teach that Jesus was sinless and had no sins to repent of. When Jesus went to John, who was baptizing people in the Jordan River, John was reluctant, saying something like, "I need to be baptized by you, and you come to me?" Jesus' reply is somewhat puzzling: "Let it be so now, for it is fitting for us to fulfill all righteousness." When Jesus came back up out of the water, the Holy Spirit descended on him like a dove, and a voice from heaven said, "This is my beloved Son, with whom I am well pleased" (Matthew 3:13-17). Jesus' baptism by John is considered the beginning of his public ministry. (Some early Christians believed that Jesus was not *born* the Son of God but was *adopted* at the time of his baptism, as evidenced by the words of the voice from heaven. This belief is called Adoptionism and was considered a heresy.)

Jesus himself did not baptize anyone, but after his crucifixion and resurrection, he told his disciples to spread their faith to all people, baptizing them in the name of the Father, Son, and Holy Spirit—a formula that is still spoken in most Christian baptisms (Matthew 28:19). This is why the ritual is often called *threefold baptism*. Oddly, though, the Book of Acts never tells of anyone using the Father-Son-Spirit formula, but baptizing only in the name of Jesus—which is why some Christian groups baptize only in the name of Jesus, and are known as "Oneness" Christians or "Jesus Only" Christians.

Baptism in the Bible was by immersion, that is, the person went fully under the waters, usually in a river or lake (harking back to the practice of John in the Jordan River). Many Christians still prefer to do baptisms outdoors (weather permitting), and some denominations do not consider a baptism valid unless it is by immersion. Some churches have pools called baptisteries behind the pulpit, so that any time of year persons can be immersed for baptism. For many centuries, the person being baptized has worn a white robe, symbolizing the beginning of a new and pure life. Often the wall behind the baptistery has a painting of the Jordan River, the place where John baptized Jesus. Some Christians have felt so strongly about immersion that they have published versions of the Bible where they substitute the word "immerse" for "baptize."

Other denominations practice "sprinkling," with the minister placing his hand in a bowl of water and then placing it on the person's head. Others pour a small amount of water onto the person. The countless paintings showing the baptism of Jesus are probably wrong historically, since they show Jesus and John standing ankle deep in water, with John pouring water on Jesus' head. The artists were probably not even aware that biblical baptism was by immersion. Issues of climate and health make immersion impossible for some people.

Regardless of the form used, baptism had several meanings. It symbolized cleansing, washing away one's past wrongs. It also symbolized death and resurrection, identifying with what happened to Jesus himself (Romans 6:4). Going under the water symbolized dying, coming back up again symbolized a new life.

For most Christians, baptism is the rite of passage into becoming a member of the church, a sign that one is a full-fledged believer and wants to be considered part of the faith community. But one issue Christians strongly disagree on is the baptism of infants. There is no mention of baptism of infants in the Bible, and so some Christians insist on "believer's baptism," baptizing only people old enough to decide for themselves if they want to be part of the church. The Book of Acts says that entire "households" were converted to Christianity and baptized, which at least suggests that children (and infants too?) were baptized.

Jesus' baptism is an important day for Christians, and has for centuries been celebrated on January 6, called Epiphany. This is a "double holy day," since it commemorates the wise men bringing gifts to the infant Jesus as well as the beginning of Jesus' adult ministry, beginning with his baptism.

John the Baptist prophesied that Jesus would baptize people not with water but with the Holy Spirit. (Mark 1:8). Some Christian groups, such as Pentecostals, place emphasis on the "baptism of the Spirit," and regard it as more important than baptism with water (which makes sense, given John's prophecy). Baptism of the Spirit is not a church ritual but something that happens spontaneously, with the person somehow aware that he has been "filled with the Spirit," often shown by the ability to speak in unknown tongues (SEE PAGE 365).

Barabbas
The people's (wrong) choice

Here is a case of a very minor biblical character who has intrigued people for centuries. The Gospels relate that at the trial of Jesus in Jerusalem, Pilate, the Roman governor, offered to release to the Jews one prisoner, since it was the custom to do so at Passover time. The people were given the choice—Jesus, the prophet accused of blasphemy by the Jewish council, or Barabbas, a notorious murderer and revolutionary. The council's cronies stirred up the mob to shout for Barabbas, so Barabbas was released and Jesus crucified (Mark 15:7-15). This could not have pleased Pilate and the Romans, since Barabbas definitely was a rebel, probably one they would have trouble with in the future.

We know nothing else about the man. Since he had taken part in a rebellion, he was probably a Zealot, and chances are he went back to the other Zealots and continued to engage in anti-Roman acts.

Preachers have had a field day with Barabbas, since his name simply means "son of a father"—in other words, "anybody." It might have even been a false name. As preachers view it, the innocent Jesus literally died in place of the guilty Barabbas, which symbolizes the core of Christian preaching—Jesus dying in place of everyone, every "son of a father."

Par Lagerkvist, a Swedish author who won the Nobel Prize for Literature, wrote a novel, *Barabbas*, in which the title character leaves prison and goes back to his low-life cronies to discover that his woman has become a Christian. She dies by stoning, and later when Barabbas is imprisoned again, he is chained to a prisoner who is a Christian. In the end, Barabbas himself is crucified. The novel was made into a film released in 1962. Barabbas appears in practically every movie about Jesus, and such films often try to draw a contrast between Jesus' way of peace—a spiritual revolution—and Barabbas' way of violence. He is usually depicted as surly, unclean, and profane, a clear contrast to the meek Jesus. Belgian author Michel de Ghelderode wrote the 1928 play *Barabbas*, and it is still staged.

Barnabas

Paul's shadow

Barnabas's original name was Joseph, a common name in those days, but he was nicknamed Barnabas, meaning "son of encouragement." A Jew born on the island of Cyprus, he lived in Jerusalem and sold his property to give to his fellow Christians there (Acts 4:36-37). When Saul the Christian-basher converted to Paul the Christian, it was Barnabas who vouched for him to the skeptical Christians (Acts 9:26-29). Paul and Barnabas were commissioned as missionaries and traveled widely, spreading the faith to both Jews and Gentiles. In one town, Barnabas and Paul were mistaken for the gods Zeus and Hermes because they had worked miracles (SEE PAGE 389). Barnabas and Paul were both present at the Council of Jerusalem (SEE PAGE 77), where it was agreed that Gentile converts to Christianity did not have to be circumcised. Alas, the two friends parted company, and Paul took Silas as his new missionary partner (Acts 15:36-41). Paul mentioned Barnabas in several of his letters. Acts refers to Barnabas as an "apostle" and also "prophet" and "teacher" among the early Christians. Mark, the author of the earliest Gospel, was Barnabas's kinsman, and an old tradition says that he wrote the Gospel at the urging of Barnabas. An early document called the Epistle of Barnabas almost made it into the New Testament, though whether Barnabas actually wrote it is in doubt. Also doubtful is the tradition that he wrote the Letter to the Hebrews, which *did* make it into the New Testament. Barnabas is an important character in Felix Mendelssohn's great oratorio *St. Paul*.

Barnabas is considered the patron saint of his birthplace, the island of Cyprus. The Catholic and Orthodox churches observe June 11 as the Feast of St. Barnabas.

Bathsheba and David
Adultery can be murder

The most famous case of adultery in history involved the king of Israel, David (ALSO SEE PAGE 87). The king already had several wives and concubines, but one day after his afternoon nap he saw Bathsheba bathing in a house nearby. As it happened, she was the wife of one of his valiant soldiers, Uriah, but he sent for her anyway, and they made love. Bathsheba became pregnant. Hoping to cover himself, David had Uriah sent home from the front for a "love furlough," but the dedicated soldier wouldn't sleep at home with his wife, saying it wasn't right to do so when his fellow fighters were sleeping in the field. David resorted to nastiness: he had Uriah sent to the thickest part of the fighting, ordering the other soldiers to fall back. Uriah was killed, David and Bathsheba married, and all seemed well—temporarily.

Apparently God was watching, because the prophet Nathan confronted the king, but in a stealthy way. He told the king a story about a poor man who pos-

David and Bathsheba's Child Dies
II Samuel. Chapter 12, Verses 15-23.

sessed one lamb that he kept as a pet. A wealthy neighbor with many sheep and cattle took the poor man's lamb and served it up as dinner for a guest. (The rich man was David, who had many wives but took another man's wife.) David was furious, shouting that such a horrible man deserved to die. Nathan uttered one of the most famous accusations in history: "Thou art the man!" He told David that because of his adultery with "the wife of Uriah" (note Nathan's choice of words) and his sending Uriah to his doom, violence would plague his family forever, and the child Bathsheba was carrying would die. The child did die, and David had to face rebellions throughout his reign, including one by his favorite son, Absalom. The David and Bathsheba story is found in 2 Samuel 11 and 12. Bathsheba did bear another son later, Solomon, who became king after David died. Thus she appears in Jesus' genealogy in Matthew 1, where she is called "the wife of Uriah."

In the Book of Psalms, Psalm 51 is attributed to David as his heartfelt confession of sin after being confronted by Nathan. The touching poem admits fault and begs for God's mercy. It contains the often-quoted words, "Wash me and I shall be whiter than snow" and "Create in me a clean heart, O God, and renew a right spirit within me."

The story of David and Bathsheba has, of course, appealed to artists and writers over the centuries, since it has everything—lust, sex, violence, stealth, the revealing of a hidden secret, repentance, punishment for sin. Painters have particularly been drawn to the moment of confrontation when the righteous Nathan cows David with the words "Thou art the man!" Numerous plays have been written on the story, including *David and Bethsabe*, written in Shakespeare's day by George Peele. Stephen Phillips wrote a poetic drama *The Sin of David*. The top-grossing film of 1951 was *David and Bathsheba*, which pretty much excused both parties for their adultery, but tacked on a scene of repentance at the end. The affair was also part of the story in the 1985 film *King David*.

Muslims honor David, whom they call Daud, as a prophet, but they deny the Bible's story of his adultery with Bathsheba.

B.C. and A.D.
Slightly off, but still functional

Christianity began in the Roman Empire, so the early Christians dated their years as the Romans did, years being A.U.C.—*anno urbis conditae*, "from the foundation of the city [of Rome]." They also numbered years as being "in the *n*th year of Emperor X." You can see this in Luke's Gospel, where it states that Jesus began his public life "in the fifteenth year of Tiberius's reign" (Luke 3:1). As time passed, this system of dating became uncomfortable for the Christians, since some of the Roman emperors were notorious persecutors. In other words, when Christians looked back on their own history, they preferred not to date years by the reigns of persecuting emperors like Nero and Diocletian. It also made sense to honor the founder of Christianity by numbering years based on his life. So around the year 540, a monk named Dionysius Exiguus invented the Christian chronology, with the year of Jesus' birth being A.D. 1—A.D., meaning *anno domini*, "year of the Lord." The years before were B.C.—"before Christ," and there was no year zero, so 1 B.C. was followed by A.D. 1. Using the small amount of data the Gospels give about dates, Dionysius calculated that Jesus was born in the Roman year 753 A.U.C. It turned out his calculation was slightly wrong. Jesus was born before the death of King Herod the Great, and Herod actually died in the year 4 B.C. So, weird as it sounds, Jesus was born around 4 or 5 "before Christ." By the time people were aware of the slight miscalculation, it seemed pointless to re-date everything that had been written before. Wherever Christianity spread, the year number was often preceded by the phrase "year of our Lord," as is still in some legal documents.

Dionysius's system didn't catch on until about 690 or so. Once it caught on, it spread gradually, and by now it has "gone global," so that even people not remotely aware of Christianity date the years as B.C. or A.D. For religious reasons, Jews still use their own chronology, with their year 1 being (supposedly) the year of the world's creation, a year that, in Christian terms, was 3761 B.C. For everyday purposes, Jews, like practically everyone else on the globe, use the Christian chronology of Dionysius Exiguus.

the Beatitudes
Bless those words

"Blessed are the ..." These are the opening words in Jesus' famous Sermon on the Mount (SEE PAGE 335). Found in Matthew 5 (and, slightly altered, in Luke 6), they are Jesus' blessings pronounced on these people: the poor in spirit, those who mourn, the meek, those who hunger and thirst after righteousness, the merciful, the pure in heart, the peacemakers, and those persecuted for righteousness' sake. In blessing these types of people, Jesus was telling his listeners what sort of people would be part of "the kingdom of God." The Beatitudes have probably been quoted and discussed and preached more than any part of the Bible.

Incidentally, the name Beatitude comes from the Latin word *beatitudo*, "blessedness." Composer Cesar Franck wrote an 1880 oratorio, *Les Beatitudes*.

Beelzebub
The shoo-fly god

This Hebrew words means "lord of the flies." In the Old Testament it refers to a god of the Philistine people of Ekron (2 Kings 1:2). By the time of Jesus and the apostles, Beelzebub was taken to be another name for the "prince of demons," Satan. Some of Jesus' enemies attributed his miracles to the power of Beelzebub (Mark 3:22, Luke 11:15).

The most famous Beelzebub in literature is the demon in John Milton's epic *Paradise Lost*. He is not Satan himself but is Satan's right-hand demon, second in power to him: "One next himself in power, and next in crime." In Christopher Marlowe's play, *The Tragical History of Doctor Faustus*, Beelzebub is one of three devils who bring about Faustus's spiritual ruin.

English author William Golding (1911-1993) won a Nobel Prize and is best known for *Lord of the Flies*, a disturbing novel about unsupervised schoolboys that revert to savagery on a deserted island. The book's title is an allusion to the biblical name Beelzebub, though in the book it also refers to a wild pig's head, covered with flies after it is placed on a stake in a primitive rite.

Belial
Bad news boys

The Old Testament uses the phrase "sons of Belial" several times. Belial simply meant "worthlessness," so a "son of Belial" was a "good-for-nothing" (Deuteronomy 13:13, Judges 19:22, 1 Samuel 25:25). However, in the New Testament, Paul seemed to use Belial as an alternate name for Satan: "What harmony is there between Christ and Belial?" (2 Corinthians 6:15).

In John Milton's epic poem *Paradise Lost*, Belial is one of the demons (rebel angels, that is) thrown out of heaven. He is described as the lewdest of the demons, one who loved "vice for itself."

Bethany

A good locale for raising the dead

Two places in the New Testament have this name, both of them important. One was the spot where John the Baptist baptized people, including Jesus (John 1:28), but no one is sure where this Bethany was, except that it was a site on the Jordan River.

The other Bethany was a village about three miles from Jerusalem, notable as the home of Jesus' friends, Mary, Martha, and Lazarus. It was also the site of Jesus' greatest miracle, the raising of the dead Lazarus. The site today has the Arabic name el-Azariyeh (which is a morph of the name Lazarus, if you look at it closely). The name Bethany has been popular as a name for churches and religious schools, as well as a large Christian publishing house. In recent years it has been a popular name for girls, though it's doubtful whether people know its religious connection.

Bethel

The pillow place

Bethel was the site where the patriarch Jacob slept with his head on a stone and had his famous dream of a stairway to heaven (Genesis 28). (SEE PAGE 165.) Many centuries later, after Israel had divided into a southern kingdom (Judah) and northern kingdom (Israel), Israel's king, Jeroboam, set up a worship center at Bethel, the aim being to keep the people of his kingdom from worshiping at the temple of Jerusalem, which was in Judah. Apparently Jeroboam set up a calf idol at Bethel, and several of the prophets harshly condemned the Bethel shrine.

Bethlehem

Birthplace of two kings

Thanks to the familiarity of the Christmas story, most people know that Bethlehem was the birthplace of Jesus. Mary and Joseph were residents of Nazareth, several miles north in Galilee. However, the Roman census required people to return to their ancestral homes, which is why Mary and Joseph were in Bethlehem at the time of Mary's delivery. Christians believe Jesus' birth in the town was a fulfillment of the prophecy of Micah that the Messiah would be born there (Micah 5:2). Prior to Jesus' birth, the town's claim to fame was being the birthplace of Israel's most famous king, David.

Bethlehem is mentioned in countless songs and stories relating to the birth of Jesus, and it was one of the world's earliest tourist destinations, since Christians wanted to visit the birthplace of Christ. The Roman emperor Constantine built the Church of the Nativity around the year 330, supposedly on the site of the actual birth, although no one knows for sure. There are several cities in the U.S. named Bethlehem. The infamous lunatic asylum in London was once called St. Mary of Bethlehem, but in time the name morphed into Bedlam.

bishops
Overseeing, or overlooking, spirituality?

Our word "bishop" morphed from the Greek word *episkopos*, literally meaning "overseer" or "superintendent." (You can see how the word "episcopal" came into being.) The word *episkopos* is used only five times in the New Testament, once (1 Peter 2:25) referring to Christ himself. In other places it seems to refer to a leader of a local group of Christians. Centuries after the Bible was written, a bishop was the head minister in a city or town. When the church became corrupt and worldly in the Middle Ages, the word bishop fell into bad repute, and when William Tyndale translated the Bible in English in the early 1500s, he used "overseer" instead of "bishop," insisting that the saintly overseers in the Bible were nothing like the worldly, materialistic bishops of his own time.

blasphemy
Them's stoning words ...

Blasphemy refers to mocking or cursing God. One of the Ten Commandments forbids using God's name in vain, and the Jews took this so seriously that they eventually stopped mentioning his name (Yahweh) at all, substituting the word "Lord." The punishment for blasphemy was stoning to death (Leviticus 24:10-16). Sadly, some of the Bible's heroes were wrongly accused of blasphemy, including Jesus himself and also the saintly martyr Stephen (Acts 76). The priests saw Jesus as a blasphemer because Jesus proclaimed himself "the Son of the living God"—which would have been blasphemy, except that (according to the Gospels) it happened to be true.

The "unpardonable sin," a form of blasphemy, was said by Jesus to be unforgivable (SEE PAGE 374).

The Book / Bible / Scripture
Scroll down for more info

Our word "bible" comes from the Greek words *biblia* and *biblion*, plural and singular for "book." In ancient times, paper (papyrus) was often exported through the port city of Byblos in Lebanon. The name of the town eventually morphed into *biblion*, meaning "paper" and eventually "book."

You might be aware that for many years one Christian publishing house marketed Bibles under the name *The Book*. Within the Bible itself, the word "book" really means "scroll," since there were no books in biblical days. The early Christians were among the first people to use books, bound on one side with writing on both sides of the page. Scrolls were actually wasteful, since the writing was normally on just one side, plus you couldn't flip easily from the beginning to the end. The early form of book was called a *codex*.

The Bible has often been called "the Good Book" or simply "the Book." People also use "Scripture" (capital S) to refer to the Bible. Scripture simply means "written things." It is common to use "Holy" before both Bible and Scripture. "Holy Writ" is another term for the Bible.

For Jews, the word bible refers only to the writings that Christians call the Old Testament. Jews don't accept the New Testament as part of their Bible. The Jews refer to their Bible as Tanak. A relatively modern name for the Hebrew Bible, the acronym is composed of the first letters of the three parts of the Hebrew Bible; the Torah (Law), the Nevi'im (Prophets), and the Ketuvim (Writings).

Since the Bible has been regarded as a specially inspired book by many—the authoritative word of God on moral and spiritual matters—the word "Bible" has been attached to many books claiming to be the authority on a particular subject, such as *The Fisherman's Bible*, *The Corvette Owner's Bible*, etc.

the boyhood of Jesus
Wise for his years

There is only one story in the Bible between Jesus' birth in Bethlehem and his baptism at the age of thirty, but it's an important one. In Luke 2, we learn that the twelve-year-old Jesus was taken with his parents to visit the temple in Jerusalem for the Passover celebration. The family traveled with a larger group, for they had already left the city when they realized Jesus was missing. In a panic, Mary and Joseph returned to Jerusalem and found Jesus in deep conversation with the Jewish teachers in the temple. "All who heard Him were astonished at His understanding and answers." Mary and Joseph scolded him for remaining behind and frightening them. Jesus replied, "Why is it that you sought me? Did you not know that I must be about my Father's business?" At the age of twelve—which among the Jews at that time meant the age of maturity—Jesus already had a sense of his destiny and mission. This story also shows that after this, Jesus "was subject unto them" (Luke 2:51), or in other words, he was "obedient" to his parents. This is an important part of the Gospel.

This is an appealing scene, and artists over the centuries have painted numerous canvases with titles like *Christ Among the Doctors* ("doctors" meaning "teachers," in this case.) The innocent but intelligent looking child is surrounded by elderly men with expressions of awe and amazement. The Christian would be expected to see such pictures and recall that when he reached adulthood, Jesus would be condemned as a blasphemer by some of those teachers.

Luke's Gospel tells us that Jesus "grew in wisdom and stature, and in favor with God and man" (Luke 2:52). This is the sum total of what the Bible tells us of Jesus' years between his birth and his baptism around age thirty. Where the four Gospels are silent, lots of stories that didn't make it into the Bible tell tales of the young Jesus, such as making

The Boy Jesus in the Temple
LUKE. CHAPTER 2, VERSES 46-52.

birds out of clay and bringing them to life, of striking a child dead and bringing him back to life, and many others. These are sheer fiction, although in the Middle Ages most churchgoers (who weren't literate, anyway) probably weren't aware of where the Gospels ended and the legends began. One of the great cultural surprises of recent years was the religious conversion of novelist Anne Rice, famed for her tales of vampires and witches. In 2005, Rice published *Christ the Lord: Out of Egypt*, narrated by the seven-year-old Jesus, and drawing on many of the legends about Jesus' childhood.

Aside from the legends, artists have often depicted the boy Jesus going about the family trade of carpentry, although in times past some critics said it was "vulgar" to show the Son of God working in a carpenter shop—an odd accusation, since the Bible makes it clear that Jesus was a fully human person, raised in a working-class home.

the bronze serpent
Worm or snake?

As great of a leader as Moses was, the Israelites he led out of slavery constantly complained and rebelled. Numbers 21 tells how God sent poisonous snakes as punishment. When the people confessed their sins, Moses set up a bronze snake on a pole, so that those who looked at it would live. While this may strike some people as pure legend, scientists think that what the people may have suffered from was the guinea worm, a very long parasite that burrows under the skin and causes great sickness.

God Sends Fiery Serpents Among the People
NUMBERS. CHAPTER 21, VERSES 4-9.

It can be removed—slowly—by twining it little by little around a stick. The bronze snake may have been a kind of visual aid to tell the people how to cure their ailment.

The Israelites had such reverence for the bronze snake that centuries later they were worshipping it as an idol—something God strictly prohibited. They even gave it a name, Nehushtan, but King Hezekiah ordered it destroyed.

Jesus referred to himself being lifted up on the cross as a way of spiritual healing, in the way that the bronze snake led to physical healing (John 3:14-16).

Some people think that the pole with two snakes twined around it, used as a symbol of the medical profession, is based on the bronze serpent of the Bible, but in fact that symbol is based on the emblem of the Greek god Asklepios, the god of healing

the burning bush
Holy grounded

Exodus 3 has one of the great God-man meetings in the Bible in the encounter of the burning bush. Moses had fled from Egypt and was herding sheep for his father-in-law in the wilderness. On the mountain of Horeb (also called Sinai), Moses saw a bush that was on fire but not consumed by the flames. God called to him from the bush and told him to take off his sandals, for he was standing on holy ground. God told Moses he had seen the oppression of the Hebrew slaves in Egypt and would free them and lead them to the land of Canaan. Moses asked God his name, and he identified himself "the God of your fathers, the God of Abraham, Isaac, and Jacob." To chase away any doubts Moses may have had, God told him to throw his staff on the ground, and it turned into a snake, then changed back again. Moses protested his own inadequacy as a speaker or leader, but God replied that he would teach Moses what to say and would pair him with his brother Aaron, a good speaker.

Moses Is Sent to Egypt
EXODUS. CHAPTER 3, VERSES 1-12.

Occurrences like these are what the scholars call *theophanies*, or God revealing himself to man in a dramatic way. The theophany at the bush is probably the best known in the world. There is speculation that a certain type of shrub that grows near Sinai sometimes catches fire spontaneously in the heat of the sun. However, there is no scientific explanation for the voice of God coming from the bush.

The scene was one of the high points of several movies about Moses, especially the 1956 epic *The Ten Commandments*, and the 1999 animated *Prince of Egypt*. Film conveys the drama of the scene much better than the many paintings of the encounter do. An image of the burning bush has been used by many Jewish and Christian groups throughout history. In Raphael's painting *Moses Before the Burning Bush*, the head and shoulders of the gray-bearded God emerge from the bush while Moses hides his face, his flock of sheep in the background

St. Katherine's monastery has existed for centuries on Sinai on the site where, supposedly, the burning bush encounter took place.

Several garden plants are known by the name burning bush, so called because of their showy leaves or flowers.

Caiaphas

Villain in a turban

In the story of Jesus' arrest, trial, and crucifixion, the person who comes off looking worst (besides Judas, that is) is Caiaphas, who was the Jewish high priest from the year 18 to 36. In those days, the priests weren't exactly the most spiritual people in the world. They were selfish, scheming bureaucrats, living off the money that devout Jews gave to the temple in Jerusalem. In other words, the highest officials in the Jewish religion were lousy specimens of humanity. Without realizing it, Caiaphas uttered a prophecy, claiming that it was better for one man to die than have all the Jews suffer (John 11:41-53). Christians think this is exactly what Jesus did—died in place of the real sinners in the world. Like the priests and other officials connected with the temple, Caiaphas feared that if Jesus' followers caused a ruckus, the Romans might tighten their hold on the region, maybe even shutting down the temple and doing away with their priesthood.

After Jesus' arrest, he was brought to the home of Caiaphas, where a travesty of a trial took place. Caiaphas was so enraged at Jesus, calling him a blasphemer, that he tore Jesus' robe. He sent Jesus off to Pilate, hoping Pilate would have Jesus crucified as a threat against the Roman government, which is exactly what happened, though Pilate didn't cave in immediately. The Book of Acts (Acts 4:6, Acts 7:1) states that Caiaphas also persecuted Jesus' followers.

In the various Passion plays and films about Jesus, Caiaphas is usually the villain of the piece (along with the traitor, Judas Iscariot). He is shown as unspiritual, someone who chose to condemn the Jews' Messiah instead of welcoming him with open arms. As the Jewish high priest, Caiaphas has been at the center of a centuries-long controversy about Jesus' trial, with Jews accusing Christians of an anti-Semitic depiction of Caiaphas and the other priests. This is frankly not the case, since all the Jews aren't responsible for Jesus' death, but Caiaphas and his cronies definitely are. In the 1927 film *The King of Kings*, director Cecil B. DeMille showed Caiaphas as a scheming bureaucrat, the man responsible for Jesus' death, but to fend off charges of being anti-Semitic, the movie showed Caiaphas praying to God, saying he alone was responsible for what happened, not the Jews as a whole. (Given that the Book of Acts says that Caiaphas persecuted Jesus' followers, it is extremely unlikely that this "repentance" actually took place.) Caiaphas is shown as equally vile in *Jesus Christ Superstar* and *The Passion of the Christ*.

Acts 4:6 states that Annas was the high priest, which confuses some readers. Annas was actually Caiphas's father-in-law and had been high priest earlier but removed from his post by the Romans. The Jews thought the high priest was a lifetime appointment, so although Caiaphas held the post officially, many of the Jews still looked to Annas as the *real* high priest. Along with Caiaphas, Annas is presented in a bad light in such films as *The Passion of the Christ* and *Jesus Christ Superstar*.

Cain and Abel
Brotherly non-love

The first child born into the world was a murderer. He was Cain, firstborn of Adam and Eve. In Genesis 4, the farmer Cain makes an offering to God, as does his younger brother Abel, the shepherd. For a reason that is not explained, God does not accept Cain's offering. Cain is so angry that he kills Abel in the field, and when God asks Cain where Abel is, he utters the famous question, "Am I my brother's keeper?" God curses Cain, making him "a fugitive and wanderer on the earth" (Genesis 4:14). He goes to "the land of Nod, east of Eden." The phrase "the curse of Cain" refers to continual wandering.

Genesis 4:17 mentions Cain's wife—leading to that great question: Where did he get a wife if the only people on earth were Adam, Eve, and himself? The only logical answer is that she was a sister, since Genesis 5:4 says that Adam and

Eve had daughters. In some old legends, Cain refused Adam's choice of wife for him, and God's punishment was his rejection of Cain's sacrifice. Cain's source of a wife isn't the only puzzle connected with him: Genesis 4:17 says that Cain "built a city"—an odd thing for someone cursed with being a wanderer. One more puzzle: Cain laments to God that whoever meets him will kill him (presumably

Cain Kills His Brother Abel
GENESIS. CHAPTER 4, VERSES 8-15.

for being a murderer), so God gives Cain a "mark" that will shield him from attack. So who were these other potential murderers in the world—other unnamed children of Adam and Eve?

Over the centuries, various religious sects have called themselves Cainites, with such groups claiming that they honor "bad boys" like Cain and Judas, who they admire because they were misunderstood rebels who didn't slavishly obey God. In the Anglo-Saxon epic poem *Beowulf*, the murderous monster Grendel and his mother are said to be descendants of Cain. Muslim legend says that Cain and Abel each had twin sisters, and that God commanded Cain to marry Abel's twin, but Cain would not, and married his own twin. It was because of this disobedience that Cain's offering was rejected by God.

As the Bible's first murderer, Cain has fascinated authors, some of whom try to show him sympathetically. The English poet Lord Byron wrote *Cain: A Mystery*, and fellow poet Samuel Taylor Coleridge wrote *The Wanderings of Cain*. John Steinbeck's novel *East of Eden* takes its title from Genesis 4:16 and retells the story of Adam, Cain, and Abel in a modern setting. The Cain story has been depicted in a few films, such as *The Green Pastures*, where the narrator describes him as "a mean rascal." The film *The Bible ... In the Beginning* showed Cain being stingy with the offering he made to God, a plausible reason for God's rejection of it, especially since Hebrew 11:4 says Abel offered a better sacrifice than Cain did.

The old expression "raising Cain" was a euphemism for "raising hell." Presumably the wicked Cain is in hell, so raising him up is a way of raising hell up. An old legend says that the "man in the moon" is Cain.

Canaan
God's favorite property

This is one of the most-mentioned locales in the Bible. It is the region that God gave to Abraham and his descendants. It took its name from a person, Canaan, the son of Ham, who was one of the three sons of Noah. Genesis describes how God called Abraham from his home in Ur and told him to live in Canaan. The latter chapters of Genesis tell the story of Abraham's grandson, Jacob, who moved the entire clan to Egypt because of a famine. The descendants—the twelve tribes of Israel—lived in Egypt and eventually became slaves of the Egyptians, until Moses led them out, taking a full forty years to complete the journey to Canaan. They didn't settle Canaan peacefully, for they had to conquer the idol-worshipping people there first, which is told in the Book of Joshua. The conquest was never quite completed, and the Israelites were constantly falling into the worship of the Canaanites' gods, especially the fertility god Baal, whose "worship" often involved having sex with "shrine prostitutes." Jews today regard the nation of Israel as the Canaan that is rightfully theirs, as God promised Abraham.

For Christians, the name Canaan took on an entirely different meaning: it referred to heaven, the "promised land" of God's people. Christians read the Old Testament and saw the promises about living in "a land of milk and honey" as referring to heaven, not to Canaan or any place on earth. Numerous Christian hymns refer to "Canaan" and "Canaan land," always meaning heaven. Several U.S. towns are named for Canaan, including New Canaan, Connecticut.

Historians say the Canaanites were probably the first people on earth to use an alphabet.

chapter and verse
Divvying up the Word

Each book of the Bible is divided into chapters, and each chapter into shorter sections called verses. These are numbered to allow people to refer to a specific quotation in the Bible. "Exodus 20:11" means "the Book of Exodus, chapter 20, verse 11." The numbers are for the benefit of readers, preachers, scholars, and anyone wanting to find a specific saying in the Bible.

These divisions weren't there from the beginning. In fact, the chapter divisions didn't exist until about the year 1200, and were done by Stephen Langton, an English clergyman who later became England's archbishop of Canterbury. In the 1500s, a French printer named Robert Estienne created the divisions into verses. All printed Bibles use these divisions, and the printed texts show the numbers in front of each verse (or, sometimes, in the margins).

The Book of Psalms is a special case. It always existed as 150 individual Psalms and did not need to be divided into chapters. Instead of saying "Psalms, chapter 23," you would say "Psalm 23." However, the Psalms have their verses numbered as the other books of the Bible do.

These divisions have been a "Godsend" to Jews and Christians—or anyone wishing to refer to a specific place in the Bible. Instead of saying, "That quote is somewhere in Revelation," you can be specific and say, "That's found in Revelation 3:20." A preacher might say on Sunday morning, "Turn in your Bibles to Isaiah 7:14."

The phrase "chapter and verse" has come to mean that someone is being very specific—that they have "done their homework" on a subject. If someone says, "The Bible teaches reincarnation," a person could reply, "Where is that in the Bible? Give me chapter and verse." The idea is that if a person is misquoting or misrepresenting what the Bible says, other people can refer to a chapter and verse and find out if that is what the Bible really says. The term *prooftexting* means referring to specific verses to back up a belief or practice.

charismatics

No more boredom in church

In the 1960s, Christians in many churches began "speaking in tongues"—a kind of ecstatic speech referred to in 1 Corinthians 12 and 14. Those chapters speak of "gifts of the Spirit" that are bestowed on Christians, and speaking in tongues is one of the gifts. The Greek word for "gifts" is *charisma*, and the people who emphasized the gifts of the Spirit are called *charismatics*. Speaking in tongues is not the only gift, for others include healing, preaching, teaching, prophesying, etc. Churches and even denominations have been divided over the charismatic movement, with some people saying that the movement has led to more joyous, heartfelt worship services, while critics say that people who claim to have "spiritual gifts" become arrogant. Some have even said that the "gifts" were really sent by the devil to make Christians appear silly. Charismatic churches generally have worship services that allow for handclapping, swaying with the music, and other things that traditional church services lack.

cherubim

Awesome, not cute

We generally think of "cherubs" as adorable child-faced angels, but the beings called *cherubim* (plural) in the Bible are awesome, not adorable. When Adam and Eve sinned and were booted out of Eden, cherubim served to bar their way back in, equipped with "flaming swords" (Genesis 3:24).

The next time that cherubim are mentioned is in the design of the famous ark of the covenant (SEE PAGE 32). The ark was a gold-covered wooden chest, and on the top, over the solid gold lid called the "mercy seat," were the two cherubim—human-shaped figures with wings instead of arms, with their outstretched wings touching each other (Exodus 25). The space between the wings, and over the mercy seat, was considered the sacred space of God, which is why the Old Testament several times uses the phrase "the Lord Almighty, enthroned between the cherubim." The ark was eventually placed in the temple in Jerusalem, which also had carvings of cherubim (1 Kings 6:23-29).

After the temple was destroyed by the Babylonians, people still remembered the cherubim. Living in exile in Babylon, the prophet Ezekiel experienced a mysterious vision of cherubim, which he described in detail: "Their whole body, with their backs, their hands, their wings, and the wheels that the four had, were full of eyes all around. ... Each one had four faces: the first face was the face of a cherub, the second face the face of a man, the third the face of a lion, and the fourth the face of an eagle" (Ezekiel 10:12, 14). (These did not match the cherubim on the ark of the covenant, so we can assume that the ancient Israelites applied the term cherubim to any awesome heavenly creature.) Ezekiel identifies them as the "living creatures" he saw in a vision related in Ezekiel 1.

Were the cherubim a type of angel? The Bible itself doesn't say so, and most of the angels mentioned in the Bible appear very humanlike, not like the figures on the ark, nor the strange beings Ezekiel saw. But if they were heavenly beings, certainly they could be classified as angels. Long after the Bible was written, some Christian and Jewish writers liked to speculate about the different types of angels and what their duties were in the heavenly court.

Exactly how the name cherubim, or cherubs, came to be applied to plump little child angels is still a mystery.

Children of God

Not quite everyone …

The Bible says that all people are God's children, right? Actually, no. God is very seldom referred to as "Father" in the Old Testament, and the Jews are considered God's "people," but not "children." Jesus shocked many people by bluntly referring to "my Father." Christians believed that Jesus was God's Son (capital "s"), having the same "essence" (for lack of a better word) as God. Christians believed they were all children of God—*adopted*, as the apostle Paul said, but not sons or daughters in the unique way that Jesus was (Romans 8:15, Ephesians 1:5). Being "born again" brought a person into God's family (John 1:12).

One Bible verse that drives translators nuts is John 3:16, which states that "God so loved the world that he gave his only begotten Son"—or so the older translations have it. The word that is translated as "only begotten" is the Greek *monogene*, which literally means "only child." Some modern versions have "only son" or "unique son" or "one and only son"—all of them close to the meaning, but not quite there.

chosen people

Privilege equals burden

In the Old Testament, the Israelites—also called Hebrews, later Jews—thought of themselves as "chosen" by God to be his special people. God's "choice" dates back to his covenant with the patriarch Abraham in Genesis, when he called Abraham the father of a great nation that worshiped only the one true God. Abraham's descendants, the Israelites, were chosen not because they were deserved but simply because God made his own free choice. So being "special" was no cause to be conceited or cocky. On the contrary, since God gave them spiritual guidance, they were obligated to obey it—or suffer the consequences. The prophet Amos quotes God as saying, "You only have I known of all the families of the earth: therefore I will punish you for all your iniquities" (Amos 3:2). Israel had God's laws, and if they were foolish enough (or mean enough) to disobey, God would punish them—often by using some heathen, idol-worshipping nation to do the punishing. Since God was holy and righteous, his chosen people had to follow suit. In other words, if you're special, you have to *act* special.

Christ / Messiah
The one, the only, the anointed

Christ wasn't Jesus' last name. It's a title, from the Greek word *Christos*, which has the same meaning as the Hebrew word *Messiah*: the Anointed One. Anointing was a ritual of pouring or daubing a small amount of scented oil on a person's head, marking them for a special divine task. In ancient Israel, kings and priests were anointed, but the Jews were awaiting the arrival of *the* Anointed One, God's man who would deliver his people from oppression. The Old Testament is full of prophecies of the coming of a great king who would be a descendant of King David, and who would also be like the great figure Moses. Most Jews thought the Messiah would be a political liberator, driving the Romans out of the Jews' homeland. But perhaps a few thought the Messiah would have a more spiritual role—not a mighty king riding on a horse, but a servant figure, identifying with the common people, bringing spiritual deliverance. Some thought the Messiah would be a purely human figure, others thought he would be divine.

Jesus turned out not to be the political Messiah some had hoped for, and there is some speculation that Judas, who betrayed Jesus, may have done so because he was disappointed that Jesus wasn't the liberator he desired. Or, Judas betrayed him in the hope that he would finally be forced to assume the role of liberator, which did not happen. When Jesus rode into Jerusalem on Palm Sunday and was hailed by the crowd, it's probable that many of those people were hoping he would be this long-awaited deliverer, which explains why the crowd seemed to turn against him after his arrest. It is ironic that Jesus was dragged before Pontius Pilate as a political agitator or rebel, since he plainly told Pilate that "My kingdom is not of this world." Before and after Jesus, there were Jewish rebels who, for brief periods, were hailed as the political Messiah.

Bible scholars argue whether Jesus was always aware that he was God's Messiah. It was not a name he applied to himself, yet he praised the disciple Peter for stating bluntly, "You are the Christ, the son of the living God." When Jesus was arrested and questioned by the priests, they asked him if he was the Christ, but he replied, "You have said so," and referred to himself as the "Son of Man." He did see himself as the Messiah, but he clearly did not press the issue, probably because he was not the military or political Messiah so many had hoped for. The priests condemned him as a blasphemer—not for claiming to be the Messiah, but for claiming to be the Son of God.

After Jesus' resurrection and ascension, his followers were known as "brothers" or "disciples," but eventually the name "Christian" came into being, so the people of the new faith were those who believed Jesus was the Christ, or Messiah. Acts and the New Testament epistles refer frequently to Jesus Christ, or sometimes Christ Jesus. And, quite often, people simply used the single name Christ.

The word Messiah is still used to refer to Jesus, and the name is remembered as the title of one of the most famous pieces of classical music, George Frideric Handel's *Messiah*. Many of the words in *Messiah* are taken from the Old Testament's prophecy of the Anointed One. Spelled with a small "m", messiah can refer to any kind of deliverer or liberator. People speak of a "messiah complex," the condition of someone believing himself to be a divinely appointed prophet or leader.

Jews who become Christian but also maintain their Jewish traditions are known as Messianic Jews. They are accepted by Christians but often snubbed by Jews, who see them as traitors to their heritage. Messianic Jews think of themselves as "fulfilled Jews" or "completed Jews," since they have found the Messiah that Jews have always hoped for.

A "Christ figure" in a book or film is a virtuous, compassionate being who sacrifices himself for others. Millions of people who have no particular affection for Christianity, or for any religion, recognize a "Christ figure" as a good thing.

Christians / brethren
Brother believers

Even though the New Testament is a Christian book, the actual word "Christian" doesn't appear in it very much. Acts 11:26 says that "the disciples were first called Christians at Antioch," which was a large city in Syria. The apostle Paul preached his faith before the Jewish ruler Agrippa, who referred to "becoming a Christian" (Acts 26:28). Enduring persecution as a Christian is mentioned in 1 Peter 4:16. So in the whole New Testament, "Christian" appears only three times. Some people referred to them as "the Nazarene sect" (Acts 24:5), after Jesus' hometown of Nazareth, and they were also referred to as "those who belonged to the Way" (Acts 9:2).

Much more common than "Christian" are the words "disciples," "brothers," and "believers," which have the same meaning as "fellow Christians." Some modern translations of the Bible do use "Christians" where older versions more correctly had "brothers." Obviously the word "Christians" is more gender-inclusive than "brothers" (and is easier to say than "brothers and sisters").

Christmas and Epiphany
Each day is a gift

You won't find the word Christmas in the Bible. Matthew and Luke give us a lot of details about Jesus' birth, but not a clue about what time of year it was. Frankly, we have no idea. The Romans celebrated December 25 as the festival called *Natalis Solis Invicti*, "birthday of the unconquered sun." This was a winter holiday celebrating the lengthening of days. As Christianity spread, the church adopted the old holiday, and as early as the year 336 Christians were celebrating it as the birthday of the "Sun of Righteousness," Christ. In time it was called the Feast of the Nativity, "nativity" coming from a Latin word meaning "birth."

The holy day called Epiphany, celebrated on January 6, commemorates the visit of the wise men to the baby Jesus. The Greek word *Epiphaneia* means "appearance" or "manifestation." The wise men's visit means Christ has appeared to the Gentiles (non-Jews). (At times Epiphany was referred to as the Feast of the Three Holy Kings, based on the old legend that the wise men were kings.) The "twelve days of Christmas" refers to the span from Christmas to Epiphany. (Thus the "twelfth day of Christmas" is January 5.) In some countries, people exchange gifts on Epiphany instead of Christmas, in memory of the gifts the wise men brought. Epiphany also commemorates Jesus' baptism in the Jordan River, which began his public ministry, and also his first miracle, turning the water into wine at the wedding in Cana.

Christ Is Born
LUKE. CHAPTER 2, VERSES 15, 16.

Incidentally, Easter was celebrated as a holy day long before Christmas and Epiphany were.

church
The "no walls" kind

The word "church" occurs many times in the New Testament, but never once does it refer to a building, since the early Christians met in homes or outdoors. The Greek word translated as "church" was *ekklesia*, meaning simply "assembly," which is why one large denomination today calls itself Assemblies of God. *Ekklesia* is at the root of our word "ecclesiastical," meaning "having to do with the church." In the 1500s, when William Tyndale made the first translation of the New Testament into English, he used "assembly" instead of "church."

Some churches today are aware that people often think of church services as boring, so many of them opt for other biblical names for their gatherings: assembly, temple, tabernacle, fellowship, etc.

circumcision
Covenant cutups

Around the globe and throughout history, circumcision—cutting off the foreskin of males—has been practiced as a religious rite by Jews and Muslims and as a sanitary measure in modern surgery on infants, boys reaching puberty, or on adult men. In some cultures it is simply tradition, but for the ancient Israelites, it was a sign of God's covenant with them, a practice begun when the patriarch Abraham was told by God to circumcise all males at the age of eight days (Genesis 17), which is still a Jewish practice. The Philistines, the coastal dwellers who were notorious for oppressing Israel, did not practice circumcision (many of the other surrounding nations did), so Israelites referred to the Philistines contemptuously as "the uncircumcised" and themselves as "the circumcision." They took circumcision so seriously that they even believed the angels were circumcised. (This belief isn't found in the Bible, incidentally.)

Throughout the history of the world, Jews have been mocked for circumcising their male infants, and even today some people regard it as a barbaric tribal custom that ought to be discontinued. In the period between the Old and New Testaments, the Greeks who settled in the territory of Israel became the cultural trendsetters, and some Jewish men had surgery performed to "uncircumcise" themselves so they would fit in with their Greek friends. Needless to say, these were Jews that did not take their religion seriously.

The custom was to circumcise a male child at eight days old, at which time its name was officially given (Luke 2:21). Ceremony was involved, the act being called "the covenant of our father Abraham," harking back to Genesis 17. Of course, the circumcision of an eight-day-old infant is no guarantee that he will grow up into a saintly man. Israel's prophets were aware of this, so they constantly preached that if the person's heart wasn't right, circumcision meant nothing (Jeremiah 4:4).

This idea was picked up by the first Christians. Even though Jesus and his disciples were Jews (and presumably circumcised), the faith spread to Gentiles, and some Jewish Christians believed that male Christians had to be circumcised. The matter was settled at the Council of Jerusalem (Acts 15), which decided circumcision was not necessary to become a Christian. The apostle Paul sounded like one of the Old Testament prophets when he wrote that "circumcision is of the heart" (Romans 2:29).

Uncircumcised men were not allowed into the Jerusalem temple itself, only the outermost court (called the Court of the Gentiles, appropriately enough). Acts 21 tells of a riot that ensued when the apostle Paul's enemies thought he had brought an uncircumcised man, Trophimus, into the temple.

Joshua 5 tells of the circumcision of all the Israelite men who had been during the forty years' journey from Egypt to Canaan. The circumcision was done with flint knives, and the site where it was done was called Gibeath-Haaraloth—"hill of foreskins." An even more painful story to read is found in Genesis 34, where Jacob's sons Levi and Simeon get revenge for the rape of their sister, Dinah. When the rapist agrees to marry the sister, Jacob insists that the men in his family be circumcised. And "on the third day, when they were sore," Simeon and Levi attacked and killed them all.

Muslims practice circumcision even though the Koran does not mandate it. They too regard themselves as children of Abraham, as the Jews do. Although Christians have never believed it was necessary, the Orthodox Church of Ethiopia does practice circumcision. For many centuries the Christian men of Europe regarded circumcision as a barbaric and shameful practice—since it was associated with Jews and Muslims.

The Eastern Orthodox churches celebrate January 1 as the Feast of the Circumcision of Our Lord. Some other churches refer to it as the Feast of the Holy Name of Jesus, since Jesus (like all Jewish children) was given his name on the eighth day after his birth, the same day as his circumcision.

A medical note: in the ancient world, where personal hygiene standards were low, circumcision did serve a medical need, with circumcised men less prone to certain below-the-waist problems. Whether people in those times knew that or not is debatable. In all likelihood they acted out of habit—and in the case of the Jews, as a reminder of their covenant with God.

cleansing the temple
Merchandising madness

We generally think of Jesus as exuding warmth and kindness, but he could show righteous anger on the right occasion. One of these was when he entered the temple courts in Jerusalem and saw the moneychangers and the sellers of sacrificial animals doing a brisk business. These businessmen were providing legitimate service—selling the animals that people offered up as sacrifices, and also exchanging non-Jewish coins for the Jewish shekels, the only currency the temple would accept. Jesus was angry not at their trade, but at what we would

Jesus Purifies the Temple
JOHN. CHAPTER 2, VERSES 13-17.

call price-gouging—and also the whole atmosphere, making the temple more like a market than a house of worship. Jesus made a whip out of cords and drove the sellers out, overturning their tables. While doing so, he quoted Isaiah 56:7, "Is it not written, `My house shall be called a house of prayer for all nations'? But you have made it a `den of thieves'" (Mark 11:17). Jesus' violent act—known in Christian tradition as the "cleansing of the temple"—angered the Jewish authorities, who made money off the system. Not surprisingly, "the scribes and chief priests heard it and sought how they might destroy him" (Mark 11:18). Some of the early Christians thought the cleansing of the temple was a fulfillment of the prophecy of Zechariah 14:21: "There shall no longer be a trader in the house of the Lord on that day."

While artists have tended to focus on the meek, kind Jesus, the cleansing of the temple, showing Jesus in a more assertive mood, is an appealing subject. Jacopo Bassano's *Purification of the Temple* (c. 1580, National Gallery, London) is a riot of beasts and human bodies, conveying the confusion of the scene. In the many films about Jesus, the cleansing is always a key scene. Perhaps the best cleansing scene is in the 1973 film of *Jesus Christ Superstar*, where the sung lyrics, "You have made it into a den of thieves!" carry emotional weight.

clergy
Don't call them "Father" …

In the Old Testament, the only clergy were the priests, who were all from the tribe of Levi, and who lived off sacrifices and other offerings made by the people. There were still priests in the New Testament period, but also rabbis, who had studied the Law of Moses and were considered experts. Rabbis were not paid for their services, however. Neither were the Christian ministers in the Bible, for they served the Christian communities out of dedication to God, not for any material gain. The apostle Paul spoke of various offices that Christians held in the churches—prophets, teachers, apostles, administrators, healers (1 Corinthians 12:27-29, Romans 12:3-8). Three of his epistles—1 and 2 Timothy, Titus—are called the Pastoral Epistles because he discusses the qualifications for being an *episkopos* or *presbuteros* or *diakonos*. *Episkopos* is usually translated as "bishop" but sometimes "overseer" (which is what it literally means). *Presbuteros* is usually translated "presbyter" or "elder" (the literal meaning). *Diakonos* is usually "deacon."

There is a lot of debate over whether the offices were interchangeable, or whether Paul intended the titles to be permanent fixtures among Christians. One thing is certain: these men were *not* required to be celibate, for Paul seems to have assumed most of them were married men (1 Timothy 3:4). The idea of celibacy for clergy was adopted centuries later, with the Catholic Church basing the practice on the fact that both Jesus and Paul were unmarried men, and also the fact that Paul recommended the single state for Christians capable of resisting sexual temptation (1 Corinthians 7:1-8).

Regarding clergy's use of titles like "reverend" or "father" or "doctor," the New Testament is clearly against them. Jesus told his disciples to strive to be servants of people, not their masters, and that being addressed as "father" was wrong, for God was the only true Father (Matthew 20:26-28, Matthew 23:9). In fact, Matthew 23 pretty much condemns all the "showy" aspects of religion—pompous titles, a distinctive form of dress, special places to sit in worship services. Jesus gave a stern warning: "Whoever exalts himself will be humbled, and whoever humbles himself will be exalted." The many pictures and statues showing bishops and other church officials dressed in rich robes and distinctive hats are ironic, considering Jesus' words. The many religious orders who take vows of poverty, such as the Franciscans, take Jesus' words more seriously.

Communion / Lord's Supper / Eucharist
Meal with meaning

The church ritual called Holy Communion, or the Lord's Supper, or the Eucharist is a commemoration of Jesus' Last Supper with his disciples before he was arrested, crucified, and resurrected. As Jesus broke the Passover bread for the disciples, he told them, "This is my body," and passing the cup of wine, he said, "This is my blood of the new covenant. Do this in remembrance of me." From the earliest days, Christians did as Jesus instructed, celebrating the ritual every time they gathered together, breaking bread, drinking wine, and recalling the words Jesus spoke to his disciples. The New Testament gives the impression that an actual meal was prepared, but in later times the bread and wine were given in small amounts, which is still the case in most churches. The bread is often only a small wafer, with the wine (or grape juice) given in thimble-sized cups. Other churches serve actual bread and pass around a common cup of wine, which is closer to what occurred with Jesus and the disciples.

One of the saddest stories in the history of religion is how Christians have persecuted each other over the issue of what the Lord's Supper involves. For centuries the Catholic and Orthodox churches have taught that Jesus' words were literal: When he said, "This is my body" and "This is my blood," he meant what he said. Whenever the Lord's Supper is celebrated, the bread and wine actually become (in some mysterious way) the body and blood of Jesus. This mysterious

The Holy Communion
Matthew. Chapter 26, Verses 26-28.

transformation is called *transubstantiation*. With the Protestant Reformation in the 1500s, some people questioned the old belief, and said the important part of the Last Supper was Jesus saying, "Do this in remembrance of me." Most Protestants regard Communion as just a reminder of what took place at the Last Supper.

The early Christians were accused of human sacrifice and cannibalism because they spoke of eating the flesh and drinking the blood of Jesus—but they were referring to the bread and wine used in Holy Communion, of course. The rumor about cannibalism persisted for many years and was one reason the early Christians were persecuted.

Corinthians
Living morally in an ancient Vegas

In the ancient world, "Corinthian" was another way of saying "whore." The large, cosmopolitan port city's patron goddess was Aphrodite (no surprise), and her large temple had a thousand "priestesses" (more accurately, "temple whores"). There was a Christian fellowship in this Greek metropolis as early as the year 52, and it was trying to survive in a moral cesspool—and often failing, which is why the apostle Paul wrote two of his most important letters to the Corinthian Christians. Acts 18 shows that Paul established the church in Corinth, and 1 and 2 Corinthians were written to address the moral and spiritual problems there. In 1 Corinthians he urged the people to heal their divisions and to crack down on openly immoral members, including one brazen man who was cohabiting with his stepmother. In one passage, Paul reminded the people that their bodies belonged to God, and they had no business giving them to prostitutes (1 Corinthians 6:12-20). He urged single Christians to stay single and celibate if they could, but better to marry than to sleep around. He discussed the variety of spiritual gifts different Christians had, and in the eloquent 1 Corinthians, chapter 13, claimed that genuine love for others was greater than any spiritual gift—in fact, love would remain when everything else had passed away. He also discussed the divisive issue of "speaking in tongues." 1 Corinthians, chapter 15 is a prophecy of what will happen at the time of the resurrection, when believers would put on a new "spiritual body" for their life in eternity. Some of the verses from this chapter were set to stirring music in Handel's *Messiah*.

In 2 Corinthians, Paul reminded the Christians that "if anyone is in Christ, he is a new creation—the old has passed away, the new has come" (2 Corinthians 5:17). He urged the people to aid fellow Christians in distress, reminding them that "God loves a cheerful giver" and that "we reap what we sow" (2 Corinthians 9:6-8). Paul got very personal and lamented having a "thorn in the flesh," an affliction he had prayed to have removed, but his suffering made him more dependent on God.

The two letters are some of the most studied and most quoted parts of the New Testament.

Council of Jerusalem

The cutting edge question

The early Christians were all Jews, but as the gospel spread to Gentiles (non-Jews), a question arose: Should Christians have to obey all the Jewish laws? To be painfully specific, did male converts have to undergo the Jewish ritual of circumcision?

In times past, the Jews required that converts had to be circumcised before they were fully considered Jews. Would that also be true for Christians?

Acts 15 describes a crucial Christian gathering in Jerusalem, where the apostle Peter told the assembly that conversion to Christianity was a spiritual matter, so circumcision must not be required. The apostle Paul, who was already converting Gentiles, backed him up in this matter, and the council drafted a letter to non-Jewish Christians, telling them to avoid immorality but making no mention of mandatory circumcision.

The council's decision was an important one because it meant that Christianity was something more than just an offshoot of the Jewish religion. It was a universal faith for the whole world, something spiritual, and the old laws of the Jews did not necessarily apply. Keep in mind that in these days before anesthesia, circumcision for an adult male was extremely painful. Aside from that, many Gentile men regarded circumcision as a tribal relic from the Jews' past, something that had nothing to do with loving God and your fellow man.

creeds
Faith in a nutshell

A creed is a summing up of basic beliefs, something to be memorized by a person who adheres to a religion. The early Christians' essential creed was simple: Jesus is Lord. The apostle Paul stated a form of this: "If you confess with your mouth that Jesus is Lord and believe in your heart that God raised him from the dead, you will be saved" (Romans 10:9).

Over time, the Christian creeds got a little more detailed, most of them stating a belief in (1) God the Father and Creator; (2) Jesus the Son of God who was crucified, resurrected, and taken into heaven; (3) the return of Jesus to earth as judge of all mankind; (4) the power of God as the Holy Spirit; and (5) eternal life. One of the oldest creeds is called the Apostles' Creed, though it wasn't written by the apostles themselves. Millions of Christians worldwide recite the Apostles' Creed every Sunday. Another common creed, longer than the Apostles', is the Nicene Creed, named after a Christian council held in the year 325. All creeds are, in theory, based on the Bible. All of them acknowledge a belief in the Trinity (SEE PAGE 368)—that God exists as Father, Son, and Holy Spirit. All of them state that Jesus was both divine and human, and some of them go into detail explaining just how he was both at the same time.

cross and crucifixion
Brutality turned into salvation

It is ironic that many people wear crosses on necklaces or earrings, since crucifixion was a truly horrible thing. We aren't absolutely sure who invented crucifixion, but it was probably the ancient Persians, since we know that the Persian emperor Darius crucified 3,000 political prisoners five hundred years before the time of Jesus. The Romans used it as the most common form of capital punishment for political agitators, pirates, and slaves. (Romans citizens were beheaded, which was considered a quicker and more merciful death.) Usually the condemned man was whipped, then made to carry the crossbeam (the *patibulum*) to the crucifixion site, where the upright post was already fixed. (In other words, the many pictures and movies that show Jesus carrying a "full cross" are probably not correct.) Capital punishment in those days was a very public thing, since the idea was to remind any would-be criminals that the law was strict. Crucifixions were usually done on hills or by roadsides. This public humiliation was part of the punishment, and as the Gospels make clear, people passing by felt no shame in insulting the crucified man.

The condemned man would be stripped of his outer clothing, with his wrists attached to the crossbeam with rope or nails. (Nails went into the wrist, not the hand itself.) The feet were either bound or nailed. The Romans crucified their victims nude, but made an exception for Jewish men. As stated in the Gospels, a sign (called a *titulus*) was nailed over the person's head, stating his name and his crime. (In some cases, it was hung around the person's neck.) The *titulus* over Jesus had the inscription "Jesus of Nazareth, King of the Jews," but most crosses in art have

Jesus Dies on the Cross
JOHN. CHAPTER 19, VERSES 25-30.

simply INRI, the abbreviation of the inscription in Latin. Death was caused by exhaustion or heart failure, and some victims lingered for days. Death could be hastened by using an iron club to break the legs. Jesus died fairly quickly, probably because of the brutal beating he had already received.

It's debatable whether crucifixion was the most horrible punishment ever devised, but certainly it was among the worst, as anyone who saw the film *The Passion of the Christ* is aware. The Gospels don't provide details about the crucifixion for an obvious reason: the first readers of the Gospels had probably seen men crucified and knew how brutal it was. Thus the Gospels use the bare words "they crucified him." The Roman politician and writer Cicero stated that crucifixion was the "most cruel and most repulsive" means of execution, and many people agreed.

The Gospels make it clear that Jesus' crucifixion did not take him by surprise. He had already told his disciples that on this visit to Jerusalem he would be crucified—then rise again.

The cross is mentioned numerous times in the New Testament, the key idea being that Jesus, the Son of God, was innocent and deserved no punishment. The early Christians believed that Jesus was the ultimate sacrifice, someone guiltless dying in the place of all sinners. Putting your faith in "the cross" meant you believed that Jesus' painful death had given you salvation, putting you in a right relationship with God. The symbol of this horrible form of capital punishment became the symbol of salvation. It is, of course, one of the most common religious symbols in the world.

A cross that also has an image of Jesus' body on it is usually called a *crucifix*, not cross. Interestingly, the earliest crucifixes did not show Jesus in agony but triumphant—on the cross, but clothed, head erect, sometimes wearing a crown—the Son of God triumphing over death, a figure called the *Christus triumphans*. Later crucifixes showed Jesus in agony—the *Christus patiens*. As the church became wealthy and worldly, crosses and crucifixes in churches were often made of gold or ivory and even encrusted with jewels. In the Middle Ages, the Crusaders who fought the Muslims often had crosses on their armor and shields. In fact, the name Crusader comes from the Spanish *cruzada*, meaning "marked with a cross."

Jesus told his followers to expect persecution, and tradition says some of them were crucified. A very old tradition says that the apostle Peter, about to be crucified, told the Romans he was not worthy to die the same death as his master—so the Romans obliged him by crucifying him upside down. The Roman emperor Constantine, who converted to Christianity in the year 312, abolished crucifixion in the empire. It didn't completely die out, however, and in the 1500s Japan had an anti-Christian purge in which it crucified many of the Christians in that country.

The conversion of Constantine occurred in the year 312. Before a major battle, he saw a vision of a cross in the sky, with the words, "In this sign conquer." He inscribed the cross on his soldiers' shields and won the battle. His conversion changed the course of European history, since he ended the persecution of Christians and paved the way for the faith to become the only tolerated religion in the empire.

Helena, the mother of Emperor Constantine, made a trip to the Holy Land and claimed she found the actual cross Jesus had been crucified on. (Needless to say, archaeology was not very scientific in those days.) As centuries passed, probably a trainload of splinters from the "true cross" were sold and traded, and some church authorities insisted that the wood, since it had touched Jesus, was able to miraculously multiply. In the 1500s, leaders of the Protestant Reformation openly mocked this cult of "true cross" splinters and insisted that faith in Christ, not possession of splinters, was the important thing in Christian life.

Many Catholic churches have the fourteen "stations of the cross" within their walls. These are marked by pictures showing Jesus from the moment of his condemnation to the burial of his body in the tomb. It is a devotional exercise for people to walk to each station in sequence, meditating on what happened and offering up prayers. The circuit is also called the *Via Crucis* ("Way of the Cross") or *Via Dolorosa* ("Way of Sadness"). The city of Jerusalem, of course, has the actual stations themselves, and many Christian tourists still follow the path. While the names of many roads in Jerusalem are translated into English, Hebrew, and Arabic for their signs, the name Via Dolorosa is used in all three languages. Composer Franz Liszt's 1879 choral work *Via Crucis*, with words from the Bible, has solo parts for Jesus and Pilate, with the chorus representing the women of Jerusalem.

One of the oldest writings in English is the long poem *The Dream of the Rood*, composed in Anglo-Saxon (Old English) sometime around the year 700. The word "rood" meant "cross," and the poem is a theological meditation on the meaning of Jesus' suffering.

No one knows exactly what type of wood Jesus' cross was made from, but in the realm of legend, several types of tree that don't grow straight up were said to supply the wood of the cross—the tree was so shamed at having supplied the wood to crucify the Son of God that, afterward, its trunk and branches grew crooked instead of straight. The dogwood, live oak, and several other crooked-trunked trees are thought to be the "embarrassed" tree.

crown of thorns
Headwear (not) fit for a king

Three of the Gospels report that part of Jesus' humiliation after his arrest was the mocking of him as "king of the Jews," in which the Roman soldiers draped him with a cast-off robe, giving him a reed for a scepter, and, worst of all, pressing a crown of thorns onto his head. Bible scholars argue about just what thorny plant was used, but the point is that Jesus not only endured a horrible scourging

Jesus With the Crown of Thorns
Matthew. Chapter 27, Verses 27-30.

on his back, but some nasty wounds on the head as well. We don't know whether the thorny crown remained on his head after he was nailed to the cross, but every artwork and film shows it that way, which is appropriate, since there was a sign affixed over Jesus' head reading "Jesus of Nazareth, King of the Jews."

Luke's Gospel omits the crown of thorns incident. Luke seemed to be trying to make the story as appealing as possible to Roman readers, so he simply chose not to include the episode of Jesus being crowned and mocked by the soldiers. ("Spin" existed in the ancient world, obviously.)

In the 1930s, a German film about Jesus was titled *Golgotha* in its homeland, but released as *Crown of Thorns* in the United States. Paintings with the title *Christ Crowned with Thorns* are too numerous to count, and references to the crown of thorns are common in pop culture (think of the song "American Pie" with its mention of a "thorny crown"). Several thorny garden plants are known by the name crown-of-thorns. Some orders of Catholic monks modeled their distinctive tonsures (hairstyle) on the crown of thorns, with the head being shaved on the top and at the nape, leaving a ring of hair around the head, a visual reminder of Christ's crown of thorns.

In the Middle Ages, many individuals and churches claimed to possess the crown of thorns—or, at least, one of the thorns from it. The French scientist Blaise Pascal (1623-1662) had his faith deepened when his niece was healed of an ailment by the "Miracle of the Holy Thorn." There was big business in relics that had (supposedly) actually touched Jesus himself, such as the wood of the cross, the nails, the cup used at the Last Supper, etc.

Dagon
Zapped by the ark

The chief god of the Philistines is mentioned only a few times in the Bible, but in some very colorful stories. The most dramatic is the final act of Samson in the Book of Judges. The muscleman Samson, shorn of his hair, was captured and blinded by the Philistines. While in prison, his hair grew back and so did his strength. Taken to the temple of Dagon to be mocked by the people, Samson literally brought the house down by pushing two pillars apart (Judges 16).

Later, the Philistines captured Israel's sacred chest, the ark of the covenant, and set it in the temple of Dagon. The next morning they found the Dagon idol lying face down, its head and hands broken off. Naturally, they returned the ark to Israel (1 Samuel 5).

The last mention of Dagon is in the story of King Saul. After his defeat by the Philistines, they hung his severed head in the temple of the god (1 Chronicles 10:10).

the Damascus road experience
History's most famous 180

One of the most dramatic stories in the New Testament is found in Acts 9, where the devout Jew Saul (later re-named Paul, SEE PAGE 275) is on his way to the city of Damascus to arrest Jews who have become Christians. On the road there, he is blinded by a light from heaven and hears the voice of Jesus saying, "Saul, Saul, why are you persecuting me?" His traveling companions see the light but do not hear the voice. He has to be led into Damascus, where a Christian named Ananias restores his sight and introduces him to the other Christians in the city. The Jews of Damascus are not pleased that their chief heretic-hunter has turned Christian, and they

The Conversion of Saul
ACTS. CHAPTER 9, VERSES 3-9.

plot to kill him. The Christians help Saul escape by lowering him in a basket over the city walls. Much of the Book of Acts tells of the career of the former persecutor who becomes the most famous witness to Christianity.

The story became part of the language, with "Damascus road" referring to any dramatic, life-altering experience. Artists have been fascinated by the episode, depicting Paul lying on the ground, blind, while his companions stare in puzzlement. (The Italian artist Caravaggio painted it numerous times.) *Damascus Road*, an outdoor drama dealing with the life of Paul, has been presented in the Great Smoky Mountains for many years.

Daniel
The lions den fellow

The Book of Daniel is one of the most-read books of the Old Testament, one with stories adults often read to children because the hero is a highly moral young man, and also because the stories show young people triumphing in adversity. The old Sunday school song "Dare to Be a Daniel" reminded children that clean living meant God would watch over them in times of trouble.

Daniel and his three friends were among the Jewish exiles that had been taken to Babylon after the Babylonians conquered their homeland. The four attractive and intelligent boys were groomed to be aides in the court of the Babylonian king Nebuchadnezzar. The king had a mystifying dream about a statue made of four metals, and when his court wizards couldn't interpret the dream, Daniel could, explaining that the metals represented four kingdoms of the future. (Bible readers have for two thousand years been arguing about just which nations were represented by the metals—although we know that the statue's gold head represented Nebuchadnezzar himself, for Daniel told him so.)

For this, Daniel and his friends were promoted to high office, but later they got into trouble for not bowing down to a huge gold idol the king had set up. As faithful Jews, they would not bow down to an idol. The king had the three friends—Shadrach, Meshach, and Abednego—thrown into a fiery furnace. Miraculously they survived, and the king saw a fourth person walking among them in the furnace, one who "looked like a song of the gods." Christian theologians have speculated that this fourth person in the furnace was an angel—or perhaps God himself—or Christ, putting in a "preview" appearance before his actual birth centuries later. The Old Testament Apocrypha contains a short book called the Song of the Three Young Men, which is supposedly the prayer of the three in the fiery furnace. English composer Benjamin Britten wrote an opera *The Burning Fiery Furnace*. The popular church play *It's Cool in the Furnace* is based on this story.

Later Nebuchadnezzar had another puzzling dream, and Daniel interpreted it to mean the king would go mad and live in the wilds, crawling on all fours, which happened exactly as he prophesied. (SEE PAGE 253 for more about Nebuchadnezzar.)

Another famous incident from the book is chapter 5, where the Babylonian ruler Belshazzar holds a grand feast, using the vessels from the Jews' temple to drink from. A disembodied hand writes four words on the wall, sending the people into a panic. Daniel interprets the words to mean that the Babylonians are about to be conquered by the Persian Empire, which happens that very night. The story is the source of the phrase "handwriting on the wall." Artists have had a field day with this scene, showing the gaudily clad Babylonians quaking with fear over the spectral hand.

With the Persians in power, Daniel becomes an aide to the king, Darius. The king issued a decree that no one could pray to any god or man except Darius himself. The faithful Daniel would not do so, so the king had him thrown into a den of lions. The next morning, Daniel was unharmed, protected by the Lord. The image of Daniel in the lions' den has been a favorite for artists, who depict Daniel praying while the lions look on him hungrily. Often the scene shows human bones scattered on the ground.

Chapters 7-12 of the book are very different from the first, containing visions of the future, very similar to the New Testament's Book of Revelation. This type of writing is called *apocalyptic* (SEE PAGE 306). As with the Book of Revelation, readers have been puzzling for centuries over the meaning of Daniel's visions of the end of time.

Catholic Bibles contain other stories that are added to Daniel, one telling the story of a virtuous Jewish woman named Susanna, another showing how Daniel exposed the priests of the false god Bel. Daniel saves Susanna from being executed, so he gained a reputation as a fair judge, the source of the phrase "a Daniel come to judgment" in Shakespeare's play *The Merchant of Venice*. George Frideric Handel wrote an oratorio about Susanna and Daniel, and Daniel is also featured in his oratorio *Belshazzar's Feast*.

Eastern Orthodox Christians honor Daniel and his three friends as saints and celebrate them on December 17.

David
Loving, but not always wisely

The Bible speaks of David as "a man after God's own heart" (1 Samuel 13:14). Maybe it's appropriate that his name actually means "beloved." He was Israel's great king, psalm-writer, and military leader—but also an adulterer, overly indulgent father, and a failure on several other fronts. His story is the fullest biography of anyone in the Old Testament, and the Bible shows him (as it shows all its heroes) "warts and all." The Bible gives us David the shepherd boy, harpist, poet, slayer of the giant Goliath, bosom friend of Jonathan, loyal servant (and prey) of the paranoid King Saul, husband of many wives, a military man—David was so many things, and "all charisma." In spite of his obvious failings, Israel remembered him as an ideal king, an emotional man so God-obsessed that he danced publicly when the ark of the covenant was brought into Jerusalem. Israel had reasons to regret it had ever asked God for a king, but David was, in the final analysis, a *good* king, loyal to God and people near him. Historically, David's forty-year reign was from about 1010 B.C. to 970 B.C.

David's saga is told in 1 and 2 Samuel, 1 Kings, and 1 Chronicles. The books of Samuel are somewhat misnamed, since David is really the principal character, although they were (supposedly) written by Samuel. For more about the key episodes in David's life, see the entries for Samuel, Saul, Jonathan, Goliath, Bathsheba, Michal, and Absalom.

David's birth in the little town of Bethlehem led to the idea that Israel's savior-king, the Messiah, would be born in Bethlehem. It was, of course, Jesus' birthplace centuries later, and during his lifetime, many people referred to him as the Son of David.

David was highly regarded in the New Testament period. After Moses and Abraham, he is the Old Testament character most mentioned in the New Testament. In the Middle Ages, nine famous warriors in history were called the Nine Worthies, and three of them were from the Bible: David, Joshua, and (from the Apocrypha) Judas Maccabeus.

One oddity about the name David: He is the only person in the Bible with the name.

David is the subject of countless artworks and works of literature. David as the killer of Goliath is a favorite for sculptors (SEE PAGE 134 for more on Goliath). Several artists have painted *King David in Prayer*, recalling his important (but less dramatic) role as psalmist. So far no film has been able to capture his life, partly because it simply doesn't fit into a two-hour form. The 1985 film *King David* tried, but failed. Joseph Heller's 1984 novel *God Knows*, narrated by the elderly David,

David Slays Goliath
I SAMUEL. CHAPTER 17, VERSES 45-51.

looks at the events of the Bible from a humorous perspective. Elmer Davis's novel *Giant Killer* stuck closer to the Bible. Author Roark Bradford retold the stories in the dialect of Southern blacks in *Ol' King David and the Philistine Boys*. Poets Abraham Cowley and Thomas Elwood both wrote long poems about the king with the title *Davideis*. Playwright James Barrie, best known for *Peter Pan*, also wrote *The Boy David*, which is somewhat sympathetic to Saul. American poet Stephen Vincent Benét wrote the long poem *King David*. Swiss composer Arthur Honegger wrote a 1921 opera *Le Roi David* (*King David*), and French composer Darius Milhaud wrote an opera *David* in honor of the 3,000th anniversary of Israel. The English poet Christopher Smart wrote a lengthy *Song to David*, praising David's many virtues, especially his writing of the Psalms.

One closing tidbit: An old tradition says that David is one of the four kings in a deck of playing cards.

Day of Atonement / Yom Kippur

It doesn't get more solemn than this ...

This was the most important of Israel's holy days. The high priest offered sacrifices for the sins of all the people, in a ritual described in Leviticus 16. The priest slaughtered a goat and sprinkled its blood on the lid (the "mercy seat") of the ark of the covenant. Another goat suffered a different fate: the high priest would lay his hands on the goat, symbolically laying on it the sins of the people, then drive it off into the wilderness. (This was the so-called "scapegoat.") With the destruction of the temple in the year 70, and the end of the Jewish priesthood, the rituals mandated in Leviticus had to be "spiritualized" for use in the synagogues—no more priest, blood, or goats. But the confession of sins remained, along with the people forgiving each other.

The word *atonement* means "at-one-ment"—that is, bringing God and man together, after human sin had caused them to separate, spiritually speaking. After the ritual, God and man were "at one." In the New Testament, a new idea is presented: people no longer need the annual ritual of the Day of Atonement, for Jesus, the innocent Son of God, is the final sacrifice, so his death on the cross creates atonement once and for all.

The Jewish calendar year opens with Ten Days of Repentance, the first of these being Rosh Hashanah. Yom Kippur, the Day of Atonement, is the tenth day, and on that day no work is to be done, nor are Jews to eat, drink, wash, or have sexual relations. Devout Jews may spend the entire day at their synagogues in worship, prayer, and meditation. The final worship concludes with the blowing of the *shofar*, a trumpet made from a ram's horn. Yom Kippur is the tenth day of the Jewish month Tishri, and because the Jewish calendar is lunar, not solar, the date varies on standard calendars, with Yom Kippur occurring in late September or early October.

In the long-running conflict between Arabs and Israelis in the Middle East, one memorable incident occurred October 6, 1973, when Egyptians and Syrians attacked Israel on Yom Kippur, something that shocked Jews worldwide. By the time the so-called Yom Kippur War ended on October 24, Israel had recovered all the territory it lost on October 6.

deacons
Helping hands and minds

The word comes from the Greek *diakonos*, meaning "helper" or "one who carries out the commands of another." They are mentioned in the New Testament as helpers of the apostles, and Acts 6 describes the appointment of the first seven deacons, one of whom was the eloquent Stephen, the first Christian martyr. Although the early Christian ministers were all men (as far as we know), a woman named Phoebe was apparently a female deacon, and presumably there were others (Romans 16:1). Different Christian groups apply the name deacon in different ways. In some churches, being a deacon is a step on the way to being an ordained minister, but in some churches deacons are laymen who form a kind of governing board in the church.

the Dead Sea
Not quite, but really close

This is the lowest point on planet earth, 1,290 feet below sea level. The surrounding area is bleak and desolate, but tourists to Israel often swim in the Sea, which has such a high salt content (25 percent, compared to 5 percent in ocean water) that floating is easy. The high salt concentration also means that almost no plants or animals live in it. (It isn't quite "dead," but darn near it.) The Bible sometimes calls it the Salt Sea (Genesis 14:3), Sea of the Arabah (Deuteronomy 3:17), or the eastern sea (Joel 2:20). The muddy Jordan River empties into the Sea. It was considered Israel's eastern border, but the Bible mentions it only as a geographical reference point, since the area is not a favorable spot for living in. Historians speculate that the destroyed cities of Sodom and Gomorrah might lie underneath the Sea. In fact, in times past it was called the Sodomitish Sea.

Deborah
Woman of substance

Ancient Israel was pretty "sexist" by our standards, but certain outstanding women made their presence felt. One was Deborah, Israel's only female judge, and also a prophetess. Judges 4:5 says, "She held court under the Palm of Deborah ... and the Israelites came to her to have their disputes decided." But like the other "judges," she was primarily a military deliverer. Her partner in getting the Canaanites off Israel's back was the military man Barak, but the real star of the Deborah-Barak story is a woman named Jael. She lured Sisera, the enemy leader, to her tent, tucked him in for a nap, then while he slept drove a tent peg through his head.

Chapter 5 of Judges is the "Song of Deborah," her very militant victory song recounting the defeat of Sisera. The song contains the line "the stars in their courses fought against Sisera." Author Shelby Foote used *Stars in Their Courses* as the title of his book about the Civil War Battle of Gettysburg. Salomon de Bray's painting *Jael, Deborah, and Barak* (1635) shows a stern and very buxom Jael, who holds a mallet and looks directly at the viewer. Deborah is an old woman, her hands pressed together in prayer. Barak wears black armor. Composer George Frideric Handel wrote an oratorio about Deborah, and the modern Italian composer Ildebrando Pizzetti wrote the opera *Deborah and Jael*.

demons / unclean spirits / exorcism
Call them "Legion"

Demons are not really important in the Old Testament, but very important in the New Testament, where they are invisible spirits that can cause humans mental and physical suffering. Jesus had power over the demons (also called evil spirits or unclean spirits) and could cast them out with just a word. Jesus' enemies accused him of having power over demons because he was in league with Beelzebub, the prince of demons (Matthew 12:24), and some said he himself was possessed by a demon (John 7:20). But most people were deeply impressed with Jesus' power and saw it as a sign that God's kingdom was already present on earth. One of Jesus' followers, Mary Magdalene, had seven demons in her until Jesus expelled them (Mark 16:9). The most notable case of his power over demons was the healing of a man who went naked, living among tombs, and could not even be restrained by chains. When Jesus asked the demon inside the man what its name was, the demon replied, "My name is Legion, for we are many." Jesus sent the legion of demons into a herd of pigs, which then jumped off a cliff (Luke 8:26-39). The people of the village were awed to see the former maniac now sitting "clothed and in his right mind." Jesus told his disciples that they too would have power to drive out demons (Luke 9:1, 10:17).

Jesus' acts of casting out demons have been called exorcism, but that isn't quite correct. Exorcisms usually involve reciting a long ritual, but in Jesus' case the expelling of demons was instantaneous, for "he cast out the demons with a word" (Matthew 8:16).

Some people get the impression that all mental and physical ailments in the Bible were attributed to demons, but that isn't so. Some people are described as "sick" or "epileptic" or even "lunatic"; these are distinguished from people afflicted by demons.

The apostle Paul referred to demons in several ways: "rulers," "authorities," "powers of this dark world," or "spiritual forces of evil in the heavenly realms" (Ephesians 6:12, NIV). The demons were also considered evil angels, for Jesus referred to "the Devil and his angels" (Matthew 25:41).

The early Christians believed the gods worshipped by the pagans were actually demons, leading human beings into false religion, occult practices, witchcraft, and immorality. This belief explains why John Milton, in his great epic poem *Paradise Lost*, gave most of the demons the names of pagan gods.

Regarding the name Devil—in the Bible there is only one Devil (also called Satan) but numerous demons, who do Satan's bidding, with Satan's kingdom set in opposition to God and his angels (Ephesians 2:2).

Throughout history, belief in demons seems to go in cycles, with one age being skeptical, another believing strongly in demonic power. The 1973 film *The Exorcist* sparked new interest in demonic possession and led to numerous horror movies where the villains were demons instead of the usual monsters and aliens. (The film named the demon Pazuzu, the actual name of a demon honored—or feared—by the ancient Assyrians.) Christian missionaries in Third World countries still testify to the reality of demon possession, and also the power of casting them out.

What do demons look like? Nothing at all, since, like Satan, they are invisible spirits. Artists have often depicted them as monsters, frequently with bat wings, fangs, claws, etc. The famous hermit St. Anthony of Egypt lived in the wilderness and claimed to be tormented by horrible demons, and artists have let their imaginations run wild as they paint the placid saint surrounded by all sorts of grotesque demons combining animal and human features. In a sense, these paintings are the ancestors of the demons and monsters of horror films. Closer to the depiction of demons in the Bible are films like *The Exorcist* that show a normal human being made ugly and vile by the power of the demon within.

Russian author Fyodor Dostoyevsky's novel *The Possessed* takes its title from the New Testament's concept of demon possession. In fact, the book's original Russian title *Besy* means "the demons." Dostoyevsky saw the political radicals of his day as demonic.

Devil / Satan

We stand accused

The name Satan in Hebrew means "adversary," and he is mentioned only a few times in the Old Testament, most famously in the Book of Job, where Satan is a member of God's heavenly court. When God praises Job's righteous living, Satan says that Job is good only because it brings him material rewards. Satan here is not so much a tempter or evil being as he is a kind of heavenly prosecutor, pointing out people's flaws or weaknesses to God.

Satan is mentioned numerous times in the New Testament, where he is also called the Devil (*Diabolos*—Greek for "accuser" or "slanderer") and the evil one. His aim is to tempt people and separate them from God, and he has incredible power on earth, even being called "prince of this world" (Luke 4:6, 2 Corinthians 4:4). Sinful people belong to him, and their evil ways have their source in him. He has power over an army of demons, who do hurt to mankind. (Note: There is only one Devil, but numerous demons. Some old translations that use "devils" are not correct.) He is behind pagan religions and the occult (Acts 13:10).

Jesus himself had a fateful encounter with Satan, being tempted by him immediately after his baptism (SEE PAGE 358). Jesus passed this test, and part of his mission on earth was to destroy the Devil's kingdom (John 12:31, Luke 10:18). Casting out demons from people was part of this mission. Christians will be tempted by Satan but can resist through confidence in God's power, since they have the "whole armor of God" (Ephesians 6:11).

In the end times, Satan will summon up the antichrist (or "Beast") and will appear to triumph over the forces of good, but he will be thrown with wicked people into the lake of fire and brimstone (Revelation 20:10).

What does the Bible say about Satan's appearance? Not much. In Revelation he is a red dragon with horns, but Revelation is highly symbolic, and Satan is in fact an invisible being like all demons. But the red dragon image lies behind most of the popular images of Satan, who is often red and horned, but in human shape. In art he has also been depicted as a serpent, based on the story of the serpent tempting Adam and Eve in the Garden of Eden, though, in fact, the Eden story does not say the serpent was Satan. Revelation 12:9 refers to Satan as "that ancient serpent." Most Jews and Christians have assumed that the serpent was the shape Satan took to deceive Adam and Eve. Artists often depict Satan with goatlike hooves because Jewish legends refer to Satan and the demons as *seirizzim*, "goats."

One notable attribute of Satan is his falseness. The Bible says he is the "father of lies" who can "masquerade as an angel of light" (John 8:44, 2 Corinthians 11:14), an idea reiterated in William Shakespeare's line "The Devil hath power to assume a pleasing shape."

Jews and Christians have also identified Satan with Lucifer, the bright angel whose pride led him to rebel against God and be cast out of heaven (SEE PAGE 223). This belief is behind such literary classics as John Milton's epic poem *Paradise Lost*, which deals with Lucifer and his fellow rebel angels warring against God, being cast down to hell, then attempting to thwart God by leading the first human beings into sin. Satan in this poem is one of the great creations of literature, a fascinating character who finds it "better to reign in hell than serve in heaven." Many readers have wondered if Milton really admired Satan for his spunk, but by the end of the poem, Satan and the demons are made to look like selfish, egotistical fools. Satan's crime is in trying to be a god—the same sin he tempts Adam and Eve into.

Satan is also in Milton's sequel, *Paradise Regained*, in which he tempts Jesus. Milton makes Satan the spokesman for all the great literature and philosophy of the pagans, but in the end, pagan culture is shown to be hollow, based on pride, egotism, and the worship of false gods.

In Dante's masterpiece *The Divine Comedy*, Satan is in the lowest part of hell. He is a hideous being with batlike wings and three mouths, which gnaw eternally on Judas Iscariot (who betrayed Jesus) and Brutus and Cassius (who betrayed Julius Caesar). In John Bunyan's allegory *The Holy War*, the devil (named Diabolus) tries in vain to capture the city of Mansoul.

Satan has been a character in countless other works of literature, and not always as the bad guy. Some authors have admired Satan for his willingness to rebel against God, and Satanism has always existed (usually underground) as a way of rebelling against Christianity. For some writers, Satan is a good character because he leads Adam and Eve out of their childlike innocence into a more interesting world where they control their own destiny instead of relying on God. For example, Italian poet Giosue Carducci's 1870 *Hymn to Satan* celebrates Satan's rebellious nature and mocks religion. In some stories, such as the two movie versions of *Bedazzled*, Satan is more of a prankish mischief-maker than a true enemy of God.

Various people, both real and fictional, have been said to be the offspring of Satan or one of his demons. The magician Merlin of the King Arthur legends was said to be the son of Satan and a mortal woman.

Aside from the biblical names Satan, Devil, the evil one, Lucifer, and Beelzebub (SEE PAGE 53), Satan has been called Old Nick, Clootie, Samael, Asmodeus, even Old Hornie. Prince of Darkness is one of the most familiar, and although it sounds biblical, the actual name isn't found in the Bible.

Satan's original role as heavenly prosecutor in the Book of Job still exists in the name "Devil's advocate." The Catholic Church, when deciding whether or not to declare a certain person as a saint, has an official called the Devil's advocate, whose duty is to try to prove that the person is not worthy of sainthood.

Christian theology has never taught that the Devil *makes* people sin. The old line of comic Flip Wilson—"The Devil made me do it"—isn't found in the Bible, where people are responsible for their own sins, with the Devil only tempting them. In a sense Satan, though he is evil, serves a useful purpose, testing people's moral fiber.

For Muslims, the evil one is Shaitan, or Iblis, lord of the demons who try to lead people astray.

Diaspora
Homeless but faithful

When the Babylonians conquered the Israelites in 586 B.C., they sent many into exile in Babylon and other regions. Years later the Israelites were allowed to return to their homeland, but many stayed in Babylon or settled in other areas of the Middle East. Since the only Jewish temple was in Jerusalem, they visited there if possible, but in their own lands, religious life centered around their synagogues. The word Diaspora, meaning "dispersed" or "scattered," refers to Jews who lived away from the original homeland. Eventually there were more Diaspora Jews than Jews living in the homeland.

In the New Testament period, Disaspora Jews lived throughout the Roman Empire, including faraway Rome itself. This proved to be an advantage for the first Christian missionaries. Since most of them were Jews, they could travel throughout the empire and present their teachings about Jesus the Messiah in any Jewish synagogue, since Jews everywhere longed for the Messiah.

Eventually, Christians came to use Diaspora in another sense: not the Jews, but all Christians, since they were God's people scattered over the face of the earth. Two New Testament letters—James and 1 Peter—are addressed to "the Dispersion."

Dinah
Sex, violence, deceit, etc.

One of the most interesting, and unsettling, stories in the Bible concerns Dinah, the one daughter of the patriarch Jacob. Dinah was raped by Shechem, the son of a local chieftain. This rape story had a twist: After raping her, Shechem decided he actually loved her and asked his father to arrange the marriage. Jacob and his twelve sons weren't pleased that Dinah was raped, but they held their peace when Shechem made an honorable proposal of marriage. Two of Jacob's sons, Simeon and Levi, agreed to the marriage, on one condition: Shechem and all the men of his tribe would have to be circumcised. In this pre-anesthesia age, circumcision for adult men was not a minor thing; it incapacitated the men for

several days. On the third day after the circumcision—"when they were sore,"
Genesis says—Simeon and Levi came to Shechem's city and killed all the males,
making off with all the livestock and goods as well. Jacob was horrified, since
the act would probably lead to vengeance from the locals. Simeon and Levi
excused themselves with, "Should he treat our sister like a prostitute?" The
story is found in Genesis 34.

Dinah is an attractive name and has been fairly popular as a name for girls. We
can assume most parents bestowing the name aren't too familiar with Genesis 34.

disciples
The hand-picked twelve

In the Bible, a disciple was a learner, or pupil. In those days, a disciple treated
his teacher with immense respect, treating him like a beloved father figure.
Jesus had numerous disciples, but a special select group of twelve were the
most important, traveling with him as he worked miracles and taught the
crowds that came out to hear him. Some of the disciples left their homes and
family to follow after him, which tells us they were deeply devoted to him
and his message.

Why were there twelve? One explanation is that there were twelve disciples
because there were twelve "tribes" of Israel, the descendants of the patriarch
Jacob's twelve sons. By choosing twelve special learners to be his followers,
Jesus was starting a "new Israel," one based not on family trees, but on spiritual
devotion.

Although the disciples have been honored for being Jesus' closest followers,
the Gospels depict them "warts and all," often behaving foolishly and rashly, mis-
understanding his message. And of course, one of the disciples, Judas Iscariot,
became a traitor, leading the priests' henchmen to arrest Jesus by night. Most
of the disciples fled in fright after Jesus' arrest, as Jesus himself predicted. After
Jesus' death and resurrection, the eleven remaining disciples chose another man,
Matthias, to replace Judas. From that time on they are usually called apostles
(those "sent out") instead of disciples. In the Book of Acts, all Christians are
referred to as disciples. One large Christian denomination in the U.S. calls itself
the Disciples of Christ.

divine right of kings
Oily politicians

In ancient times, a king was often thought to represent the people's god (or gods) on earth. He was not only his nation's military commander and chief judge, but also a sacred person, so killing him was not just murder, but sacrilege as well. Israel went many centuries with no king because the people believed their only true king was God. When the Israelites begged the prophet Samuel to give them a king, Samuel warned of the oppression, taxation, and other bad things that would follow. But God directed him to anoint a king—anointing being the ritual of pouring scented oil on the person's head, a sign of his dedication to God. The first king, Saul, was a disappointment, so God ordered Samuel to anoint a new king-in-waiting, the young David. Saul and David were rivals, and several times Saul tried to kill David, but David refused to do violence against "the Lord's anointed one," Saul. But when David himself became king, his own son, Absalom, had no qualms about trying to depose (and perhaps kill) his father.

Sometime around A.D. 700, kings in Europe renewed the Bible's custom of anointing, the anointer usually being the chief bishop in the country, or sometimes the pope. Elaborate rituals developed, and people were expected to believe that their king, no matter how incompetent, cruel, or corrupt he might be, was still "the Lord's anointed," so rebelling against him would be unthinkable. History proved that not everyone was afraid to kill or depose the anointed ones, but the rebels always knew that they would be accused of committing a sin against God. Once the new king was securely established, he too would be anointed, and the people would be told that he ruled "by the grace of God." This belief that the king was sacred is known as the *divine right of kings*. The belief was supposedly rooted in the Bible, but in fact the Bible approves of deposing tyrannical and immoral rulers like Ahab and Jezebel. In general, the greater the incompetence of the king, the more insistent he was that he was "the Lord's anointed." Some kings obsessed with their "divine right" were among the worst rulers in history. Tsar Ivan the Terrible of Russia is a classic case, with his belief that he could put to death any of his subjects at will (and he did on several occasions).

As Europe became more secular and less religious, the belief in the divine right of kings became a joke for most people. In the 1700s, English poet Alexander Pope mocked "the right divine of kings to govern wrong." In the 1770s, some of the Founding Fathers claimed that since all human beings had one common ancestor in Adam, the world was a "level playing field," with no individual having any God-given right to dominate others. The pro-king forces said, in reply, that only kings had inherited Adam's right to rule over other creatures.

doves
Spirited lovebirds

Doves and pigeons (which are the same, actually) are found over most of the globe and were familiar birds in biblical times. Their first mention is in the story of Noah in Genesis. With the earth flooded, Noah sent out a dove, which returned to the ark, since it found no place to light. A week later, he sent it out again and it brought back a green olive leaf. A week later he sent the dove out once more and it did not return, so he knew that dry land was to be found (Genesis 8:6-12).

Doves mate for life (which is why they are connected with weddings) and are mentioned more than once in the Song of Solomon, the sensuous love song found in the Old Testament.

The most memorable instance of a dove appearing was at the baptism of Jesus, when he saw "the Spirit of God descending like a dove and coming to rest on him" (Matthew 3:16) or, in Luke's account, "the Holy Spirit descended on him in bodily form, like a dove" (Luke 3:22). Because of this incident, Christians have long associated the Holy Spirit with the dove, which is why Christians who place a great deal of emphasis on the Spirit (Pentecostals and charismatics) often use the dove as their symbol. The dove almost always appears in pictures of Jesus' baptism, and also in some pictures of the Trinity (SEE PAGE 368).

Easter

Pre-chocolate, pre-bunny

Since Jesus was resurrected on the first day of the week, the first Christians considered every Sunday a day to celebrate his resurrection, which is why it came to be called "the Lord's day." Over time, some began celebrating the resurrection as an annual event as well. It was first called *Pascha*, the Greek word for Passover, which was natural since Jesus' death and resurrection occurred near the Jewish feast of Passover, and the apostle Paul referred to Jesus as "our Passover lamb" (1 Corinthians 5:7). Jesus, called the "lamb of God" several times in the New Testament, was regarded as the perfect and final sacrifice for man's sins.

In the year 325, the Council of Nicaea decreed that Easter would be celebrated each year on the Sunday following the first full moon after the spring equinox (March 21).

Until about the last century, Easter was considered a much more important holy day than Christmas, since the New Testament makes it clear that the resurrection of Jesus was the key event of all time. The word Easter is not actually found in the Bible.

Ecce homo

He was the Man

Countless paintings have the title *Ecce Homo*—Latin for "Behold the man." These are the words Pontius Pilate spoke to the crowd when he presented the beaten

Jesus, with a crown of thorns pressed onto his head, wearing a cast-off purple robe from the Roman soldiers to mock him as "king of the Jews." Some people view the Gospel narrative as being too hard on the Jewish authorities, but the Romans come off looking bad too, since the soldiers seem like cynical sadists. It is easy to understand why the episode has been painted so often, since it contrasts the innocent and bloody Jesus with the bloodthirsty priests and the brutal Roman soldiers. It is a point of high drama, since Pilate is showing the crowd the suffering Jesus, hoping they will not want him punished further. Right after he says, "Behold the man," the Jewish authorities shout out, "Crucify him!"

The German philosopher Friedrich Nietzsche, who despised Christianity, gave the title *Ecce Homo* to a book about himself.

Ecclesiastes
The "been there, done that" book

One of the most interesting, and most puzzling, books in the Bible is Ecclesiastes, which claims to be the work of "the son of David, king in Jerusalem." That refers to Solomon, the very wise and very wealthy king of Israel, who is also supposed to be the author of Proverbs. Both Proverbs and Ecclesiastes are considered Wisdom literature (SEE PAGE 294), but Ecclesiastes seems to be "anti-wisdom," with chapter 2 lamenting, "what happens to the fool will happen to me also. Why then have I been so very wise?" In fact, the author seems pessimistic and cynical, finding no pleasure in anything—wisdom, wealth, worldly pleasures, hard work. A phrase that crops up again and again in the book is "vanity of vanities, all is vanity"—or in more modern translations, "useless, useless" or "pointless, pointless." Everything that people value, the book says is "a chasing after the wind."

How did this seemingly cynical book get into the Bible? One reason is that the wise Solomon was supposed to be the author. Another reason is that the book concludes with, "Fear God and keep his commandments, for this is the whole duty of man." In other words, after whining about how boring and meaningless life is, the author comes back to the Bible's basic idea: obey God and trust him, and put no stock in the things that most people consider important.

In spite of its cynicism, the book is very quotable, and many authors have dropped "vanity of vanities" into their works, including William Makepeace Thackeray, who used the phrase at the end of his classic novel *Vanity Fair*. "Vanity of vanities" also inspired the genre of painting called the *Vanitas*, a still-life picture with objects arranged to remind the viewer of the transience and uncertainty of life. Chapter 3 has been widely quoted. It begins, "To everything there is a season, and a time for every purpose under heaven. A time to be born, a time to die…" Back in the 1960s that passage founds its way into the lyrics of the song "Turn! Turn! Turn!" by the rock group The Byrds. It has been recorded by many other artists, though it's doubtful any of them know the words are from the Bible.

The Jews were slow to accept the book onto their list of "inspired" books, and it has never been a favorite of theirs, nor of Christians. Some Jews read the book aloud at the holiday of Succoth, or the Feast of Booths. It is never quoted or referred to in the New Testament, which indicates that the Jews living at the time of Jesus were not fond of this cynical, skeptical book.

Eden
Man's home (briefly)

We have no idea where the Garden of Eden is, or was, and some say it exists only in legend. The Book of Genesis says the garden had a river that divided into four rivers, two of them being the Tigris and Euphrates, which are real rivers in the region now known as Iraq. Wherever it was, the name Eden means "delight," which was appropriate, since it was a place without pain or conflict, and the two humans inhabiting it could eat from "trees that were pleasing to the

The Expulsion From Eden
GENESIS. CHAPTER 3, VERSES 23-24.

eye and good for food." Eden didn't last, however, since Adam and Eve disobeyed God by breaking the one rule he imposed on them: Do not eat from the tree of knowledge of good and evil. Tempted by the sly serpent, they did eat and were driven out of their innocent, clothing-free paradise. There was no way back, for the way into Eden was blocked by an angel with a flaming sword.

For a place so important in the history of the human race, Eden is not mentioned much in the Bible. The prophet Isaiah spoke of a future time when Israel's deserts would become "like Eden" (Isaiah 51:3), which has come to pass, since arid sections of Israel are now irrigated to produce fruit trees. Ezekiel refers several times to "Eden, the garden of God."

Although the Eden story is a brief one, the name of the garden is familiar to everyone, and many places on the map (including nudist camps, for obvious reasons) describe themselves as "Edens."

Egypt
Land of the pharaohs—and slaves

With the exception of Israel, no nation is mentioned more often in the Bible than Egypt. The ancient civilization along the Nile River was always connected with the key event in Israel's history, the exodus from slavery, led by Moses. Because of the years of bondage in Egypt, and because the pharaoh resisted their liberation, Israel always had a low opinion of Egypt.

The later chapters of Genesis reveal that the Hebrews left their homeland (Canaan) due to a famine, which is the setting for the famous story of Joseph, who became the right-hand man of Pharaoh and saved his father Jacob and eleven brothers from starvation. Jacob and his sons settled happily in Egypt, but as recorded in Exodus 1, the Egyptian pharaoh made slaves of their descendants until they were delivered by God and Moses. The pharaoh of this oppressive period is never named in the Bible, but historians believe he was Rameses II (the name he was called in the films *The Ten Commandments* and *Prince of Egypt*), who was a notorious builder (and also one who had previous pharaohs' names on monuments rubbed out and his own name inscribed). Besides being an oppressor nation, Egypt was also notorious for worshipping dozens of gods in the shapes of animals, something the Israelites abhorred. Egyptian practices like observing a "sacred bull" to determine the will of the god Apis seemed absurd to them—likewise constructing huge, elaborate tombs to bury the mummified bulls.

For hundreds of years, Egypt was considered the home of sorcery and occult practices. This is partly due to the Book of Exodus, in which Pharaoh's court magicians managed to duplicate a few of the miracles performed by

Moses (Exodus 7). They are not named in the Old Testament, but in Jewish tradition they are called Jannes and Jambres, as we see in the New Testament (2 Timothy 3:8). The Jews always were repulsed by sorcery, and Jannes and Jambres were the embodiment of occult dabbling, which, the Jews believed, God detested.

Egypt was still a powerful empire long after the Israelites left it. Apparently Israel—or at least its king—got over the traditional hostility toward its former oppressor, because Solomon married Pharaoh's daughter, a sign that Israel was becoming a nation to reckon with. (The Bible also says that Solomon's many marriages to foreign wives led him down the wrong spiritual path.) The alliance between Israel and Egypt didn't last beyond Solomon's lifetime. During the reign of his son, a pharaoh named Shishak attacked Jerusalem and carried off Solomon's valuable temple treasures (2 Chronicles 12:9). The saintly king Josiah was killed while battling Egyptian forces, and afterward the pharaoh (named Necho) set up his own puppet king in Jerusalem (2 Kings 23:29-35). In the time of the prophet Jeremiah, Israel tried to play one big power (Babylonia) against another (Egypt). Jeremiah scolded his people for looking upon Egypt to save them from the Babylonians. When the Babylonians conquered Judah in 586 B.C., many of the Jews, including Jeremiah, fled to Egypt. And, much later, Joseph, Mary, and the infant Jesus fled to Egypt to avoid the massacre of the infants of Bethlehem by King Herod.

One of the Bible's classic lines regarding Egyptians is this lovely sentiment from the Song of Solomon: "I liken you, my darling, to a mare harnessed to one of Pharaoh's chariots."

Ehud

Israelite versus cellulite

The Bible generally doesn't say much about people's physical appearance, but it does state that Eglon, the king of Moab, was extremely obese. In Judges 3, we learn that Moab had Israel under its heel for many years, and God's chosen deliverer for Israel was a man named Ehud, who is mentioned as being left-handed. He went to meet with Eglon to present Israel's tribute money, and informed the court that he had a secret message for the king. All the servants left. When Ehud and Eglon were left alone, Ehud surprised the king by drawing out with his left hand the sword he had concealed on his right leg. He plunged it into the king's belly "and the fat closed over the blade." Ehud made a swift getaway and rallied the troops of Israel, letting them know Moab's portly king was dead.

El
The short but almighty name

Lots of names in the Old Testament include the ending "*el*." *El* is the Hebrew word meaning "God." All those names with *el* have their own meanings. For example, Daniel means "God is judge." There are numerous others: Samuel, Ezekiel , Joel, Israel, Elijah, Elisha, Bethel, etc. (Bethel meant "house of God," Elijah meant "Yahweh is God"—all "el" names had meanings.)

El is the shortest name for God. Sometimes the plural form *Elohim* is used, such as in the opening of the Bible: "In the beginning Elohim created the heavens and the earth." Although it's plural, it is still translated "God" because it is a kind of "royal plural." After Elohim creates the world, he says, "Let us make man in our image"—note the "our."

In the Hebrew Old Testament, God is often *El* or *Elohim*, but is also *Yahweh*, his actual name, which in English Bibles is usually translated "Lord." Sometimes God is *El Shaddai*—which most Bibles translate as "Almighty God." The form *Yahweh Elohim*, "the Lord God," also occurs.

elders
Gray and respectable

The ancient world had a higher opinion of senior citizens than we do today, and both Jews and Christians considered it a duty to respect the aged. Among the early Christians, the elders were highly honored, especially if they had wisdom to go along with their age. Several of the New Testament letters refer to elders, and each Christian fellowship had a designated group who had responsibilities for worship and other church matters. The Greek word we translate as "elder" was *presbuteros*, a word that lingers in the name Presbyterian. In many churches today, an ordained minister is technically an elder (regardless of his age), but in other churches (including the Presbyterians) the elders are a kind of board of trustees for the church. In some churches, the elders have been known to work together to boot out an unpopular minister.

Elijah

The chariots-of-fire man

The prophet Elijah was one of the great men of the Old Testament, a man with enough spunk and faith to confront two very intimidating foes, King Ahab and Queen Jezebel of Israel. Jezebel was a devoted Baal worshiper, and while she lived there was a serious threat that Baal worship might supersede the worship of Israel's God.

Elijah's father is never mentioned, an odd occurrence in the Bible, where "son of" served the same purpose as a last name serves for us. Elijah suddenly appears in 1 Kings 17, dramatically prophesying a severe drought in Israel because of the worship of Baal. Hiding from Ahab, Elijah is miraculously fed by ravens in the wilderness, then sheltered by a widow, whose son he brings back to life. He also miraculously multiplies the food supplies of the poor woman.

The most famous incident with Elijah is his showdown with the prophets of Baal on Mount Carmel. Elijah is the sole prophet of God at the scene, facing 450 Baal men. Elijah turns the meeting into a crisis: the people of Israel must choose whether to serve God or Baal. The Baal prophets go into a frenzied dance, slashing themselves with knives, but nothing happens; Baal does not show. Elijah calls on the power of Israel's God, who sends down fire (possibly lightning) to burn up the sacrifice on the altar. The Israelites, deeply impressed, declare themselves for God, and they execute the Baal prophets. The long drought finally ends, and as King Ahab drives his chariot back to his home, Elijah outruns him on foot.

After Jezebel promises to have him killed, Elijah flees into the wilderness. He goes to Mount Horeb (also called Sinai), the mountain where Moses met God centuries earlier. God calls on him there, and Elijah witnesses a powerful wind, then an earthquake, then a fire—then finally, a "still, small voice" (1 Kings 19:12). The voice reminds him that there are other devoted people in Israel besides Elijah.

Afterward, Elijah takes Elisha as his protégé. Ahab dies but is succeeded by his equally wicked son, Ahaziah. Elijah prophesies that Ahaziah will die. When fifty of the king's soldiers try to capture Elijah, they are destroyed by fire from heaven.

Elijah's end is dramatic: instead of dying, he is taken to heaven in a chariot of fire drawn by horses of fire. Even after he is gone, his cloak, given to Elisha, is so powerful that Elisha can part the waters of the Jordan River with it.

Elijah's saga (found in 1 Kings 17-19 and 2 Kings 1-2) is a colorful one, full of miracles and confrontations with evil rulers, and his encounter with God himself on Mount Horeb. Centuries later, the prophet Malachi predicted that Elijah would return before "the great and awesome day of the Lord." In the New Testament, Jesus told his followers that the wilderness prophet

Elijah Ascends to Heaven
II Kings. Chapter 2, Verses 11-13.

John the Baptist was the Elijah predicted by Malachi (Matthew 11:14, Luke 1:17). Some people thought Jesus himself was the predicted Elijah (Matthew 16:14). At the dramatic episode called the Transfiguration (SEE PAGE 367), Elijah and Moses both appeared, conversing with Jesus. Elijah had become the symbol of all of Israel's prophets, while Moses represented the Law of God. Elijah and Moses were both "deathless," since Elijah had been taken to heaven in a fiery chariot, while Moses had been mysteriously buried by God himself. Also, both Moses and Elijah had encountered God on Mount Sinai.

Christians have been aware for centuries that many of the miracles done by Elijah were also performed by Jesus—bringing a dead child to life, miraculously multiplying food, etc. Also, both Elijah and Jesus were taken up into heaven. With the exception of Moses, Elijah is the Old Testament man most-mentioned in the New Testament. Revelation 11:3 says that Moses and Elijah are the two preachers of repentance in the end times who will be killed by the Beast.

The Old Testament refers to Elijah as a "hairy man"—which could mean he had a hairy body or that he wore the rough hair garments sometimes worn by prophets.

Elijah is mentioned twice in the Koran, under the name Ilyas, and he is honored as the champion of monotheism. Eastern Orthodox Christians observe July 20 as the feast day of Elijah, the "Glorious Prophet." For Jews, Elijah is the forerunner of the Messiah, and a cup of wine is poured for him at the Passover meal, where he is always the "unseen guest." In some Jewish legends, Elijah is actually an angel who only appears to be a man—an idea based on his being taken into heaven, and also the fact that his father and mother are never mentioned.

Elijah is a "character," and artists have enjoyed painting him in his dramatic confrontation with the Baal prophets, with Elijah often shown as a shaggy-bearded muscular man in a rough cloak. He also appears in the many paintings of the Transfiguration. English poet-artist William Blake is one of many artists to paint *Elijah in the Chariot of Fire*. The incident is also the source of the old spiritual song "Swing Low, Sweet Chariot." Oddly, his colorful story has not yet been adapted into a film. In Herman Melville's novel *Moby-Dick*, a man calling himself Elijah tells the book's narrator, Ishmael, to beware of sailing on Captain Ahab's ship for it is doomed, a prophecy which proves true at the book's end. Composer Felix Mendelssohn's great choral work *Elijah* includes the episode of the priests of Baal. Because Elijah was fed by ravens in the wilderness, Christians have used the raven in artwork as a symbol of God providing for his people.

The phrase "still, small voice" from Elijah's story has become part of the language. Also, "Elijah's mantle," referring to the cloak that Elijah gave his protégé Elisha, has come to refer to succession to the office of a great man.

In the Roman Catholic Church the monks and nuns known as Carmelites trace their foundation back to Mount Carmel, where Elijah had his famous showdown with the Baal prophets. An old tradition says that Elijah himself started a monastery on the mountain.

Elisha

Following a tough act

The prophet Elisha was the protégé and successor of the fiery prophet Elijah. He was present when Elijah was taken into heaven in a fiery chariot. Elijah threw down his mantle (cloak) to symbolize that Elisha was to continue his work as prophet (2 Kings 2). Elisha struck the waters of the Jordan River with the cloak, and the river parted. (From this comes the phrase "Elijah's mantle," meaning a great man passing on his abilities and work to another man.)

Like his master, Elisha performed many amazing miracles, including purifying undrinkable water and poisoned stew, raising of a dead child, and causing a lost ax head to float on the waters. When Elisha was mocked as a "bald-head" by some pesky boys, he cursed them, and they were devoured by two bears from the woods. (Elisha's baldness might have been his natural state, but it's also possible he had a shaved head, as some prophets did.) Elisha healed Naaman, a Syrian army captain, of leprosy. Elisha would not accept payment for the healing, but his greedy servant, Gehazi, did, and for that Gehazi was cursed with leprosy. On another occasion, the Syrians tried to capture Elisha, but he was protected by chariots and horses of fire. The Syrians were struck with blindness. Elisha was also credited with having second sight (2 Kings 2-8).

Like Elijah, Elisha opposed the idol-worshipping family of King Ahab. Elisha engineered the anointing of Jehu to be the next king of Israel, and Jehu killed off the entire family of Ahab and had the wicked queen, Jezebel, killed also (2 Kings 9)—just as Elijah had prophesied.

Elisha's death was a normal one, and he was not taken to heaven in a fiery chariot as Elijah was. However, he had such amazing power that a dead man thrown into his grave was brought to life again by coming into contact with Elisha's bones (2 Kings 13:20-21).

In the New Testament, Elisha was mentioned by Jesus as a prophet of Israel who performed miracles—signs that God loved all people, not just the people of Israel (Luke 4:27).

The Eastern Orthodox Christians observe June 14 as the feast of Elisha. The Muslims' Koran refers to him as Al-Yasa and honors him as a great prophet.

Elizabeth

Never too late for motherhood

At the beginning of Luke's Gospel we meet the aged Elizabeth and her husband Zechariah the priest, both of them "righteous before God," but childless.

While Zechariah is serving in the temple, the angel Gabriel tells him that Elizabeth will have a son who will "be filled with the Holy Spirit, even from his mother's womb." (Because he doubts the angel's words, poor Zechariah is struck with muteness until the son is born.) The aged Elizabeth gives birth to John the Baptist, the wilderness prophet whose ministry paved the way for Jesus (Luke 1). Elizabeth is a relative of the Virgin Mary, who visits her during her pregnancy, both of them rejoicing in their miraculous conceptions. Elizabeth greets Mary with the words, "Blessed art thou among women, and blessed is the fruit of thy womb" (Luke 1:42). The visit is celebrated by Roman Catholics on May 31 as the Feast of the Visitation. Elizabeth's words to Mary are the basis of the familiar Catholic prayer, the Ave Maria (Hail Mary).

Although she is a minor character in the Bible, Elizabeth has intrigued artists, who have delighted to show her with the infant son John in paintings with Mary and the baby Jesus. Mary the virgin mother and Elizabeth the elderly mother are both signs of God's power to work miracles.

Enoch

Walking to heaven

You may not have heard of Enoch, but you have heard of his famous son, Methuselah, who lived to be 969 years old. But Enoch himself is an interesting—and mysterious—character, because the Bible says "Enoch walked with God, and he was not, for God took him" (Genesis 5:24). In the Bible, "walked with God" means "pleased God by his behavior." In other words, Enoch was a saint. But what is meant by "God took him" is not clear. Jews and Christians have taken it to mean that Enoch did not die but was taken by God to heaven. In the New Testament, the Letter to the Hebrews mentions Enoch in its listing of people of faith.

Though he is mentioned only twice in the Bible, Enoch's name became attached to a whole body of literature claiming to be his revelations to mankind after he was taken into heaven. A book known as 1 Enoch was widely read by Jews and Christians. Ethiopian Christians include it in their Bibles. Some Jews believed he was the Messiah, who was taken to heaven by God but would return in the future to save Israel from its enemies.

Esau / Edom
Hairy situations

E

Esau was the twin brother of Jacob, the sons of Isaac and Rebecca. While pregnant, Rebecca was told by the Lord that the twins she was carrying would be the ancestors of two warring nations. Esau was technically the firstborn of the two and, if you can believe Genesis 25, was hairy from his birth. As adults, Esau was an outdoorsman and the favorite of Isaac, while Jacob was a stay-at-home and his mother's pet.

As oldest son, Esau would get the lion's share of the inheritance, but Genesis has two stories of how the wily Jacob tricked Esau out of it. In Genesis 25, Esau comes in from the hunt, is ravenously hungry, and foolishly sells his inheritance (the "birthright") for some stew Jacob is cooking. Genesis 27 says that while Esau was out hunting game for Isaac, Rebecca told Jacob to wrap goatskins around his smooth arms to fool his nearly blind father into giving him the special blessing due to Esau, the elder son. The ruse works, Isaac thinks Jacob is Esau, and he gives him the blessing—something that once spoken

Jacob's Reconciliation With Esau
GENESIS. CHAPTER 33, VERSES 1-7.

could not be retracted or given again. Esau was furious, and resolved to kill Jacob. Rebecca sent Jacob to her brother's home to keep him safe. Jacob spent years avoiding his irate brother, but in Genesis 33, the two brothers reconcile tearfully.

Esau was also called Edom, and his descendants were the Edomites. The Lord's word to Rebecca proved true, for the Edomites were often at war with the Israelites, the descendants of Jacob. The Edomites were often subservient to Israel, but never for long. The brief Book of Obadiah is one long rant against the Edomites for aiding the Babylonians when they conquered Jerusalem. In between the Old and New Testaments, the Jews conquered the Edomites again and forced them to convert to Judaism. The family of Herod was among the Edomites conquered, and one reason the Jews detested King Herod was his Edomite ancestry.

Jews in the New Testament period referred to the Roman Empire as Edom, probably a way of criticizing it without the Romans being aware.

eschatology
Boning up on the future

Eschatology is the study of the events at the end of time—the Greek *eschaton* meaning "end." Several books of the Bible claim to reveal "signs" of the end times, notably The Book of Revelation, Daniel, the Gospels, and several of Paul's letters. Throughout history, preachers and authors have always known they could attract an audience by revealing the "right" interpretation of these prophecies. Jesus himself said that no one knows the day or hour of the Last Judgment (Matthew 24:36), which ought to tell interpreters not to get too certain about their beliefs.

Books about eschatology may not be correct (who can prove if they are or not?), but many have sold hugely, not only books about the Bible and theology, but also fiction. One of the great publishing success stories of recent years has been the *Left Behind* series, twelve novels and several "prequels" dealing with the end of time.

Essenes
The Dead Sea scrollers

In the New Testament period, the Essenes were a group of Jews living a kind of monastic life in wilderness areas and waiting for the final conflict between good and evil. Most of them were unmarried, and they shared their simple possessions, believing themselves to be God's "righteous remnant." The very old writings known as the Dead Sea Scrolls were probably the possession of the Essenes, so we have them to thank for preserving some of the oldest copies of books of the Bible, as well as Biblical commentaries. The Essenes aren't actually mentioned in the Bible, but it's possible that John the Baptist was connected with them in some way.

Esther

Queen at a crucial moment

The Book of Esther is unusual, since it comes in two versions: one that mentions God, one that doesn't. Jewish and Protestant Bibles have the "godless" version, which doesn't mention even prayer. The longer version, found in Catholic Bibles, mentions God and prayer many times. So why two versions? The Hebrew version is probably the older of the two. The longer version that mentions God is in Greek; its later additions to the book are all religious.

In both cases, the Book of Esther tells the story of the court of ancient Persia, where many Jews lived in exile after being conquered by the Babylonians. The Persian king has a banquet and orders his wife to "show off her charms" to his drunken male guests. She refuses, and the king's counselors decide that if the king's wife can be "uppity," every wife in Persia might follow her lead. The king casts his wife aside and holds an empire-wide "beauty pageant," choosing a new wife from among the most beautiful girls. His choice is young Esther, who is (unknown to the king) Jewish. Her elevation to queen happens at a time when the king's Jew-hating right-hand man, Haman, is plotting to destroy all the Jews in the kingdom, starting with Mordecai, Esther's surrogate father. At Mordecai's urging, Esther reveals she is a Jew to her husband and tells of Haman's plot. Haman is hanged on the high gallows that he had intended for Mordecai. Instead of the Jews being exterminated, they are allowed to defend themselves. All ends happily, and the book ends with the institution of the Jewish holiday of Purim. The name of the holiday, incidentally, comes from the casting of lots—*pur*—to determine the day of extermination.

People still puzzle over the two versions of the book. Purim was often celebrated with a lot of drinking and rowdiness, and some scholars think the original Hebrew version of Esther was "godless" because its authors didn't want God's name connected with the riotousness of Purim. The longer version, they think, had religious additions for the purpose of making Purim into a more religious holiday instead of a secular one. At any rate, the Book of Esther (the short version) is read in its entirety on the Feast of Purim. Neither the short nor long version of Esther has been as popular among Christians, since the Jews in the story turn on their Persian exterminators and do not provide a good example of "turn the other cheek." Still, it does show God (even if he is not mentioned) as leading his people through a great crisis. Although it is easy to doubt whether the story actually happened, its picture of anti-Semitism in the ancient world is close to the truth.

The book calls the Persian king by the name Ahasuerus. This was probably the ruler Xerxes, who reigned from 486 to 465 B.C.

The Book of Esther has a colorful setting in the court of the Persian emperor, so scenes from the book have often been painted by artists. There are numerous renderings of *Esther Before Ahasuerus*, since the scene of her pleading for her people is an emotional one. Claude Vignon's 1624 version in the Louvre is very impressive. The great French dramatist Jean Racine's 1689 play *Esther* is based on the story. Composer George Frideric Handel's first oratorio was *Haman and Mordecai*, later retitled *Esther*. The book has been filmed a few times, notably the 1960 film *Esther and the King*, starring a very young Joan Collins as Esther, and the 2006 film *One Night with the King*.

Since she was beautiful, devout, and heroic, Esther's name has been a common one among Christians, even more so among Jews. In Jewish legends, Esther's beauty remained ageless throughout her long life.

evangelicals
The born-again band

The name comes from the Greek *euangelion*, translated as either "good new" or "gospel." Of course, all Christians claim to believe in the Gospel (the message of Jesus being Lord and Savior), but evangelicals are Christians who take a more literal view of the Bible, who favor a more traditional morality, and who are more likely to emphasize evangelism than social issues. There is no real divide between evangelicals and fundamentalists, though fundamentalists are more likely to emphasize personal issues such as total abstinence from smoking and alcohol, staying away from movies and pop music, etc. Fundamentalists are less "worldly" than evangelicals, while evangelicals try to be less worldly than the culture at large. There are some denominations that are entirely evangelical; in the more liberal denominations, there are also evangelicals. As a general rule in Christian history, people identifying themselves as evangelicals are dissenters from the established church, either wanting to break away or to make the church closer to that of the New Testament period. In the Reformation period (the 1500s), Protestants who broke from the Catholic church were called evangelicals, and later groups in the Church of England called themselves the same name. *Time* magazine, which did several stories on the evangelicals in the U.S., dubbed 1976 "the year of the evangelical."

Evangelists
Gospelizers

Our word "evangelist" comes from the Greek word *euangelion*, meaning "good news" but often translated "gospel." An evangelist is someone who spreads the Gospel (the story of Jesus, that is). When you see Evangelist with a capital E, it refers to the authors of the four Gospels in the New Testament—Matthew, Mark, Luke, and John. They are called the four Evangelists, and are often depicted in paintings and sculptures, sometimes together, sometimes separately. Centuries ago, the four somehow became associated with the Bible's description of "living creatures" with four faces: a man's face, a lion's, an ox's, and an eagle's (Ezekiel 1:10, Revelation 4:7). In artwork, Matthew is often depicted with a man (or angel) nearby, Mark with a lion, Luke with an ox, and John with an eagle. Naturally, the four Evangelists are also shown writing on scrolls.

excommunication
Outside the box

Since the very beginning, Christians felt compelled to exclude certain members from fellowship, either because of moral lapses or teachings opposed to Christian belief. There was no fine or physical punishment involved. The person was simply barred from the group, in the hope that he would repent and eventually come back. Some of Paul's letters refer to this practice (1 Timothy 1:20, 1 Corinthians 5:5, Titus 3:10). It wasn't until the 300s that the church actually began to execute heretics. When the practice began, many Christians were scandalized, wondering how loving Christians could take the life of another human being.

The Catholic Church still has an official ritual for excommunication. Most other churches will, on rare occasions, remove an immoral member from the group.

The Jews practiced a form of excommunication, and Jesus warned his followers that they would be excommunicated (Luke 6:22).

Exodus
The world's most famous exit

Exodus is the name of the second book of the Old Testament and also the key event in that book, in which the Hebrew slaves were liberated from Egypt by Moses and the power of God. Exodus means, appropriately, "going out." The first book of the Bible, Genesis, ends with Jacob and his twelve sons living in Egypt

The Egyptians Drown in the Red Sea
EXODUS. CHAPTER 14, VERSES 26-31.

to escape a famine at home. In Exodus, their descendants are made slaves by the Egyptians, and their labor is so harsh they cry out for a deliverer, and God sends them Moses. As a young adult, he had killed an Egyptian overseer, fled to the wilderness, and was called by God, who spoke to him from a burning bush. Moses and his brother Aaron confront the Egyptian pharaoh and demand he free the slaves.

Pharaoh resists, and God sends ten plagues to vex the Egyptians. Pharaoh frees the slaves, then changes his mind and pursues them into the desert. Trapped at the edge of the sea, the Israelites panic until God miraculously parts the waters for Moses, allowing them to cross, but then drowns the Egyptian troops. Camped out in the wilderness by Mount Sinai, the people wait anxiously as Moses goes to the Mount to meet with God and is given the Ten Commandments (chapter 20) and other laws. Probably the Exodus occurred around 1240 B.C.

The Exodus from Egypt is the most important event of the Old Testament, one that generations of Jews have never forgotten. It is referred to many times in the Old and New Testaments, and the Book of Exodus is quoted several times in the New Testament. For Jews, it was evidence that God had singled them out to be a special people in the world, the first receivers of God's moral laws. Aside from its spiritual value, millions of people have found the story inspiring because it shows an oppressed people being freed from a tyrannical empire. Moses' words to Pharaoh, "Let my people go!" have inspired freedom fighters throughout the centuries, and certainly it has inspired slaves and their sympathizers. American author Henrietta Buckmaster's 1941 novel *Let My People Go* is about the Underground Railroad that led slaves to freedom.

The Jewish holiday of Passover is an annual commemoration of the Israelites being "passed over" by the angel who struck down the Egyptians' firstborn—the last of the ten plagues and the one that convinced Pharaoh to free the slaves.

Numerous episodes from Exodus have been depicted in painting and sculptures, notably Moses and the burning bush, Moses confronting Pharaoh, Moses on the mountain, and the parting of the sea. George Frideric Handel wrote an oratorio, *Israel in Egypt*, and Carl Philipp Emanuel Bach wrote one titled *The Israelites in the Wilderness*. The Exodus story has been filmed numerous times, twice by director Cecil B. DeMille, both titled *The Ten Commandments*, with the 1956 version being one of the most famous biblical films ever made. Although the film has been accused of being "too Hollywood," it has made millions of people familiar with the story of Moses and the Exodus. Two TV mini-series have been made, *Moses the Lawgiver* and, most recently, *The Ten Commandments*. A 1999 animated movie *The Prince of Egypt* was a surprising success. Novelist Leon Uris used the title *Exodus* for his 1958 book about the establishment of the modern nation of Israel.

(For more about Moses himself, SEE PAGE 247.)

Ezekiel
Deep, deep visions

One of the strangest books in the Bible is the book of the Old Testament prophet Ezekiel, who was one of the Jews taken into exile in Babylon after the Babylonians conquered their homeland. His book opens with a vision of some shiny, metallic "living creatures" with four faces and four wings, and shining above them was the throne of God. It's generally assumed that the "creatures" were types of angels, but in 1968 author Erick von Daniken published his book *Chariots of the Gods*, a huge seller that put forth the theory that what Ezekiel saw were aliens, a theory many people still believe.

Probably the most memorable part of the book is chapter 37, where Ezekiel is set down in a valley full of dry bones, and where God asks him, "Can these bones live?" This had a spiritual meaning: Could people who are spiritually dead live again? (The answer was yes, of course.) This chapter is the source of the old spiritual about "dem dry bones" that "hear the word of the Lord."

The Prophet Ezekiel
Ezekiel. Chapter 1, Verses 4-5, 9-10, 26-28.

Ezekiel believed he had been chosen by God to be a "watchman for Israel," offering the exiled Jews comfort but also scolding them for their sins (Ezekiel 3:16). He was especially hard on the priests and prophets, who he saw as not giving the people the moral guidance they needed. (He himself was both priest and prophet, a rare combination.) Some of his moral insights are significant; for example, he tossed aside the idea that children can be punished for the sins of their parents. Instead, each person is responsible for his own sins.

Along with Isaiah and Jeremiah, Ezekiel is considered one of the Major Prophets in the Old Testament, so-called because their books are longer than the twelve Minor Prophets. In artwork, Ezekiel is often depicted as a white-bearded man with a wild look about him, which is appropriate considering the visions he had. Raphael's *The Vision of Ezekiel*, (1518) plays very loosely with the prophet's vision: the gray-bearded, bare-chested God, accompanied by three angels, rides on the wings of the eagle and the winged ox and lion.

A type of Jewish mysticism, called Merkabah, became popular in the period between the Old and New Testaments. The Merkabah mystics would fast and recite hymns of praise in the hope that they would experience visions of God and the angels as Ezekiel did.

In the movie *Pulp Fiction*, one of the characters quotes a long verse from the Book of Ezekiel—but the quote is totally fictional, not found in Ezekiel or anywhere else in the Bible.

Ezra

Moses, act II

Ezra was the Jewish priest who led a major religious reform after the Jews returned from their long exile in Babylonia. Ezra read them the Law of Moses and insisted they live their lives according to it. For this reason, Ezra is regarded by the Jews as a kind of second Moses, renewing the old Law. Ezra insisted that Jewish men married to non-Jewish women had to divorce their wives. Many of the Jews believed their exile in Babylon was God's punishment for their immorality, so they honored Ezra as the leader of a moral reform to keep from being exiled again. He is a prominent character in the Old Testament's Books of Ezra and Nehemiah. Tradition says he was the author of 1 and 2 Chronicles, as well as the Book of Ezra. There are also several apocryphal books that are supposedly by him, all of them named Esdras instead of Ezra. Jews have a higher regard for Ezra than Christians do, and the Book of Ezra is seldom read by Christians. The Muslims' holy book, the Quran, states that the Jews believed that Ezra was the son of God, which is not correct, although it does indicate that the Jews (at the time of Muhammad, anyway) held Ezra in high regard.

faith healing
The body-spirit connection

Several healing miracles are found in the Old Testament, mostly done by the prophets Elijah and Elisha. In the New Testament, the great healer was Jesus himself, who healed the blind, mute, lame, and on a few occasions brought the dead back to life. The healings were evidence of divine power, but also of the faith of the person being healed. In one locale Jesus (his own hometown, Nazareth) did few miracles because of the people's lack of faith (Matthew 13:58), and after one healing he told the person, "Your faith has made you well."

Skeptics tend to mock the healing stories, saying that the only time a healing appears to occur is when the person's condition was "all in his head." This was probably true in some cases, but then, people in Jesus' time were pretty skeptical too, and yet many of them truly believed he had healed people. He told his disciples they would also be healers, and several of their miracles are reported in the Book of Acts. In fact, healing miracles have been reported throughout history, but the skeptics abound, many of whom are churchgoers. Notable Christian leaders like Martin Luther and John Calvin said that miracle healing can still occur, but that they were performed by Jesus and his apostles to convince people of God's power. In other words, they taught that the age of miracles is already past.

There have been plenty of shyster faith healers over the years who employed fakers to pretend to be lame or deaf to be healed by the preacher in front of a large audience. However, some of the healers seem genuine. We are probably more appreciative of the body-spirit connection than they were in ancient times, so it would probably be wise to keep an open mind about healing miracles. Several popular movies, including *Resurrection*, give sympathetic depictions of people with a miraculous power to heal.

fire and brimstone
Pure hell

We know what fire is, but just what is brimstone? It is an old name for sulfur, something common in volcanic areas. (In the Middle Ages, the English word for sulfur was *burn-stone*, which eventually morphed into *brimstone*.) When the Book of Genesis says that God destroyed the immoral cities of Sodom and Gomorrah with fire and brimstone, it may be referring to a volcano (Genesis 19:24). The Book of Revelation says that at the end of the world Satan and all unbelievers will be cast into a lake of fire and brimstone where they will burn eternally (Revelation 14:10, 19:20, 21:8). This is why "fire and brimstone" is another way of saying "the fires of hell."

the fish symbol
Christ on the bumper

You've probably seen the familiar fish emblem on auto bumpers but also on key chains, pendants, etc. The Greek word for fish was *ICHTHUS*, and some of the early Christians took the letters as a monogram for *Iesous CHristos THeou Uios Soter*—"Jesus Christ, God's Son, Savior." Some of the bumper plaques have the name JESUS inside, while some have the actual Greek word ΙΧΘΥΣ. Christians have been using the fish as a symbol of their faith since ancient times. Four of Jesus' disciples were fishermen, and he said if they became his followers, he would make them "fishers of men"—gathering souls instead of fish.

flagellation
Don't punish yourself

Flagellation means scourging or whipping, a punishment most famously inflicted on Jesus, shown in gory detail in the film *The Passion of the Christ*. Roman scourges had pieces of metal or bone attached to the lashes, thus the whipping was so brutal that some people died from it; the harsh whipping may explain why Jesus died relatively quickly on the cross. But generally when people speak of flagellation, they mean self-whipping, something practiced for centuries by a minority of Christians. Though the Bible does not mention such practices, the apostle Paul spoke of beating his body to keep his worldly impulses in check, and also stated that he bore on his body "the marks of Christ" (1 Corinthians 9:27, Galatians 6:17). He did not mean literally beating his body, but was referring to self-control, and as for the "marks of Christ," he meant the literal scars he had received from being persecuted as a Christian, since he had been scourged five times (2 Corinthians 11:24). But some Christians have chosen to whip themselves, even to the point in drawing blood. St. Thomas More, the "man for all seasons" who was executed by King Henry VIII of England, was a highly intellectual man, yet he beat himself. Flagellation is supposedly practiced in some parts of South America, but not with church approval. The practice was mocked in a Monty Python film, which showed robed Christians chanting and knocking themselves in the head with wooden boards.

footwashing
At your service …

Some Christians include a ritual washing of each others' feet in some of their worship services. In some churches it is done once a year, on Maundy Thursday, the day of the Last Supper and the day before Good Friday. The practice is based on John 13, where Jesus, just before he was arrested, washed the feet of his twelve disciples. They were perplexed, since he was their master and footwashing was normally the task of a servant, but he was demonstrating that they too ought to humbly serve mankind. Greece, Rome, and other ancient cultures looked down on servanthood, thinking that the best people were made to rule, not serve, but Jesus took an entirely different view.

forty
Well-rounded number

Forty is a number of special significance in the Bible. In Genesis, the rains that caused the great flood fell for forty days and nights. Moses spent forty days with

God on Mount Sinai. It took the Hebrew slaves forty years to travel from Egypt to their new home in Canaan. Goliath taunted the Israelite army for forty days. Saul, David, and Solomon each reigned as king for forty years. The prophet Elijah fled to the wilderness and was fed by ravens for forty days. In the Book of Jonah, the city of Nineveh had forty days to repent. After his baptism, Jesus was in the wilderness for forty days, being tempted by Satan. After Jesus' resurrection, he was on earth for forty days, then ascended into heaven. In Old Testament Law, criminals could be punished by no more than forty lashes—but in practice they only delivered thirty-nine, for fear of a miscount.

the four horsemen of the Apocalypse
Nothing to do with football

"Apocalypse" is another title for the Book of Revelation, the book that describes the ultimate showdown between God and evil. In one of its visions, four figures are mounted on horses: Conquest on a white horse, War on a red horse, Famine on a black horse, and Death on a pale horse. "Pale" is actually a poor translation, since the Greek word *chloros* here is more like "sickly green"—the color of a rotting corpse, an appropriate color for death (Revelation 6:1-8).

Some of Revelation's symbols are puzzling, but the four horsemen are easy to interpret: they symbolize the horrors that will occur at the end of time. They have been depicted in many artworks, notably a frightening engraving by the great Albrecht Durer, who included it in his chilling illustrations for the Book of Revelation. *The Four Horsemen of the Apocalypse* was used as the title of a World War I novel by the Spanish author Blasco Ibanez, made into a classic silent movie with Rudolph Valentino. Fiction writer Katherine Anne Porter's 1939 book *Pale Horse, Pale Rider* takes it title from the description of Death riding on a "pale" horse.

Gabriel

Announcer, but not trumpeter

Gabriel, along with Michael, is the only angel in the Bible given a name. In the Old Testament, he is mentioned twice in the Book of Daniel as the heavenly interpreter of Daniel's vision (Daniel 8:16, 9:21). Daniel speaks of Gabriel being "in swift flight," which suggests a winged angel.

Gabriel is more closely connected with the events of Jesus' birth. In Luke's Gospel, Gabriel appears in the temple while the aged priest Zechariah is offering incense. He tells Zechariah that his aged wife Elizabeth will give birth to a son who will "make ready a people prepared for the Lord." Because Zechariah doubts this angel who claims to "stand in the presence of God," he is struck mute until the child is born. The child of the aged couple grows up to be the prophet John the Baptist.

The second birth is even more miraculous than the first, since no human father is involved. Gabriel goes to Nazareth to tell the Virgin Mary she will give birth to "the son of Most High." Mary is puzzled, since she has not been with a man, but the angel says "the Holy Spirit will come upon you, and the power of the Highest will overshadow you; therefore, also, that Holy One who is to be born will be called the Son of God (Luke 1:35)."

That is all the Bible says about Gabriel. Why he came to be considered the trumpeter at the Judgment Day is not clear. Jesus said that angels would blow the trumpet on that fateful day (Matthew 24:31), and the apostle Paul said the Lord would descend "with the shout of an archangel, and with the trumpet of God" (1 Thessalonians 4:16). There are also seven angels (all nameless) in the Book of

Revelation. But none of these passages particularly connects Gabriel with the trumpet of judgment.

As with Michael, both Christians and Jews wove a number of legends around the angel Gabriel. Some say that Michael guides the movements of the sun, while Gabriel guides the moon. Some say it was Gabriel who wrote the Ten Commandments on stone on Mount Sinai. Since the Bible says Gabriel announced to Mary that she would bear Jesus, a legend grew that it was also Gabriel who announced Jesus' birth to the shepherds near Bethlehem. Another legend says it was Gabriel who buried Moses in his unmarked grave.

Michael and Gabriel are both considered "archangels," but Gabriel is not called this in the Bible. The simple fact that he was named, while other angels were not, suggested to Bible readers he must have been very important, thus an archangel, not an ordinary angel.

Gabriel appears as an important figure in John Milton's *Paradise Lost*, where he aids Michael in defeating Satan and the rebel angels. He also appears in *Jerusalem Delivered*, Italian poet Torquato Tasso's epic poem about the First Crusade. Gabriel appears in thousands of paintings showing him announcing to the Virgin Mary that she will bear the child Jesus, an incident Catholics refer to as the Annunciation. Traditionally, Gabriel is the patron saint of postal workers.

Gabriel, like Michael, is mentioned in the Koran, where his name is Jabrail, or Jibril. He is also called the "Faithful Spirit" who delivers the divine revelation to Muhammad. He is actually a more important figure in Islam than in Christianity.

Galilee
The Messiah's home turf

Jesus' hometown of Nazareth was in the region called Galilee, the northern part of the Holy Land. Although he was born in Bethlehem and was crucified and resurrected in Jerusalem, most of his public life was spent in Galilee, and all his disciples (except possibly the traitor, Judas) were Galilean men. His first miracle was at Cana in Galilee, and his "base" in his years of preaching and healing was not in Nazareth but the town of Capernaum on the shore of the Sea of Galilee. The lion's share of his work was done among Galileans.

Judea, the region around Jerusalem, had a kind of superiority complex, thinking of the Galileans as bumpkins, and not as religious as the people of Judea. In John's

Gospel, some of the religious leaders said Jesus could not be the Messiah, since prophecy said the Messiah would come from Bethlehem, meaning they weren't aware of his birth in Bethlehem (John 7:40-51). Apparently the Galileans had a distinctive accent, since Peter, after the arrest of Jesus, was identified as a Galilean by his speech (Matthew 26:73). Because Jesus was a Galilean, he was sent after his arrest to be interrogated by Herod, ruler of Galilee, who mocked Jesus and returned him to Pilate for trial.

Jesus Calms the Winds and the Sea
MATTHEW. CHAPTER 8, VERSES 23-27.

The Sea of Galilee, mentioned many times, is actually a large freshwater lake, called by several other names, including Gennesaret, Kinnereth, and Tiberias. The Jordan River enters the lake at one end and flows toward the Dead Sea at the other. On the shores of the lake, Jesus called four fishermen to be among his disciples. Jesus calmed a fierce storm on the lake (Mark 4:39) and on one occasion walked on the lake's storm-tossed waters (Mark 6:45-53). It is the lowest freshwater lake on earth.

The English poet A. C. Swinburne, no friend of religion, is the source of the line "Thou hast conquered, O pale Galilean / The world has grown gray from thy breath." Swinburne thought the influence of Christianity on the world was bad, that the "pale Galilean" (Jesus) had made people value weakness instead of strength. Julian, the last non-Christian emperor of Rome, had been reared as a Christian but hated the religion, and he wrote the work *Against the Galileans*.

Genesis / creation
Begin at the beginning

The Book of Genesis tells of the creation of the world and the story of the ancestors of the Jews. Genesis is the Greek word for "beginning," and the book's first words are, "In the beginning God created the heavens and the earth." In many creation myths, the gods make the world out of some pre-existing material, but in Genesis the creation is *ex nihilo*—Latin for "out of nothing." God simply gives the word, and things come into being. He creates light, divides it into night and day, then creates the dry land, plants, sun, moon, stars, animals, then finally creates man "in the image" of God. On the seventh day, God rests from creation, and later in the Bible, God commands people to observe the seventh day (the Sabbath) as a day of rest also. While other ancient stories have several gods involved in creation, in Genesis there is only one God, who creates everything with a sense of purpose and declares it all "good." In almost all ancient religions, the sun and moon were worshipped as gods (often the chief gods), but in Genesis God creates light even before the sun and moon are created—and Genesis refers to them not as divine beings, but as the "greater light" and the "lesser light."

The whole creation takes place in six "days," and people still squabble over whether the days are literal twenty-four-hour days, or long periods of time. The majority of Christians and Jews today do not believe the world was made in six twenty-four-hour days, but many still stand by the key belief that God created everything and had a purpose in doing so. Many also believe in the evolution of the human species but hold Genesis' teaching that of all creatures, only man was made in the image of God. Interestingly, in the early twentieth century, some of the Christians who described themselves

The First Day of Creation
GENESIS. CHAPTER 1, VERSES 1-5.

as Fundamentalists were willing to accept evolution, so long as they could still affirm that evolution was God's plan, not mere coincidence or random chance. Today, defenders of the Genesis account point out that the first thing God created was light—something that fits quite well with the "Big Bang" scientific theory. And no scientist would argue with the creation sequence of heavenly bodies, plants, animals, and finally human beings. (Too bad the two sides in this old debate can't sit down together and seek out common ground.)

The Genesis account of creation differs radically from creation accounts of other ancient religions, mostly because there is no conflict of gods, no stories of a god or gods fighting with a pre-existing ocean and subduing it. (For example, in Babylonian myth, the god Marduk killed the evilwater dragon Tiamat after a long battle and made earth and sky from the two halves of her corpse.) Genesis is also the only ancient account in which humankind is created "in the image of God." In Genesis, creation is full of purpose, one God creating things and calling them "good."

Some very old versions of the Bible contained prefaces or footnotes to Genesis, stating that the creation took place in 4004 B.C. This "fact" was determined by James Ussher, the chief bishop of the Irish church in the 1600s. Ussher published a book with the Latin title *Annales Veteris et Novi Testamenti*—"Chronicles of the Old and New Testaments." Ussher started with a sound idea: we know the historical dates for several events in the Bible (such as the Babylonian conquest of Jerusalem, which took place in 586 B.C.). Working backward from dates like this, and taking note of the genealogies that mention how long certain people lived, Ussher calculated that the universe was created in 4004 B.C. He wasn't the first person to try to compute the date. Some Jewish scholars had earlier calculated the date of creation as 3761 B.C.—not far off from 4004. Ussher's date was included in some printings of the King James Version beginning in 1701.

Following the creation story, the Book of Genesis tells of mankind's disobedience (called the Fall), Cain's murder of his brother Abel, the great flood sent as punishment for human sin, then God's calling of Abraham to be the ancestor of a chosen people (the Hebrews, later called Israelites, then Jews). The book concludes with the colorful stories of Abraham's grandson, the wily Jacob, and the emotional story of Jacob's favorite son, Joseph, sold into slavery but eventually made the right-hand man of the Egyptian Pharaoh.

The creation story itself has been told and retold numerous times. It is the subject of Franz Joseph Haydn's oratorio *The Creation* and French writer Guillaume du Bartas's epic poem *La Semaine (The Week)*. The creation was depicted dramatically in the opening sequence of the 1966 movie *The Bible ... In the Beginning*.

The other important characters and stories of Genesis are covered in entries on Adam and Eve, Cain and Abel, Noah, the tower of Babel, Abraham, Jacob, and Joseph.

Gentiles
Or "heathen," if you prefer

Simply put, a Gentile is a non-Jew. The Hebrew word is *goyim* (plural), and in English Bibles it can be translated "Gentiles," "the heathen," "the pagans," or even "the nations."

The Gentiles were not in a covenant relationship with God, as Israel was, and most Gentiles worshipped idols of many gods. Many of them did not practice circumcision, and the Bible at times refers to Israelites as "the circumcised" and the Gentiles as "the uncircumcised." In the Bible, Gentile is generally a derogatory term.

Still, the Old Testament contains hints that God was not the Jews' "tribal God," but one who loved everyone, even Gentiles. The Book of Ruth says that the grandmother of King David was a Gentile, a woman from Moab. The Book of Jonah has the prophet Jonah going to the pagan city of Nineveh and preaching repentance.

In the New Testament, Jesus and his original disciples were Jews, but several Gentiles in the Gospels are shown as being people of faith, including some Roman soldiers. Jesus at times criticized the Gentiles for their repetitious prayers (Matthew 6:7) and their materialism (Matthew 6:32), but his harshest criticisms were for his fellow Jews. In the Book of Acts, the apostles spread the faith everywhere, and the great apostle Paul, a Jew, becomes known as "apostle to the Gentiles," a title he took pride in (Romans 11:3, Galatians 2:8). At the famous Council of Jerusalem (SEE PAGE 77), the Christians leader decided that Gentile converts to Christianity did not have to obey the ritual laws of the Old Testament, including circumcision. Paul claimed that Jesus Christ had broken down the barrier between Gentiles and Jews (Romans 10:12). (Paul may have been thinking of a literal barrier: the Jerusalem temple did not allow Gentiles to enter its inner precincts on pain of death. Christianity was its own religion, not just a "stepchild" of the Jewish religion.) It was not long before the Gentile Christians greatly outnumbered Jewish Christians.

Luke was the only Gentile author of any books of the Bible (he wrote his Gospel and also Acts). In Proverbs, chapter 31 is said to be the proverbs of a certain King Lemuel, and since he was not one of the kings of Israel, we can assume he was a Gentile king.

Gethsemane

Midnight in the garden of agony

According to the dictionary, a "Gethsemane" is "a place or occasion of great mental or spiritual suffering." At the time of Jesus, Gethsemane was a sort of garden or park near Jerusalem. Jesus and his disciples went there the night he was arrested. Before the arrest, Jesus—who knew what was about to happen—went off alone to pray, begging God, "Father, if it is possible, let this cup pass from me; nevertheless, not as

I will but as you will" (Mark 14:36). The "cup" meant the "cup of suffering" he was about to drink from. While Jesus prayed, the disciples, who were supposed to keep watch, had fallen asleep. A mob appeared, and Judas, the traitor, gave his master Jesus a kiss, the sign to the mob that he was the one to arrest.

The scene of Jesus praying and agonizing in Gethsemane has been a favorite one for artists, who often gave their paintings the title *The Agony in the Garden*. Usually the picture shows the disciples sleeping nearby, emphasizing that Jesus is

Christ's Agony at Gethsemane
LUKE. CHAPTER 22, VERSES 39-44.

truly alone as he faces death. The one by Andrea Mantegna (c. 1430-1506) in London's National Gallery shows the "garden" as a rocky, forbidding place, the appropriate setting for what occurred there. Other painters continued this tradition of depicting Gethsemane as anything but peaceful and serene. *The Agony in the Garden* by El Greco (1541-1614) is almost surreal, with the sad but accepting face of Jesus. Movies about Jesus' arrest and death inevitably include

the Gethsemane scene, notably Mel Gibson's *Passion of the Christ*, which opens in Gethsemane and has Jesus confronting a very sinister Satan.

Gideon
A jarring leader

If you ever stayed in a hotel, you've seen the Bibles bearing the name and logo of the organization called the Gideons. They take their name from one of the "judges" (military deliverers) in the Book of Judges. Chapter 6 relates Gideon called by an angel of the Lord to be Israel's deliverer, even though Gideon protests he is a mere nobody. Gideon doubts whether the visitor is a real angel, until the angel sets some food afire by touching it. Gideon was apparently a skeptic by nature, for later he tested God by "laying out the fleece" (SEE PAGE 407).

Gideon and his three hundred men managed to fight off the Midianite raiders, even though badly outnumbered. The men rattled the sleeping Midianites by blowing trumpets and breaking jars. (It is this type of jar that the Gideons use as their logo.)

Gideon worked to stamp out worship of the pagan god Baal, and he was so effective that he was nicknamed Jerubbaal, meaning "fights against Baal." The people offered to make him king, but he modestly refused. ("I will not rule over you, the Lord will rule over you.") Gideon was an effective leader, and the land was at peace for forty years.

The Call of Gideon
Judges. Chapter 6, Verses 16-24.

Gideon had, amazingly, seventy sons. One of them, Abimelech, was a ruthless character who killed his brothers and had himself made king over Israel. The rogue was killed when a woman dropped a millstone on his head.

The Gideons International organization, incidentally, was founded in the U.S. in 1899 and chose the name Gideon because of the judge's "humility, faith, and obedience." The Gideons distribute Bibles not only to hotels but also hospitals, nursing homes, military bases, prisons, and schools.

the golden calf
Idol when they were idle

In one of the great ironies of history, while Moses was on Mount Sinai receiving the commandment not to make idols, his fellow Hebrews were at the foot of the mountain engaging in an idol-worshipping orgy. Prior to going up the mountain, Moses had delivered the word of God to the people: obey God's commands and be blessed; disobey and suffer the consequences. The people were told to keep off the mountain—in fact, they couldn't even touch it. While on the mount, Moses met God face to face and received the Ten Commandments, along with many other laws. The mountain smoked and rumbled, and there were even mysterious blasts of a heavenly trumpet. But Moses spent so much time away from the Hebrews that they grew restless. With a little arm-twisting, they persuaded Moses' brother Aaron to make them an idol. Aaron took their gold jewelry and created

The Idolatry of the Golden Calf
Exodus. Chapter 32, Verses 1-4, 5-19.

a golden idol. The translations usually call it a calf, but it was probably in the form of a young bull, which in ancient times was worshipped as a fertility god. Proving himself to be a not very loyal brother, Aaron announced that this golden god was the god who delivered them from Egypt. The people ate and drank and, as the text says, "played"— implying some sexual hijinks, which were generally part of pagan worship.

On the mountain, God told Moses he intended to destroy these immoral people, but Moses begged him not to. When Moses went down and saw what happened, he broke the stone tablets the laws were engraved on. He had the idol burned and ground into powder, pouring it into water and making the people drink it. The Lord also sent a plague on the people, though the Bible doesn't specify what it was. The Koran mentions the incident, approving of God's anger at the people for their worship of an idol.

One reason the Jews never forgot the golden calf incident is that after Israel split into two separate kingdoms, the northern kingdom, which kept the name Israel, no longer had Jerusalem and its temple, so the king set up two worship sites—both of them with golden calf images. Whether the people actually worshipped them or not was a moot point, because the more devout Jews were scandalized at an animal image at their worship sites. The people in the southern kingdom, Judah, thought that Israel was hopelessly mired in idolatry, allowing calf idols that were constant reminders of the awful incident at Sinai.

This episode, found in Exodus 32, is one of the great dramatic moments in the Bible, a high point of the 1956 film *The Ten Commandments*, and painted by countless artists. Composer Arnold Schoenberg captured it musically in his opera *Moses und Aron*.

the Golden Rule
Morality in a nutshell

In Matthew 7:12, Jesus told his listeners, "Whatever you wish that men would do to you, do so to them." In other words, treat people as you wish to be treated. This rule, he says, is a summation of all the rules contained in the Law (the five books of Moses) and the Prophets (the historical and prophetic writings). Christians have come to refer to it as the Golden Rule, "golden" meaning "best" or "most important."

Over the years, many businesses claiming to operate under Christian principles have used the name Golden Rule. Department store entrepreneur J. C. Penney originally called his stores the Golden Rule Stores, and there is a Golden Rule insurance company.

The English king Alfred the Great (849-900) sought to rule as a Christian and believed the Golden Rule could serve as the foundation for law and justice—in the negative form of "Do not do others what you would not wish done to you."

Golgotha / Calvary
Capping the skull

All four Gospels state that Jesus was crucified on a site called the Skull, which the Jews called by the Aramaic name Golgotha. Luke's Gospel uses the Greek word for skull, *kranion*, but more often than not Christians have used the Latin name, Calvary, familiar from countless sermons and hymns, as well as a common name for churches. (There are almost no churches named Golgotha, certainly none named Kranion.) Though people speak of Jesus' crucifixion on a hill, the Bible doesn't mention a hill, and no one knows for sure why the site was called the Skull. Were there human skulls lying around, or animal skulls? Or did the shape of the site somehow remind people of a skull? Travelers to the Holy Land have been trying to locate the precise site for centuries. The only guidance, other than the name Skull, is that John's Gospel says the site was outside the city walls of Jerusalem (John 19:20). Since the Romans crucified criminals in very public places, it makes sense that Golgotha might have been a hill.

Because the innocent Jesus was crucified there, the names Calvary and Golgotha have both come to mean any place or incident of unjust suffering. One legend says that Golgotha was the site where Adam died—the first sinner died there, but the Savior of sinners died there as well, so the belief goes.

Modern Swiss composer Frank Martin wrote an oratorio titled *Golgotha*.

Goliath

Huge and armored vs. small and mobile

This Philistine warrior's name has become a synonym for "giant." (The Philistines were a pagan people living on the coastal plain near Israel, and they were notorious for raiding the Israelites—and also for being uncircumcised.) The hulk Goliath was over nine feet tall, and his spear shaft was like a weaver's rod, with an iron point weighing six hundred shekels (1 Samuel 17:7). He challenged Israel to send its best man out for a one-on-one showdown. No one accepted until the shepherd boy David came forward. King Saul was impressed with his courage, and said to him, "Go, and the Lord be with you." David wore no armor, only his shepherd's bag, a sling, and "five smooth stones." Goliath was amazed and appalled that this was the best man Israel could send—but David, with one stone from his sling, felled the giant, then cut off Goliath's head with his own sword. The Philistines panicked and fled. This was the deed that set David on the road to fame in Israel.

The Bible tells us that when David went out to face Goliath, he took "five smooth stones," not just one. Why five? Were the other four his back-ups? No, indeed. Goliath had four brothers (who, we must assume, were probably as large and fierce as he was), so the other stones David carried were just in case the other four brothers showed up. As it turned out, the four brothers of Goliath did later die battling with David and his soldiers (2 Samuel 21:22).

This is one of the most appealing stories in the Bible. The young boy David versus the hulking Goliath has stirred the creative juices of thousands of authors, painters, and sculptors. Perhaps the most famous statue in the world is Michelangelo's thirteen-foot-tall *David*, showing the young (and naked) shepherd boy, poised with his sling, ready to take on the giant Philistine. (This David is notoriously *not* circumcised, one of the greatest goofs in the history of art.) Other sculptors like Donatello chose to depict the triumphant lad with the severed head at his feet. The poet Michael Drayton penned the 1630 narrative *David and Goliath*, and American author Elmer Davis (1890-1958) wrote the novel *Giant Killer*, and there are countless plays and novels dealing with what is probably the most famous (and lopsided) one-one-one confrontation in history.

Beginning in the 1950s, several cheaply made Italian movies—the "sword and sandal" genre—were built around a hulking muscleman named Goliath, but he was not connected with the Philistine giant of the Bible. The real Goliath was depicted in the 1961 movie *David and Goliath*, starring Orson Welles as Saul.

Was Goliath purely a legend? Maybe not. In November 2005, archaeologists digging at Tel es-Safi, a site in southern Israel that may be the Philistine city of Gath, unearthed a shard of pottery with the name Goliath. The shard dates from around 950 B.C. While it does not prove the biblical Goliath existed, it does prove that Goliath was an actual Philistine name from that period.

Good Friday
Horrible, but good in the long run

Good Friday is the annual observance of Jesus' trial and crucifixion. On the previous night, Jesus celebrated the Passover meal with his disciples (known to Christians as the Last Supper), then was betrayed by Judas and arrested. Early the next day he was brought to the Roman governor Pilate for trial. Pilate questioned him and found no fault in him, but was coerced into giving Jesus the death penalty by the Jewish priests, who envied Jesus' popularity and feared him as a troublemaker. Pilate had Jesus flogged (a brutal punishment that was sometimes fatal), then crucified between two thieves on the site called Golgotha. Jesus was taken from the cross and buried in a tomb belonging to Joseph of Arimathea. Christians believe he was resurrected on the following Sunday, the day celebrated as Easter.

All four Gospels provide details about the events of Good Friday, an important day for Christians because they believe Jesus' crucifixion is the sacrifice that brings God and sinners into harmony again. This is why it is *Good* Friday, despite the horrible events that occur. It has also been called Holy Friday, and Eastern Orthodox Christians know it as Great Friday. The Gospel accounts differ slightly, but together we get a fairly clear picture of the events of the day. Luke's Gospel includes Jesus being sent by Pilate to the Jewish ruler Herod, then sent back to Pilate again. The Gospels record the words Jesus spoke from the cross, seven utterances in all, known as the "seven words from the cross" (SEE PAGE 336).

Most churches have some kind of service on Good Friday, with readings from the Gospels about the events of the day. Some churches will drape a black cloth over a cross, symbolizing the death of Jesus. The cloth will be removed on Easter morning. Roman Catholics and some Christians fast on Good Friday as a sign of mourning. Another legend has it that Adam and Eve were expelled from Eden on a Friday, so God allowed Christ, making amends for their sin, to die on a Friday.

Good Shepherd
(see Shepherd of Israel)

Good Samaritan
(See Parable of the Good Samaritan)

Gospel
You've got good news …

The word gospel comes from the Anglo-Saxon *godspell*, meaning "good news," the same meaning as the Greek *euangelion* in the New Testament. To the early Christians, the good news was that Jesus, the Son of God, taught, performed miracles, was crucified, and was then resurrected—and that these events brought salvation to the people who believed in him. Strictly speaking, that story is *the* Gospel, and there is no other. The four Gospels in the New Testament—Matthew, Mark, Luke, John—aren't telling four different stories. They are the same story, but "according to" the four different witnesses. In other words, the Gospel of Matthew is really "the one Gospel, as told by Matthew." The authors of the four Gospels are often referred to as the four Evangelists (SEE PAGE 115) because they presented the *euangelion*, the good news.

The four Gospels in the New Testament weren't the only gospels written—far from it. There were literally dozens of gospels in circulation in ancient times, most of them claiming to be the work of one of Jesus' apostles—the Gospel of Thomas, Gospel of Peter, etc. Archaeologists frequently find fragments of these old writings, and we now have a good idea of what they were like. They usually have words in common with the four Gospels in the New Testaments but also contain "secret" teachings that Jesus passed on after his resurrection. Centuries ago the church authorities branded these gospels as "false" or "heretical," which is why they weren't included in the Bible. The four Gospels in the New Testament are "the real ones," written by people who actually witnessed the events, or who had talked to people who had. Since Christians traditionally regarded the four Gospels as the most important truths revealed to mankind, the phrase "gospel truth" came to refer to anything that was indisputably true.

In Catholic, Orthodox, and Episcopal churches, every worship service includes a reading from one of the Gospels, along with a reading from an epistle (or Acts), an Old Testament book, and one of the Psalms.

Gospel music is the name given to Christian songs that emphasize the personal aspects of faith—joy in believing in Jesus and regarding him as friend and guide, the joy of fellowship with other believers, and sorrow over one's sins.

the Great Commission
The evangelism mandate

If Christian evangelism offends you, be aware that it was commanded by Jesus himself. Matthew's Gospel (Matthew 28:19-20) ends with the risen Jesus giving his disciples this mandate: "Go therefore and make disciples of all the nations, baptizing them in the name of the Father and of the Son and of the Holy Spirit, teaching them to observe all things that I have commanded you; and lo, I am with you always, even to the end of the earth." This is known as the Great Commission, and it is the source of the baptism ritual of baptizing the person "in the name of the Father, Son, and Holy Spirit" (also known as the Trinity). Christian evangelists and missionaries believe they are obeying the Great Commission.

Greek
Common ground

Jesus and his earliest followers spoke the Aramaic language (SEE PAGE 31), but the entire New Testament was written in Greek, which many Jews spoke as a second language. In the eastern part of the Roman Empire, Greek was used as the common language of communication, since it was understood by more people than the Romans' language, Latin. When Jesus was crucified, a sign was placed above his head with the words "Jesus of Nazareth, King of the Jews" in Greek, Aramaic, and Latin so that anyone passing by could read it.

The Greek used by the New Testament authors was called *Koine* (meaning "common") Greek. In a few places in the Gospels, the writers gave the Aramaic words used by Jesus, then translated them into Greek. Since the Gospels were written in Greek, they could be read much more widely than if they had been in Aramaic or Latin.

By the time of Jesus, there was already a translation of the Old Testament into Greek. It was called the Septuagint, and when the New Testament writers quoted the Old Testament, it was the Septuagint they were quoting.

Why had Greek become the language of people far from Greece? Chalk it up to the conquests of Alexander the Great, who spread the Greek language and culture over the large empire he created. This occurred in the period between the Old and New Testaments. Eventually Rome conquered most of Alexander's empire, and although the Romans considered themselves the "master race," they always had a slight inferiority complex where the Greeks were concerned. Romans who considered themselves intellectual or cultured would learn Greek. As late as the year 180, Roman emperor Marcus Aurelius wrote his *Meditations* in Greek, not Latin.

During the Middle Ages, Latin became the dominant language of the church, and few scholars in Europe could even read Greek. The Latin Bible, called the Vulgate, was *the* Bible for centuries. In the 1500s, the leaders of the Protestant Reformation insisted on making new translations of the Bible from the original Greek and Hebrew. William Tyndale produced the first English New Testament translated from Greek. Koine Greek is still taught in many Christian colleges and seminaries so that future ministers and teachers can read the New Testament in its original form.

The original Greek manuscripts of the Bible had no punctuation, no lowercase letters, and no spaces between words, so the text LOOKEDSOMETHING-LIKETHIS.

Hallelujah
Just translate it

It won't surprise you that this familiar Hebrew word means "praise the LORD." Literally, it means "praise Yah," *Yah* or *Yahweh* being the name for God, but pious tradition always substituted "the LORD" for the actual name Yahweh. The word occurs many times in the Psalms, usually as "praise the LORD" instead of "hallelujah," and it made its way into Greek (which has no letter *H*) as *Alleluia*. It does not appear in the New Testament until The Book of Revelation, notably in Revelation 19:6: "Alleluia! For our Lord God Almighty reigns." Handel set it to beautiful music as the "Hallelujah Chorus" in his *Messiah*. "Hallelujah" is a vital part of Christian song and worship.

hats
Head on down to church

Women in some churches would not dream of showing up without wearing a hat. The hat-for-church tradition is based on 1 Corinthians 11, where the apostle Paul said that in worship services, men should have their heads uncovered, while women's must be covered. Paul's logic in this odd chapter is not easy to fathom, and most Christians treat the whole discussion as one that no longer applies to contemporary churchgoers. Woman who follow the instructions of the chapter may not be aware of Paul's words, but may simply be doing what other women in their church do. Paul's words are the basis of all nuns (until very recently) wearing some kind of head covering.

heaven and hell
Eternal choices

It surprises many people that the Bible says relatively little about heaven and hell. In fact, in the Old Testament the Israelites apparently believed that all people who died went to a shadowy region called *Sheol*, which was neither heaven nor hell, but was not as pleasant as life on earth. Sheol was not so much an afterlife as an afterdeath. (The ancient Greeks had a similar belief, with all people ending up in Hades.) Some old translations of the Bible translate *Sheol* as "hell," but this isn't correct. The Israelites sought to enjoy life on earth (while living morally, of course), and they believed that a person lived on by having a good reputation and as many children as possible. However, some very late parts of the Old Testament affirm a belief in heaven and hell, notably Daniel 12:2, which says that after death the good will be given eternal life, while the wicked receive "everlasting contempt."

By the time of Jesus, most Jews believed in an afterlife called heaven, or also called "Abraham's bosom." The wicked would be sent to hell, generally thought of as a place of burning. In fact, the Greek New Testament uses the word *Gehenna*, which referred to the Hinnom Valley near Jerusalem, a rubbish dump that was endlessly burning. The Hinnom Valley was where people had sacrificed their children to the god Moloch, so to Jews it was a wicked, horrible place. (Gehenna is the source of the Muslim term for hell, Jahannam, which is described in the Koran as a burning pit.) While Jesus is often thought of as loving and compassionate, he believed in both heaven and hell, as seen in such parables as the sheep and the goats (Matthew 25), where the bad receive eternal punishment, the good receive eternal life. The parable of Lazarus and the rich man pictures poor Lazarus the beggar at Abraham's side in heaven, while the rich man who snubbed him is burning in hell (Luke 16). Jesus also referred to hell as the "outer darkness," where there is "gnashing of teeth," meaning a state of regret (Matthew 8:12).

The Book of Revelation has the most vivid images of heaven and hell, with hell described as a lake of fire and brimstone in which Satan and wicked people are thrown, to be tormented eternally (Revelation 20:10). Heaven is described as a city made of pure gold, with gates of pearl, and no sun or moon because the glory of the Lord lights it. Jewels glisten everywhere, and more importantly, "God will wipe away every tear from their eyes." Revelation also depicts the saints in heaven wearing white robes and playing harps.

In 2 Peter 2:4, the word translated "hell" is the Greek word *Tartaros*—the place, in Greek myths, of torture and agony for evil people. According to 2 Peter, the angels who rebelled against God were sent there to be chained in gloomy darkness until the Day of Judgment. The New Testament also uses the Greek word *abyssos* for hell—the source of our word *abyss*.

When the New Testament was written, many Jews believed there were seven heavens, the seventh being the best, of course. Paul mentions in 2 Corinthians 12:2 that he knew of a man (possibly himself) who had a vision of being caught up in the third heaven.

Many popular images of heaven and hell are drawn from the Bible—burning forever in fire and brimstone, heaven with pearly gates, white robes, harps, etc. The idea that people in heaven become winged angels is not in the Bible, however. Neither is the idea of purgatory, a place where people destined for heaven have to spend time "cleaning off" their sins before entering God's presence. (Purgatory is an important belief in Roman Catholic dogma.) The Bible nowhere says that hell is underground.

Heaven and hell have inspired some of the classics of world literature, including Dante's *Divine Comedy*, where the poet is given a tour of hell, purgatory, and heaven, meeting many famous sinners and saints. (Dante's hell was full of surprises—even some of the popes were there!) Dante's name for hell was *inferno*, from the Latin word *infernus*, which is the root of our word *infernal*. John Milton's epic poem *Paradise Lost* opens with Satan and his followers landing in hell after they rebelled against God and were thrown out of heaven. The capital of hell is Pandemonium, meaning "all demons." John Bunyan, author of *Pilgrim's Progress*, also wrote *The Holy City* (heaven) and *A Few Sighs from Hell*. C. S. Lewis's *The Great Divorce* shows people from hell being given a brief "furlough" in heaven, though most of them choose to return to hell. The old legend of Don Juan, a notorious playboy who ends up being dragged into hell, has been treated in many books and plays, as has the story of Faust, the scholar who sells his soul to the devil. For many centuries, theatres in Europe had a "hell-mouth," a door painted to look like an evil face, which would open and receive a wicked character—such as Faust and

H

Don Juan—into hell. The Marc Connelly play *The Green Pastures* pictures heaven as a pleasant fish fry, not far from Jesus' statement that heaven is a banquet.

Many people today claim they don't believe in hell, but many films still feature hell, sometimes comically, sometimes not. It is an unpleasant reality in *What Dreams May Come* and *The Black Hole*. The hells in films like *Beetlejuice*, *Stay Tuned*, *The Devil and Max Devlin*, and *Highway to Hell* are horrifying, but funny. In times past, when the word hell wasn't used in polite company, people often used euphemisms—such as Hades and (believe it or not) Halifax.

Hebrew
Lordly language

Hebrew was the language of ancient Israel, written from right to left instead of from left to right. Almost all of the Old Testament was written in Hebrew, with some later parts in Aramaic. Hebrew has twenty-two consonants and no vowels, but centuries ago some scholars known as the Massoretes went through the Old Testament and added "vowel points" so that readers would know how to pronounce the words.

By the time of the New Testament, most Jews (including Jesus and the apostles) spoke either Aramaic or Greek instead of Hebrew. The Old Testament had been translated from Hebrew into Aramaic and Greek. Jewish scholars continued to learn Hebrew, but by about the year 135 it was a "dead" language, no longer actually spoken by many people. That would change in the twentieth century, when Israel was re-established as a nation, with Hebrew as its official language (although most Israelis speak at least one other language besides Hebrew).

Throughout the Middle Ages, few Christians bothered to learn Hebrew, since the church used only the Vulgate, the Latin Bible that had been produced around the year 400. (Jerome, translator of the Vulgate, worked from the Hebrew and called upon Jewish scholars to aid him in his work.) In the 1500s, the leaders of the Protestant Reformation insisted that translations of the Bible be made from the original Hebrew and Greek, so many universities began teaching both languages. Hebrew is still taught in many Christian and Jewish colleges and seminaries so that future generations will be able to translate the Old Testament accurately.

In earlier times, both Jews and Christians tended to assume that Hebrew was the original language of mankind—which made sense, since the Book of Genesis, telling of the creation of the world, was in Hebrew. It was assumed that Adam and Eve spoke Hebrew—and so did God, when he spoke to humans. Even in the Middle Ages, when few Christians bothered to learn Hebrew, they regarded it as the "holy tongue."

Yiddish, the language of Jews in Germany and Eastern Europe, is written in Hebrew letters. Essentially it is an old German dialect with many words borrowed from Hebrew. The name Yiddish is from the old German word *judisch*, meaning "Jewish." Most of the Jewish immigrants to the U.S. in the late 1800s and early 1900s spoke Yiddish.

Hebrews (letter)
Receivers unknown

The Letter to the Hebrews is one of the mysteries of the New Testament, since its author and recipients are unknown. Its title is based on the fact that the letter quotes the Old Testament often and tries to prove that Jesus was greater than Hebrew figures like Moses and Aaron and Israel's prophets. Jesus is described as the great high priest in heaven, mediating between sinners and God, and making the Jewish priesthood unnecessary. In fact, Jesus is not only the ultimate priest, but the ultimate sacrifice also. Chapter 11 of the letter is often quoted. It is the "Faith Hall of Fame," commending people of faith in times past, such as Noah, Abraham, Moses, and others. They are a "cloud of witnesses" watching Christians and urging them on in the life of faith. The letter reminds readers their faith may be tested in the sinful world, but this is God's way of disciplining them, training them to be better.

Some old Bibles attribute the letter to Paul, but it isn't written in his style, and most Bibles now admit it is anonymous.

Herod Antipas
A man even Jesus didn't like

Throughout his life, Jesus seemed to be plagued by someone named Herod. The king called Herod the Great was the paranoid fiend who massacred the infants of

Bethlehem, hoping to kill the newborn "king of the Jews" (SEE PAGE 145). His son, named Herod Antipas, but simply called "Herod" in the Gospels, was also a nasty character, though not quite as much as his father. Herod Antipas ruled the district of Galilee, the district where Jesus grew up and preached. Like his father, Herod Antipas kissed up to the Romans, notably by ruling from his new city of Tiberias, named in honor of the Roman emperor, Tiberius. The large lake called the Sea of Galilee in the Gospels even got a new pro-Roman name, Lake Tiberias.

Herod is most famous for beheading Jesus' kinsman, the prophet John the Baptist. (See the entry on Herod's step-daughter, Salome. SEE PAGE 321.) Herod reluctantly had John imprisoned and later beheaded, and though an unspiritual man, he seems to have thought that John, a righteous man, had some divine power. His wife, Herodias, bore the real grudge against John, since he condemned her for divorcing Herod's brother and marrying Herod.

After John's execution, Herod speculated that this Jesus from Nazareth might be John come back from the dead (Mark 6:16). He didn't particularly fear or respect Jesus, because some of his court followers—called "Herodians"—connived with the Pharisees about ways to kill Jesus (Mark 3:6). On one occasion, the Herodians told Jesus to leave their region because Herod wished to kill him. Whether this was a bluff or a serious threat is not known. Jesus' reply, however, was direct enough: "Go tell that fox, I will drive out demons and heal people today and tomorrow, and on the third day I will reach my goal" (Luke 13:32, NIV). Then he gave the Herodians some assurance: he was on his way to Jerusalem and would perish there, not in Herod's region of Galilee. People have puzzled over what Jesus meant by "that fox." Did he mean crafty? Or did he mean "insignificant as some wild animal"? Perhaps both. Whatever it was, he didn't mean it as a compliment. Herod is the one individual in the Gospels that Jesus spoke of with contempt.

As it turned out, Jesus would eventually meet Herod face to face in Jerusalem. After his arrest and his first meeting with Pilate, Jesus was sent to Herod. Knowing that Jesus was from Galilee, Pilate decided to let Herod, the ruler of Galilee, handle the case. Herod was "greatly pleased" to finally meet this prophet from Nazareth—not for any spiritual reason, but because he hoped Jesus might perform a miracle. But Jesus' reply was memorable: "He made no answer" (Luke 23:9). It was the one case in the Bible where Jesus had nothing whatever to say to a person who spoke to him. Herod's soldiers mocked Jesus, dressing him in a purple robe and scorning him. Then Herod sent him back to Pilate. The episode ends with a puzzling revelation: "That day Herod and Pilate became friends—before this they had been enemies." Herod may have mocked Jesus, but he found nothing in him deserving of execution, which Pilate pointed out to the priests, to no avail.

Luke's Gospel is the only one that reports Jesus' encounter with Herod. Perhaps the other authors knew nothing about it or simply didn't think it was important. It serves the purpose of showing that the Jews' own rulers were as bad, or worse, than the Romans.

By the way, Herod's official title was "tetrarch," meaning someone who rules a fourth part of a kingdom. His father Herod had been a full-fledged king. Herod died in the year 39, not mourned by the Jews.

Herod Antipas has been depicted in numerous paintings in connection with his beheading of John the Baptist, or with the silent Jesus standing before him. He has also been featured in plays and movies about Jesus' life in connection with Jesus' trial. In *Jesus Christ Superstar*, Herod is a cynical buffoon, daring Jesus to "walk across my swimming pool." In Mel Gibson's *Passion of the Christ* he is more cynical, but in neither movie does Jesus speak a word to him, as Luke's Gospel says.

Herod the Great
"Great" ain't "good"

Historical characters known as "the Great" aren't necessarily *good* people, which is certainly true in this case. Herod wasn't even a true Jew, yet he ruled for years as king of the Jews thanks to his having licked the boots of the Roman emperor Augustus. The Roman Senate showed their appreciation by making him king for thirty-two years. He imitated the Romans' fascination with Greek culture and surrounded himself with Greek advisors. People favoring Greek culture were called Hellenists, and Herod was one, and the Jewish high priests he appointed were Hellenists also. Herod was an Idumean, not a Jew. The Jews hated him for being a foreigner and for being a Roman puppet. He tried to win their love by his many building projects, including his renovation of the temple in Jerusalem, making it far more beautiful than the original one built by Solomon. The Jews loved the temple but hated him. (In one of history's great ironies, Herod's temple would be destroyed in the year 70 by ... the Romans.) Herod impressed the Romans and scandalized the Jews by building temples to the pagan gods—and to his Roman patron, Augustus. He built a new port city and named it Caesarea, another tribute to the Romans. He rebuilt the old city of Samaria in honor of Augustus, and lived there as a pagan, not a Jew.

He may have been a "great" builder, but his morals were rock-bottom. Much of his wealth came from the copper mines of Cyprus, where slaves toiled away without seeing the sun, fed in troughs like livestock. The amphitheatres he built were the scenes of bloody gladiator contests and the sensuous plays the Greeks and Romans loved. Herod was pathologically suspicious and paranoid, growing worse as he aged. He murdered one of his wives (he had eight) along with her sons and brother, and killed his own first-born son. Matthew's Gospel tells us that the visit of the magi, who were seeking a newborn "king of the Jews," caused Herod to order the massacre of the infants of Bethlehem (Matthew 2). His brutal act failed, for Joseph, Mary, and the baby Jesus had fled to exile in Egypt. He died after much pain and agony.

Herod was succeeded as king by his son Archelaus, who was just as vile as his father. After Herod's death, Joseph, Mary, and the child Jesus went to live in Galilee, which was outside of Archelaus's district (Matthew 2:21-23). Archelaus had a huge effect on the history of the region because his subjects hated him so much they reported him to Rome. Instead of replacing him with another "king of the Jews," the Romans made Judea a province of the empire and installed a Roman governor. Jesus' trial and crucifixion under the Roman governor Pilate were an indirect result of Archelaus's mismanagment of his kingdom.

One of Herod's sons executed the prophet John the Baptist and mocked Jesus before his crucifixion. A grandson persecuted Jesus' apostles and had one of them beheaded. But the depraved family soon lost its power and influence, while the new faith lived on. So much for earthly power.

Herod has been a fixture in dramas and films about Jesus. In plays from the Middle Ages, he was usually portrayed as a ranting tyrant, and Shakespeare in his *Hamlet* used the expression "it out-Herods Herod," referring to a ranting style of acting. Herod is an important character in French composer Hector Berlioz's oratorio, *L'Enfance du Christ* (*The Childhood of Christ*).

A word about reading the New Testament: The authors used the name "Herod" to refer to Herod the Great, to his son Herod Antipas, to a grandson Herod Agrippa, and to a great-grandson Herod Agrippa II, all of them important characters in the Gospels and Acts. They had one thing in common: they were really nasty people.

Hezekiah

Witnessing the miracles

One of the few decent kings in the Bible was Hezekiah, king of Judah and friend of the prophet Isaiah. According to 2 Kings, Hezekiah "did what was right in the eyes of the Lord," tearing down the worship sites of the false gods. During Hezekiah's reign, the Assyrian king Sennacherib threatened to attack Jerusalem, so Hezekiah bribed him with gold and silver taken from the temple. When the Assyrians still threatened, the prophet Isaiah assured Hezekiah that the Lord would protect the land from the Assyrians. Sure enough, an angel struck down the 185,000 soldiers of the Assyrian army. Sennacherib was punished by being murdered by two of his own sons (2 Kings 19).

Later, Hezekiah was dying from an illness, but he prayed, and God gave him fifteen more years. Unfortunately, the king foolishly showed his treasures to the ambassadors from Babylon, and Isaiah prophesied that in the future Babylon would conquer and carry off those treasures. The prophecy came true generations later, when the Babylonians sacked Jerusalem and deported most of the people. Hezekiah consoled himself that at least the tragedy would not happen in his own lifetime. Oddly, the good king was succeeded by his immoral son Manasseh.

high places

Most friends up there are bad ...

It is pretty much universal that people think of their god, or gods, as being "up there." Since ancient people couldn't ascend into the skies, they did the next best thing and situated their worship places on hilltops and mountains—which in the Bible are the "high places." (The Hebrew word *bamah* means literally "elevation.") Numerous times the Old Testament mentions pagan worship shrines being on these "high places." They were not only the scene of worshipping false gods, but the worship often involved orgies and human sacrifice. The Israelites were commanded by God to avoid such places and destroy the sites (Numbers 33:52). A handful of kings, such as Hezekiah, destroyed the high places, while wicked kings like Manasseh did not. The saintly king Josiah did a national "cleansing" of all high places (2 Kings 23:1-25).

Readers today probably don't know the significance of "high places." Some modern Bible versions like Today's English Version use such phrases as "pagan places," "pagan hill shrines," or "hilltop shrines." Ironically, Jerusalem's temple to God was on a mountain, and even today Christians like to build their churches on elevated sites.

the Holy Grail
Wine, with or without jewels

You won't find the word "grail" in the Bible, but the New Testament tells the story of the Last Supper, in which Jesus, taking the Passover meal with his disciples, refers to the cup of wine with the words, "This is my blood of the new covenant" (Matthew 26:28). According to legend (not the Bible itself), the cup Jesus used at the Last Supper was used by one of his followers (usually Joseph of Arimathea) to catch the blood of the crucified Jesus. (Some say that Joseph of Arimathea also possessed the Roman spear that pierced Jesus on the cross.) The cup was passed on from Joseph to others, and magical powers were associated with it. The Catholic Church teaches that the wine used in Holy Communion becomes the actual blood of Jesus. During the Middle Ages, Christians thought that if their own cup of wine could magically become Jesus' blood, imagine the power of the real cup Jesus had used. The legend of the cup—the Grail—became connected with the tales of King Arthur and the Knights of the Round Table. According to the Arthur legends, the knights sought the Grail because it could heal diseases and wounds. It had moved from the realm of Christianity into the realm of "white magic."

The first written version of the grail legend was Chretien de Troyes's *Le Conte del Graal*, composed sometime before 1190. Richard Wagner's famous opera *Parsifal* deals with the grail legends. Some of the legends say that Arthur's famous Round Table was the actual table used at the Last Supper (unlikely, since the Round Table seated 150 people). Glastonbury, England, has the Chalice Well, and supposedly the Grail, brought there by Joseph of Arimathea, lies at the bottom of the well and gives the waters amazing healing properties. The water contains rust, and people said this was due to the staining of the water by Christ's blood in the Grail.

The Grail legend was at the core of the popular movie with *Indiana Jones and the Last Crusade*, in which Indiana seeks (and finds) the Grail and uses it to cure his wounded father. But long before Indiana Jones, a thousand tales and songs spoke of the "quest for the Holy Grail." Artists frequently depict it as a splendid object—gold, encrusted with jewels, etc. But the Indiana Jones movie probably had it right: the actual cup used at Jesus' Last Supper was a very plain earthenware cup. The film *Monty Python and the Holy Grail* was a spoof of the legends of the grail and King Arthur (with some randy women hanging out a "Grail lantern" to lure in the knights). The film got recycled into the hit Broadway play *Spamalot*.

In 1916, Arabs near the site of the ancient city of Antioch claimed they found the actual Holy Grail. Dubbed by the media "the chalice of Antioch," it was a silver cup engraved with figures of Jesus and the apostles. People with wild imaginations believed this actually was the cup used by Jesus at the Last Supper—overlooking the unlikelihood of Jesus and the apostles having a "commemorative cup" specially made for that occasion. Archaeologists believe the cup was probably made in the fourth century. The finding of the chalice of Antioch resulted in a novel (later a film) called *The Silver Chalice*, concerned with the making of the chalice for the Last Supper.

Regarding the word "grail": it's probable that it originated in the French phrase *sang real*—"royal blood," meaning the blood of Jesus. Over time *sang real* got changed into *san greal*, which morphed into English as "Holy Grail." The other possibility is that "grail" came from a Middle English word *graal*, meaning simply "bowl."

the Holy Innocents
Royally butchered

One sad event connected with the birth of Jesus is known as the massacre of the Holy Innocents. The wicked and paranoid Jewish king Herod was disturbed at the visit of the wise men (Magi), who were looking for a newborn "king of the Jews," so hearing that the child had been born in Bethlehem, he ordered his soldiers to descend on the town and slaughter all the male children under two years of age.

He failed to accomplish his purpose, however, because an angel had warned Joseph, husband of the Virgin Mary, to flee to Egypt with the newborn Jesus (Matthew 2:13-18). The early Christians were aware that Jesus' birth and survival was in a sense an echo of the birth of Moses centuries earlier: a deliverer had been born, and through the workings of God, had escaped a slaughter of children.

In Christian tradition, the murdered children are regarded as the first martyrs. The Feast of the Holy Innocents is celebrated on December 28 by Catholics, December 29 by Eastern Orthodox. In the past, the day was also known as Childermas and was kept as a day of fasting and mourning. However, over time some tomfoolery came to be associated with the day, such as the custom of parents whipping their children in bed to remind them of the suffering of the Holy Innocents. (Presumably this whipping was done in play.) In many Catholic countries, the day came to be associated with merrymaking and practical jokes.

The slaughter of the Holy Innocents is a dramatic (and gruesome) incident and has been the subject of many works of art, which typically show the mothers of Bethlehem looking on with horror as their infants are killed. Also common in art is the scene known as *The Flight into Egypt*, which typically shows Joseph on foot, leading a donkey that is carrying his wife and the baby Jesus. Often the pictures will show a winged angel somewhere nearby, a sign of God's protection for the family.

the Holy Land
Sacred vacation spot

Israel and parts of Jordan and Lebanon have been called "the Holy Land" for centuries, since they have sites sacred to Jews, Christians, and Muslims, particularly the ancient city of Jerusalem. People of all three faiths have been making pilgrimages—journeys to sacred places—since ancient times. In the New Testament period, Jews from far away often journeyed to Jerusalem, since it had the one temple devoted to their God. Christians have been traveling there for centuries, visiting locales associated with Jesus and the apostles—Jerusalem, Bethlehem, Nazareth, and others. In fact, the religious wars known as the Crusades were waged with the goal of keeping the Holy Land accessible to Christian pilgrims, since the Muslims conquered the region and occasionally harassed Christians. Today there are plenty of travel agencies sponsoring Holy Land tours, although tourists have to keep close watch on the news, given the frequent violence in the region.

Holy of Holies
A room with a view (of God)

In the days of Moses, Israel's worship centered on a large tent, called the Tent of Meeting, or Tabernacle. In the innermost part of the Tent was the gilded chest called the ark of the covenant (SEE PAGE 32), kept in a special area called the Holy of Holies (or "Most Holy Place" in some Bible versions). On a few select days, Israel's high priest would enter the Holy of Holies, where the ark symbolized the presence of God. On the annual Day of Atonement, the priest would sprinkle blood on the ark, symbolizing a sacrifice for all the people's sins.

The Tabernacle (which had the advantage of being portable) was eventually replaced by the beautiful temple King Solomon built in Jerusalem. Like the Tent of Meeting, the temple had a Holy of Holies.

The ark of the covenant disappeared, probably at the time the Babylonians destroyed the temple in 586 B.C. When a new temple was built, it had a Holy of Holies, but there was nothing inside it—something that surprised the Roman general Pompey when he conquered Jerusalem in 63 B.C.

In the New Testament, the Letter to the Hebrews states that all believers now have access to the Most Holy Place, because Jesus offered himself up as a once-for-all sacrifice (Hebrew 10:19). The old religion with the high priest as the only person with direct access to God has disappeared. In the year 70, the Romans destroyed the temple, which has never been rebuilt, so there is no longer a Most Holy Place in the Jewish or Christian religions.

Holy Spirit / Holy Ghost / Spirit of God
Separate, equal, and powerful

Christians believe there is one God, but he exists as three "persons"—Father, Son, and Holy Spirit—known as the Holy Trinity. The Spirit is mentioned in the Bible at the very first words of Genesis, which says that God's Spirit moved over the face of the earth's waters. In fact, the Hebrew word translated "Spirit" is *ruach*, which can also be translated "breath." The same is true for the Greek word *pneuma* in the New Testament. In the Old Testament, the Spirit seems to empower certain special individuals for certain tasks. In the New Testament, however, Jesus promises his disciples they will all be empowered with the Spirit, which happens dramatically on the day of Pentecost when the Spirit comes upon the twelve disciples with the sound of a mighty wind and "tongues of fire." The disciples are able to speak in unknown languages, and they preach the gospel everywhere (Acts 2). The New Testament speaks of every Christian having the Spirit within them, giving each believer a "spiritual gift" that benefits the whole fellowship in some way (1 Corinthians 12). The Christians saw the workings of the Spirit as fulfilling the words of the prophet Joel, who predicted a time when the Spirit would empower many people (Joel 2:28-29).

Because the Spirit descended in the form of a dove at Jesus' baptism, the dove is often used as a symbol of the Spirit, especially Christians who consider themselves Pentecostals and charismatics. When you see a dove bumper sticker on someone's car, chances are that person regards himself as part of a "Spirit-filled" church. Artists have almost always shown the dove over Jesus' head at his baptism, and sometimes the scene is depicted as the Holy Trinity, with God the Father (generally a white-bearded male figure, but sometimes just a radiant glow) watching from heaven. Some hymns refer to the Spirit as "heavenly dove," and some use the term "Comforter," a word Jesus used to refer to the Spirit (John 14:16).

While the Spirit was important to the earliest Christians, he was largely forgotten for many centuries, except that baptisms continued to mention Father, Son, and Spirit. Some theologians taught that the "gifts of the Spirit" mentioned in the New Testament were no longer necessary in the church, and that they ceased after the time of the apostles. Creeds continued to mention the Spirit, but most Christians were probably not aware of how often the Spirit is mentioned in the Bible. One of the great controversies in Christian history resulted from a theological battle over whether the Spirit "proceeds" from the Father and Son, or just from the Father. The disagreement contributed to a permanent split (known as the Great Schism) between Roman Catholics and Eastern Orthodox churches, though probably most Christians hadn't the slightest knowledge (or concern) over the matter.

Early in the twentieth century, the Pentecostals began to preach often about the Spirit and his gifts, and "Spirit-filled" churches have a more emotive form of worship service, often with hand clapping, swaying, lively music, etc.

In older English translations of the Bible, such as the King James Version, the term "Holy Ghost" was used, but most Bibles now use "Holy Spirit." An order of Catholic monks devoted to missions in Africa is called the Congregation of the Holy Ghost.

Holy Week
Triumph, tragedy, then happy ending

Holy Week is the name given to the seven days from the day Jesus and his disciples went to Jerusalem until Jesus' resurrection a week later. Holy Week begins with Palm Sunday (SEE PAGE 266), the day Jesus rode into Jerusalem on a humble donkey and was hailed by many people as the one who "comes in the name of the Lord." Jesus and his twelve disciples had gone to Jerusalem to celebrate the Passover festival. The week was an eventful one, with Jesus driving the moneychangers out of the temple court (SEE PAGE 357), debating with the Pharisees and the Jewish priests, teaching the crowd, sharing the Last Supper with the disciples, then being betrayed, arrested, tried, flogged, and crucified, then resurrected on Easter morning. The week includes not only Palm Sunday but Maundy Thursday (the night of the Last Supper and the arrest), Good Friday (the trial and crucifixion), and Holy Saturday (mourning for the dead Jesus). Easter, the day of resurrection, is the "happy ending" to the week.

For centuries Christians have emphasized the events of Holy Week, also called Great Week, and many churches have special ceremonies and readings for worship services. Many Christians, especially the newly baptized, wear white on Easter, a sign that the mourning for Jesus was over, that God and Jesus had triumphed over death.

homosexuality
As old as Sodom …

Putting it bluntly, yes, the Bible does condemn homosexual behavior. The first mention of it is the story of the wicked cities of Sodom and Gomorrah, in which two angels visit the home of Lot in Sodom and tell him to flee the city, since God is about to destroy it. The men of the city surround Lot's house and order him to send out the two angels (who look like men) so they can have sex with them. The story is the root of the word sodomy.

Homosexual activity is condemned in the Old Testament (Leviticus 18:22, 20:13) and the New Testament (Romans 1:26-27, 1 Corinthians 6:9, 1 Timothy 1:10). In the Old Testament period, pagan gods were worshipped with fertility rituals that often involved men having sex with "shrine prostitutes"— some female, but some male. Israel's prophets warned against such activity. In the New Testament period, homosexual behavior was tolerated among the Greeks and Romans, but the apostle Paul insisted that people who practiced such behavior could not enter heaven (1 Corinthians 6:9-11). Putting it another way, you could be a homosexual, or be a Christian, but you couldn't be both. Throughout most of its history, Christianity has taken its cue from Paul and insisted that homosexual behavior is wrong. The modern world has grown much more accepting of homosexuals, and more liberal Christians insist that the old rules no longer apply, while conservative Christians stick by the words of Paul.

One deep friendship that has caused a lot of speculation was the bond between David and Jonathan in the Old Testament. The two were closer than brothers, and when Jonathan died in battle, David went into deep mourning, lamenting than Jonathan's love "was extraordinary, passing the love of women" (2 Samuel 1:26). An interesting sentiment from David, a man of multiple wives and concubines, and numerous children. Entire books have been written attempting to "prove" the two men had a sexual relationship.

Hosea
The one married to Gomer (don't laugh)

Hosea was one of the prophets of Israel, a man whose married life became an illustration of God's relationship with Israel. God ordered Hosea to marry a woman named Gomer, who was a "wife of whoredom," which could mean she was a literal prostitute, or that she engaged in the ritual sex that was often part of pagan worship. She was unfaithful, naturally, but she bore Hosea several children, and God himself gave them descriptive names like No Mercy and Not My People. Hosea, like other prophets, saw idolatry as a form of "whoring" or not being faithful to the true God. The Book of Hosea is a plea to Israel to return to its "husband" (God) or disaster would strike. It did, for not long after the time of Hosea, Israel was conquered by the Assyrians.

Hosea is a very quotable book, with such striking phrases as "they sow the wind, and they reap the whirlwind" (8:7) and "you have plowed iniquity and reaped injustice; you have eaten the fruit of lies (10:13)." Like all the prophets, Hosea was aware that people could be immoral even though they were going through the motions of religion. God tells Hosea that "I desire steadfast love and not sacrifice, the knowledge of God rather than burnt offerings" (Hosea 6:6).

H

idolatry

Image problems

One of the Ten Commandments reads, "You shall not make for yourself any carved image, or any likeness of anything that is in heaven above, or that is in the earth beneath" (Exodus 20:4). In other words, no idols, no statues, no pictures should be bowed down to. Israel's God was invisible, not something that could be "localized" into any kind of object. Israel was different from every culture around it, for it's practically a universal thing: people want to honor or worship a material thing. In ancient times, they made images of gods that were like immoral people—fickle, unpredictable, and very promiscuous. The Israelites believed that you became like the thing you worshiped. If you worshiped a holy God, you became holy yourself. If you bowed down to a promiscuous fertility god or goddess, you became like them. The Israelites noticed that worship of fertility gods tended to turn into a drunken orgy—more like a fraternity party than what we normally associate with the word *worship*. So the great prophets had to preach the message over and over: worship the invisible, holy God, and don't bow down to these immoral gods of nature—who really don't exist anyway.

the Incarnation

What if God was one of us?

The word incarnation is from Latin and means "in the flesh." Christians apply it to Jesus, believing he was fully a human being but also, in some unexplainable way, God in the flesh. The New Testament refers to him many times as the "Son of God," but also makes clear that he *was* God, something that wasn't absolutely certain until he came back from the dead.

The ancient Greeks and Romans had myths about their gods occasionally walking the earth in human form. The story of Jesus differs in that Jesus was actually born as a human infant and lived out a full human life, even dying, before being resurrected. He differed from the Greek gods-in-disguise in another way: he was loving and compassionate toward human beings, while the Greek gods were often lecherous and mischievous when they moved among humans.

Christians consider the Incarnation to be part of the gospel ("good news") message. Many churches have the name Church of the Incarnation.

INRI
Cross talk

You have probably seen pictures of the crucified Jesus with a plaque over his head reading "INRI." There was indeed a sign affixed to the cross, since this was the practice with all crucified persons. (The Romans called this the *titulus*.) According to the Gospels, the sign was written with the same words in three different languages—Aramaic, Latin, and Greek—so that anyone passing by would be able to understand the words. The words in English are "Jesus of Nazareth, King of the Jews." In Latin the words were *Iesus Nazarenum Rex Iudorem*, which artists usually abbreviated to INRI.

According to John's Gospel, the sign on the cross offended the Jewish priests, who went to Pilate and told him the sign should read, "This man said, 'I am the king of the Jews.'" Pilate's terse reply was, "What I have written, I have written (John 19:22)."

Isaac
Patriarch, Generation II

The hundred-year-old Abraham and his ninety-year-old wife Sarah finally had a son, Isaac, as God had promised. But after a few years, God put Abraham to the test. He commanded Abraham to "take now your son, your only son, Isaac, whom

The Sacrifice of Isaac
GENESIS. CHAPTER 22, VERSES 2-12.

you love, and go to the land of Moriah, and offer him there as a burnt offering" (Genesis 22:2). The man was horrified, since it must have seemed unlikely he and his aged wife Sarah would ever produced another son. But this was Abraham, the man of total faith. So he obeyed the command (reluctantly, we can imagine). The naive boy Isaac asks his father why there are fire and wood but no sheep for a sacrifice. Abraham answered, "God will provide." Abraham bound the child with ropes and raised his knife to kill him—a tense moment, we may assume—but he was stopped by an angel, who said, "Do not lay your hand on the boy, or do anything to him; for now I know that you fear God." The angel said that because of Abraham's total trust, God will surely bless him.

It is worth noting that many ancient nations near Israel practiced child sacrifice. Israel always condemned it. The early Christians saw the sacrifice of Isaac as a symbol of Christ's sacrifice by his Father, God. Abraham's total trust in God made him the great role model of faith for Jews and Christians.

Muslims, incidentally, tell the story very differently. In their tradition, Abraham (*Ibrahim*) comes near to sacrificing his favorite son Ishmael (*Ismail*), not Isaac. The Arab Muslims believe they are descendants of Ismail.

Artists have been intrigued by the subject, and there are countless paintings of the aged Abraham with his knife raised over his son, with the angel appearing in the nick of time. In fact, the sacrifice of Isaac was a favorite subject in the earliest Christian art, found in tombs and catacombs. Perhaps the best-known painting is *Abraham Sacrificing Isaac* (1635) by Rembrandt. A winged angel stays Abraham's arm, the knife falling in mid-air. Abraham has his hand over his son's eyes. In the 1600s, Caravaggio did at least two paintings on the subject, and it was sculpted by Donatello in bronze in the 1400s. An early silent film was titled *The Sacrifice of Isaac*. The popular 1966 film *The Bible … In the Beginning* covered Genesis from the creation of the world to the sacrifice of Isaac.

Isaac was the middle generation between Abraham and Jacob, all three being ancestors of the Israelites, God's "chosen people." When God revealed himself to

Moses in the burning bush centuries later, he referred to himself as "the God of Abraham, Isaac, and Jacob." Isaac has been a common name among Jews, and Christians often use "Ike" as the nickname form.

In his old age, Isaac became blind, and his wife Rebecca and son Jacob managed to play a nasty trick on Isaac's favorite son, Esau (SEE PAGE 111). The name Rebecca has been commonly used for women, despite the Bible's depiction of her as a schemer.

The ancient city of Hebron in Israel has the cave that, tradition says, is the burial place of Isaac and Rebecca.

Isaiah

Prophecy enough for two men

Isaiah was one of the great prophets of the Old Testament, his book being first among the Major Prophets, and also the longest. Isaiah chapters 1 through 39 are full of scolding the people for their immorality and warnings of what will happen if they don't repent. Isaiah was a spiritual-political advisor to King Hezekiah, one of the few kings with any morals. Isaiah advised Hezekiah to be an "isolationist," relying on God for protection instead of on foreign nations. Chapter 6 contains the famous vision in which Isaiah sees God in the temple and accepts God's calling to be his prophet. (SEE PAGE 334.) Isaiah refers to God as "the Holy One" thirty times. Isaiah 7:14's words, "a virgin shall conceive and bear a son," were believed by Christians to be a prophecy of the Virgin Mary bearing Jesus.

Chapters 40 through 66 are very different in tone and style, and they are often called the Book of Consolation, since chapter 40 begins with the words, "Comfort ye my people" (words used at the opening of Handel's *Messiah*). These later chapters predict the coming of a "Suffering Servant," a man (or possibly a whole nation) who will obey God perfectly and atone for the people's sins through suffering. The early Christians believed these sections—which they called the "Servant Songs"—were prophesies of Jesus. Isaiah also prophesied that a "remnant" of the people would be spiritually saved, an idea the early Christians applied to themselves.

Chapter 20 states that the prophet went "naked" for three years. As in other places in the Bible, "naked" doesn't mean "stark naked," but simply "indecent." Probably Isaiah was wearing his loincloth—the equivalent of a man today walking in

The Prophet Isaiah
ISAIAH. CHAPTER 9, VERSES 6-7;
CHAPTER 53, VERSES 4, 5, 12.

public in his briefs. Since his aim was to draw attention to his message, he probably succeeded.

The book has been the center of controversy for centuries, since most scholars believe the two sections of the book were by two different men living in different periods. It is possible the second section was by another prophet named Isaiah, or by a disciple of the first Isaiah. Both sections have been read and loved by generations of Jews and Christians, and Isaiah is the most quoted prophet in the New Testament, quoted fifty-six times in all. Yiddish-American author Sholem Asch made him the subject of his 1955 novel *The Prophet*.

One bit of useless but interesting trivia: Isaiah named one of his sons Mahershalahasbaz—the longest name in the Bible. Isaiah's wife was referred to as a "prophetess," which may mean simply the wife of a prophet, or, that she made prophecies herself.

A tradition says that Isaiah was martyred—by being sawn in half—under the wicked king Manasseh. A Christian writing called the Ascension of Isaiah claims to tell the story of his martyrdom and of his trip through the seven heavens, where he sees a vision of Christ. The Orthodox churches commemorate Isaiah on May 9.

Ishmael
The very contemporary matter of Abraham's favorite son

Abraham, the man Jews consider their spiritual and physical ancestor, had been promised by God that he would be the father of a great nation—yet as the years passed by, Abraham and his beloved wife Sarah had no children. Abraham fathered a child by his wife's maid, Hagar, and the child was named Ishmael, a name that means "may God hear." After Ishmael was born, Hagar became rather haughty toward her mistress, so Sarah drove both mother and child into the wilderness, but an angel of God saved them from perishing (Genesis 16). The nation of Israel was descended from Abraham's son Isaac, but Genesis records that a great nation was descended from Ishmael also. The name Ishmael came to refer to any outcast from society, because of the prophecy in Genesis 16 that "he will be a wild man, his hand will be against every man, and every man's hand against him."

The Arabs believe themselves to be descendants of Ishmael, called *Ismail* in the Koran. Arabs and other Muslims believe that the great shrine of the Ka'ba in their holy city of Mecca was built by Abraham and Ismail. The Koran, in contrast to the Bible, says that Ismail, not Isaac, was the favorite son of Abraham, and was the son who came near to being sacrificed. (This means they believe that Jews and Christians deliberately distorted the true story of Abraham.)

Poor Hagar and the child Ishmael in the wilderness have been the subject of many paintings, including the touching *Hagar in the Desert* (1835) by the French painter Corot. But culturally speaking, the most famous Ishmael is the narrator of Herman Melville's classic novel *Moby-Dick*, which begins with the words "Call me Ishmael." Writing in the 1800s, Melville assumed his readers were familiar with the Bible, and that they would immediately assume that a character named Ishmael was a rootless type, a nomad, like the adult Ishmael of the Bible.

Israel

Man, tribe, nation, or idea?

Israel is the most-mentioned nation—and group of people—and person—and idea—in the Bible. The word first occurs in Genesis 32, where the patriarch Jacob wrestles all night with a heavenly visitor who bestows on him the name Israel, meaning "struggles with God" (or, according to some scholars, "let God rule"). Jacob's twelve sons were the ancestors of the twelve "tribes" that collectively were known as Israel. The descendants were sometimes called *Israelites*, sometimes *children of Israel*. Most Israelites thought of themselves as belonging to both Israel and to their tribe. Moses, for example, was from the tribe of Levi, meaning he identified as both Levite and Israelite. (For more about the twelve sons/tribes, SEE PAGE 371.)

The name Israel didn't originally apply to a specific place. The land Jacob and his sons dwelled in was called Canaan, and it was the land God had promised to Abraham, Jacob's grandfather. Jacob's sons settled in Egypt because of famine in Canaan, and they lived in Egypt many years, with their descendants eventually becoming slaves until Moses led them back to Canaan. The Book of Joshua tells of the Israelites move into Canaan and the allotment of certain lands for each tribe. The Book of Judges tells that the tribes were not united but were a loose federation, all with the same God. Union came when Saul was anointed king over Israel. David made Jerusalem Israel's capital, and his son Solomon built the temple there. From Saul through Solomon, the twelve tribes were united as a nation, Israel.

After Solomon's death, his son Rehoboam alienated the ten northern tribes. They broke away, chose their own king, and kept the name Israel. Rehoboam reigned over the southern two tribes, Judah and Benjamin, with the nation being called Judah. The Books of Kings tell the parallel stories of the kings of Israel and Judah. The Assyrians conquered Israel in 722 b.c., and the Babylonians conquered Judah in 586. From that point on, the name Israel ceased to refer to any locality. It referred to all people who traced their descent from Jacob, wherever they might live. They were "children of Israel," even if Israel was not on any map. Their God was the "God of Israel."

When Israel ceased to exist on the map, a new idea came into being: a person did not have to be *born* into Israel but could *convert* to the faith. Gentiles (non-Jews) could become part of God's people, converts known as *proselytes* (SEE PAGE 294). This paved the way for an important idea in the New Testament: Christians were the "new Israel," regardless of their ethnic background, since they accepted Jesus as the Messiah that Israel had hoped for. The apostle Paul, who was proud of his descent from Israel, was the "apostle to the Gentiles," writing, "through the gospel the Gentiles are heirs together with Israel, members together of one body, and sharers together in the promise in Christ Jesus" (Ephesians 3:6). Christians adopted the Old Testament as their own book, applying all of God's promises to Israel to themselves.

The nation of Israel that exists today came into being in 1948. People of that country are called Israelis, not Israelites.

(For more about the use of the word "Jews," SEE PAGE 179.)

J

And you thought you knew your alphabet …

Here's a bit of shocking news: neither Greek nor Hebrew has the letter J—or the J sound, either. When you see the letter J in a name in the English Bible (Jesus, Jews, Elijah, Jerusalem), the sound in the original languages was Y. The Greeks used their letter *iota* as both the vowel I and the consonant Y. In the Greek Bible, Jesus' name was *Iesous*, which was pronounced *Yesus*. Hebrew had the consonant *yodh*, with the Y sound, and Old Testament names that have J in the English Bible had a *yodh* in the original Hebrew. Elijah was pronounced Eliyah.

How did this happen? Centuries ago, the English made no real distinction between I and J. Both letters, if they appeared before a vowel, had the Y sound. Over time, they stopped using I in front of vowels and used only the letter J. As the centuries passed, the sound morphed from the Y sound to the J sound we use in words like "jump" and "jet." The Germanic languages—German, Dutch, Danish, Swedish, etc.—still pronounce the letter J as a Y.

Jabez

So much from so little

Jabez is such a very minor character in the Bible that he was almost forgotten, until the book *The Prayer of Jabez* became a huge seller, spinning off various sequels and other products. Jabez's brief prayer, found in 1 Chronicles 4:10, is simply asking God to bless him and keep him from harm. "And God granted what he asked."

Jacob
The original smoothie

Jacob was the son of Isaac and grandson of Abraham, but his true claim to fame was being the father of twelve sons who became the ancestors of the twelve tribes of Israel, Israel being Jacob's new name after his famous wrestling with God (SEE PAGE 166). Jacob was the twin brother of Esau, a hairy man who liked to hunt, while Jacob was a stay-at-home mama's boy with smooth skin. Jacob managed to trick Esau out of his inheritance and Isaac's blessing (SEE PAGE 111), and Esau was so angry that Jacob ran away to live with his mother's brother Laban. He fell deeply in love with his cousin Rachel and agreed to serve Laban for seven years in order to have Rachel as a wife (Genesis 29). When the seven years were up, tricky Jacob got his comeuppance: his uncle told him it was the local custom to marry off the eldest daughter first, so Jacob had to marry Leah, Rachel's older (and less attractive) sister, whom he did not love. He had to labor for seven more years, though he had the consolation of being married to both Rachel and Leah at the end of the weeklong marriage celebration. Jacob's dream at Bethel is described in more detail on the following page.

Jacob had four sons by Leah, two each by two of his concubines, but none by Rachel. At long last Rachel gave birth to Joseph, then Benjamin, and as the sons of his old age, they were doted on. From Genesis 37 until the end of the book, the main character is Joseph, sold by his brothers as a slave, then made right-hand man of the Egyptian Pharaoh (SEE PAGE 196). Due to a famine, Jacob and the other eleven sons settle in Egypt, where Joseph provides for them. At the end of his life, Jacob pronounces prophetic blessings on his sons (Genesis 49). Since he was a high-ranking official in Egypt, Joseph ordered Jacob's body embalmed in the Egyptian manner, which required forty days, then a caravan took Jacob's body to the family burial ground in Canaan.

Jacob's story is interesting, but he is hardly an admirable character, although Bible commentators and preachers often try to find some spiritual meaning in his story. He comes across as a contemptible sneak and a not very wise father, given his spoiling of Joseph. However, Jacob's debt of seven years labor to take Rachel as his wife is one of the most appealing love stories in all the world. The Jews have honored him as their ancestor, and Jacob has been a common name for Jewish men. In the New Testament, several important characters were named Jacob—though in English versions of the Bible, the name had morphed into James. Muslims regard Jacob—*Yakub*—as a prophet. The Latter-day Saints (Mormons, that is) used the phrase "the order of Jacob" to refer to the practice of polygamy, which they approved of.

Jacob is an important character in the rock opera *Joseph and the Amazing Technicolor Dreamcoat*, which opens with the song "Jacob and Sons." He has also been the subject of several fine TV movies. He is featured in Nobel Prize-winning author Thomas Mann's epic masterpiece *Joseph and His Brothers*, in "The Tales of Jacob."

The ancient city of Hebron in Israel has the cave that, tradition says, is the burial place of Jacob and Leah.

Jacob's dream
Stairway to heaven

A stone doesn't make a comfortable pillow, but on one occasion it certainly induced an amazing dream. Jacob stopped for the night in the wilderness, in flight from his irate brother Esau, the man he cheated out of his inheritance. While asleep with his head on a stone, he dreamt of angels walking up and down a staircase into heaven. Somewhere above the staircase, God (always invisible, of course) renewed with Jacob the covenant he had made with Jacob's grandfather, Abraham, and pronounced a blessing on Jacob's descendants (who would come to be called Israel). When Jacob awoke, he said, "Surely the Lord is in this place … This is none other than the house of God, and this is the gate of heaven" (Genesis 28:16-17). Appropriately, he named the spot Bethel, meaning "house of God."

In British tradition, the Stone of Scone that sits underneath the monarch's coronation chair was the stone pillow where Jacob laid his head on the night of his famous dream.

In the King James Version, the stairway is referred to as a "ladder," and anyone who attended church camp probably remembers singing the old spiritual "Jacob's Ladder." The name was also given to the rope ladders used on ships.

Bethel itself, since it meant "house of God" has been a common name for churches and religious schools, and even for a number of cities in the U.S. In the 1700s and 1800s, churches in England that were Nonconformist (not connected with the established Church of England) were frequently named Bethel, so much so that if someone heard the name "Bethel," they would assume it was a Nonconformist church.

Jacob's dream of the angels on the stairs has fascinated artists over the centuries. The angels in their robes walking in mid-air make a striking contrast to the snoozing Jacob with his head on the stone, William Blake and many other noted artists committing the scene to canvas. Several children's toys and plants have been named "Jacob's ladder," and a favorite old camp song is the plaintive "We Are Climbing Jacob's Ladder."

Jacob wrestling God
All night, and no holds barred

Among the many colorful events in Jacob's life, one that stands out is the story of Jacob literally wrestling with God—or God's angel, anyway. Genesis 32 tells of Jacob camped out in the wilderness, running away from his irate brother Esau. He meets a "man" who wrestles with him until daybreak. This mysterious wrestler manages to pull Jacob's hip out of its socket, then demands to be let go, but Jacob famously replies, "I will not let you go unless you bless me." The "man" then bestows a new name on Jacob: "Israel," meaning "struggles with God" because Jacob has "struggled with God and with men, and have prevailed." Jacob never learns the mystery man's name, but is convinced he has seen God face to face.

Jacob Wrestles With the Angel
GENESIS. CHAPTER 32, VERSES 24-31.

This strange story is the source of the name Israel, a name still found on the world map. The scene has been a favorite of artists, usually a tense depiction of two men locked in what appears to be a to-the-death match. Artist Paul Gauguin did a famous painting called

Vision After the Sermon, Jacob Wresting With the Angel. Eugene Delacroix also did a famous painting of the story, *Jacob Wrestling with the Angel* (1861, Paris), showing a muscular and large-winged angel struggling with the equally muscular Jacob in a wild landscape.

James the apostle
Reigns in Spain

The brothers James and John were two of Jesus' twelve disciples. These sons of Zebedee were both fishermen, and part of Jesus' "inner circle" that also included Peter. Jesus called the brothers "sons of thunder," probably because they asked him to destroy some inhospitable villagers (Luke 9:54-56). James, John, and Peter were present with Jesus at the glorious Transfiguration (Mark 9) and at the time of his arrest in the garden of Gethsemane (Mark 14:33-42).

James had the distinction of being the first disciple martyred for his faith. In the persecution of Christians under Herod Agrippa I, James was put to death with the sword (Acts 12:2)—that is, beheaded. This Herod Agrippa was the grandson of the Herod who had massacred the infants of Bethlehem when Jesus was born and the nephew of the Herod Antipas who executed John the Baptist.

In the Middle Ages, a legend grew that James's mortal remains were moved from Jerusalem (where he died) to a site that would become the city of Santiago de Compostela, in northwestern Spain. There was already a tradition that the apostle had preached the gospel in Spain before he died in Jerusalem. In the year 813, some Spanish shepherds were summoned (so the story goes) by a star to the site of the still-preserved body of James. How did it get there? Another legend: after his execution in Jerusalem, James's body was put in a boat—made of marble!—which miraculously floated to the coast of Spain. (A less miraculous version of this says that James's followers carried his body by boat to Spain.)

Santiago (Spanish for "St. James") became one of the great pilgrimage centers in the Middle Ages and afterward. In a sense it was one of the earliest "tourist hot spots" in Europe, with people from all over the continent eager to visit the cathedral at Compostela, which supposedly has the body of James. In fact, it was the third-most popular destination of pilgrims, the first and second spots being Jerusalem and Rome. Those who had visited the cathedral wore a seashell (the symbol of James) as a sign they had been there. James is the patron saint of Spain, and the Catholic Church honors him with the Feast of St. James, July 25. Legend has it that during the Spanish efforts to drive the Muslim Moors out of Spain, James appeared on a white horse to rally the Christian forces. Thus James was given the title *Matamoros*—the Moor-slayer. For centuries, Spanish soldiers charged into battle with the cry "Santiago!" The Spanish had a military Order of Santiago, and membership in it was prestigious. Its members wore a red cross, with the lower bar ending in a point, meaning the cross was also a sword. The Spanish settlers in the New World thought so highly of James that they established several cities named for him, notably the Santiago that is the capital of Chile, and also prominent cities of that name in Cuba and the Dominican Republic.

James has British as well as Spanish connections. A fashionable area of central London has been called St. James's for centuries, after St. James's Palace, formerly one of the royal dwelling places, built by Henry VIII. Henry built the palace near a very old hospital for lepers named for St. James. Although the palace is no longer the monarch's home, all foreign ambassadors to Great Britain are officially described as being sent "to the Court of St. James's."

Mormons (Latter-day Saints) believe that James, along with Peter and John, appeared to Mormon founder Joseph Smith.

James is sometimes referred to as James the Greater, to distinguish him from another of Jesus' twelve apostles, James the son of Alphaeus, often called James the Less.

James the brother of Jesus
Family connections

The Gospels state that Jesus had several brothers—or, more accurately, *half*-brothers, since they were sons of Mary and Joseph, while Jesus was the son of Mary and God. (Catholics do not accept this, since they believed that Mary remained a virgin all her life, meaning the "brothers" of Jesus were actually the children of Joseph by an earlier marriage—meaning they were no blood relation to Jesus at all. In the Catholic view, the Gospels' use of the word "brothers" is in the more general sense of "family members.") Apparently the brothers did not fully appreciate who he was until after his resurrection (Matthew 13:55). One of the brothers, James, saw the risen Jesus, and James became a leader among the Christians in Jerusalem (Acts 12:17) and presided at the Council of Jerusalem (SEE PAGE 77), which decreed that non-Jews wishing to become Christians did not have to be circumcised. Acts shows that James and the great apostle Paul respected each other.

The Letter of James is notable for stating that "faith without works is dead"—meaning, if you really are a person of faith, your deeds will show it. That message—"walk the walk, don't just talk the talk"—is directed at people who pay lip service to their religion but don't act the part in their daily lives. Some people, including Reformation leader Martin Luther, disliked the letter because they thought it taught salvation by one's good deeds instead of by faith. Most Christians have appreciated the letter and approved the idea that faith and good deeds go together and can't be separated.

Christians often referred to him as "James the Just" or "James the brother of the Lord" to distinguish him from the apostle James. (To add to the confusion, Jesus had another disciple named James, generally known as "James the Less" because he was less important than the other disciple James.)

James has attracted some attention in recent years because of the finding of an artifact inscribed with his name. In 2002 an ossuary (bone box) was found in Jerusalem with the inscription "James, son of Joseph, brother of Jesus." All three names were very common in the old days, but the inscription is remarkable in mentioning a brother of the deceased. The ossuary is dated sometime between A.D. 20 and 70. The Jewish historian Josephus wrote that James brother of Jesus was stoned as a heretic in the year 63. If the ossuary really is the resting place of James's bones, this would be the only authentic archaeological find confirming the existence of Jesus.

Jehu
Baal extermination man

Israel's king Ahab and queen Jezebel were some of the most immoral rulers ever, but their wicked family was annihilated by Jehu, who was anointed by the prophet Elisha. Jehu killed the kings of both Judah and Israel as vengeance against Ahab's dynasty. Queen Jezebel faced Jehu defiantly from a palace window, but two of her servants threw her down when Jehu ordered them, and the dogs devoured her body. Jehu and his men slaughtered seventy of Ahab's descendants. In 2 Kings 10, we learn that he annihilated all the worshippers of the false god Baal by telling the people they should gather together for a worship service for Baal. The worshippers were killed, and the Baal temple made into a latrine. The Lord rewarded Jehu by letting him and his descendants rule for four generations.

In times past, a "jehu" was someone who drove fast and furiously, based on 2 Kings 9:20: "The driving is like the driving of Jehu … for he drives furiously."

Jephthah
The worst parental promise ever

Many ancient cultures practiced some form of human sacrifice, often the sacrifice of children. Israel did not, regarding it as a horrible thing. One very sad story about child sacrifice is the saga of Jephthah, who was one of the "judges" (military deliverers) in the Book of Judges. The son of a prostitute, Jephthah was booted out of his father's home by his half-brothers, and he gathered around him a group of homeless rogues who were superb fighting men. The band was asked to help fight off the Ammonites, and Jephthah agreed, but he made the rash vow that if he was victorious, he would sacrifice the first thing that came out his doors when he returned home. Alas, the first thing that came out was not a sheep or cow, but his one daughter, greeting him with tambourine and dancing. She asked him to postpone the sacrifice for two months so she could retire to the hills to lament her fate (dying young, while still a virgin). The Book of Judges is at least reticent about the sacrifice: it only says that Jephthah "did with her according to his vow" (11:39).

Jephthah's story, found in Judges 11-12, also contains the famous episode of pronouncing the word shibboleth correctly (SEE PAGE 416).

George Frideric Handel wrote an oratorio about Jephthah.

Jeremiah
Tear ducts fully functional

Jeremiah was one of the great prophets of the Bible. He claimed that God had destined him to be a prophet even before his birth (Jeremiah 1:4). Jeremiah's mission was to preach doom to the Jews unless they changed their wicked ways. He claimed the people were "wise in doing evil, but how to do good, they know not." Chapter 9 begins, "O that my head were waters and my eyes a fountain of tears," thus he is often called the "weeping prophet." Like most prophets with such a message, Jeremiah found himself in trouble with the authorities, and also with the false prophets who told the king the optimistic messages that he wanted to hear (the "yes men" of the ancient world). Wicked King Jehoiakim received a scroll written by Jeremiah, and he showed his contempt by using the scroll as fuel in his fireplace. The priest Passhur had Jeremiah beaten and put in the stocks. On another occasion, the prophet was thrown into a well. Although shy and sensitive by nature, Jeremiah was bold enough to stand up to kings, priests, and false prophets. Jeremiah's warnings of doom were fulfilled when the country was conquered by the Babylonians, and Jeremiah joined the many

Jeremiah's Lament
JEREMIAH. CHAPTER 1, VERSES 1-5, 11-12.

Jews who sought refuge in Egypt. According to one tradition, Jeremiah hid the famous ark of the covenant in a cave. Another tradition says that Jeremiah's fellow Jews in Egypt finally had enough of his preaching and stoned him to death.

The "weeping prophet" is considered to be the author of the brief Book of Lamentations (SEE PAGE 212), which bemoans the destruction of Jerusalem by the Babylonians. The word "jeremiad" came to refer to any kind of sad lament. A "jeremiah" is anyone bearing a message of doom.

Jeremiah is quoted many times in the New Testament, and the Gospels state that some people believed Jesus to be Jeremiah come back to earth again. There is much spiritual depth in the Book of Jeremiah, particularly his prophecy of a time when God would write his laws on people's hearts. Many verses from Jeremiah became part of the language, such as, "Can the leopard change his spots?" and "Is there no balm in Gilead?"

Parts of the Book of Jeremiah are written in the third person, which is one reason we know Jeremiah so well. These parts are probably by his friend, disciple, and secretary, Baruch.

As one of the major prophets, Jeremiah has often been depicted in art, usually as a bearded man weeping. Donatello's marble statue *The Prophet Jeremiah* (c. 1425) shows a beardless and clearly sad man. On Michelangelo's Sistine Chapel ceiling,

Jeremiah's head rests on one hand, the picture of despondency. Rembrandt's 1630 *Jeremiah Lamenting the Destruction of Jerusalem* shows an old and very sad man, with, oddly, his elbow resting on a large book labeled "Bible." American composer Leonard Bernstein's Symphony No. 1 is known as the *Jeremiah*.

The Eastern Orthodox churches observe May 1 as the feast of Jeremiah.

Jericho
Where Joshua fit de battle

Jericho is a notable city in the Bible, also notable in world history because it may very well be the oldest city in the world, inhabited as far back as 8000 b.c. Chapter 6 in the Book of Joshua tells of it being the first Canaanite city conquered by the Israelites, who were led by Joshua after the death of Moses. The conquest itself was a miracle, with God ordering Joshua to have the people march around the city, while priests carried rams-horn trumpets and the ark of the covenant. At the blast of the trumpet the people shouted, and (as the old spiritual says) the walls come a-tumblin' down. The Israelites killed everyone in the city, except the prostitute Rahab and her

The Walls of Jericho Fall
JOSHUA. CHAPTER 6, VERSES 12-17, 20.

family, who had sheltered Israel's spies earlier. The site was under a curse for many years and inhabited. In the New Testament period it had become a sort of resort town, where Herod the Great had a palace. Jesus passed through Jericho, healing the blind and dining at the home of the repentant tax collector Zacchaeus (Matthew 20:29, Luke 19). Jesus' parable of the Good Samaritan is set on the narrow, robber-infested road that ran from Jerusalem to Jericho.

Jericho, which was also called the "city of palms," lives on in the old spiritual ("Joshua Fit De Battle Of Jericho") and perhaps because of that song, the name is associated with the Bible. Several U.S. towns are named Jericho, and in the apocalyptic thriller movie *End of Days*, the hero's name was John Jericho.

Jericho is the lowest city on the face of the earth.

Jerusalem
City central

Jerusalem is the most mentioned city in the Bible, and probably the most mentioned city in the world's literature; it is considered a holy city by Jews, Christians, and Muslims. The city originally belonged to a people called the Jebusites, but Israel's King David captured the city around 1000 B.C. and made it his capital, bringing Israel's sacred ark of the covenant there and making it Israel's religious center. David's son Solomon built the fine temple to God that stood on Mount Moriah for several centuries. When Israel split into two nations (Israel and Judah) after the death of Solomon, the king of Israel built religious shrines in his country so that worshippers would not need to visit the temple in Jerusalem, which was in Judah.

Jerusalem was looted by the Babylonian empire in 586 B.C., and the temple was destroyed. Most of the population of the city was deported to Babylon, living in exile there for many years. The Book of Lamentations in the Old Testament is a sad poem about the desolation of the city. In 538 B.C., the Persians conquered the Babylonians and allowed the Jewish exiles to return, and the rebuilding of the city began, including a new temple on the old site. The return is described in the Books of Ezra and Nehemiah.

The Greeks under Alexander the Great conquered the area and introduced Greek culture to the region. The Jews staged a revolt against the Greek rulers, and for a time Jerusalem was once again the Jews' capital, but then the Romans conquered the region. They installed the immoral Herod as king over the area. Herod renovated the temple, turning it into an architectural wonder, although the Jews despised him.

As an infant, Jesus was taken to the temple by Mary and Joseph. He also went there with them when he was twelve, and he discussed the Old Testament Law with the Jewish teachers, amazing them by his wisdom. Jesus and his disciples visited Jerusalem more than once. Jesus lamented Jerusalem as "the city that stones the prophets," even though it was considered God's holy city. He foresaw that he would meet his fate there, and though he was hailed as Messiah when he rode into Jerusalem on a donkey at Passover season, that same week he was

J

Return of the Exiles to Jerusalem
EZRA. CHAPTER 1, VERSES 1-5.

arrested and condemned by the Jewish authorities and the Roman governor, Pilate. He was crucified and buried near the city, and after he was raised appeared to his disciples there. In the Book of Acts, the apostles began their evangelizing work in Jerusalem, and the saintly Stephen was stoned there, becoming the first Christian martyr. The famous Council of Jerusalem (SEE PAGE 77) met to decide whether non-Jews who became Christians had to obey the Jewish laws. Among the Jewish Christians in Jerusalem, Jesus' brother James played a leading role. Another James, one of Jesus' disciples, was executed in the city, the first apostle to die for his faith.

Jesus was not the political Messiah that most of the Jews hoped for. Others tried to play that role, and a major Jewish revolt against Rome erupted in the year 66. The Romans crushed the revolt and destroyed the temple in 70. The spiritual center of Judaism shifted from Jerusalem to the small town of Jabneh, where an academy was established, with the Jews learning that their religion could survive without a temple. (The Romans were tolerant of the Jews' religion, as long as it didn't lead to rebellion.) After crushing the final Jewish revolt in 135, the Romans renamed the city Aelia Capitolina and prohibited any Jews from setting foot in it, although Christians were allowed, since they had not participated in the revolt. A temple to the Roman god Jupiter was erected on the former temple site. Three centuries later, when the Roman empire became Christianized, Jews were allowed to return to the city, which was called Jerusalem again, and Christians began to build churches there, including one that is supposedly on the site where Jesus was crucified. Christians visiting the city follow "the Way of the Cross," a sequence of places associated with Jesus' trial and crucifixion.

The Muslims conquered the area in the year 638, and in 691 they built the Dome of the Rock shrine. They made the building magnificent, because they wanted it to rival or surpass the Christians' Church of the Holy Sepulchre, supposedly built over Jesus' tomb. In the Middle Ages, the Crusaders were sometimes in control of Jerusalem (but more often not), and they built numerous new churches. (In some of the periods when the Crusaders ruled, Jews and Muslims were barred from the city.) The city remained in Muslim hands until the twentieth century, when the new nation of Israel was established, although Muslims still have access to their holy places in the city. The fact that the Dome of the Rock sits on the very spot where the Jews' temple once stood has been a cause of strife between Muslims and Jews.

The Book of Revelation ends with a vision of "the holy city, new Jerusalem," with streets of gold and pearly gates—and no temple, for there was no need of one, since God was present in the city.

Although Christians have a fondness for the literal city of Jerusalem, most Christian hymns and sermons tend to focus on the heavenly Jerusalem of Revelation. The many Psalms in the Bible that refer to Jerusalem are often interpreted by Christians as referring to heaven. The followers of Swedish writer Emanuel Swedenborg organized as the Church of the New Jerusalem.

A reverence for the city and its history was apparent in the many medieval maps that showed Jerusalem as the literal center of the world.

Jesse
Messiah stock

We remember Jesse because we remember his famous son, Israel's best-known and best-loved king, David. In a day when there were no last names, David was "the son of Jesse," and Jesse's name figures in the genealogies of the kings of Israel—and of Jesus also.

Since he was the ancestor of a long line of Jewish kings (not to mention the Messiah), Jesse's name has been used fairly often for naming boys. But Jesse is most famous for being depicted in church windows and paintings as the "Jesse tree," showing Jesse lying on his back asleep, with a tall tree or vine with its "roots" in his groin area and the branches of the tree showing the names or pictures of the Jewish kings, ending with Jesus, of course. (It usually looks more like a candelabrum than a plant.) The image is based on a prophecy of the Messiah in Isaiah 11: "There shall come forth a shoot from the stump of Jesse, and a branch from his roots shall bear fruit. And the Spirit of the Lord shall rest upon him." For Christians, this "branch" was Jesus Christ.

Jesus
The king not of this world

In his own language, Aramaic, his name was *Yeshua*, a variation of the Old Testament name Joshua. In the earliest Christian writings, all in Greek, his name was *Iesous*. Even the most confirmed skeptics have to admit he was one of the most amazing men of history, someone who made such an impression on people that they referred to him by numerous titles: Christ (Messiah), Lord, Savior, Son of God, Prophet, the Lamb of God, the Word, Redeemer, Servant of God, and Son of Man, the name he used himself. Most of these names and titles are covered in separate entries, as are most of the key events in his life: Christmas, boyhood, baptism, temptation, parables, Sermon on the Mount, crucifixion, resurrection, ascension. Most of the key people in his story are also covered separately: the Virgin Mary, Joseph, Herod the Great, John the Baptist, Satan, Peter, Andrew, James, John, Matthew, Mary Magdalene, Judas Iscariot, Caiaphas, Pilate, Herod Antipas, Thomas. This entry is designed as a general overview of the man.

Two of the Gospels (Matthew and Luke) report that he had no human father, but that Mary, a virgin of Nazareth, conceived through the power of the Holy Spirit.

The Angel of the Lord Proclaims the Savior's Birth
LUKE. CHAPTER 2, VERSES 8-14.

Because of a Roman census, Mary traveled with her husband Joseph to Bethlehem, where Jesus was born in a stable and visited by shepherds who knew of the birth through an angel, and later by the magi who brought expensive gifts. The family lived in Nazareth, though they visited Jerusalem when Jesus was twelve, at which time he amazed some of the Jewish teachers with his spiritual depth. No more is heard of his boyhood or youth, except that he pursued the trade of his legal father, Joseph, who was a carpenter. Around age thirty, he was baptized by his kinsman, John the Baptist, then went to the wilderness for forty days, being tempted by the devil with power and public acclaim, but he refused the temptations. He began a public life lasting about three years, announcing that "the Kingdom of God" was at hand. One sign of the kingdom was that Jesus healed numerous illnesses and cast demons out of people. On a few occasions he even brought the dead back to life.

In his teaching, he emphasized that the Jewish code of laws was a good thing, but that people had become too concerned with the details of the laws and forgotten the most important goals: loving God and loving one's neighbor. People considered him a great prophet, but unlike the prophets, who began their statements with, "Thus says the Lord," Jesus stood on his own authority. Jesus addressed God directly as "Father," so he was conscious of himself as the Son of God.

Jesus chose twelve disciples to travel with him and learn from him. They were devoted to him but frequently misunderstood his teachings and could be fickle and selfish. In time they came to see him as the Messiah (Christ) that the Jews had longed for. Jesus had no ambition to be a military or political leader, for his "kingdom" was a spiritual one. It is probable some of his followers expected him to be a military Messiah.

Most of his life was spent in his home district of Galilee, but he and the disciples journeyed to Jerusalem for the Passover celebration, and he prophesied he would be killed there. Though he entered the city to the acclaim of crowds, the Jewish religious leaders saw him as a dangerous troublemaker, one who saw through their hypocrisy, and who was more popular with the people than they were. For reasons that are unclear, one of his disciples, Judas, went to the priests and offered to lead them to Jesus at night so they could arrest him without drawing the attention of the crowds. Jesus was arrested and his disciples fled in fright. He was interrogated by the priests and condemned as a blasphemer (not for claiming to be Messiah, but for claiming to be God's Son). The Roman governor, Pilate, believed he was innocent and no threat, but he caved in to the priests' demand for an execution. Jesus was brutally beaten, then crucified, and while hanging on the cross forgave his enemies. He was buried the same day, but came back from the dead, as he promised his disciples. Later they watched him being taken up into heaven. The early Christians believed his death on the cross was a kind of sacrifice, that of a perfectly innocent man dying in place of sinful mankind. The crucifixion mysterioulsy reconciled God and man. It was believed that people who put their faith in Jesus would inherit eternal life. It was also believed he would some day return to earth on the clouds of heaven, judging the living and the dead for their deeds.

J

Jesus' story is told in the four Gospels of the New Testament—Matthew, Mark, Luke, John. There were dozens of other Gospels in circulation, but in time the Christian community saw these four as being closest to reality. The Book of Acts tells of how the disciples of Jesus spread the belief in him as the Son of God, starting with the Jews in their homeland, but taking the faith to non-Jews throughout the Roman Empire.

The Bible says nothing about Jesus' appearance. One Gospel (Luke) says he was around thirty when his public life began, so presumably he was about thirty-three when he was crucified. He was probably bearded, like most Jewish men, and would have had dark, shoulder-length hair, probably parted in the center. As a carpenter, and as someone who traveled often on foot, he was probably somewhat lean and muscular. In the earliest Christian art, Jesus appeared young and beardless—at least in those cultures where beards were rare. In fact, the earliest images of Jesus show him in the pose of the Greek god Aristaeus—a young, beardless man carrying a lamb across his shoulders. (This was natural, since Aristaeus was a god of healing, and unlike most other Greek gods, he was almost always kind, not malicious.) Most artists gave little thought to whether their images of Jesus reflected his own time and culture. In Europe, Jesus was often depicted as fair-skinned and fair-haired, and his clothing was that of the artists' time, not Jesus'. In the Renaissance, Jesus was frequently shown as having the perfect bodily proportions that fascinated artists of that age—an attractive physique, but probably not the physique of a first-century Jewish carpenter.

Christianity is a global phenomenon, and Jesus has been depicted with the skin and hair of practically every locale on earth—probably not authentic, but at least a sign that Jesus was "one of us," as the Bible teaches. One of the most popular images of Jesus is the twentieth-century *Head of Christ*, by German artist Werner Sallman. As a response to people who said pictures of Jesus showed him as frail and feminine, Sallman depicted Jesus with a pleasant smile but with bronzed, outdoorsy skin, dark brown eyes, and an overall rugged look—both tough and tender—probably closer to the real Jesus than the Jesus of Renaissance art, and also an image that could please both men and women.

Jesus' words and deeds made a deeper impression than his appearance. He had many enemies in his lifetime, and throughout the centuries many people have mocked his statements about loving one's enemies and turning the other cheek. However, such teachings also have admirers, not all of them Christian. His life story has inspired countless books, plays, films, and songs, most of them trying to be faithful to the story found in the Bible. But he has also inspired "revisionists" who believe the Gospels in the Bible covered up the story of the "real Jesus." Some critics have even said Jesus never existed, that he was a fictional Messiah that some of the Jews invented. No one seriously believes this now, although plenty of people doubt his miracles and his resurrection.

The early Christians believed Jesus was the Christ (Messiah), and very quickly adopted the habit of referring to him as Jesus Christ, or sometimes Christ Jesus. In all his epistles, the apostle Paul almost always adds Christ to the name of Jesus. Over time, some people even dropped the name Jesus, simply referring to him as Christ.

When did Jesus live? Centuries ago a Christian scholar miscalculated the year A.D. 1—that is, year 1 *Anno Domini*, "year of our Lord." The scholar thought Jesus was born in the year 1, but we're pretty certain he was born about 4 or 5 B.C. (Yes, weird as it sounds, he was born "before Christ.") Pontius Pilate was governor from 26 to 36, so Jesus' arrest and crucifixion had to happen in that period. Probably Jesus' public ministry spanned about three years and he was crucified (and, Christians believe, resurrected) in about the year 30 or so.

Since Christians thought of Jesus as divine, they applied the commandment against taking God's name in vain to Jesus' name also. So Christians regarded it as a sin to say "Jesus Christ!" or "Holy Jesus!" in jest or anger. Because of this, a number of euphemisms sprang up: Jeepers Creepers, Judas Priest, Jiminy Cricket, Jeez, etc.

Jews
Israel's survivors

The word "Jew" actually comes from the tribe of Judah, who was one of the twelve sons of Jacob. The word isn't used in the earliest parts of the Bible, where Jacob's descendants are called Israelites or "children of Israel," or sometimes Hebrews. Israel was one nation until it split in two during the reign of King Rehoboam, the son of Solomon. The ten northern tribes continued calling themselves Israel, and the two southern tribes (Judah and Benjamin) took the name Judah. Israel was conquered by the Assyrians, who dispersed (or killed) its people. Judah was conquered by the Babylonians, who sent most of the people into exile. To the

Babylonians, they were "Jews," people of Judah. However, the people still thought of themselves as "Israelites" even though the nation of Israel had ceased to exist politically.

In the Gospels of Matthew, Mark, and Luke, the only people who use the word "Jew" are the Romans and the Magi. John's Gospel uses the word many times, not referring to Jews in general, but to the Jewish priests and temple officials—the Jewish "establishment" that was mostly hostile to Jesus.

Jezebel
Queen of mean

Here's a name that still rings a bell with people, even if they have only the vague notion that it means "a bad woman." In 1 Kings, she is indeed a *very* bad woman, and married to a very bad man, King Ahab of Israel. Jezebel's father was a priest-king of Sidon, so she grew up worshipping gods other than Israel's God. Worse, she was dedicated to stamping out the worship of God in Israel and turning the whole nation to the religion of her god, Baal. She also believed if the king wanted something, even someone's ancestral property, he could take it, leading to the nasty incident of her husband seizing the vineyard of Naboth (SEE PAGE 16). She faced quite a foe in the person of the fiery prophet Elijah, who staged a famous showdown between himself, the prophet of God, and a whole horde of Jezebel's Baal prophets. Elijah won, the Baal prophets were killed, and Jezebel swore to hunt Elijah down and destroy him. She didn't, but the fact that he fled from her indicates she was a power to be reckoned with.

As it turned out, Jezebel's fatal foe was Jehu, who had been chosen by God to exterminate all of Ahab's Baal-worshiping progeny—and wife. In a scene that seems made for a movie, Jezebel met Jehu not by cowering or begging for mercy but with her hair and makeup applied, dressed to kill (literally). Her last words were a sneer thrown at Jehu: "Had Zimri peace, who slew his master?" Jezebel was reminding him that Zimri had killed the king of Israel, took his place—then reigned seven days before dying himself. But Jehu had the last word: he ordered two servants to shove her out a high window. When men came to bury her, then found not a body but only her skull, hands, and feet. Fulfilling the prophecy, Jezebel had been eaten by dogs (2 Kings 9:30-37).

According to 2 Kings, Jezebel's chief sins were an autocratic monarchy and the introduction of the worship of Baal. Later generations tended to forget those important things and remember her as the "painted woman," probably because 2 Kings says she "painted" her eyes before her fatal encounter with Jehu. The name "Jezebel" has come to suggest a loose woman, even though the Bible says nothing about Jezebel's sexual morals. It does, however, speak of her "whoredoms," but it's in the spiritual sense, trying to get Israel to "whore after" the god Baal instead of being faithful to God (2 Kings 9:22). The ancient Israelites assumed that someone who would "whore" spiritually would "whore" literally as well, and based on what we know about pagan religions, they were right. In the New Testament, the Book of Revelation speaks out against a woman called Jezebel, who was leading Christians astray with her teachings (Revelation 2:20).

Throughout history, any queen who displeased her subjects was referred to as a "Jezebel," particularly if her religion irked her subjects. Queen Mary I of England, who is known as "Bloody Mary," persecuted Protestants, who labeled her a "Jezebel." Later, her half-sister Elizabeth I jailed and executed Catholics, and Catholics called *her* a Jezebel. Catherine the Great of Russia was often called a Jezebel. In America's colonial period, Anne Hutchinson took her Christianity seriously but made the mistake of criticizing Puritan ministers. She was known as the "American Jezebel," and she was banished from Massachusetts and later died in an Indian massacre. Many of the Puritans said that she deserved a violent death (as Jezebel did), considering her unorthodox religious views. Probably the most famous royal Jezebel of all was Mary Queen of Scots, a Catholic ruling a kingdom that was no longer Catholic, and opposed by the fiery preacher John Knox, who minced no words when confronting the Jezebel on the throne. Mary died by beheading.

Aside from royals, any woman who is manipulative, scheming, or immoral is likely to be called a "Jezebel." Bette Davis won an Oscar for playing a manipulative, cold-hearted Southern belle in the 1938 film *Jezebel*.

Because Jezebel "painted her eyes and adorned her hair" before her fatal encounter with Jehu, many people associate make-up with an immoral character, and Christian women who refuse to wear make-up point to Jezebel as a kind of negative role model.

Such a colorful character has been depicted by numerous artists. Andrea Celesti's painting *Queen Jezebel Being Punished by Jehu* shows the body of the queen lying

J

on the pavement while dogs lick at her, Jehu looking on. John Masefield (1878-1967), England's poet laureate, wrote a verse drama, *A King's Daughter*, dealing with Jezebel. Jezebel was the subject of a rather bad production with Paulette Goddard titled *The Sins of Jezebel*.

Job
Made to last

"Why do good people suffer?"—that's the theme of the Old Testament's Book of Job. Wealthy and also saintly, Job is tested when God allows Satan to afflict Job with all kinds of troubles. (Here, Satan is more of a tester than a tempter. He wants to prove to God that Job is good only because it "pays.") Job's children and wealth are taken, his skin is afflicted with boils, and his wife urges him to "Curse God and die!" But Job replies, "Shall we accept good from God and not accept adversity?"

A different test comes in the form of his three so-called friends—with the colorful names Bildad, Eliphaz, and Zophar. They come to give comfort, but the more they talk, the more certain they are that if Job is suffering, he must have brought it on himself. They are determined to find some logic and purpose in the suffering, but Job continues to insist that he has done nothing wrong. The speeches of Job and the three friends on the subject of God's justice are priceless.

All their chattering ends when God himself appears "out of the whirlwind." God never answers the puzzle of why good people suffer. God speaks of how amazing and complex his universe is, and Job, confronted with his awesome Creator, knows that there is no answer to the painful question. At the book's end, God restores Job's fortunes and scolds the three friends for speaking about things too deep for them. God hasn't "explained" why good people suffer, he's only sent the message: "I'm in charge of things—trust me."

The book ends very happily. Job's fortunes are restored to him, and though his children have all died, he

Job Laments His State
JOB. CHAPTER 19, VERSES 8-11, 25-27.

has more children, including three daughters who are described as very beautiful. The Freemasons have a girls' auxiliary organization called the International Order of Job's Daughters.

Job has intrigued people for centuries. Artist-poet William Blake was inspired to do some fine (and surreal) illustrations of the book. Albrecht Durer's painting *Job and His Wife* (c. 1504, Frankfurt), shows the wife dumping a bucket of water on the nearly naked, despondent Job. Is she trying to cleanse him or bring him to his senses? Georges de la Tour's *Job Mocked by His Wife*, c. 1630, shows the wife holding a candle of the near naked man. *The Patient Job* by Gerard Seghers, in Prague, shows the bare Job with his three friends on the left, his scolding wife on the right, with Job's eyes cast up to heaven. Poet Archibald MacLeish wrote a Pulitzer Prize-winning play, *J.B.*, telling Job in a modern setting. More recently, playwright Neil Simon did a humorous version of the story in his play *God's Favorite*. Poet Robert Frost wrote *A Masque of Reason*, an amusing dialogue between God, Job, and Job's wife. At the end of this long poem Frost writes, "Here endeth Chapter Forty-three of Job." (Job in the Bible has 42 chapters.) English author H. G. Wells (1866-1946) best known for his science fiction novels, also wrote *The Undying Fire* (1919), a modernized version of the Book of Job. English composer Charles Parry wrote an oratorio about Job, and Ralph Vaughan Williams composed music for a ballet on the subject.

A very old Jewish tradition makes Moses the author of the Book of Job, but no one actually knows who wrote it. Muslims honor Job—*Ayub*—as one of the prophets.

Joel
The Spirit-predicting man

Joel was one of the prophets of the Old Testament and is frequently quoted by Christians because he seemed to predict some key events among the first Christians. In Joel 2, God promises a time when "I will pour out my Spirit on all flesh; your sons and your daughters shall prophesy, your old men shall dream dreams, and your young men shall see visions." Christians believe the prophecy came to pass when the first believers showed evidence of being empowered by the Spirit, as seen in the Book of Acts, chapter 2. Joel has some other striking phrases, notably the command to "beat your plowshares into swords, and your pruning hooks into spears; let the weak say, 'I am a warrior'" (Joel 3:10). Joel used the phrase "the valley of decision," which has been used as the title of a novel and film. Like all the prophets, Joel predicted doom if the people did not repent of their sins, but assured them that God would welcome them back if they mended their ways.

John the apostle
The born-again Gospel man

John was one of two disciples (Matthew was the other) who wrote Gospels, the stories of Jesus' life. John was in a privileged position to do so because he and his older brother James, along with Peter, formed a kind of "inner circle," the three being closer to Jesus than the other disciples. John is also credited with writing three epistles (1, 2, and 3 John) and the mysterious last book of the Bible, the Book of Revelation. Thanks to his writings, this Galilean fisherman is known worldwide.

Like all the disciples, John was capable of speaking and acting foolishly at times. Jesus referred to James and John as "sons of thunder" (Mark 3:17), which apparently was a compliment, but when the two of them asked him if they could have special places in heaven, Jesus told them they didn't know what they were asking for (Mark 10:35-45). Peter, John, and James were present at the amazing event called the Transfiguration (Matthew 17), where Jesus appeared to be conversing with the long-dead Moses and the prophet Elijah. The three were also the only disciples present when Jesus agonized in the Garden of Gethsemane before his arrest.

When Jesus was arrested after his betrayal by Judas, the disciples fled and hid, but John is mentioned as being present at the cross, and while on the cross, Jesus gave his mother Mary into John's keeping (John 19:26-27).

Throughout John's Gospel, John never refers to himself by name. Instead he refers to "the disciple whom Jesus loved." At the very end of the Gospel, he writes, "This is the disciple who is bearing witness about these things" (John 21:24). While it isn't certain that "the disciple whom Jesus loved" was John, most scholars believe it was.

In the Book of Acts, the apostles John and Peter heal a crippled beggar, which gets them into trouble with the Jewish authorities. Acts 3-4 describes the encounter, including the apostles' reply to their accusers: "Whether it is right in the sight of God to listen to you more than to God, you judge." Later, Peter and John preached to the Samaritans (Acts 8:17-25).

John's Gospel is radically different from the other three Gospels, Matthew, Mark, and Luke. Those three, similar in so many ways, are called the Synoptic Gospels. The Gospel of John starts not with the story of Jesus' birth or baptism, but with Jesus as "the Word of God," who existed from all eternity. His Gospel omits all the parables and most of the miracles that the other Gospels include. Instead it has the story of turning the water into wine at the wedding at Cana; Nicodemus the teacher coming to Jesus in secret and being told he must be "born again"; the famous incident of the woman about to be stoned for adultery; the washing of the disciples' feet by Jesus; and, most famous of all, the raising to life of Jesus' dead friend Lazarus (John 11). John's Gospel also includes several "I am" speeches by Jesus, in which he announces, "I am the bread of life," "I am the resurrection," "I am the good shepherd," and "I am the light of the world." This Gospel contains the story of the disciple Thomas, who doubts Jesus has been resurrected until he has seen him himself.

Certainly the most famous verse in the Gospel is John 3:16: "For God so loved the world he gave his only begotten Son, that whosoever believes in him should not perish, but have everlasting life." This is a good summary of the whole New Testament, which is one reason the verse has been so often displayed on posters held up at sporting events. It is also a verse that gives translators fits, because the Son is described by the Greek word *monogene*—literally, "an only child." John's meaning was that Jesus was God's divine Son in a unique way, while Christians are sons and daughters of God "by adoption." The King James Version used "only begotten Son," but most people today probably do not know what "begotten" means, so modern translations use "only Son" or "unique Son." One reason some very conservative Christians stick with the King James Version is that they believe its translation of 3:16 is the only correct one.

The three epistles of John are not as widely read as his Gospel, but 1 John is a beautiful example of spirituality, emphasizing *love*, a word often found in his Gospel. The letter contains the important words "God is love." The other two epistles, 2 and 3 John, have the distinction of between the two shortest books in the Bible.

What about the Book of Revelation? The book itself names John as its author, but this was a common name, and no one is certain it was John the

J

Apostle. It does have some things in common with the Gospel, including numerous mentions of *the lamb of God*. Bible scholars have noticed that the Greek of the Gospel of John and the Greek of the Book of Revelation are extremely different, so in all likelihood the John who wrote Revelation was not John the Apostle. Many old Bibles refer to the book as "the Revelation of St. John the Divine."

As an important apostle, John was the subject of many legends. While the other eleven apostles all died as martyrs, John supposedly died of old age, though he was at one time sentenced by the Roman emperor Domitian to be executed by being plunged into boiling oil, but miraculously survived. A book claiming to be the Acts of John was circulated, saying that he became Jesus' disciple while very young, which explains why artists have almost always shown him as a young man with no beard. A fairly old tradition, which might be based on fact, says he was exiled by the Roman emperor to the barren Greek island of Patmos, where he saw the visions he recorded in the Book of Revelation. In some legends he did not die but was taken into heaven like the prophet Elijah.

John's image has appeared in paintings and sculptures since early times, usually as the youngest of the disciples, although the icons of the Eastern Orthodox churches show him as an old, white-bearded man holding his Gospel. As one of the four Evangelists (authors of the Gospels), he is often depicted with an eagle, the symbol of his Gospel. The Eastern Orthodox churches refer to him as "John the Theologian," and Orthodox icons often show him on the bleak isle of Patmos, the sky filled with the visions from the Book of Revelation. The Italian painter Titian's *St. John the Evangelist on Patmos*, painted on a ceiling, is a stunning depiction of John receiving the Revelation from heaven, with God the Father, surrounded by angels, seated on the clouds. The great French painter Nicholas Poussin also did a *St. John on Patmos*, although Poussin made the island look attractive, while the real island (named in Revelation 1:9) was a bleak, rocky place. In the countless paintings of the Last Supper, John is always show on one side of Jesus, sometimes with his head resting on Jesus, since the Gospel says he reclined on Jesus (John 13:23).

In the Catholic Church, his feast day is December 27, and the Eastern Orthodox commemorate his death on September 26. Mormons (Latter-day Saints) believe John, along with James and Peter, appeared to Mormon founder Joseph Smith. Because of his importance (and also the importance of another John, the

Baptist) the name John has always been a popular one in Christian countries (as John, Jean, Juan, Giovanni, etc.) In Rome, the most important church after the St. Peter's Basilica, is the St. John Lateran cathedral.

In plays and films about Jesus, John plays a special part, since he is the only disciple present at the crucifixion. He was also, along with Peter, the first disciple to see that Jesus' tomb was empty (John 20:4). In films he is, as in artwork, usually depicted as young and beardless. Composer Johann Sebastian Bach wrote a *St. John Passion*, a choral work using texts from John's Gospel.

John the Baptist
The camel-hair prophet

According to Luke's Gospel, John the Baptist's parents were the aged Zechariah and Elizabeth, very devout people, but childless in an age when being childless was considered bad. The angel Gabriel appeared in the temple where Zechariah was serving as a priest and announced that Elizabeth would conceive a child. Because Zechariah doubted the angel, he was made mute until the child, John, was born. Elizabeth had a young relative named Mary, whose conception was even more astounding, since Mary was a virgin (and the mother of Jesus, of course). When Mary arrived for a visit, Elizabeth reported that her unborn child "leaped" in her womb.

The next we hear of John he is living in the open, preaching to people the need to repent of their sins and be baptized in the Jordan River. John had a definite "look"—a rough garment of camel's hair, and he was living on wild locusts (grasshoppers, that is) and honey. The angel Gabriel had foretold that John would act "in the spirit and power of Elijah … to make ready a people prepared for the Lord" (Luke 1:17). Elijah was the great prophet of the Old Testament who was taken to heaven in a fiery chariot. Later, the prophet Malachi predicted that Elijah would return again to earth, with God saying, "I will send you Elijah the prophet before the great and coming day of the Lord comes" (Malachi 4:5). The Jews didn't believe in reincarnation, but many of them did believe that John was the Elijah-like prophet Malachi had predicted. Some people even thought John was the Messiah the Jews had awaited, but John made it clear he wasn't. There was someone greater coming, he said. He was merely "preparing the way" for this person. John baptized people in water, but this "greater one" would baptize with the Holy Spirit.

John's Gospel (written by the apostle John, not by John the Baptist) begins by saying, "There was a man sent from God, whose name was John …" This Gospel says John was not "the light" but came to "bear witness to the light"—the light being Jesus.

John was present at the beginning of Jesus' public life. Jesus came to John for baptism, although John was reluctant, since Jesus had no sins to repent of. Jesus was baptized, hearing a voice from God saying he was "well pleased" with his beloved Son.

Like a true prophet, John did not sugarcoat his message. When the Pharisees and Saducees, people who thought themselves very religious, came to him for baptism, he called them a "brood of vipers" (Matthew 3:7). He warned that when the Messiah came, he would burn up everything useless with "unquenchable fire." When tax collectors (whom everyone hated) came to him, he told them to collect no more than was legal. Soldiers who came to him were told not to extort money from people with threats. In other words, he told people with authority not to abuse it.

John preached against Herod Antipas, the ruler of Galilee, for marrying his brother's wife, Herodias. Herod finally threw John in prison but hesitated to execute him, since the people thought so highly of John. But the poor prophet met his end thanks to Salome (SEE PAGE 321), the daughter of Herodias. Her dancing pleased her stepfather so much, he offered to give her whatever she liked. At her mother's urging, she asked for, and got, the head of John the Baptist brought in on a platter. The superstitious Herod feared that Jesus might have been John, raised from the dead. (In the legends of King Arthur, it was said that Arthur's famous sword, Excalibur, was the sword used to behead John.)

In Christian tradition, John is considered the forerunner of the Messiah, and also the first of the prophets after a long silence. (The Jews had gone hundreds of years with no guidance from prophets, only from the Law.) Jesus told his own followers that John was (in a figurative sense) the prophet Elijah that had been predicted. Jesus also told them, "Among those born of women there has not risen one greater than John the Baptist" (Matthew 11:11). Andrew and John, who had both been disciples of John, later became disciples of Jesus.

Because of his importance in the life of Jesus, and because he had such a distinctive look, John has been the subject of countless paintings and sculptures over the centuries. He is often shown as rough and shaggy, in his camel-skin tunic and, oddly, holding a lamb, which refers to his identification of Jesus as "the Lamb of God who takes away the sin of the world" (John 1:29). Caravaggio painted John dozens of times, usually as a young beardless man, nearly nude, accompanied by a sheep. The saint was so highly regarded that Francis I, king of France, had himself painted by Jean Clouet as John the Baptist in 1518, holding a lamb and a cross—and with an Asian parrot in the background. Donatello sculpted John in both wood and bronze, the 1457 bronze version being prominent in the Siena Cathedral. Carel Fabritius's 1640 *Beheading of John the Baptist* in Amsterdam actually shows the headless body beneath the head on the platter. Giotto's

The Baptism of Jesus
MATTHEW. CHAPTER 3, VERSES 13-17.

frescos of the life of John, completed 1320, are in the Santa Croce church in Florence. El Greco painted John numerous times, always as bearded and wiry. Da Vinci's John in the Louvre, c. 1515, is young, curly-haired and beardless, not even remotely evoking the John of the Bible. Raphael's John, c. 1518, is also a pretty boy. Titian's 1542 John is one of the most striking, with a bearded, shaggy-haired, and very muscular figure. This one has some depth in his face, as if he's sorrowing over his people's sins. He also is seen as a baby in paintings of "the Holy Family," that is, Mary, Joseph, and the baby Jesus, along with his own mother Elizabeth. In Christian art, John is the most common infant after Jesus himself. The most common image of John shows him baptizing Jesus in the Jordan River, a scene often found in baptisteries (the pools in churches used for baptisms). His beheading—or, rather, Salome looking at his bodiless head—has been a favorite subject. The French sculptor Rodin did a famous life-size (and nude) *St. John the Baptist Preaching*, now in London's Victoria and Albert Museum. After Jesus and Mary, John has probably appeared in more paintings and sculptures than any other person from the Bible.

Numerous places on the map have been named for John the Baptist, including the oldest city under the U.S. flag, San Juan, Puerto Rico—its full name being *San Juan Bautista*, which used to be the name of the whole island. Thousands of other churches and cities have been named for him. The cathedral in Turin, Italy, is named for him, and it houses the famous Shroud of Turin, which many people believe is the burial cloth of Jesus. One of the oldest Christian buildings on earth is the Church of St. John the Baptist in Jerusalem.

The Gospels say that John ate "locusts and honey," and locusts could mean real locusts (grasshoppers, that is), but could also mean the pods of the carob plant, which is why carob pods have been called "St. John's bread." The popular medicinal herb St. John's wort takes its name from the old custom of picking it on the eve of John's feast day (June 24). In Europe, it used to be a custom to light bonfires on the night of St. John's Day to ward off bad luck.

The Catholic and Eastern Orthodox churches have several holy days dedicated to John, including January 6, Epiphany, which celebrates Jesus' baptism (and also the visit of the Magi). John's birth is celebrated on June 24 and his beheading on August 29. The holy day of Visitation, May 31, commemorates the visit of the Virgin Mary to John's mother Elizabeth. The Muslims regard John (*Yahya*) as a holy prophet, although the Koran does not mention his baptizing or his execution. The Great Mosque in Damascus, Syria, claims to have his head, which was visited by Pope John Paul II in 2001 (the first visit of a pope to a mosque, by the way). A religious sect called the Mandaens, found in Iraq and Iran, trace its roots back to the disciples of John. The Mandaens regard Jesus as a false Messiah. Mormons believed that John the Baptist appeared in a vision to their founder, Joseph Smith.

John has been the subject of numerous works of literature, partly because of his beheading at the instigation of Salome. He is an important character in Oscar Wilde's tragedy *Salome*, in Richard Strauss's opera based on that play, and in Hermann Sudermann's play *The Fires of St. John*. In all three of these, Salome is in love with John. (In Wilde's and Strauss's versions, John has the name Jokanan.) In movies about the life of Jesus, John is a major character, and probably none has played him more memorably than Charlton Heston in the 1965 film *The Greatest Story Ever Told*. In *The Last Temptation of Christ*, John is portrayed as a slightly mad character (as is Jesus himself). One of the earliest oratorios ever written was Alessandro Stradella's 1676 work *San Giovanni Battista (St. John the Baptist)*.

Jonah and the whale
Such a fish story …

If there's one Old Testament prophet people know the name of, it's Jonah, the man who found himself in the belly of a whale and somehow survived it.

As a matter of historical record, one man actually did survive being swallowed by a whale. His name was James Bartley, and he was on his first voyage on a whaling ship in February 1891, near the Falkland Islands off the coast of South America. One the crew members harpooned a sperm whale (the only whale with a mouth big enough to swallow an adult human). It submerged, then resurfaced under the longboat, scattering the men into the air and ocean. The whale was caught, killed, and butchered on the deck of the ship. Much to everyone's surprise, the stomach was moving, and the ship's doctor cut it open to find an unconscious James Bartley. He had spent about fifteen hours inside the whale. The digestive juices had burned off all his body hair and bleached his skin white. The poor man wisely became a shoemaker and never went to sea again. On his tombstone are the words, "A Modern Jonah." His story doesn't prove that the tale of Jonah is true, of course, but it does make you wonder.

In the Bible, Jonah was ordered by God to go to Nineveh, the capital of the Assyrian empire, to tell its inhabitants to repent (chapter 1). Jonah had no desire for the Assyrians, Israel's enemies, to repent and be saved, so he took passage on a ship, which was struck by a fierce storm. Jonah managed to stay fast asleep in the hold of the ship. The people on the ship cast lots to determine which of them was the cause of the storm. Jonah, who knew the storm was God's way of reminding him of his duty, asked to be thrown overboard. "The Lord had prepared a great fish to swallow Jonah." Inside the whale, Jonah prayed. After three days, the whale vomited him up on dry land, and Jonah went on to Nineveh, as the Lord had commanded. His message was a simple one: "Yet forty days, and Nineveh shall be overthrown." Much to his surprise (and regret) the pagans in Nineveh, even the king himself, did repent. Jonah went into a long pout until the Lord reminded him that the people of Nineveh, and even their beasts, mattered to him: "Should I not pity Nineveh?"

The book's point: God loved the people of pagan Nineveh, not just the people of Israel, his "chosen" people.

The book tells us nothing about the period that Jonah lived in, nor the name of the king of Assyria. Jonah's name is mentioned in 2 Kings 14:25, as "Jonah son of Amittai, the prophet from Gath Hepher." Jesus compared Jonah's stay in the whale to his own burial and resurrection, referring to it as the "sign of Jonah" (Matthew 12:40). Jesus also said that "the men of Nineveh will stand up at the judgment with this generation and condemn it; for they repented at the preaching of Jonah, and now one greater than Jonah is here."

The Book of Jonah is included among the twelve Minor Prophets, the last section of the Old Testament. His book is very different from the other eleven, since his is a narrative, while the other eleven consist of warnings and prophecies.

Among Jews, the Book of Jonah is read in its entirety in synagogues on the annual Day of Atonement. The book is a touching tale of sin and forgiveness, and thus highly appropriate for the Jews' annual festival of divine mercy.

For the Muslims, Jonah (called *Yunus* in the Koran) is sent by the god Allah to convert the pagans of Nineveh. He tells them to repent, but they do not and he leaves, but afterward the sky appears fire-red, so the Ninevites repent. Jonah sets sail and is swallowed by whale, which coughs him up on land, and he goes back to Nineveh, where the already repentant people await his spiritual guidance. In Muslim legend, the whale that swallowed Jonah is one of the ten animals that enter heaven.

The story of Jonah has intrigued some notable writers. Laurence Housman (1865-1959) wrote a play about Jonah, *The Burden of Nineveh*. American poet Robert Frost wrote *A Masque of Mercy*, in which the "Fugitive" is the prophet Jonah, running away from God. In Frost's poem, the Fugitive is named Jonas Dove—the name Jonah in Hebrew literally means "dove." The English composer John Taverner wrote *The Whale*, a cantata based on the Jonah story. American author Robert Nathan wrote the novel *Jonah*.

Jonah's story is colorful, to put it mildly, but somehow Hollywood never got around to making a film about Jonah and his adventure. Jonah finally did hit the big screen in an animated film aimed at the very young, *Jonah: A Veggie Tales Movie*, using the popular Veggie Tales characters.

The story of Jonah got a lot of public exposure during the famous 1925 "monkey trial," in which former statesman William Jennings Bryan took the stand to defend the truth of the Bible. Lawyer Clarence Darrow asked Bryan if he truly believed Jonah had been swallowed by a whale. Bryan replied that, no, the Bible claimed it was a "great fish," not a whale. Bryan was right, of course, since it does say "great fish." (We know today whales are mammals, not fish.)

Based on the incident of the miraculous gourd vine in Jonah chapter 4, author Zora Neale Hurston titled one of her novels *Jonah's Gourd Vine*.

The Eastern Orthodox churches celebrate September 22 as the feast of St. Jonah the Prophet.

Jonathan

David's bosom buddy

Male bonding reached its high point in the deep friendship between Jonathan, son of Israel's King Saul, and the shepherd boy David, who later became king himself. David and Jonathan were both gritty soldiers, and they loved and admired each other. In the words of 1 Samuel 18, "the soul of Jonathan was knit to the soul of David, and Jonathan loved him as his own soul." Alas, Jonathan's father Saul had many excellent qualities, but he could be moody and paranoid, and he resented David's increasing popularity with the people. He ordered Jonathan to kill David, but Jonathan would not. (Note: If David became king, then Jonathan, the king's son, would *not* become

The Friendship of David and Jonathan
I SAMUEL. CHAPTER 20, VERSES 40-43.

king. See the problem Jonathan faced in being so fond of David?) Jonathan walked a thin line, trying to be a good son, but also devoted to his best friend. At one point his moody father even tried to kill him with a spear for siding with David.

Both Saul and Jonathan died while fighting the Philistines. David's famous lament is in 2 Samuel 1:19-27. It contains the line, "How the mighty are fallen," but also contains the phrase, "I am distressed for you, my brother Jonathan; you have been very pleasant to me, your love to me was wonderful, surpassing the love of women." (One theologian published a book called *Jonathan Loved David*, claiming to prove the two men were homosexual lovers.) It is possible, but doubtful, since David, who had several wives and numerous children, proved that he was perhaps overly fond of female company, and Jonathan himself fathered children. Whatever the nature of their relationship, they had a friendship of such depth that most people can hardly comprehend it. Most men who ever lived wished for such a "buddy."

the Jordan River
Not wide, but widely known

By world standards the Jordan is small, but it is Israel's largest river, and it is connected with some of the most important events in the Bible. Most notable is the Israelites' crossing while it was in flood. According to Joshua 3, the water from upstream stopped flowing as the people, led by priests carrying the ark of the covenant, crossed over on dry land. The great prophet Elijah, just before he was taken into heaven, struck the

Jordan with his cloak and the waters parted. His successor prophet, Elisha, healed the Aramean military leader Naaman of leprosy by having him wash in the Jordan.

In the Gospels, the Jordan was the site where John the Baptist baptized repentant sinners. Most importantly, it was where John baptized Jesus (Matthew 3:13-17, Luke 3:21-22). This event has been for centuries one of the most popular subjects for artists, and the Jordan River is probably one of the most painted rivers in the world. Baptisteries (shallow pools in churches used for baptisms) often have the Jordan River depicted on a wall behind the pool. For centuries, visitors to the Holy Land have brought back some Jordan River water to use in baptisms (for baptism by *sprinkling*, that is—bringing back enough water for baptism by *immersion* would be quite a task).

Because of the Old Testament story of Elijah crossing the Jordan before he was taken into heaven, "crossing the Jordan" passed into the Christian vocabulary as a phrase referring to death. Hundreds of Christian hymns refer to the Jordan, for once one has "crossed Jordan," one is in heaven. (In many of these songs, Jordan is described as "deep" and "wide," which is certainly not true of the real Jordan.) In the time when slavery existed in America, slaves used "crossing the Jordan" to mean crossing the Ohio River into the northern states where slavery was illegal. Thus all the black spirituals about crossing the Jordan had a double meaning—release from this world's troubles by dying and entering heaven, or crossing the Ohio River to freedom. The phrase was still familiar enough in the twenty-first century that a TV series was titled *Crossing Jordan*. The films *Here Comes Mr. Jordan* and *Heaven Can Wait* had a character named Mr. Jordan, an angel whose duty it was to escort newly deceased people to heaven.

In the twentieth century, the name Jordan was given to the predominantly Muslim nation east of Israel. The region had long been known as the Transjordan, meaning "beyond the Jordan." In biblical times the region consisted of the nations of Edom, Moab, and Ammon—all three being thorns in Israel's side. The centuries-old feud continues to this day, as the Muslims of Jordan and other nations contest Israel's right to any of the land around the Jordan River.

Joseph, the husband of Mary
History's most famous stepfather

Though just a carpenter, Joseph was descended from King David and his hometown was (like David's) Bethlehem. He resided in the village of Nazareth, but returned to Bethlehem for the Roman census. According to Matthew's Gospel, Joseph was engaged to Mary, but she became pregnant by the Holy Spirit. Joseph, "a just man," did not want to disgrace her, so he opted to divorce her quietly. But in a dream, an angel told Joseph to marry Mary, who had conceived miraculously. Later, when wicked King Herod ordered the death of all male infants in Bethlehem, another dream warned Joseph to flee with the family into Egypt. A later dream told him to return to Israel and live in Nazareth.

As an adult, Jesus was referred to as "the carpenter's son," and Jesus himself followed the same trade. More than once Jesus is called "Joseph's son," although Luke mentions that Jesus was the son of Joseph "as was supposed." Legally, not biologically, Jesus was Joseph's son, and the genealogies in Matthew and Luke trace Joseph's family tree, not Mary's. Joseph is not mentioned again after he and Mary take Jesus to Jerusalem when Jesus is twelve years old. We can assume that he died before Jesus reached adulthood.

Artists have given us many pictures of Joseph, particularly in Nativity scenes and the countless paintings with the title *The Holy Family*. Joseph is almost always shown as a much older man than Mary. The Bible gives no data on his age. According to Catholic tradition, Mary was not only a virgin when Jesus was born but *remained* a virgin throughout her life. Where the Gospels mention Jesus as having "brothers," Catholic tradition assumes that these must have been Joseph's children from an earlier marriage. It is probably for this reason that he is shown as older than Mary. (Also, whatever Joseph's age, Mary was probably very young when she married, typical of Jewish brides of that era.) El Greco's painting *St. Joseph and the Christ Child*, c. 1600, shows Joseph as a relatively young man. This is also true in Francisco de Herrera's 1648 rendering. But Georges de La Tour's 1640 *The Dream of St. Joseph* shows him as an old, bald man, sleeping while a female angel puts the dream into his head. In Rembrandt's 1655 rendering, Joseph is an old man, and both the angel and Mary are present in the picture. The popular TV movie *Jesus of Nazareth* (1977) broke with tradition and showed Mary and Joseph as both very young when they married. In many artworks, Joseph is depicted with the tools of a carpenter.

For some curious reason, in pictures of Joseph, Mary, and the child Jesus, Joseph is usually show in red, Mary in blue. (A few species of flower that have both red and blue blossoms are called Joseph-and-Mary.) The familiar white Easter lily is usually called the Madonna lily (after Mary), but has also been known as the St. Joseph's lily.

J

Joseph has never been as revered a figure as his wife Mary, but he is still beloved in Christian tradition. Affection for him is seen in the common use of his name for boys in all Christian countries—Joseph, Jose, Giuseppe, Jozef, etc. (aided by the fact that the Joseph in the Book of Genesis was also an honored figure). There are numerous town, schools, and churches named for him. He has long been the patron saint of carpenters, and of manual laborers in general. Christians in several countries recognize him as their patron saint, including Belgium, China, and Peru. The Catholic Church celebrates May 1 as the Feast of St. Joseph the Worker, honoring his role as protector of all working men. He is also honored with a feast on March 19, and since 1870 Catholics have held that he is Patron of the Universal Church, second only to his wife Mary as most honored among the saints.

Incidentally, the Catholic Church does not give its approve to the old practice of home-sellers burying a statue of St. Joseph in the lawn, hoping it will help the home to sell more quickly.

Joseph, Jacob's son
The dreamy kid with the colorful coat

One of the best and emotionally rich stories in the Bible is found in Genesis 37-50, the saga of Joseph, eleventh and favorite son of the patriarch Jacob. Jacob doted on the boy, who was the son of Jacob's favorite wife, Rachel, and gave him a lovely "coat of many colors." The older brothers were jealous, particularly when Joseph reported dreams of his brothers and parents bowing down and honoring him. The brothers plotted to kill him, then left him in a pit, but finally sold him into slavery in Egypt. There, he served an official named Potiphar, who found Joseph to be a trusted servant. The randy wife of Potiphar tried to seduce Joseph, who refused her; she cried "Rape!" (The Old Testament in the original Hebrew says Potiphar was a *saris*, a eunuch.) Joseph was thrown into prison, where he interpreted the dreams of two other prisoners. One of them, a servant of Pharaoh, told Pharaoh that Joseph could interpret Pharaoh's troubling dreams. Joseph did so, predicting a famine—seven productive years followed by seven "lean years." The grateful Pharaoh made him Egypt's prime minister, in charge of planning for the famine. The rest of Genesis tells of his brothers' journey to Egypt in search of food. They failed to recognize the brother they wronged, but eventually he revealed himself to them in an emotional scene—"I am Joseph, your brother"—and they are reconciled, and the elderly father Jacob came to Egypt to see his lost son. Joseph married an Egyptian wife and she bore him two sons, Manasseh and Ephraim, who became the ancestors of two of the twelve tribes of Israel.

Joseph's story is one of the Bible's masterpieces, full of drama and sentiment. Joseph is a role model of a young man keeping his courage and morals in adversity. Jews and Christians saw it as an example of God providing for a person of faith in difficult circumstances. Christians saw his deliverance from the pit and from prison as foreshadowing the resurrection of Jesus. Joseph's colorful life has been depicted often by artists, and many (notably Rembrandt) were drawn to the incident with Joseph and Potiphar's wife. In Tintoretto's *Joseph and Potiphar's Wife*, c. 1555, (in the Prado, Madrid), the wife is naked and wearing a string of pearls as she grasps at Joseph's cloak. Andrew Lloyd Webber and Tim Rice gave the world the musical fancy *Joseph and the Amazing Technicolor Dreamcoat*, which proved that even

a biblically illiterate public would pack the houses to see a reenactment of a story from Genesis (if it had bouncy music, anyway). The German Nobel Prize-winning author Thomas Mann was one of many authors drawn to the Joseph saga, leading to his epic *Joseph and His Brothers*, which took him sixteen years to write. Joseph symbolizes the sensitive, artistic person who uses his gifts for the good of others. In England, Charles Jeremiah Wells (1800-1879), a

Joseph is Sold Into Egypt
GENESIS. CHAPTER 37, VERSES 23-28.

friend of poet John Keats, became famous for *Joseph and His Brethren* (1876), a long dramatic poem in blank verse. The great Dutch poet Vondel (1587-1679) wrote a dramatic play *Joseph in Egypt*.

Composers have been attracted to the Joseph saga. George Frideric Handel wrote the oratorio *Joseph and His Brethren* (1744), and French composer Etienne Mehul (1763-1817) wrote an opera on the subject. The story has been popular in films as well, with its exotic setting in Egypt and its theme of reconciling brothers. Probably the best film made of the story was Turner Network Television's long Emmy-winning version, which had Ben Kingsley as Potiphar.

Because Joseph was sold into slavery by his brothers, antislavery writings in the 1700s and 1800s often referred to him. In fact, America's first antislavery book was *The Selling of Joseph*, written by New England author Samuel Sewall (1652-1730).

Joseph's name made its way into the language in various ways. In times past, a "Joseph" was a young man who successfully resisted sexual temptation. A long flowing robe, especially a colorful one, was a "Joseph" or "Joseph's coat," and poorer families in Appalachia and elsewhere made quilted coats of fabric scraps, calling them "coats of many colors." Various colorful garden plants are known by the name "Joseph's coat."

Alas, a sad note: Modern Bible translations are probably correct in discarding "coat of many colors" and using "coat with long sleeves"—more correct, but certainly less colorful.

Muslims honor Joseph—*Yusuf*—as a prophet. In Muslim legends, the wife of Potiphar is named Rahil or Zuleika.

Joseph of Arimathea
Friendly witness

Here is a classic case of a minor biblical character as the subject of some colorful legends. In the Gospels, Joseph is described as a member of the Jewish ruling council, but also, secretly, an admirer of Jesus. He did not approve of the council condemning Jesus, and after Jesus' death he had Jesus buried in his own family tomb, obtaining permission from the Roman governor, Pilate.

That is all the Bible tells us, but legend tells much more. Supposedly he obtained the cup Jesus used at the Last Supper and, at the cross, caught Jesus' blood in it. This cup exists in the realm of legend as the Holy Grail (SEE PAGE 148). In legend, Joseph took the Grail with him to England, where he preached the new faith and established the famous Abbey of Glastonbury, which has long been associated with King Arthur and the Grail legends. He also possessed the Roman spear that pierced the side of Jesus on the cross. Some of these tales were found in the Gospel of Nicodemus, composed in Glastonbury centuries after the time of Joseph.

Joseph is depicted in the many paintings of Jesus' body being taken down from the cross (usually titled *Deposition from the Cross*). In many plays and films about Jesus he is often shown as the one member of the Jewish council who tries to have Jesus judged fairly.

Because of his connection with the burial of Jesus, Joseph is the patron saint of funeral directors. The Catholic Church celebrates his feast day on March 17 (meaning he is overshadowed by the much more famous saint of that day, Patrick).

Joshua

Following the Moses acts

Joshua was the successor to Moses after the Israelites arrived in the land of Canaan after being led out of slavery in Egypt. Prior to assuming Moses' mantle, Joshua had been one of the Israelite spies sent by Moses to the land of Canaan. Most of the spies were intimidated by the Canaanites and their fortified towns, but Joshua and another spy, Caleb, encouraged the Israelites to proceed with the conquest of Canaan. After much complaining and hand-wringing, the Israelites did so (Numbers 13-14).

The Book of Joshua tells the story of the conquest of Canaan and the division of the land among the twelve tribes of Israel. The book opens with God telling Joshua to observe the laws given to Moses and reminding him that "the Lord your God is with you wherever you go" (Joshua 1:9). Chapter 2 tells of Israelite spies in the city of Jericho, which in chapter 6 is taken without a battle, since the Lord himself causes the city's walls to fall (SEE PAGE 172). Chapter 3 tells of the famous miracle of the flooded Jordan River parting as Israel's priests pass through carrying the ark of the covenant. Chapter 10 tells of the miracle at Gibeon, where the sun "stood still" while the Israelites defeated their enemies in battle. (The book is extremely violent, and many readers today find it distasteful to read.) In chapter 23, Joshua reminds the people that though God has helped them defeat their enemies in Canaan, he can give the land back to their enemies if the people do not follow the divine laws. A verse from the book that Jews and Christians frequently quote is Joshua 23:15: "As for me and my house, we will serve the Lord."

Joshua was a privileged character; of all the thousands of Israelite slaves that Moses led out of Egypt, he was one of only two that survived to enter the land

The Appointment of Joshua
NUMBERS. CHAPTER 27, VERSES 18-23.

of Canaan. (The other was fellow spy Caleb—the only two men who had enough faith to encourage the Israelites to conquer Canaan.)

Several scenes from the book have been popular subjects in artworks, notably the crossing of the Jordan River and the fall of Jericho. George Frideric Handel wrote an oratorio, *Joshua*. He is an important character in the 1956 film *The Ten Commandments*. American author Timothy Dwight published the long narrative poem *The Conquest of Canaan* (1789), based on the book of Joshua—which he clearly intended to have parallel the Founding Fathers and the building of a new "Canaan" in America.

Joshua's name, incidentally, was actually *Yehoshua*, which in New Testament times was spelled *Yeshua*—the name we know as Jesus. The name means "the Lord saves."

In the Middle Ages, nine famous warriors in history were called the Nine Worthies, and three of them were from the Bible: Joshua, David, and (from the Apocrypha) Judas Maccabeus.

Josiah
A diamond among the coals

The rulers in 1 and 2 Kings are mostly a bunch of rogues, with the Bible stating that most of them "did evil in the sight of the Lord." One of the few exceptions was the saintly Josiah, whose reign is described in 2 Kings 22-23. His reign began at age eight, when his wicked father Amon died. Josiah "did what was right in the eyes of the Lord" (in 2 Kings 22:2). He repaired the temple in the Jerusalem, but more importantly, he launched a moral reform after the high priest found an old copy of the Book of the Law (probably the Book of Deuteronomy, the fifth book of the Old Testament). Josiah decided to order the nation's life around the Book of the Law, and he stamped out the worship of Baal and other false gods. Sacrifice of children to the god Moloch was ended. Josiah also instituted the observance of the Passover holiday, which had been forgotten for centuries. "There was no king like him, who turned to the Lord with all his heart and with all his soul, according to all the Law of Moses, nor did any like him arise after him." Sadly, at age thirty-nine he was killed in battle against the invading Egyptians. In the next generation, the nation was conquered by the Babylonians, who destroyed the temple he had renovated.

A tradition says that Josiah is one of the four kings in a deck of playing cards, the others being David, Solomon, and Hezekiah. The four of them were among the few Jewish kings who were respectable men.

Judas Iscariot
Never trust the treasurer ...

With the exception of Satan, Judas may be the most famous villain in history. Judas was among Jesus' disciples, and was trusted enough to be the band's treasurer (John 12:6). Since Jesus chose his twelve disciples, we can assume that Judas was, at first, a sincere follower. But the Gospels make it clear that he was, or became, a bad character, thieving from the group's common treasury, of which he was in charge. Luke's Gospel says that Satan entered into Judas (Luke 22:3-6). The Gospels tell us that Judas went to the Jewish priests and offered to lead them to Jesus at night so they could arrest him. (A daytime arrest might have caused a revolt among the people in Jerusalem.) The "blood money" the priests paid him for the betrayal was thirty pieces of silver. (Exodus 21:32 sets thirty pieces of silver as the price of a slave, so the priests did not have a high opinion of either Jesus or Judas.) Judas led an armed band to Jesus in the Garden of Gethsemane, identifying Jesus with a kiss—the infamous "kiss of Judas." (There was nothing sexual in the kiss, incidentally, as a disciple greeting his master with a kiss was common in that culture.)

Matthew's Gospel says Judas repented of his deed and returned the money to the priests, then hanged himself. According to Matthew, the priests used the "soiled" money to buy a field, called the Field of Blood, to be used for burying foreigners. The Book of Acts, though, says Judas himself bought the field, then fell headlong in it "and all his bowels gushed out." At any rate, the two accounts agree that he came to an unpleasant end. Acts also mentions that the remaining eleven disciples filled Judas's place with a new man, Matthias.

The name Iscariot puzzles scholars, for it could mean he came from a town called Kerioth, or that he was connected with the Jewish revolutionaries called the Sicarii, famous for assassinating Roman officials and Jews who collaborated with them. If he was one of the Sicarii, he may have followed Jesus in the hope he was a political Messiah who would lead a revolt against Rome. Jesus was not that sort of Messiah, of course, which is why so many plays and films depict Judas betraying Jesus either because he was disappointed, or because he hoped that being arrested would provoke Jesus to begin the revolt. If this was Judas's goal, he was guilty of the same thing Satan was guilty of when tempting Jesus to choose power, trying to get him to be a political-military leader.

Long ago artists found ways of making Judas look different from the other disciples, notably by making him a redhead (a tradition followed in the film *The Last Temptation of Christ*). In the thousands of paintings of the Last Supper, he is always shown with one hand on the bag containing the thirty pieces of silver. He is also featured in the many paintings showing the kiss in the Garden of Gethsemane.

In Christian tradition, he is the supreme villain, the man who (whatever his motive) treacherously betrayed the Son of God. In Dante's famous poem *The Divine Comedy*, in the lowest circle of hell, Judas is gnawed eternally by the teeth of Satan. The twentieth century became kinder to Judas, however, wanting to "understand" him, so he has been portrayed somewhat sympathetically in *Jesus Christ Superstar* and *The Last Temptation of Christ*. In fact, in *Superstar* he is a frustrated idealist, and a more appealing character than the other disciples. More recently, *The Passion of the Christ* was less sympathetic, but showed Judas so tormented by guilt that he saw no way out except to hang himself. American poet Robinson Jeffers's *Dear Judas, and Other Poems*, depicts Judas favorably, as one who thought Jesus would be jailed briefly instead of crucified. Popular novelist Taylor Caldwell make the betrayer the subject of her book *I, Judas*. Judas is a soloist in Jules Massenet's oratorio *Mary Magdalene*, and in Edward Elgar's oratorio *The Apostles*.

In the section on Words and Phrases based on the Bible (page 404), you'll find many examples of Judas's name.

A very ancient Gospel of Judas, discovered in the 1970s, made the news when it was published in April 2006 by *National Geographic*, who marketed the book as an archaeological find of huge importance. The Gospel does not claim to be *by* Judas, but *about* him, showing him to be the favorite disciple of Jesus, one to whom Jesus revealed secret teachings not revealed to the other disciples. In this Gospel, Jesus *wants* Judas to betray him. The Gospel was one of many circulated in ancient times among the Gnostics, whose religion was for centuries a rival to Christianity.

Jude
Living down a bad name

The name "Judas" was very common in the New Testament period, and Jesus actually had two disciples of that name, one being the infamous traitor, Judas Iscariot. (John 14:22 specifically refers to the good Judas as "not Iscariot.") Matthew's and Mark's Gospels refer to an apostle named Thaddeus, who was probably the same as this Judas, who has often been called simply "Jude" to distinguish him from the bad Judas. Supposedly, the brief Letter of Jude in the New Testament was written by this Jude.

The Bible tells us little about the man, but somehow, in the 1700s, he became the "Patron Saint Of Lost Causes." Many Catholics had come to believe that the little-known saint had a huge "treasury of merit" to draw upon, since he was neglected and thus seldom prayed to. In fact, the Catholic Church observes October 28 as the Feast of Simon and Jude (Simon was Jude's brother, and also a disciple of Jesus). The Eastern Orthodox Church celebrates June 19 as the Feast of Judas, "Apostle and Brother of the Lord." The name St. Jude is perpetuated in the name of the famous St. Jude Children's Hospital, a favorite charity of the late entertainer Danny Thomas.

Judges
Armor, not black robes

Unfortunately, The Book of Judges is the most poorly named book in the whole Bible. The Hebrew title for what we call the Book of Judges is *Shopetim*—not really "judges" in our modern sense, but something more like "liberators" or "military leaders." The period of the judges fell between the times of the Israelite settlement in Canaan (described in the Book of Joshua) and when the nation got its first king, Saul. The Book of Judges repeats a familiar story: The Israelites forget the true God and worship idols; God allows a neighboring nation to punish them; they beg for a deliverer, and God sends them a mighty man to help fight off the enemy. Then the pattern repeats itself. A total of fifteen judges are listed, some of them little more than names. The most famous judges were Gideon, Samson, Jephthah, and the one female judge, Deborah. The theme of the book is "In those days Israel had no king: everyone did as he saw fit" (Judges 21:25, NIV). This is especially seen in chapter 19, a sordid tale of attempted homosexual rape and violent sex. In fact, with its stories of violence, sex, treachery, and even child sacrifice, it is the closest the Bible has to an X-rated story. The writers weren't trying to titillate, but to warn readers that, "This is how rotten life becomes when people forget God." Judges is a contrast to the gentle story of the Book of Ruth, which takes place in the time of the judges.

Judith
Dinner ending with a bang

The Book of Judith belongs to the Old Testament Apocrypha, meaning it is accepted as divine Scripture by Catholic and Orthodox Christians, but not by Protestants. Judith is a beautiful and virtuous Jewish widow who saves her town from the invading army of Holofernes. She has dinner with the general, who becomes drunk and lecherous and expects a sexual payoff. Judith gives him something else entirely: While he is in a drunken stupor, she cuts off his head with a scimitar. His army panics and is routed by the Jews, who honor Judith for her courage and craftiness.

With its mix of violence, sex, and intrigue, the story has been a popular subject for art, plays, and film. The pioneering silent film-maker D. W. Griffith filmed *Judith of Bethulia*. French author Jean Giraudoux also wrote a play about Judith. The film and some of the plays make the story more psychologically complex by giving Judith feelings of attraction for Holofernes. In art, Judith is often shown either holding the severed head of Holofernes or raising the sword aloft over him.

Judith is one book of the Bible that is definitely fiction, not history. The book's chronology and geography are incorrect; whoever wrote it was clearly trying to tell a "Once upon a time" type of tale, not depict a real event in history. Still, whatever the story's historical content, it is touching and inspiring.

The name Judith means "Jewess," by the way.

J

the keys of the kingdom
If only we knew the real meaning …

You may be aware that a coat of arms with two large keys is associated with the Catholic Church, specifically with the Vatican in Rome. The image of the two keys crossed to form an X has made its way into countless paintings. So what do the keys mean? The Gospels tell us that at a crucial moment, Jesus asked his twelve disciples who people believed he was. The disciple Peter had the right answer: "You are the Christ, the Son of the living God." Jesus blessed him and said, "You are Peter, and on this rock I will build my church, and the gates of Hades shall not prevail against it. And I will give you the keys of the kingdom of heaven, and whatever you bind on earth will be bound in heaven, and whatever you loose on earth will be loosed in heaven." (Matthew 16:16-19).

Roman Catholics interpret this as Jesus commissioning Peter (whose name means "rock") as the first pope, with all popes afterward having "the power of the keys." Thus the keys are the symbol of the papacy. Non-Catholics generally believe that the "rock" that is the foundation of the church is not Peter himself but the confession Peter made. "The keys of the kingdom" does not refer to earthly power (as some of the later popes believed) but to defining what is the Lord's will.

A popular novel of the 1940s was titled *The Keys of the Kingdom*, and its hero was a Catholic priest.

the kingdom of God
The Son arrives, the reign begins

The phrase "kingdom of God" occurs many times in the Gospels, and it is a poor translation, because it isn't referring to a place with actual boundaries, but to the condition of being under God's rule. "Reign of God" would probably be more appropriate. Jesus began his public work with the announcement that "the kingdom of God is at hand, repent and believe in the gospel" (Mark 1:5). He was proclaiming that the way to extend God's rule over the world was one person at a time, each person choosing to obey and follow God—in other words, reversing the sin of Adam and Eve, who chose to disobey God and give in to the serpent's temptation to "be like gods."

Jesus talked constantly about the kingdom, comparing it in parables to many things, such as a priceless pearl that a merchant found so valuable that he sold everything he had to buy it. He stated that the Jews' religious leaders not only weren't part of the kingdom, but tried to prevent others from entering (Matthew 23:13). Tax collectors and prostitutes who repented would enter into the kingdom ahead of the "respectable" people (Matthew 21:31). Satan was in some ways the "god of this world," but Jesus' power to drive out demons was evidence that Satan's kingdom was giving way to the kingdom of God (Matthew 12:28). The kingdom of God is already present, but also future, since Jesus anticipates a time when Satan is fully defeated.

In all four Gospels, the arrested Jesus was brought before Pilate and charged with being "king of the Jews." Pilate asked Jesus if it was so, and in John's Gospel Jesus gave the famous reply, "My kingdom is not of this world"—an answer Pilate couldn't grasp, since a Roman official had no conception of a "spiritual kingdom" (John 18:36). Many people who followed Jesus probably hoped he would be the military and political Messiah they longed for, a genuine king of the Jews who would boot out the Romans. Jesus was definitely not that kind of king.

Matthew's Gospel, incidentally, almost always has "kingdom of heaven" instead of "kingdom of God," but the meaning is the same.

Jesus is referred to as "king" in countless hymns and poems written over the centuries. Several works of literature have titles referring to him as king, including *The King Nobody Wanted* and Dorothy L. Sayers's twelve-part radio play *The Man Born to Be King*. Edward Elgar's 1906 oratorio about the spread of Christianity is titled *The Kingdom*.

Writing around the year 400, the influential theologian St. Augustine wrote that "the church is the kingdom of heaven on earth."

King James Version
Royally beautiful

The best-known and most quoted version of the Bible in English was published in 1611, with the approval of King James I of England. The King James Version, or KJV as it's often called, was not really a translation but a revision of earlier English Bibles. Even so, it won the public's affection after a few decades and was *the* English Bible for several centuries, and generations of English and Americans read and quoted it. It was the one book that English-speaking people everywhere had in common. All of the familiar biblical phrases found in the latter part of this book are from the KJV. Writers and public speakers used its names and phrases and expected their audience to know the source of the words. The English language changed over the centuries, of course, and "King James English" was no longer as understandable as it once was. By the mid-1900s, newer and more accurate translations were produced. None of them has become *the* English Bible the way the KJV did. Among Christians today, there is still a small minority who are KJOs—the "King James only" people who insist it is the most accurate version available, which is not strictly true; certainly its phrases are more memorable than any other English version ever published. The English themselves, by the way, have always referred to it as the Authorized Version, not the King James Version.

King James married and fathered several children, but he was actually fonder of attractive young men. He also fancied himself extremely wise and well-read, and liked to be thought of as a new Solomon, the Old Testament king famous for his wisdom. With his extreme ego, James would have been immensely pleased that the Bible named for him was read and loved by English-speaking people for more than three centuries.

King of Kings
Great title for a movie (or two)

Three times in the New Testament, Jesus Christ is referred to as "King of Kings and Lord of Lords"—in other words, Ruler above all other rulers. The title is interesting because Jesus made it clear that he was not a political king (something the Jews had hoped their Messiah would be), but rather a spiritual one, whose kingdom "is not of this world." In the Old Testament, several rulers of Babylon and Persia are referred to as "King of Kings," but their kingdoms were "of this world." Jesus' message was that the greatest power, the only kind that endures, is spiritual power.

"King of Kings" is a familiar phrase, partly because it is part of the Hallelujah Chorus in George Frideric Handel's choral work *Messiah*. It has also been used as the title for two popular movies about Jesus, the 1961 version taking great care to point out that the Jews hoped for a political king who would lead them in a revolution. The phrase has been used in hundreds of Christian hymns and is also a popular name for churches.

kiss of peace

Keep it respectable …

Some Christian churches still practice the "kiss of peace" (or "sign of peace"), which can be a light peck on the cheek but just as often is an embrace or clasping of hands. It is based on the Letters of the Paul in the New Testament, in which he urged his readers to "greet one another with a holy kiss." The practice is also rooted in Jesus' command to be reconciled to one's enemies before coming to the altar (Matthew 5:23-24). In the early years of Christianity, the pagans in the Roman Empire heard about the "kiss of peace" and spread the rumor that Christian worship consisted of people engaging in promiscuous sex.

kosher

The straight and narrow diet plan

The Hebrew word kosher literally means "proper." The kosher laws, mostly found in chapter 11 of Leviticus, govern the proper choice and preparation of foods. All plant foods may be eaten, but there are laws against certain "unclean" animals, notably the pig, but also shellfish or any sea creature lacking fins and scales. (Catfish, because they don't have scales, are forbidden.) Certain types of birds are forbidden, but none of the ones named in Leviticus are normally eaten anyway.

(The laws include bats among the list of forbidden birds. It's doubtful that many people have been tempted to break the rule against eating bats.)

Aside from prohibiting certain creatures as food, the laws stipulate how the animals must be slaughtered before cooking. Over the centuries the Jews elaborated on the rules in Leviticus, and now hey are so complex that a specially trained *shohet* has to inspect the carcasses of animals killed for food. In the early 1900s, some humane groups claimed the kosher ritual of animal slaughter was cruel, but studies showed that the method (involving one swift stroke of a knife across the main arteries in the neck) was as quick and painless as any other method.

The kosher laws prohibit any mixing of meat and dairy products (Exodus 23, Deuteronomy 14), and devout Jewish homes keep separate sets of dishes and utensils for meat and for dairy. Over the centuries, the Jews' enemies have mocked them for their avoidance of certain foods, especially since so many cultures love pork and shellfish. The ancient Romans thought pork was the finest of meats, so it appalled them that Jews would not eat it.

Most of the early Christians were Jews and out of habit continued to abide by the kosher laws. However, Acts 10 tells of the apostle Peter's vision of a tent filled with unclean animals, with a voice from heaven telling Peter to "kill and eat." Peter resists, saying he will not touch any unclean foods, but the divine voice declares that all things are clean. The message of the vision was that Peter should carry the faith to non-Jews, but early Christians also took it as a sign that the kosher laws no longer applied. Also, the Gospels report that Jesus himself pronounced that all foods were "clean" (Mark 7:19).

Although most Christians are pleased to be free from the diet restrictions of Leviticus, certain Christian groups have voluntarily chosen to abide by the old laws, notably the Seventh-day Adventists.

the Lamb of God

But were they silent?

Lambs, along with other beasts, were used in Israel's sacrifices for sin. The most notable slaughtering of lambs was in connection with Passover ritual, in which each family was to kill and eat a lamb for the Passover meal. Like all sacrificial animals, the Passover lamb was to be "without defect."

For most people, a lamb combined images of innocence and also of sacrifice. Thus Jesus was referred to as the "Lamb of God," most memorably by John the Baptist, who pointed Jesus out and said, "Behold! The Lamb of God who takes away the sin of the world!" (John 1:29). Since Jesus' crucifixion occurred near the time of Passover, the early Christians made a connection between his death and the killing of the Passover lamb. Paul stated that Christ, our Passover lamb, has been sacrificed (1 Corinthians 5:7). And 1 Peter 1:19 refers to Christ as "a lamb without blemish and without spot."

The Book of Revelation, the Bible's last book, could be called "the book of the Lamb." In its many symbolic visions, the Lamb clearly represents Christ, who, at the end of the world, triumphs over the powers of evil. Revelation 5:12 tells of a hymn of praise to the Lamb: "Worthy is the Lamb who was slain to receive power and riches and wisdom, and strength and honor and glory and blessing!" George Frideric Handel set this to music in the last segment of his *Messiah*.

The Latin phrase *Agnus Dei*, still used often in worship, means "Lamb of God," a reflection of John the Baptist's words about Jesus. Artists associate John with these words, which is why John is so often depicted holding a lamb in his arms.

The Roman Catholic mass contains the *Agnus Dei* invocation, asking the Lamb of God to have mercy and grant peace to the worshippers.

Lamentations
Wail of a book

The brief book of Lamentations follows Jeremiah in the Old Testament, and Jeremiah (the "weeping prophet") was supposedly the author. It consists of five poems lamenting the fall of Jerusalem (and the whole Jewish nation) to the Babylonians, who burned the temple, looted the city, and deported many of the people. The book actually has hope in it, seen in verses like, "The Lord is good to those who wait for him, to the soul who seeks him" (Lamentations 3:25). The book ends with, "Restore us to yourself, O Lord, that we may be restored."

Jews read the entire book aloud in their synagogue each year on the ninth day of the month of Ab, the anniversary of the destruction of the temple. Many Christian churches read portions of the book in worship services held on Good Friday and the following day, Holy Saturday, making a connection between the sadness over Jerusalem with the sadness over the crucifixion of Jesus. Many composers have set Lamentations to music.

Last Judgment / Judgment Day
Opening the divine ledger book

In both the Old and New Testaments, prophets taught that there would be a Last Judgment, or Judgment Day, when people's deeds on earth would be accounted for. Hypocrites will be exposed for what they are, and saints will be rewarded in heaven, while the wicked will be sent to hell. Most of the Old Testament prophets predicted a "day of the Lord" that would bring joy to the righteous but woe for the wicked.

People like to think of Jesus as loving and merciful, but many of his parables and teachings emphasized a coming day of judgment, notably in the parable of separating the sheep (good) from the goats (bad), found in Matthew 25. Other phrases in the Bible refer to the Judgment Day: day of the Lord, day of Christ, the last day, etc. In some places in the New Testament, it is simply referred to as "that day," on the assumption that the readers would know "that day" was the Day of Judgment.

People have been speculating for centuries about just when the Last Judgment will occur, but in fact the Bible is clear that no one knows the day or hour except God himself (Matthew 24:36-50). A key teaching of Jesus was, "Be ready at any time to be judged by God." The famous Apostles Creed, for example, states Jesus will "come to judge the living and the dead."

The Last Judgment has been a favorite subject of artists for many centuries. One of the most famous artworks ever painted is *The Last Judgment* in the Vatican, the work of Michelangelo. Unveiled in 1541, it is on the wall of the Sistine Chapel altar and is forty-eight by forty-four feet. At the top is heaven, with Christ as judge of the world and Mary at his side. Around him are apostles, patriarchs, and martyrs. The angels in the painting have no wings, the saints no haloes. In the center are the souls who have been judged: on the left, the blessed ascend to heaven, on the right the damned fall. The book of the elect is small and light, while the book of the damned is so large that two strong angels must hold it. At the bottom are the demons. Supposedly Pope Paul III, at the unveiling, said, "Lord, charge me not with my sins when Thou shalt come on the day of judgment." Michelangelo was neither the first nor last artist to paint the scene. Fra Angelico and Luca Signorelli painted frescoes of the Last Judgment in Orvieto cathedral in Italy, with green and purple devils clawing at the people in hell. Many Orthodox churches feature a *deesis*, which shows Christ enthroned in majesty, the Virgin Mary on one side, the apostle John on the other, usually as a central group in the Last Judgment, John being there for his connection with Revelation. The Judgment has also inspired many composers, including Georg Philipp Telemann, who wrote an oratorio *The Day of Judgment*. Many composers have created music to accompany the Latin poem *Dies Irae* (day of wrath) by Thomas of Celano. Colonial American poet Michael Wigglesworth wrote the long poem *The Day of Doom*, which was probably the first best-selling book in the colonial period.

"Judgment Day" has long been a part of our language, sometimes referring to the divine Judgment Day, at other times referring to some other future day of reckoning.

the Last Supper

Leonardo and a zillion others

Thanks to countless artists, this is one of the most famous events in the Bible. Before his arrest and crucifixion, Jesus shared a Passover meal with his disciples. The meal included wine and bread. Knowing what was about to happen, Jesus took the bread and told his disciples, "This is my body which is given up for you; do this in remembrance of me." Then he took the wine and said, "This cup is the new covenant in my blood, which is shed for you." At that moment the disciples probably did not know the significance of what he said. Afterward, Jesus went with the disciples (except Judas, the betrayer) to the Garden of Gethsemane, where he prayed to be spared death, but was arrested after Judas betrayed him to the Jewish authorities.

Most Christians celebrate the Lord's Supper, also called Holy Communion, or the Eucharist. Christians have argued over whether the wine and bread are really the blood and body of Christ (which Catholics believe), but all agree that the Lord's Supper is a reminder that Christ gave up his life as the ultimate sacrifice for human sin. It is one of the key incidents in Jesus' life, and Acts and the epistles affirm that the early Christians took care to celebrate the Lord's Supper regularly. Apparently the first Christians celebrated it weekly, but in later times Protestants have observed it less often, doing so monthly or even quarterly.

The scene of the Last Supper has intrigued artists because of its drama and tension. Jesus knows he is about to be betrayed and executed and that Judas is the betrayer. The other disciples are perplexed and inquisitive, not knowing the night will end with Jesus' arrest. Leonardo da Vinci painted the most famous *Last Supper* of all—not for public viewing, but for the dining hall of a monastery in Milan. (Many monasteries had paintings of the Last Supper on the dining hall walls. As the monks ate, they would have their minds on the most important meal ever eaten.) Painted directly on the wall as a fresco, da Vinci's masterpiece began to decay even before da Vinci's death, but it has been restored in recent years. Like practically every other painter of the dramatic scene, da Vinci painted Jesus and his disciples as if they were contemporaries of the artist—that is, in chairs seated at a table and dressed in biblical garb (or what the artists *thought* was biblical garb. In fact, Jesus and the disciples would have been reclining on low couches or sitting on the floor. In da Vinci's depiction, the traitor Judas has his hand on a bag, which holds the thirty pieces of silver he received for agreeing to lead the temple soldiers to Jesus. Albrecht Durer's 1523 woodcut of the *Last Supper* actually shows John asleep on the table, with Jesus' arm around him. Tintoretto's 1581 *Last Supper* in Venice shows the disciples—except Judas—with glasslike haloes. The Spanish surrealist painter Salvador Dali (1904-1989) gave the subject a bizarre twist in his *Sacrament of the Last Supper*, in which Jesus is ghostly white and beardless. (Tourists in Jerusalem can visit the Coenaculum, a small room that is reputed to be the site of the Last Supper.)

The Last Supper has been a key scene in the many movies about Jesus, and it was spoofed (rather offensively) in the film *M*A*S*H*. In the legends of King Arthur, the famous Round Table in Arthur's court was reputed to be the table of the Last Supper.

Latin

Speaking as Rome …

How did Latin become the "church language"? It didn't start that way. In the New Testament period, the international language used in much of the Roman Empire was Greek, not the Romans' own language, Latin. Most of the earliest Christian writings were in Greek, including all of the New Testament. As more Christians lived in the city of Rome, more literature was written in Latin. Tertullian, who lived in north Africa, was probably the first important theologian to write in Latin. Around 400, the scholar Jerome produced the Vulgate, the Bible written in Latin; in time it became *the* Bible for Christians in western Europe, so much so that people didn't bother translating from the original Greek and Hebrew any more. The Catholic Church taught that the Vulgate was inspired by God just as the original writings were. Even when most people in Europe stopped speaking Latin, the church continued to use it for writing religious books. Since the common people couldn't read Latin, the Bible was a "closed book" for most of the population. With the Protestant Reformation in the 1500s, the Bible was translated from the original into the languages people actually spoke (German, French, English, etc.).

Jerome's Vulgate is no longer read, but many of the passages of the Bible used in worship services still retain the Latin names he gave them, in particular the opening words of a passage. For example, Psalm 92 was known for years by its first words in Latin, *Bonum est confiteri*—in English, "It is a good thing to give thanks." Psalm 130 was known as the *De profundis*, Latin for "Out of the depths." The Catholic Church doesn't use Latin as often as in times past, but some of these Latin titles for Psalms and other passages are still used, partly because many classic choral works based on these passages are still sung in churches.

Lazarus
Back from the tomb

Lazarus and his two sisters Martha and Mary were close friends of Jesus, so close in fact that after Lazarus died and had been in the tomb for four days, Jesus came and raised Lazarus from the dead with the words "Lazarus, come forth." Found in John 11, the story not only shows Jesus' miraculous power, but also his human-ness, for the Gospel states that "Jesus loved Martha and her sister and Lazarus." It also contains the shortest verse in the Bible, "Jesus wept," a sign that Jesus was a human being, and not a distant, emotionless god. According to the Gospel, the raising of Lazarus was what made the priests and Pharisee resolve to arrest Jesus and have him executed. Not surprisingly, they also resolved to kill Lazarus, since he was a witness to the power of Jesus.

Lazarus Raised From the Dead
JOHN. CHAPTER 11, VERSES 39-44.

The raising of Lazarus is considered the greatest miracle of Jesus (aside from his own resurrection, of course). Jesus had raised other people from the dead, but the Lazarus story is unique because Lazarus was undeniably dead, having been so long in the tomb. Also, Jesus told Lazarus's sister Martha that the raising of her brother would be a preview of what would eventually happen to all people of faith.

Although the miracle is told in only one Gospel (John), almost every novel, play, or story dealing with Jesus shows the raising of Lazarus. The miracle has been painted countless times, with artists sometimes showing Lazarus already pale and decomposing. In any movie about Jesus the miracle is one of the high points.

American playwright Eugene O'Neill wrote *Lazarus Laughed*, a strange play about Lazarus's life after being raised from the dead. Franz Schubert wrote a cantata-opera called *Lazarus, or the Feast of the Resurrection*. The Catholic Church observes December 17 as the feast of St. Lazarus.

There is another Lazarus in the Bible, a character in one of Jesus' parables (SEE PAGE 267).

lectionaries
Words in seasons

Catholic, Episcopal, and some other churches use a *lectionary* in their worship services. This is a set of passages from the Old and New Testaments, assigned to each Sunday and holy day in the year. Most churches follow a three-year cycle, and in most of them, each day's reading consist of an Old Testament passage, a Psalm, a Gospel passage, and an epistle passage. Many of the readings are geared toward the season of the year. For example, the readings for Christmas are from the Gospel stories of Jesus' birth and from the Old Testament prophecies of the Messiah. The key purpose of lectionaries is to make sure that the most important passages from the Bible are read aloud in worship services. Critics of lectionaries complain that the passages are generally read with no comment and that churchgoers generally don't pay much attention to them. At the time of the Protestant Reformation in the 1500s, many preachers broke from the use of lectionaries.

Christians adopted the use of lectionaries from the practice of synagogues (Luke 4:16, Acts 13:15).

Lent
After the Mardi Gras

Lent is the forty-day period before Easter, beginning on Ash Wednesday and ending on Holy Saturday. The season has been observed since about the fourth century, and it began as a way of commemorating Jesus' forty-day period after his baptism, when he fasted in the wilderness and was tempted by Satan. The rules for fasting are very strict; for example, in the Eastern Orthodox Churches people are only allowed one meal per day, eaten after sundown, and no meat, fish, or eggs the entire forty days. The rules were gradually relaxed in other Christian churches to the point where each Christian chooses "to give up something for Lent," maybe a favorite food, to make at least a small personal sacrifice during Lent. The major idea of Lent is that people should do soul-searching and make spiritual preparation before the festive day of Easter, a day of joyous celebration of Jesus' resurrection. Because Lent used to be a period of strict fasting in most churches, the Tuesday before Lent was a day of feasting and partying, and still is in locales like New Orleans that celebrate Mardi Gras ("Fat Tuesday").

Lent is not actually mentioned in the Bible. The name comes from the Old English word *lencten*, meaning "springtime." Early Christians referred to the period by the Greek name *Tessarakoste* or the Latin *Quadragesima*, both meaning "fortieth."

leprosy
Society's outcast illness

The most mentioned disease in the Bible is leprosy, and ancient people had a horror of it, not fully understanding its causes or cures. Leprosy is a hideous condition, causing spots on the skin that thicken and turn into ulcers, which lose their covering of skin and then cause deformity and paralysis. Leviticus 13 deals in great detail with diagnosing the condition, in a "pre-scientific" fashion. It stipulates that the leper had to live "outside the camp" and wear torn clothing and disheveled hair, and would have to call out "Unclean! Unclean!" when he passed by. People in advanced stages of leprosy ended up in leper colonies, much cut off from the life of the community.

We now know that the ancient words for leprosy actually referred to any disfiguring skin disease, not just true leprosy, which is called Hansen's disease. Some of the so-called lepers in the Bible had conditions we today would call eczema or psoriasis, which are relatively easy to treat. Given the difficulty in curing any of these in ancient times, and the fact that so many skin conditions (though not all) are contagious, excluding lepers from society made sense, even though it seems terribly cruel to us.

In the Old Testament, the wonder-working prophet Elisha healed Naaman, a Syrian captain, by having him bathe in the waters of the Jordan River. Uzziah, one of the kings of Judah, contracted leprosy and had to live in quarantine until he died (2 Chronicles 26:21).

In the Gospels, Jesus healed numerous lepers, sometimes with nothing more than a touch and the words, "Be clean." On another occasion, ten lepers called out to him from a distance and begged for healing. "And as they went they were cleansed." One of them went back to Jesus, bowing and thanking him, leading Jesus to wonder why only one of the ten bothered to express gratitude (Luke 17:11-19). Jesus told his followers that the healing of lepers was one of the signs that the Messiah had come (Matthew 11:5).

letters / epistles
Non-instant messaging

Some of the most important "books" of the New Testament are actually letters written by and to the early Christians. Most of them are by the great apostle Paul, who played a founding role in some of the first Christian communities. There are also letters by Peter, James, John, and Jude—and the Letter to the Hebrews, whose brilliant author remains a mystery. All of the Letters in the New Testament were written in Greek.

Is there a difference between "letter" and "epistle"? Some Bibles call them letters, others epistles. Generally speaking, epistles were more "public"—intended for a large group instead of an individual. The letters/epistles included in the New Testament have all been extremely public—not only widely read in their own time, but over the centuries.

Even the most public of the letters often had a personal touch. Paul's Letter to the Romans, the longest and deepest of his writings, was sent to a group of Christians he did not know well. But at the end of the letter he greeted some of the Roman Christians by name. Several of his letters urge the recipients to "greet one another with a holy kiss."

Paul and others used a scribe or secretary in writing. We know this because 1 Corinthians ends with the words "I, Paul, write this greeting with my own hand"—a kind of "seal of authenticity."

Paul's letters, from Romans through Philemon, are called the Pauline Epistles. The others are called the Catholic or General Epistles, since they are not addressed to a particular group of Christians but to all Christians everywhere. The shortest books in the Bible are 2 John and 3 John, two very brief letters by the apostle John. The first books of the New Testament to be written were Paul's two letters to the Thessalonians, both written around the year 52, roughly twenty years after the crucifixion and resurrection of Jesus.

In Catholic, Orthodox, and Episcopal churches, every worship service includes a reading from one of the epistles or the Book of Acts, along with readings from the Gospels, the Psalms, and the Old Testament.

Lord

The spelling is important …

In the Bible, the word Lord occurs in three forms. Written as "lord," it refers to a human master. Written as "Lord," it refers to God and also (in the New Testament) to Christ. Written "LORD" (note the small caps), it indicates the divine name Yahweh in the Old Testament. The Jews had such a reverence for the name of God that when they read the Bible aloud, instead of saying Yahweh, they would substitute the Hebrew word *Adonai*, meaning "Lord." Most English Bibles follow the old custom of printing "LORD" where the Hebrew had *Yahweh*.

For Jews, the only true Lord was God himself, but the first Christians saw Jesus as the divine Son of God and referred to him as Lord also. One of the oldest statements of Christian belief was "Jesus is Lord" (Romans 10:9). The first Christians believed Jesus had ascended into heaven and was at "the right hand of God," and either God or Jesus could be called "Lord." In the New Testament period, followers of other gods, such as Isis or Serapis, often referred to their god as "Lord." Trouble came for the Christians when some of the Roman emperors required all people to publicly acknowledge the emperor as the only Lord—something the Christians refused to do, and which sometimes lead to their persecution and death.

In the modern world it is hard for us to grasp how much meaning the people of ancient times attached to the word "Lord." For us, "Lord" is just another way of referring to God. For the Jews and Christians, it was more than that. They lived in a world where one person could literally own another, so calling anyone

"Lord" acknowledged that you were that person's possession, that you served him without question. Referring to God or Christ as "Lord" was a way of saying, "He's the Boss, I do what pleases him."

The Book of Revelation refers to Jesus as "King of Kings, and Lord of Lords," a phrase made famous by the "Hallelujah Chorus" of Handel's *Messiah*.

the Lord's Prayer

Proto-prayer

Given how short this famous prayer is, it's worth quoting the whole thing here: "Our Father which art in heaven, hallowed be thy name. Thy kingdom come, Thy will be done in earth, as it is in heaven. Give us this day our daily bread. And forgive us our debts, as we forgive our debtors. And lead us not into temptation, but deliver us from evil: For thine is the kingdom, and the power, and the glory, for ever. Amen" (Matthew 6:9-13). The prayer is found in Jesus' famous Sermon on the Mount (SEE PAGE 335). Jesus began it by saying, "Pray after this manner." In other words, he intended it to be a *model* for people's prayers, not necessarily repeated word for word itself. In fact, just before he taught the Lord's Prayer, he told his listeners not to use "vain repetitions, as the heathen do" (Matthew 6:7). Whatever his intention was, people have prayed it ceaselessly over the centuries. It has been set to music countless times, and many churches include it as part of their regular worship services.

the lost tribes of Israel

Corporate losses

How can a whole tribe of people be "lost"? It can't, but its people can be scattered abroad so that they lose their sense of group identity. That was what happened to the ten northern tribes of Israel, which were conquered by the Assyrians in 722 B.C. (2 Kings 17). The people who weren't killed in the conquest spread throughout the Assyrian empire. Most of them probably were assimilated and ceased to think of themselves as Israelites. Since their fate is unknown, countless legends have sprung up about the "lost tribes." For example, they are the ancestors of American Indians, or of the British, or other equally silly ideas. Behind all those legends is the idea that since Israelites were God's chosen people, he must have looked after them and settled them somewhere else on the globe—in America, maybe. In fact, even some respected American colonial leaders like William Penn and Roger Williams speculated that the Indians might have been descendants of the ancient Israelites, despite all evidence to the contrary.

Lot and his wife
Salt of the earth (literally)

Lot was the nephew of the patriarch Abraham, and according to Genesis 19, he and his family were the only residents of the sinful city of Sodom that God chose to save. Genesis tells the sordid story of two divine visitors who are almost raped by the men of Sodom. The visitors strike the lecherous Sodomites with blindness and tell Lot to flee the doomed city. The family flees, and God rains down fire and brimstone (possibly meaning a volcano) on Sodom. The angels had told the family not to look back, but Lot's wife did, and she became a pillar of salt. (Jesus told his followers "Remember Lot's wife!" as a warning not to look back on one's past.) The Jews remembered Lot as a righteous man who was saved from the punishment sent on Sodom for its "sensual conduct" and "lawless deeds" (2 Peter 2:6-8).

Considering Lot's righteousness, the second part of his story is bizarre. He and his two daughters live in a cave without any other men nearby. The women get their father drunk, sleep with him, and each bears him a child. The two children become the ancestors of hostile neighbor nations, the Moabites and the Ammonites, two neighbor nations of the Israelites.

Guido Reni's painting of *Lot and His Daughters Leaving Sodom*, found in London's National Gallery, amazes people familiar with the story in Genesis, since the three people look very unhurried considering they are fleeing a city about to be destroyed by fire from heaven.

Archaeologists believe the cities of Sodom and Gomorrah are now covered by the waters of the Dead Sea, which explains why in times past the Dead Sea was sometimes called the Sea of Lot and the Sodomitish Sea. A rock formation found near the Dead Sea is traditionally pointed out to tourists as Lot's petrified wife.

Muslims regard Lot—whom they call Lut or Luth—as a prophet.

the love chapter
Paul's high point

If you've ever attended a wedding, you may have heard someone read a long and eloquent description of true love. This is the famous "love chapter" found in 1 Corinthians 13. In it, the apostle Paul describes love as "patient" and "kind," never rude or arrogant or resentful. Love "bears all things, believes all things, hopes all things, endures all things. ... Love never ends." The chapter ends with the statement that faith, hope, and love endure, "but the greatest of these is love."

Regrettably, our word "love" has multiple meanings, most of them having little to do with the unselfish *agape* Paul is discussing. The Greeks had several distinct words for love. One was *philia*, which was friendship. Another was *storge*, love for family members. And of course, there was *eros*, sexual love, or any "feels so good!" love that involved a huge chunk of selfishness. *Agape* meant the selfless "neighbor love" that Christians were supposed to have for all people, especially fellow believers. Paul actually wrote the chapter to tell Christians that although "spiritual gifts" were important, the most important of all was genuine, unselfish love.

The King James Version uses the word "charity" instead of "love." That was actually a better translation of *agape*, but it no longer has the same meaning for us because we think of "charity" as referring to welfare. So we are stuck with using "love," but at least 1 Corinthians 13 makes it clear just what kind of love is most important.

It wasn't unusual in times past for families with three daughters to name them Faith, Hope, and Charity. The Puritans who settled New England were fond of the names, and since Paul referred to charity as "the greatest of these," Charity by itself was a popular name for a girl.

Lucifer
Such a bright beginning

We use this as an alternate name for Satan or the devil, but the name actually means "light-bearer." It occurs just once in the Old Testament, Isaiah 14:12-15: "How art thou fallen from heaven, O Lucifer, son of the morning! how art thou cut down to the ground, which didst weaken the nations! For thou hast said in thine heart, I will ascend into heaven, I will exalt my throne above the stars of God… Yet thou shalt be brought down to hell." (King James Version). This passage is actually referring to the proud king of Babylon, but generations of Bible readers believed that Lucifer was Satan, an angel who tried to exalt himself too high, rebelled against God, and was cast out of heaven. Throughout Christian history, Lucifer was (and still is) used as another name for Satan.

The apostle Paul mentions that Satan "masquerades as an angel of light" (2 Corinthians 11:14, NIV). And in speaking to Timothy of the spiritual qualifications for pastors, Paul states that he must not be "a novice, lest being puffed up with pride he fall into the same condemnation as the devil" (1 Timothy 3:6). Jesus told his followers that "I saw Satan fall like lightning from heaven" (Luke 10:18), which Christians applied to the Isaiah passage quoted above. Clearly the early Christians believed that Satan/Lucifer had become conceited and changed from angel to devil. In John Milton's epic poem *Paradise Lost*, Lucifer's name is changed to Satan after he rebels against God and falls from heaven. Strangely, though, the name wasn't totally discredited, and there were some prominent Christian leaders named Lucifer. (The name's real meaning, "light bearer," still carried weight.) The name Lucifer has often been used, usually in a comic sense, for villains in various plays and movies, including the sneaky cat in Disney's animated *Cinderella*.

The Dutch poet Vondel (1587-1679) wrote a tragedy, *Lucifer*. American playwright Arthur Miller, famous for *Death of a Salesman*, also wrote *The Creation of the World and Other Business*, in which God and Lucifer are among the characters. Lucifer is one of three devils who appear in Christopher Marlowe's tragedy *Dr. Faustus*. In Dante's *Divine Comedy*, Lucifer is the ruler of hell.

The first matches that man used for starting fires were quite vile-smelling. Their sulfurous fumes reminded people of something hellish—like Satan himself. So the first matches were often called Lucifers.

Luke

Writer, artist, doctor

Luke wrote one of the four Gospels and is also the purported author of the Book of Acts. We know little about Luke except that for a while he was a traveling companion of the apostle Paul, who referred to him as "Luke the beloved physician" (Colossians 4:14). Tradition says he was a Gentile, not a Jew. Considering how much attention his Gospel and Acts devote to the Jewish temple, Luke was probably a "God-fearer," a Gentile who practiced the Jewish religion. Luke's Gospel is similar to Matthew's and Mark's, but he includes several stories not found elsewhere, notably the events relating to the birth of John the Baptist; the angels' appearance to the shepherds when Jesus was born; and several favorite parables, including the prodigal son and the good Samaritan. His Gospel also includes the story of the arrested Jesus being taken before the cynical Herod, and the story of Jesus ascending into heaven after his resurrection. As the author of the Book of Acts, Luke has been called the first historian of Christianity. Luke accompanied Paul into Macedonia, the first time the gospel had been preached in Europe. In some of his letters written from prison, Paul refers to Luke as a faithful companion (2 Timothy 4:11).

In both Luke's Gospel and in Acts, he addresses himself to someone named Theophilus. Since the name means "one who loves God," we aren't sure if it was an actual person's name, or if he intended the writings for anyone who loved God.

In Luke's Gospel and in Acts, he paints a fairly rosy picture of the Romans. His Gospel does not mention (as the other three do) that Jesus was cruelly mocked by the Roman soldiers, who crowned him with thorns. And the Roman governor Pilate looks best in Luke's account. Probably Luke wanted to make the new faith as appealing as possible to Roman readers. Luke's Gospel is the least Jewish of the Gospels—for example, he never uses the word *rabbi*, but always *teacher* or *master*. The place where Jesus was crucified Luke calls *Kranion* instead of the local Aramaic name Golgotha (although both names mean "skull").

Tradition has it that Luke was an artist, and that he painted a portrait of Jesus' mother. Thanks to this tradition, he is the patron saint of artists, and there have been numerous art schools with names like Academy of St. Luke, the one in Rome being very famous. In the early 1800s, a group of German artists lived and worked together in a vacant monastery, calling themselves the Brotherhood of St. Luke, though others referred to them as the Nazarenes. The English author Taylor Caldwell wrote a popular novel about him, *Dear and Glorious Physician* (1959). He is also a prominent character in the novel and film *The Silver Chalice*, in which he is involved in the making of the cup used at Jesus' Last Supper.

L

As one of the four Evangelists (authors of the Gospels), Luke himself has often been depicted in art, and (appropriately enough) he is shown with the tools of an artist. He is also depicted with an ox, possibly because his Gospel opens with the story of Zechariah the priest sacrificing in the temple. Catholic and Orthodox Christians celebrate October 18 as the Feast of St. Luke. The phrase "St. Luke's summer" used to refer to a warm period around October 18 (the same as our phrase "Indian summer").

Lydia
Born to the purple

Lydia was a woman in charge of business, a merchant in fine purple fabrics which were made (very expensively) from the dyes of certain seashells. Lydia met the apostle Paul, and "the Lord opened her heart to respond to Paul's message." He baptized her and her entire household, and she allowed Paul and his fellow missionaries to lodge in her home (Acts 16:11-15).

---

the Magnificat
Mary exuberant

Mary, Jesus' mother, plays an important role in the first chapters of Luke's Gospel, which tells of her receiving the news that she would bear the Son of God and that her aged cousin Elizabeth had also conceived. Mary goes to visit Elizabeth (which is known as the Visitation), and rejoices at her own and Elizabeth's good fortune, in a prayer beginning, "My soul doth magnify the Lord." In the old Latin Bible, this passage began with the word *Magnificat*, and that name has been used to identify the hymn, in which Mary praises God because "he has looked on the humble estate of his servant … from now on all generations will call me blessed"—a prophecy that certainly came true, considering the honor paid to Mary by Catholics and Eastern Orthodox.

The Magnificat's words have been set to music many times, notably by Johann Sebastian Bach.

---

make-up
The right way to face God

In many churches, women wear no make-up at all, or very little. The practice is based on 1 Peter 3, where the apostle tells Christian women, "Do not let your adorning be external—the braiding of hair, the wearing of gold, or the putting on of clothing—but let your adorning be the hidden person of the heart with the imperishable beauty of a gentle and quiet spirit, which in God's sight is very precious." This makes no mention of make-up per se, but some of the more conservative Christian churches have a tradition of no make-up, no jewelry, and no flashy clothing for women members.

Malachi
The John and Jesus prophet

Malachi is the last book of the prophets, and also the last book of the Old Testament. Christians see in his book prophecies of both Jesus and John the Baptist. Malachi predicted the coming of "the sun of righteousness" with "healing in its wings" (Malachi 4:2, NIV), which is seen as a prophecy of Jesus. Malachi also prophesied that before the "day of the Lord" (judgment day) arrived, God would send Elijah the prophet (Malachi 4:5). This is the source of the Jews' belief that Elijah (or an Elijah-like prophet) would appear before the Messiah came. Jesus and the early Christians believed that John the Baptist was that prophet. Jews, since they do not accept Jesus as Messiah, still await the coming of the Elijah-like prophet.

Christians who believe strongly in tithing (giving a tenth of one's income to the church) like to quote Malachi 3:10, in which God promises to "open the windows of heaven and pour down blessing" on people who tithe.

George Frideric Handel's *Messiah* includes some verses from Malachi: "But who may abide the day of his coming, and who shall stand when he appeareth? For he is like a refiner's fire ... and he shall purify the sons of Levi" (3:2-3).

The name, by the way, is pronounced "mal-uh-ky."

Mammon
Worldly goods (or bads)

According to Jesus, "you cannot serve both God and mammon." Many modern versions of the Bible have "money" instead of "mammon," but a better translation would be "material things." When people put too much trust in material things or love them too much, they cannot love God (Matthew 6:19-24, Luke 12:15-17).

Thanks to the use of the word "mammon" in the King James Version of Matthew 6:24, the word has been used for centuries to refer to materialism.

In John Milton's epic poem *Paradise Lost*, the name Mammon is borne by one of the rebel angels who was thrown out of heaven along with Satan. The poem says that even while he lived in heaven, Mammon was material-minded, more fascinated by the gold streets than by the presence of God. In Edmund Spenser's long poem *The Faerie Queene*, Sir Guyon is tempted in the "den of Mammon," which adjoins Hell. In both poems, Mammon is the personification of the evils of wealth. In Ben Jonson's 1610 play *The Alchemist*, Sir Epicure Mammon is a worldly sensualist.

manna and quail
Simple diet, but enough

One of the great miracles in the Bible was the long-term provision of food for the Israelites in their forty years of journeying from Egypt to Canaan. Though wandering through a bleak wilderness, the people were given a constant supply of manna, which was white, sweet-tasting, and apparently nutritious. It was sent by God every night and was collected in baskets in the morning (Numbers 11, Exodus 16).

Scholars have tried to find some natural explanation for what manna was, but clearly the Bible was talking about something miraculous by God himself. Their other form of food, however, was quail. Migrating in large flocks, quail often settled down exhausted in a place to rest, making it easy to catch and eat them (Exodus 16, Numbers 11). While the provision is "natural," believers would add that the quails' arrival at the right time was God's doing.

As a miracle food sent from God, the name *manna* has been used by many religious agencies. Christians and Jews have found spiritual meaning in manna, believing that God continues to provide for his people spiritually so they are never hungry.

The sending of manna has intrigued artists. Tintoretto's 1577 painting *Miracle of the Manna* shows the manna wafting down like snowflakes as the Israelites catch it in baskets. On a nearby mountainside, God's figure appears as a kind of shadow.

M

Mark

First with the pen and ink

Mark is a fairly minor character in the New Testament, but since he wrote one of the four Gospels (and the earliest one), he is important. In the Book of Acts, he is a cousin of the missionary Barnabas, and he accompanied Barnabas and the apostle Paul on some of their first missionary journey. For an unknown reason, he offended Paul, who would not take him on the second journey, so Paul went one way and Barnabas and Mark another. Mark went with Barnabas to the island of Cyprus, and got back in Paul's good graces, because he was in touch with Paul during Paul's imprisonment in Rome (Philemon 24, Colossians 4:10). He was privileged to know not only the great apostle Paul, but Peter as well, and Peter referred to him as "Mark, my son" (1 Peter 5:13). "My son" might be just a term of affection, but it also might meet that Peter had converted Mark to Christianity, and regarded him as his spiritual "son." This is all we know for certain about Mark.

His connection with Peter is very important because a very old tradition has it that Mark wrote down his Gospel from Peter's recollections. Since Peter was the chief among Jesus' disciples and eyewitness to important events, Mark became the recording secretary for Peter's remembrance of Jesus. The tradition is almost certainly true, and Mark's Gospel served as a framework for those of Matthew and Luke, which use many of Mark's stories word for word. Mark's Gospel doesn't start with Jesus' birth but with his baptism by John. It was probably written for Gentiles (non-Jews) because it doesn't quote the Old Testament the way Matthew's Gospel does. Unlike the other Gospels, it doesn't contain many teachings or parables, but it is a Gospel of action, with Jesus performing healings and other miracles. Mark's Gospel is the shortest of the four, and also the most frustrating because the original ending of the Gospel seems to have been lost centuries ago. Most Bibles have two or even three "possible" endings for the Gospel, which include material about the risen Jesus appearing to his disciples.

One item that Mark's Gospel includes is the curious detail that when Jesus was arrested, a young man with a sheet draped around him followed, but then fled—naked—when the guards seized him. The other Gospels don't include this detail, but some people have speculated that this was Mark himself, especially since this detail isn't pertinent to the story of Jesus. It may have been Mark's way of saying, "I was there that night Jesus was arrested, so you can trust me as a storyteller."

There are many legends about Mark, some of which may be based on fact. Supposedly he became the head of the church in Alexandria, Egypt, and died there. Centuries later, merchants from Venice were trading with Alexandria, which had come under Muslim control. They managed to sneak Mark's remains out of Alexandria by hiding them (so the story goes) under a load of pork, which the Muslims wouldn't dare come near. Mark's body supposedly ended up in Venice in St. Mark's Cathedral, where it still remains, and Venice's most famous public square is the Piazza de San Marco, St. Mark Plaza. He is the patron saint of Venice. Long ago his symbol—or the symbol of the Gospel he wrote—was a lion, which is also the city symbol of Venice. The Brera museum in Milan, Italy, has Gentile Bellini's painting *St Mark Preaching at Alexandria*.

Aside from his connections with Venice and Alexandria, Mark is a familiar figure in art because he is one of the four Evangelists (Gospel authors), usually shown writing on a scroll with a lion at his side. Mark has made one appearance in a film: In Cecil B. DeMille's 1927 movie *The King of Kings*, Mark is a young boy whose leg is healed by Jesus. He becomes a follower of Jesus and is present when Jesus is arrested—in fact, dozing on the lap of Matthew, who seems to be writing something down. It was DeMille's sly way of showing that the authors of two Gospels—Mark and Matthew—were actual witnesses to the life of Jesus.

The Catholic and Eastern Orthodox churches celebrate April 25 as the Feast of St. Mark.

Mark, incidentally, was a Roman name (*Marcus*, in full), and Mark's Jewish name was John. The Book of Acts uses both names, sometimes calling him John Mark.

Martha and Mary
Sisters with a difference

There are several Marys in the New Testament. One is known as Mary of Bethany because she lived there with her sister Martha and brother Lazarus. The two sisters figure in three stories in the Gospels. Luke 10:38 tells of Jesus visiting in their home, with Mary sitting at his feet listening while Martha busies herself as the hostess. She goes to Jesus and asks him to tell Mary to help her serve the guests, but Jesus tells her that Mary has "chosen the good portion." In other words, listening to your guest teach (especially if he is the Son of God) is more important that the normal household duties.

The sisters also figure in another story, the raising of their brother Lazarus after he had been buried for four days. (For more on this miracle, see page 216.)

After the raising of Lazarus, and just a few days before his arrest and crucifixion, Jesus went to their home again, and Mary took a container of expensive perfume and poured it on Jesus' feet, wiping them with her hair. (Ordinarily a host washed his guests' feet with water.) The disciple Judas Iscariot protested this, saying the expensive perfume could have been sold and the money given to the poor. But Jesus told Judas, "the poor you have with you always, but me you do not have always" (John 12). The moral of the story is that being "practical" isn't always right, that a generous and spontaneous show of emotion like Mary's can be a good thing.

Mary and Martha
Luke. Chapter 10, Verses 38-42.

Both the sisters and Lazarus appear often in artworks and literature, and rightly so, since they had a special place in Jesus' affections, and also because of the contrast of the busy Martha and the attentive Mary. Johannes (Jan) Vermeer's *Christ in the House of Martha and Mary* (c. 1645, National Gallery of Scotland) has the familiar pose; Mary sitting attentively at Jesus' feet, Jesus scolding Martha, who holds a basket. Velazquez's 1620 version in the National Gallery, London, seems more formal. In 2000, the TV movie *Jesus* had a romantic subplot in which Mary and Jesus are attracted to each other, but Jesus does not pursue the relationship because of his sense of mission. A very different situation is seen in the 1988 film *The Last Temptation of Christ*, in which Jesus on the cross has a vision of living a normal life as a family man, marrying both Martha and Mary and having children by both.

In Catholic tradition, Martha is the symbol of the "active" life, Mary the symbol of the "contemplative" life, based on their behavior in Luke 10:38-42. Martha is the patron saint of cooks and housekeepers, and her feast day is

July 29. Pope John Paul II built the Domus Sanctae Marthae—St. Martha's house—a guest residence in the Vatican. It housed the cardinals who elected his successor, Benedict XVI.

Mary Magdalene

Not the woman you thought she was …

The Mary Magdalene of *Jesus Christ Superstar* and various books and movies may have been a reformed prostitute, but the Mary Magdalene in the Bible wasn't. The Bible doesn't say much about her at all, frankly. Two of the Gospels say that Jesus had cast seven demons out of her (Mark 16:9, Luke 8:2) and afterward she became a devoted follower. She was present at his crucifixion, saw the body to its burial, and on the day of resurrection saw the angels who told her Jesus was risen. Then she became the first person to encounter the risen Jesus (Matthew 28:1-8), which she then reported to Jesus' disciples. That is all we know for certain about her.

However, Luke 7:36-50 tells the incident of "a woman who had lived a sinful life," who anoints Jesus' feet with expensive perfume, weeping while she does so. Jesus' host is not pleased, but Jesus knows she is repentant over her past life. He tells her, "Your faith has saved you, go in peace" (Luke 7:50). The woman is not named. Two verses later, Luke mentions Mary Magdalene and her seven demons being cast out by Jesus. People have imagined that the "sinful woman" and Mary Magdalene were one and the same.

In Christian tradition, Mary was a privileged person, being the first to see the risen Jesus. The Catholic and Orthodox churches celebrate her feast day on July 22. But to most people this is immaterial because they think of her as a prostitute—or *reformed* prostitute, rather. Since we know that Jesus mingled with prostitutes (and presumably reformed some of them), having a name like Mary Magdalene to attach to one of them serves a purpose. She becomes something people love: The bad girl who turns good.

As such, she has been represented in thousands of paintings and sculptures, usually shown weeping (like the nameless "sinful woman" of Luke 7) over her sins. She is also seen in many paintings with the title *Noli Me Tangere*—Latin for "touch me not," the words the resurrected Jesus says to her in John 20:17. The idea that she had been a prostitute goes back many centuries, but the fictional idea that she was in love with Jesus is recent, probably from a German novel of the 1800s. When Cecil B. DeMille made his 1927 movie *The King of Kings*, he was tempted to include a suggestion of romance between Jesus and Mary Magdalene, but dropped it from the script, fearing people would be offended. The idea came to vivid life in *Jesus Christ Superstar*, where the reformed Mary is in love, semi-platonically, with Jesus, so different from the men she knew in her past life. *Superstar* contains the scene from Luke 7, with Mary anointing Jesus' feet with the expensive perfume, and Judas complaining about the waste. In the 1977 TV movie *Jesus of Nazareth*, Mary is shown as a prostitute who reforms. The 1988 movie *The Last Temptation of Christ* not only showed Mary Magdalene as a prostitute, but showed her "at work," and with Jesus watching her, which created a huge controversy. In this film, she and Jesus had been sweethearts, but when he rejected her, she turned to a life of prostitution. Cecil B. DeMille's 1927 *The King of Kings* had Mary as a prostitute—not a common whore, but a well-paid courtesan living in luxury. However, in DeMille's movie, he follows the Bible and has Jesus cast seven demons

The Risen Christ Appears to Mary Magdalene
JOHN. CHAPTER 20, VERSES 14-17.

out of her. The 2000 TV movie *The Miracle Maker*, done in clay animation, had Jesus cast seven demons out of Mary, and she was *not* a prostitute. However, the 2000 TV movie *Jesus* had her as the reformed prostitute. In the 2004 film *The Passion of the Christ*, Mary Magdalene is not a prostitute, but, rather, the woman who was almost stoned for adultery—not in the Bible, but an interesting departure from the usual. She got an added jolt of fame in the best-selling book (later a movie) *The Da Vinci Code*, which reveals the "secret" that Mary and Jesus married and had children, and that these were the ancestors of the kings of France. Mary Magdalene is one of the solo parts in Edward Elgar's two oratorios about the early Christians, *The Apostles* and *The Kingdom*. She was the subject of an oratorio by opera composer Jules Massenet.

Regardless of whether she was a prostitute or not, Mary Magdalene's name is perpetuated in hundreds of churches and religious schools across the world.

Both Oxford and Cambridge Universities in England have a college named for her—Magdalen at Oxford, Magdalene at Cambridge. Several names for women are variations of her name—Magdalena, Madeleine, etc. Along with Jesus' mother Mary, her fame also helped perpetuate Mary as a common name for girls. The combination Maria Magdalena was common, and in fact this was the birth name of German film star Marlene Dietrich.

The name Magdalene, by the way, is probably from the village of Magdala. The English pronounce Magdalene as "maudlin," and a "maudlin home" referred to a "halfway house" for reformed prostitutes. "Maudlin" also was used as an adjective meaning "overly emotional," since many artworks showed Mary in tears, weeping over her sins.

Mary, mother of Jesus
The appeal of the virgin mother

The Bible mentions Mary only a few times, yet she is one of the most honored people of the Bible, second only to Jesus himself. According to Luke 1, she was engaged to Joseph, but while still a virgin she learned from the angel Gabriel that she would bear God's Son. Joseph was tempted to quietly break the engagement, but an angel told him to marry her, for she would indeed bear the Son of God. She and Joseph went to Bethlehem for a census, and while there she bore Jesus in a stable, where they were visited by shepherds and the Magi. Later she and Joseph presented the infant in the Jerusalem temple, where Simeon and Anna blessed him, with the aged Simeon predicting that a sword would "pierce her soul." At age twelve, Jesus went again with Mary and Joseph to the temple, where they found him conversing wisely with the Jewish teachers. Luke's Gospel says that, "His mother kept all these things in her heart" (Luke 2:51).

Once Jesus reaches adulthood, Mary is mentioned only a few times. She was present at Cana when he turned water into wine (John 2:3), his first miracle. Matthew 12:46-50 says that on another occasion, while Jesus was talking to the crowd, his mother and brothers stood outside, wanting to speak to him, and Jesus responded, "'Who is my mother and who are my brothers?' And He stretched out his hand toward his disciples and said, 'Here are my mother and my brothers! For whoever does the will of my Father in heaven is my brother and sister and mother.'"

M

John's Gospel states that Mary was present at Jesus' crucifixion, and though in agony, he spoke tenderly to her: "When Jesus therefore saw his mother there, and the disciple whom he loved standing nearby, he said to his mother, 'Woman, behold your son'" (John 19:26). The last mention of Mary in the Bible is Acts 1:14: "They [the disciples] all continued with one accord in prayer and supplication, with the women and Mary the mother of Jesus, and with His brothers."

By around A.D. 300, Mary was referred to as "Mother of God," and later the Catholic Church decreed that she, like Jesus, was sinless and that instead of dying she was taken bodily into heaven. The Protestants broke with the Catholic tradition in regard to honoring Mary—they did not see her as sinless and did not think it appropriate to call her "Mother of God" or "Queen of Heaven" or other titles that have been applied to her. Protestants also don't agree that Mary was "ever virgin." Matthew's Gospel says that Joseph married Mary but "did not know her [sexually] until she had given birth to a son" (Matthew 1:25). Since the Gospels mention Jesus having several brothers, Protestants assume that after Jesus' birth, Joseph and Mary had other children in the usual way. Catholics insist that Joseph and Mary had no children (and that Mary remained a virgin). They believe that Jesus' "brothers" were Joseph's sons by an earlier marriage, which is why Joseph is often shown as being much older than Mary. This disagreement has been going on for centuries.

The rosary devotions popular with Catholics involve meditating on twenty "mysteries" in the life of Jesus and his mother. The "mysteries" are divided into four series, each prayed on specific days of the week. The Joyful Mysteries are The Annunciation, The Visitation, The Birth of Jesus, The Presentation, and Finding the Boy Jesus in the Temple. The Luminous Mysteries are The Baptism of Jesus, The Wedding at Cana, The Proclamation of the Kingdom, The Transfiguration, and The Last Supper. The Sorrowful Mysteries are The Agony in Gethsemane, The Scourging, The Crowning of Thorns, The Carrying of the Cross, The Crucifixion. The Glorious Mysteries are The Resurrection, The Ascension, The Descent of the Spirit, The Assumption of Mary, and The Coronation of Mary as "Queen Of Heaven." The familiar Catholic prayer beginning, "Hail, Mary, full of grace," is taken from Luke's Gospel and is often known by its Latin name *Ave Maria*. It has been set to music by countless composers.

Aside from devotional prayers, the mother of Jesus has been the subject of countless paintings and statues, often referred to as Madonna ("my lady"), especially when seen holding the baby Jesus. She is often shown being approached by the

Angel Gabriel at the Annunciation, celebrated by Catholics by tradition on March 25—nine months from Christmas. She is also depicted calling upon her relative Elizabeth (the Visitation, May 31) or with Joseph and the shepherds in Bethlehem (Christmas, of course). She is depicted in paintings of the miracle at Cana and at the crucifixion. (Some churches have "memorial windows" showing Mary with the Bible verse, "There stood at the cross of Jesus his mother"—a window usually donated in memory of someone's mother, of course.) Mary is also seen in paintings of Jesus being taken down from the cross (the Deposition). In the famous image called the Pieta, she is holding the dead Christ in her arms, an image best known in Michelangelo's classic sculpture in the Vatican. These events are rooted in the Bible, while the other holy days celebrated by Roman Catholics are not—the Immaculate Conception, the Assumption, the Queenship of Mary, the Solemnity of Mary, and others. Catholics often refer to her by the abbreviation BVM—Blessed Virgin Mary. Thousands of churches are named for or dedicated to the Virgin Mary, and many others contain a Lady Chapel, dedicated to Mary, within their walls.

Mary's parents are not named in the Bible, but a very old writing called the Proto-evangelium of James refers to them as Joachim and Anna. Roman Catholics commemorate them on July 26. Eastern Orthodox churches commemorate them on September 9.

Aside from countless artworks, Mary has been portrayed in most works of literature connected with the life of Jesus. Novelist Sholem Asch (1880-1957) wrote a best-selling novel about her. Popular author Marjorie Holmes wrote *Two from Galilee*, about young Mary and Joseph. There are many others, too numerous to mention. Most recently she was a key character in Anne Rice's novel *Christ the Lord: Out of Egypt*, dealing with Jesus' boyhood.

In films about Jesus, Mary is, of course, an important character. In films directed by devout Catholics such as Franco Zeffirelli (the *Jesus of Nazareth* TV miniseries) and Mel Gibson (*The Passion of the Christ*), Mary seems to play a larger role than the Gospels would indicate, but generally Protestants have not objected much.

The name Mary was a common one in New Testament times. Written *Mary-am* in Aramaic, it was a form of the Old Testament name Miriam, the name of Moses' sister. Besides Jesus' mother, there are at least five other Marys in the New Testament. The name Mary is one of the most common women's names in Christian cultures.

Matthew
The tax man cometh

Jesus' disciples were a mixed group since they included Simon the Zealot. The Zealots were Jews who advocated violent resistance to Roman rule. And one type of man the Zealots hated was a Jew who collected taxes for the Romans. Matthew was one, and having him and Simon in the same band must have tested their capacity for building bridges. The Gospels say that Matthew was busy at work when Jesus called him to be a disciple, and that Jesus dined at his house, and was criticized for hobnobbing with social outcasts like tax collectors and other sinners. Jesus uttered his famous words, "I came not to call the righteous, but sinners." Interestingly, Mark's and Luke's Gospels refer to the man as Levi, but it wasn't unusual to bear two names, and Matthew and Levi were certainly the same person.

Tradition says that Matthew wrote one of the Gospels, the one that comes first in the New Testament. It includes most of the material in the shorter Gospel of Mark, but adds a lot of other material, notably the famous Sermon on the Mount, found in chapters 5-7, one of the most quoted sections of the Bible. Matthew's Gospel is distinctive because it quotes the Old Testament more than the other three Gospels put together. Matthew regarded many events in the life of Jesus as the "fulfillment" of passages in the Old Testament. It is probable that Matthew wrote his Gospel for Christians who were reared as Jews, since he begins the Gospel with a genealogy tracing Jesus' descent from Abraham, the physical and spiritual ancestor of the Jews. That genealogy also includes David, the king that the Jews remembered so fondly. For Matthew, Jesus was the Messiah that Jews had long hoped for.

Matthew includes several stories of Jesus encountering Gentiles who had faith—probably as a way of letting Jewish readers know they were foolish not to accept Jesus as Messiah, since even the better sort of non-Jews accepted him. Matthew's Gospel is the only one to include the story of the wise men (Magi) visiting the infant Jesus, and the related story of wicked King Herod ordering the killing of the infants of Bethlehem. It also contains often-quoted "woes" against the Jewish religious leaders, condemning their hypocrisy and legalism. Matthew's

Gospel uses the phrase "kingdom of heaven" instead of "kingdom of God," but the meaning was the same. Matthew's Gospel ends with the Great Commission, in which the resurrected Jesus commands his disciples to go and preach the gospel to all nations.

As one of the four Evangelists (authors of the Gospels), Matthew has been featured often in Christian art. Paintings show him writing his Gospel, often with an angel looking over his shoulder.

The Catholic Church celebrates September 21 as the Feast of St. Matthew, while for Orthodox churches it is November 16. Since he was a tax collector, Matthew is the patron saint of accountants, bookkeepers, and (of course) tax collectors. A tradition says he took the gospel to Parthia (now Iran) and was martyred.

In films about Jesus, Matthew is relatively unimportant, though in the silent film classic *The King of Kings* (1927), Matthew is shown writing things down, as if taking notes to use in his Gospel. Johann Sebastian Bach composed a *St. Matthew Passion*, a choral work on Jesus' crucifixion using words from Matthew's Gospel.

Maundy Thursday
Command performance

Many churches refer to the day before Good Friday as Maundy Thursday, the day of Jesus' Last Supper with his disciples, followed by his agony in the Garden of Gethsemane and his arrest. The name Maundy comes from the Latin words *Mandatum novum*—meaning "new commandment." In John's Gospel, Jesus washes the feet of his disciples—a reminder to them that the best master is one who serves others—then teaches them many things, including a "new commandment," that they love each other (John 13:34). Most churches include Holy Communion as part of their Maundy Thursday worship services, and some also include a ritual of members washing each other's feet, a symbol of being servants of each other.

In Great Britain, it has been the custom for centuries for the monarch to perform the footwashing at a Maundy Service to which the poor were invited. The custom continues, though now the sovereign distributes money instead of washing feet, and the "poor" are more likely to be people (usually older ones) singled out for selfless community service. The British mint used to produce silver coins known as *Maundy money* for the monarch to give to the poor on Maundy Thursday.

Melchizedek

What, no parents?

In the Bible, no one has a last name, so everyone is identified as "son of So-and-so" or "daughter of So-and-so." In the few cases where someone's father is not mentioned, there is a certain mystery about the person. One of these cases is the mysterious Melchizedek, a figure in the story of the patriarch Abraham. After fighting and winning a battle, Abraham encounters him for the first time: "Melchizedek king of Salem brought forth bread and wine: and he was the priest of the most high God" (Genesis 14:18). It was rare in ancient times for the same person to be both a priest and a king. Melchizedek was king of Salem, a locale identified with Jerusalem. He blessed Abraham "in the name of the most high God." Abraham gave him a tithe (a tenth) of his booty from the day's battle.

That is all Genesis tells of him, and he would be forgotten except that Psalm 110:4 refers to someone being "a priest forever, in the order of Melchizedek." What the author of this Psalm meant, no one knows. But the early Christians applied it to Jesus, believing that he was not only the "king of kings" but also a "heavenly priest" as well. In the New Testament, the Letter to the Hebrews drives this point home. Israel's priesthood traced its descent to Aaron, the brother of Moses. Many of the priests had been rather corrupt (including the ones who condemned Jesus to death), so the Letter of the Hebrews notes that there was a better priesthood, one that began earlier than Aaron's, and that was Melchizedek. Also, Abraham, the founder of the faith, had paid homage to Melchizedek, meaning Melchizedek was earlier and more important than Aaron. In fact, Melchizedek was the first priest mentioned in the Bible, so he was the "proto-type." Psalm 110:4 said this Melchizedek-type priest would be "forever," an eternal one. The Letter to the Hebrews pictures Christ in heaven, being the eternal high priest who mediates between human beings and God (Hebrews 5-7). The fact that Melchizedek's father is not named in Genesis gave the early Christians the idea that he was "eternal"—and that in some sense, Jesus Christ "was" Melchizedek. This is fitting, since Melchizedek's name means "king of righteousness."

Melchizedek blessing of Abraham has been a frequent subject for artists.

The Latter-day Saints (Mormons) have an Order of Melchizedek for their men. Following what the Letter to the Hebrews says about Melchizedek outranking the priest Aaron, the Order of Melchizedek outranks the Order of Aaron.

Micah
The Nativity prophet

Micah was one of the Old Testament prophets. He was associated with Christmas because of his prediction that the town of Bethlehem would be the birthplace of "one who is to be ruler in Israel, whose origin is from of old, from ancient days" (Micah 5:2). Christians believe the prophecy came to pass when Jesus was born in Bethlehem. The prophecy is quoted in Matthew's Gospel when King Herod's court advisors inform the wise men that the "newborn king" they are seeking would be in Bethlehem.

The Book of Micah is the source of several often-quoted lines, such as his prediction of a peaceful time when people would "beat their swords into plowshares and their spears into pruning hooks; nation shall not lift up sword against nation, neither shall they learn war any more" (Micah 4:3). Another often-quoted line: "He has told you, O man, what is good, and what does the Lord require of you but to do justice and to love kindness, and to walk humbly with your God?" (Micah 6:8).

Michal
Wife with strife

Michal was the daughter of one king and wife of another. The daughter of Israel's first king, Saul, she fell in love with Israel's rising star, the handsome, valiant David. Her father was jealous of David's rising popularity, so he told David he could marry Michal, but there was a "bride price": two hundred foreskins cut off the enemy, the Philistines (1 Samuel 18:25-27). Saul assumed David would never come back alive from that quest, but he underestimated David, who presented him with the "trophies" of his fighting. David and Michal married, and Michal had to choose between loyalty to her husband or loyalty to her father. Saul sent men to kill David, and Michal helped him escape, deceiving the men by hiding an idol in David's bed (1 Samuel 19).

This story of a loyal wife ends sadly. When David had the ark of the covenant brought into Israel, it was a festival day, and in his religious frenzy, "David danced before the Lord with all his might," bare-chested and footloose. Michal watched and "she despised him in her heart." When David came home from his grand celebration, Michal icily scolded him for making a spectacle of himself in front of all the women. David reminded her that he now reigned in place of her father, and he didn't need her approval to "make merry before the Lord" (2 Samuel 6:16-23). Apparently this ended their romantic life altogether, because the Bible says "the daughter of Saul had no child to the day of her death."

In two films made of the David saga, *David and Bathsheba* (1951) and *King David* (1985), David's adultery with Bathsheba is condoned because of Michal's behavior.

Michael the archangel
Captain of the clouds

The Bible gives names to only two angels: Michael and Gabriel. (If you count the Apocrypha as part of the Bible, there is a third, Raphael, who appears in the Book of Tobit.) Michael is named in only two books. In Daniel, he is described as a "prince," suggesting he rules over the other angels. He is also said to be Israel's divine guardian (Daniel 10:13, 21; 12:1). But most of our beliefs about Michael come from the Book of Revelation, where, at the end of the world, Michael leads heaven's angels in defeating the great dragon, who is Satan (Revelation 12:7). Also, the brief Letter of Jude states that Michael and Satan fought over who would obtain the body of the deceased Moses, and Michael won. Verse 9 of the Letter of Jude is the only place in the Bible that refers to Michael as an "archangel."

Since The Book of Revelation describes this as a "war in heaven," Michael has always been pictured in art as a very muscular, masculine figure (but always beard-less), clad in armor and carrying either a sword or spear. He is often shown standing triumphant over a hideous (and beaten) dragon. Probably the most famous image of him is *St. Michael Vanquishing Satan*, by Raphael, found in Paris's Louvre. In the painting, Michael spreads his wings wide and thrusts a spear down at the half-human, half-dragon Satan. Michael is considered the patron saint of soldiers and policemen. Throughout history, armies of Christian countries have called upon Michael for aid as they fight against unbelievers. The Crusaders, out to recover the Holy Land from the Muslims, often prayed to Michael for aid.

Probably the most famous Michael in any artwork is the enormous sculpture *St. Michael Triumphing Over the Devil*, by Jacob Epstein. This is on the front of Coventry Cathedral in England, a church severely damaged during World War II. The armor-clad Michael stands with his foot on the head of a very human-shaped (and horned) Satan.

Because he was described as leading heaven's army of angels, tradition has called him an "archangel," meaning "ruling angel," although the word "archangel" does not appear often in the Bible. For many years he was celebrated by Catholics on September 29, a day called Michaelmas. Later the church changed the celebration to one for all three archangels—Michael, Gabriel, and Raphael. For many years, Mount Gargano in Italy drew Christian pilgrims from all over Europe, in the belief that Michael had appeared on the mount in the year 492. The town near it was called Monte Sant'Angelo, Mount of the Holy Angel.

Michael and His Angels Fight the Dragon
REVELATIONS. CHAPTER 12, VERSES 7-12.

Though the Bible says little about Michael, Jews and Christians did a lot of speculating about him. Some said it was he who stopped Abraham from sacrificing Isaac. He was also supposed to be the angel that killed 185,000 Assyrians under their king Sennacherib. In fact, wherever the Old Testament has "angel of the Lord," some readers concluded this referred to Michael. Many Catholics believe that Michael came to Mary at the time of her death and took her bodily into heaven.

Michael is an important character in John Milton's epic poem *Paradise Lost*. Although the poem's main subject is the temptation of Adam and Eve, it also tells of the war in heaven (before the earth was created) between God's army, led by Michael, and the rebel angels, led by Satan. The old black spiritual "Michael, Row the Boat Ashore" is asking the angel Michael to carry the person's soul across the "river of death" into heaven.

Both Michael and Gabriel are mentioned in the Koran.

Michael became an extremely popular name for boys in the last half of the twentieth century.

Russia's large port city of Archangel was founded in 1583 and originally named Archangel Michael. Even though the Soviet Union was officially Communist and atheist, the name of the city was never changed.

In England in the 1400s and 1500s, a coin called the "angel" was in circulation, with one side bearing an image of Michael slaying Satan. The Legion of the Archangel Michael, also called the Iron Guard, was a twentieth-century military-political organization in Romania, considered fascist but, unlike other fascist movements, was overtly religious, claiming to be rooted in the Romanian Orthodox Christian tradition.

millennium
Years, or moments that seem like years?

We all know that a millennium is a thousand years, but when Christians talk about *the* millennium, they are referring to the Book of Revelation, with its prophecy of a thousand-year reign of the saints on earth, a period when Satan will be bound, then unleashed again at the end of the thousand years (Revelation 20:1-10). Since Revelation is full of symbols and numbers, readers can never be certain if anything in the book is strictly literal. Generally Bible scholars have assumed that the thousand years is symbolic, or allegorical—anything but a literal thousand years. But for the last two thousand years, many Christians have thought the thousand years would be literal and taking place on the earth. Movements and sects that believe themselves to be part of this "reign of the saints" are called *millenarian*. These movements have been a mixed bag, attracting some genuinely devout people, but also attracting shysters and misguided fanatics. Some contemporary groups that began as millenarian movements are the Jehovah's Witnesses and the Seventh-day Adventists. The Christian sect known as the Shakers referred to itself as the Millennial Church.

During the hundreds of years that Christianity was the established religion in Europe, theologians and Bible scholars taught that the millennium predicted in Revelation 20 had already taken place. More sensitive Christians looked at the corrupt church hierarchy with its materialistic bishops and philandering priests and could see that this state of affairs was definitely *not* the reign of the saints prophesied in Revelation.

One key to understanding why many Christians don't take the thousand years literally is that the Bible insists that for God (with the eternal perspective), a thousand years are like a day (Psalm 90:4, 2 Peter 3:8).

miracles
Things that can't happen, but do

People who haven't read the Bible might assume it is full of miracles from beginning to end. There are plenty of miracles, but they tend to cluster around certain key people and events. The creation of the world at the beginning is the first one miracle, even if there are some who don't believe it was done in six twenty-four-hour days. The next big cluster of miracles is in the time of Moses, when God sent plagues on the Egyptians, manna and quail to feed the Israelites, and made the dramatic parting of the Red Sea. There are a few miracles in Joshua and Judges, a handful in 1 and 2 Samuel, then come the miracle-laden careers of the prophets Elijah and Elisha. The New Testament is full of miracles, not only in the life of Jesus, but also in his apostles lives. Almost all miracles are done to demonstrate God's love and compassion for mankind. The miracle-workers in the Bible aimed to help people, not dazzle and amaze them—although the miracles did have that effect, of course.

Even skeptics admit there are plenty of things in the universe that science can't quite explain. Founding Father Benjamin Franklin, very skeptical about the Bible, claimed he believed in the miracle of Jesus turning water into wine—but that it was also a miracle the way ordinary grapevines absorb water and sun and in time produce wine. The Cana miracle, as Franklin saw it, was merely a speeding up of a process we think of as natural.

Moloch
Heavy metal deity

The gruesome god Moloch was worshipped by the Ammonites, a neighbor nation of Israel. In some worship sites, a huge metal image of Moloch was heated like a furnace while infants who had just been slaughtered were placed in its arms and burned. The sacrifice was accompanied by cymbals and other noises—probably to drown out the children's cries. Most people of Israel, especially the prophets, were appalled at human sacrifice, especially child sacrifice, even though it was fairly common in the ancient world. Many Israelites worshipped Moloch, something the prophets condemned. Some of the kings, even the wise Solomon, set up worship sites for Moloch. The wicked king Manasseh was noted for sacrificing his own sons to Moloch (2 Kings 21:6). The reformer king Josiah ended the practices. Archaeologists in the Middle East have, to their horror, dug up "foundation sacrifices"—bones of children that apparently were sacrificed at the dedication of a house or temple.

The best-known site for the horrible worship of Moloch was the Valley of Ben Hinnom outside Jerusalem. This spot had such a reputation that, in the period between the Old and New Testaments, some Jewish writers claimed that Ben Hinnom was the gateway to hell. The name eventually morphed into the name Gehenna, which is the word used in the Greek New Testament to mean "hell."

In many Jewish and Christian legends, the gods of the pagan nations were often thought of as demons, cohorts of Satan. We see this in the great epic poem *Paradise Lost* by John Milton. The well-read Milton knew Hebrew (and numerous other languages), and in his poem he refers to Moloch as the "grisly king," recalling that the name Moloch literally means "king."

In the silent movie classic *Metropolis* (one of the masterpieces of German director Fritz Lang), there is a disturbing scene in which the robot-like industrial workers appear to be thrown as sacrifices into a Moloch-like furnace. The name "Moloch!" flashes on the screen. Lang and his scriptwriter were alluding to the bloodthirsty Moloch of the Bible.

money-lending
Interesting foreigners

It is hard to imagine a society with no-interest loans, but the Old Testament law prohibited the Israelites from charging interest (Exodus 22:25)—to another Israelite, that is. The law stated that foreigners could be charged interest (Deuteronomy 23:20). As Christianity spread over the Middle East and Europe, Christians abided by the old law and did not loan at interest—but

Jews living among Christians could (and this was fine with the Jews, since Christians were "foreigners"). The old stereotype of the Jewish money-lender (as in Shakespeare's play *The Merchant of Venice*) is rooted in both Jews and Christians trying to abide by the old law against charging interest to people of one's own religion. People seem to despise money-lenders, which is one of the roots of anti-Semitism.

Moriah
Temple central

It is mentioned only twice in the Bible, but because it was a sacred spot, the name has traveled far and wide, and it seems to be a favorite name for rural churches. In Genesis, God told Abraham to go to the "region of Moriah" and sacrifice his only son, Isaac—a story with a happy ending, since an angel stopped Abraham at the last minute (Genesis 22). But Moriah's real fame was in being the location of the temple of Jerusalem, built by King Solomon (2 Chronicles 3:1). (Note that Abraham performed a sacrifice there, and later a temple, the center of sacrifices, was built there.)

People often think that Israel's temple was on Zion, but, in fact it, was on Moriah. Zion was another hill in Jerusalem, but over time the name Zion came to stand for all of Jerusalem, so that people would talk of the "temple of Zion."

Moses
Meeting God, up close and personal

Moses is one of the great men of history, revered by Jews, Christians, and Muslims as a holy prophet who delivered God's laws to mankind and led the Hebrew slaves out of Egypt. He is the most important figure in the Old Testament, honored by Jews even more than their great ancestor, Abraham, and their most beloved king, David. His story is timeless: a son of Hebrew slaves in Egypt is hidden by his mother in the river to escape a mass slaughter of Hebrew children. The infant, floating in a basket, is taken in by an Egyptian princess and raised in the luxurious court, but then finds on reaching adulthood that he is of Hebrew blood. He kills

The Discovery of Moses
EXODUS. CHAPTER 2, VERSES 1-8.

an Egyptian overseer for abusing a slave, then flees into the wilderness, finding shelter (and a wife, Zipporah) in the land of Midian, where life seems peaceful and predictable until one day God speaks to him from a burning bush and tells him he will lead the slaves out of Egyptian bondage, and many miracles will clear the way. (SEE PAGE 59 for more about the fateful burning bush encounter.) Moses and his long-lost brother Aaron confront Egypt's Pharaoh and deliver God's word: "Let my people go." The hard-hearted king refuses, but one by one the ten plagues God sends on the Egyptians break down their resistance. After the death of all the firstborn in Egypt, Pharaoh finally sets the slaves free, but once they have departed, he changes his mind and pursues them with an army. At the Red Sea (SEE PAGE 303), God parts the waters for the Hebrews to pass through, then releases the waters on the Egyptians, drowning Pharaoh's men. (See the separate entries for Exodus and the ten plagues.)

Freedom from Egypt brings no relief, for after Pharoah, Moses is threatened by rebellion and constant complaints from the Hebrews, who lament that slavery in Egypt was better than the dry, barren wilderness they pass through. God sends a miraculous food (manna) so the people will not starve, but still they complain. The people camp at the foot of the holy mountain, Sinai, and Moses ascends the mountain to receive God's law from the hand of God himself. He is gone so long that the people grow restless and fearful, and they persuade his brother Aaron to make a golden calf idol. An orgy breaks loose in the camp while Moses is speaking with God (SEE PAGE 131). Moses faces other rebellions, including his own brother and sister (Aaron and Miriam) guilty of sibling jealousy. Numbers 16 tells of the dramatic rebellion of Korah, who was jealous of the leadership of Moses and Aaron. Korah and his 250 fellow rebels were swallowed up in an earthquake. Time and time again Moses has to plead with God not to destroy the rebellious, ungrateful Israelites.

The former slaves require forty years to get from Egypt to the promised land of Canaan. Poor Moses himself never enters the land, his punishment for disobeying

God on just one occasion. He dies on Mount Nebo on the edge of Canaan and is buried by God himself, and no one knows the site of his grave. His mysterious burial was the source of legends that he did not die at all, but was taken into heaven. In the popular stage play and film *The Green Pastures*, Moses is hurt that he does not get to enter Canaan, but God consoles him by saying that heaven is much nicer than Canaan.

Moses was a privileged man in many ways, notably in that the Lord would "speak to Moses face to face, as a man speaks to his friend" (Exodus 33:11). When he came down from the mountain with the stone tablets after meeting with God, "the skin of his face shone because he had been talking with God." In fact, his face was so radiant, he had to put a veil over it (Exodus 34:29-35).

Moses was privileged in another respect: He was one of the few men who had a good relationship with his father-in-law. This was Jethro, the priest of Midian, who married his daughter Zipporah to Moses. It was while he tended Jethro's flocks that he met God in the burning bush. Exodus 18 tells of the two men greeting each other with a kiss, then Jethro offering Moses some sound advice on how to settle disputes among the bickering Israelites.

The Jews regarded Moses as a great prophet, and also as the lawgiver. In the New Testament period, Moses was the most revered man in Jewish history, the presumed author of the first five books of the Bible, and the giver of the Laws that had become the spiritual foundation of the Jewish faith. Some of the early Christians saw Jesus as a kind of second Moses, greater than the first one. Jesus himself honored Moses, and in the mysterious event called the Transfiguration, Moses and the prophet Elijah both appeared on a mountain, radiant and speaking with Jesus. Jesus was critical of the Jews who had become so obsessed with keeping every detail of the Law that they lost sight of the real goal, which he said was loving God and one's fellow man. Jesus' famous Sermon on the Mount (Matthew 5-7) is regarded by Christians as a kind of "fine-tuning" of Moses' laws, emphasizing the inner attitudes of people instead of just the outward obedience. The apostle Paul had been brought up to observe the laws of Moses faithfully, but after becoming a Christian, he believed that what guided his life was not the Laws, but God's grace. Christians continued to live by the Ten Commandments, but the many other laws delivered by God to Moses (the laws of sacrifice, the kosher food laws, etc.) were regarded as no longer binding on Christians.

M

Moses has been a popular subject for artists, and certainly one of the best-known sculptures in the world is the Moses of Michelangelo, showing the brawny, bearded Moses holding the tablets with the Ten Commandments. Many paintings depict Moses before Pharaoh, and also Moses about to destroy the stone tablets after he sees the people worshipping the golden calf idol. The finding of the infant Moses in the river has been painted many times.

Giacchino Rossini wrote the opera *Moses in Egypt*, and Arnold Schoenberg wrote the opera *Moses und Aron*. George Frideric Handel wrote the oratorio *Israel in Egypt*, most of its words taken from Exodus. English author Christopher Fry's play *The Firstborn* is about Moses. He has been the main character in one of the best-loved films of all time, the 1956 epic *The Ten Commandments*, itself a remake of a 1923 film with the same title. (For the many people who love the 1956 film, actor Charlton Heston is the definitive Moses.) The 1999 animated film *The Prince of Egypt* proved the story could be appealing and popular (and even reverent) in a cartoon format. Two TV mini-series, *Moses the Lawgiver* and *The Ten Commandments*, brought the amazing story to the small screen. His story was spoofed in the rather bad comedy *Wholly Moses!*

The various movies about Moses add material that is not found in the Bible. Exodus tells us nothing about Moses' life in the court of Egypt, but we gather from the New Testament that Jews believed that "Moses was instructed in all the wisdom of the Egyptians" (Acts 7:22). Hellenistic Jewish authors like Philo and Josephus claimed all sorts of achievements for Moses in Egypt, that he was both handsome and brilliant, the inventor of the alphabet and wise in mathematics, philosophy, and a poet to boot. Some writers even identified him with Thoth, the Egyptian god of learning.

Eastern Orthodox Christians observe September 3 as the Feast of St. Moses the Prophet. Muslims honor Moses as the prophet and apostle Musa. Moses has been a common name for Jewish boys, somewhat less so for Christians. Mormon founder Joseph Smith supposedly translated a Book of Moses, narrated by Moses himself.

The mystical form of Judaism called Kabbala (or Cabala) is supposedly based on secret teachings of Moses that were never written down, but passed on by word of mouth.

One of the most controversial books written about Moses was psychoanalyst Sigmund Freud's 1939 *Moses and Monotheism*. Although Freud himself was Jewish, he was also an atheist, and he denied the reality of the Bible's story of Moses. Freud claimed that Moses was not a Hebrew, but an Egyptian, one who believed in the monotheistic (one god) religion of the pharaoh Akhenaton. After the pharaoh's death, when the old Egyptian religion of numerous gods was reinstated, Freud hypothesized that Moses took the religion of one god to the Hebrews living in Egypt, and they made him their leader—but later killed him. Later they felt so guilty about this that they made Moses into their hero. Historians think Freud was on very shaky ground with this theory.

M

the Nazarene

Small-town flavor

Although Jesus was born in Bethlehem, he grew up in the small village of Nazareth. While Bethlehem was renowned because King David had been born there, Nazareth was of no importance. We see this in John 1:46, where one man tells another that the one the prophets predicted had appeared, Jesus of Nazareth. The other man replied, "Nazareth! Can anything good come from there?" Referring to Christ as "Jesus of Nazareth" was almost like saying "Jesus from Podunk" or "Jesus from No Place Special." Nonetheless, the small town's association with Jesus has spread its fame worldwide across two thousand years. Skeptics who doubt the truth of the Gospels admit they believe at least one thing: Jesus was definitely a man from Nazareth because none of his followers would have said he came from such a rinky-dink place unless it were true.

Jesus was a very common name in the New Testament period, so "Jesus of Nazareth" was a way of narrowing the field. ("Oh, *that* Jesus.") *Jesus of Nazareth* was the title of a TV mini-series that first aired in 1977. Sholem Asch's best-selling 1939 novel *The Nazarene* told the story of Jesus.

It is ironic that he is known as "Jesus of Nazareth" because the Gospels make it clear that his hometown did not accept him as a man sent from God—in fact, there was even an attempt on his life there (Luke 4:28-30). Jesus' response to this rejection were these words: "A prophet is not without honor except in his own country" (Mark 6:4). Jesus' "base" during his years of public life was not Nazareth, but the larger town of Capernaum on the shore of the Sea of Galilee (Matthew 4:13).

A person from Nazareth was called a Nazarene. That name has been perpetuated in the name of a Christian denomination, the Church of the Nazarene. In the early 1800s, a group of German painters lived and worked together in a vacant monastery, painting religious pictures and becoming known as the Nazarenes.

Nazirites
Gotta be the hair

Most people know that the muscleman Samson's strength had something to do with his hair. What they probably don't know is that his long hair was because he was a Nazirite. These men took a vow not to touch wine, touch a dead body, or cut their hair (including the beard). Their vows were signs of their special dedication to God, people who were "separate to the Lord." The Nazirites and their vows are described in Numbers 6. A vow could be temporary (at least thirty days) or permanent—or a parent could dedicate a child as a Nazirite, which was true for Samson, whose mother was grateful for finally bearing a child.

Two other Nazirites were important. One was Samuel, whose mother Hannah dedicated him as a child. He grew up to be Israel's judge-prophet and anointer of its first two kings. The other Nazirite was John the Baptist, the shaggy wilderness prophet who preached repentance and baptized Jesus. The Book of Acts also mentions that the apostle Paul had briefly taken the Nazirite vows (Acts 18:18).

Nebuchadnezzar
King on all fours

You might think the Bible is full of myths and legends, but some of the characters were real, among them Nebuchadnezzar, king of Babylon. In 2 Kings 24-25, we learn that Nebuchadnezzar and the pharaoh of Egypt were struggling to dominate the kingdom of Judah. Nebuchadnezzar won. In 586 B.C., his army captured Jerusalem, destroying the famous temple built by Solomon and carrying most of the people into exile, leaving only some manual laborers in the region. He blinded Zedekiah, the king of Judah, and killed his sons. All the furnishings of the temple were carted away to Babylon. The years the exiles spent in Babylon are referred to as the Babylonian Captivity (SEE PAGE 45).

Among the Jewish exiles in Babylon was a young man named Daniel, whose story is told in the book of the same name. According to the Book of Daniel, Daniel and three friends had been selected as interns for the court. Nebuchadnezzar had a puzzling dream about a statue of himself, with a head of gold, chest and arms of silver, belly of bronze, legs of iron, and feet of iron mingled with clay. His court magicians could not interpret the dream, even though the king gave them an ultimatum: interpret the dream and receive great reward, or be torn limb from limb. Daniel came forth and interpreted the dream: the head of gold represented Nebuchadnezzar himself, while the silver, bronze, iron, and clay represented inferior kingdoms that would follow. Bible readers for centuries have been arguing over just which kingdoms or empires the various metals represented.

Daniel pleased by the king by interpreting the dream, and Nebuchadnezzar fell on his face and praised Daniel's God. Daniel was made chief among the wise men of Babylon.

The king's favor did not last long. He set up a huge gold statue of himself outdoors and ordered everyone to gather together and fall down and worship it. Daniel's three friends who were faithful Jews could not do this. This was reported to the king, who ordered the three of them thrown into a fiery furnace. The furnace was so hot that the heat killed the men who threw the three Jews into it. The three young men's odd names have become familiar: Shadrach, Meshach, and Abednego. They miraculously survived the furnace, and when people looked inside, they saw a fourth man among them "and the appearance of the fourth is like a son of the gods" (Daniel 3:25). The king was amazed and awed, and he decreed that no one speak a word against the God of the three young men.

Nebuchadnezzar had another mysterious dream. In it, a great tree that provided shade and fruit was cut down by "a holy one" from heaven. Daniel again interpreted: Nebuchadnezzar would be dethroned, and would live in the wilderness like a beast and eat grass like the ox. A year later, while admiring his vast building projects, the dream came true. He was driven out of his palace and lived in the wilderness: "His hair grew long as eagles' feathers, and his nails were like birds' claws" (Daniel 4:33). After several years, the king's sanity returned, and he thanked God, admitting he had been humbled. This is the last mention of the king in the Bible.

Historians know that Nebuchadnezzar reigned from 605 to 562 B.C. and was a great builder, his most famous project being the Hanging Gardens of Babylon, considered one of the Seven Wonders of the World. However, his role as conqueror and oppressor, and his looting of the temple, followed by its burning, was something the Jews never forgot. To them he was the perfect symbol of pagan tyranny. The empire he ruled did not survive him, and it was conquered by the Persians, who allowed the Jewish exiles to return home and rebuild their temple. Later the area was conquered by the Greek-speaking Alexander the Great, who in 323 B.C., died in the palace built by Nebuchadnezzar.

The incidents in Nebuchadnezzar's story, particularly those in the Book of Daniel, have fascinated artists and writers for centuries. Poet-artist William Blake did a famous picture of the mad king down on all fours, his hair and nails so long that he looks more beast than human. The great opera composer Guiseppe Verdi wrote *Nabucco*, telling of the Babylonian Captivity of the Jews, and including the story of the king's insanity and repentance (and also some very unbiblical romantic subplots). The statue composed of the gold head and various other metals has been seen in numerous artworks and has intrigued readers who try to see it as a blueprint of world history. The story of the three men thrown in the fiery furnace is a favorite, especially with children. The mysterious "fourth man" in the furnace has caused people to wonder if this was God, or an angel, or even a pre-New Testament appearance of Christ. A very ancient poem called the Song of the Three Young Men is supposedly the prayer uttered by the three while in the furnace.

Nehemiah
Eunuch in charge

Nehemiah was a Jewish servant in the court of the Persian king. The king sent Nehemiah to Judea to help rebuild Jerusalem, which had been looted by the Babylonians. His men rebuilt the walls of Jerusalem in fifty-two days, and he approved the religious reforms of Ezra, with the people dedicating themselves to live by the Laws of Moses. As cupbearer to the king of Persia, Nehemiah was probably a eunuch. His story is told in the Old Testament's Book of Nehemiah.

Nicodemus
Admiring from the shadows

The first person to hear the words "You must be born again" was Nicodemus, a Pharisee who admired Jesus but came to him by night, which suggests he didn't want his fellow Pharisees seeing him meet with Jesus. Nicodemus was prosaic enough to take the words about "born again" literally, so he asked Jesus how it was possible to enter the womb and be born again. Jesus told him the second birth was from the Spirit, not the flesh. The dialogue with Nicodemus includes one

Jesus Talks With Nicodemus
JOHN. CHAPTER 3, VERSES 1-3, 16.

of the most quoted verses in the Bible, John 3:16: "For God so loved the world that he gave his only begotten Son, that whosoever believes in him should not perish but have everlasting life."

Nicodemus remained a cautious admirer of Jesus. When some of his fellow Pharisees wanted Jesus arrested, Nicodemus asked them if their law condemned a man without a fair hearing (John 7:40-51). After Jesus' crucifixion, he helped Joseph of Arimathea with Jesus' burial. In several films, Nicodemus is depicted as one of the Jewish leaders who was unwilling to condemn Jesus.

the Nile River
The world's largest

The Nile River of Egypt is an important river in the Bible, particularly in connection with the story of Moses in the Book of Exodus. It is never named, but simply called *ye'or*, Hebrew for "the river." (The Egyptians also called it "the river" in their own language, and still do today, calling it *El Bahr*.) In the Book of Exodus, the evil Pharaoh has the Hebrew infants drowned in the river, and Moses' mother and sister hide the infant Moses in a basket in the river, where Pharaoh's daughter finds him. The ten plagues that God sent on the Egyptians affect the river, the first one turning the Nile waters to blood. (The Egyptians considered the river sacred, so this was an insult to their river god, whom they called Apis.) One of the other plagues was the horde of frogs that came out of the bloody river.

Nimrod
Mighty daring

Genesis 10:8-9 says "Nimrod ... began to be a mighty one on the earth. He was a mighty hunter before the Lord." He was also a great builder, establishing both Babylon and Assyria, which in time became mighty empires. His name has come to mean any daring hunter, or any bold person in general. (More recently, and no no one knows exactly why, a "nimrod" means "stupid person.") In the TV series *The Wild Wild West*, the heroes' gadget-laden railroad car was named the Nimrod. In the 1966 film *The Bible ... In the Beginning*, Nimrod was depicted as the builder of the ill-fated tower of Babel.

Nineveh
Jonah's target

The largest city of the Assyrian empire was situated on the Tigris River and is mentioned several times in the Bible, particularly in the books of two prophets, Jonah and Nahum. The Book of Jonah (SEE PAGE 190) tells the story of Jonah, a Hebrew prophet who ran away when God told him to preach repentance to Nineveh. After his experience of swallowed by a whale, Jonah did as God asked, and Nineveh repented. On the other hand, the prophet Nahum prophesied doom for Nineveh and the Assyrian empire, and his prophecy came to pass when the Babylonians captured the city. His prophecy that the city would lie in forgotten ruins also came to pass, for the site was not discovered until the 1800s.

According to Genesis 10:11, Nimrod, the "mighty hunter before the Lord," built Nineveh.

N

In the New Testament, as Jesus traveled about and was rejected by many of his own people, he spoke of Nineveh as a pagan city that reacted rightly to a prophet's (Jonah's) preaching (Matthew 12:41).

Noah

Floating his stock

The famous story of Noah and the flood is found in Genesis 6-8. The human race had grown so evil that God decided blot out the whole race and start over. "But Noah found grace in the eyes of the Lord" (Genesis 6:8) because "Noah was a just man and perfect in his generations, and Noah walked with God" (Genesis 6:9). At the ripe age of five hundred, Noah had three sons—Shem, Ham, and Japheth. God told Noah to build an ark so he and his sons and their wives could ride out the flood—along with a pair of every animal on earth, of course. God gave the precise dimensions of the ark, and when Noah

The Arc Rests Upon Arat
GENESIS. CHAPTER 8, VERSES 5-19.

had gathered all the creatures together, "the Lord shut him in." The rain continued for forty days and nights, blotting out the human race. (The ark was not a ship, and had no rudder or any means of navigation. It was like a giant life preserver, and where it landed was left to God.)

The waters did not subside for a hundred and fifty days. The ark came to rest on "the mountains of Ararat." To determine if dry land had yet appeared, Noah sent forth a dove, but since it found nowhere to rest, it returned to the ark. A week later, he sent the dove out again and it returned with an olive branch in its beak, a sign that the waters were subsiding. The dove with an olive branch has become the universal symbol of peace.

With his family and animals safe from the ark, Noah made an offering to the Lord, and the Lord promised he would never again destroy the earth with a flood. (This is the first time an altar for sacrifice is mentioned in the

Bible.) The sign of this promise was the rainbow—"my bow in the clouds (Genesis 9:13)."

God told Noah's three sons to "be fruitful and multiply"—sensible advice, since they were the only people on earth. Chapter 10 of Genesis lists the descendants of Noah's three sons, and generally speaking, Ham was the father of modern day Africans, Japheth the modern day Europeans, and Shem the Middle Easterners, which is why Jews and others regard themselves as "Semites," descendants of Shem. Anthropologists use "Semites" to refer to a group of ancient peoples with related languages, including the Hebrews, Canaanites, Assyrians, Babylonians, and Arabs.

Noah seems to be a heroic man, building his ark by God's order and probably being mocked by his neighbors. In spite of his goodness, Genesis records a sordid story: Noah "planted a vineyard" (supposedly he was the inventor of wine-making), got drunk on his own wine and lay naked in his tent. Ham saw what happened, found it amusing, and told his two brothers. Being more respectful of their father than Ham, Shem and Japheth walked backwards into Noah's tent and draped a cloth over him without looking at him. For being disrespectful, Ham's descendants were cursed by Noah (Genesis 9:26). For centuries, some people used this curse as justification for keeping Africans (supposedly the descendants of Ham) as slaves.

One often overlooked element in Noah's story: He was 500 years old when God told him to build the ark, 600 when it was finished—that's 100 years of labor. Noah died at the ripe age of 950, coming close to the record of his grandfather Methuselah at 969. In fact, if the chronology in Genesis is correct, Methuselah didn't die of old age, but died because of the flood.

The Noah story has fascinated people for centuries. There are many versions of flood stories around the world, but the one in Genesis is different, since God sends the flood for a reason (human wickedness) and Noah is saved for a reason (he is a good man). The ark became a symbol of good people surviving when the wicked perished, and for the early Christians the ark symbolized their hope of heaven. The word "ark" has come to mean any place of refuge from destruction. In fact, the movie *Schindler's List*, about the saving of Jews from the Nazis, was based on a book titled *Schindler's Ark* by Thomas Keneally.

In a sense, Noah was a "second Adam," since he was the new father of the human race. Happily, he was a better and more obedient man than the first

N

Adam. He is mentioned several times in the New Testament as a man of deep faith. The Book of Ezra (Ezra 14:14) holds up Noah as one of the three good men, along with Daniel and Job. Jesus told his followers that the Day of Judgment would arrive unexpectedly, just as the flood did in the time of Noah (Matthew 24:36-39).

In the Koran, however, Noah's wife, named Waila, tries to persuade people that Noah is insane. In Muslim legend, the dove Noah sent out from the ark is one of the ten animals that are in heaven.

Because of the ills that have come from alcohol abuse, some Jews attributed Noah's winemaking to Satan himself. According to legends, Satan fertilized the grape vines with blood from a lamb, a lion, an ape, and a pig. The meaning of the four beasts' blood: when drinking, a man becomes docile (the lamb), then fierce (the lion), then silly (the ape), and ends up wallowing in the mud (the pig).

Noah and the ark have been favorite subjects for artists, who have delighted in depicting the parade of animals making their way into the ark. The less pleasant subject of Noah drunk and naked has also been painted many times, as a warning that even good people can do foolish things on occasion. The famous Sistine Chapel paintings by Michelangelo depict Noah in both situations. In Michelangelo's depiction of the drunken scene, the three sons are naked as well. Possibly the most famous painting of the tipsy Noah is Giovanni Bellini's *The Drunkenness of Noah*, painted c. 1515. In this depiction, Noah is not inside his tent but lying on the ground in a stupor, his three sons draping him with a cloth, one curious, one snickering, one looking away dutifully.

On stage, Noah's story was dramatized by noted playwright Clifford Odets in *The Flowering Peach*. Comedian Danny Kaye starred in the Broadway musical *Two by Two*, based on the Odets play, with music by Richard Rodgers. ("Two by two" refers to the pairs of animals taken into the ark, of course.) In the Middle Ages, Noah was a popular subject for mystery plays, and in plays dealing with him, his wife is often depicted as a shrewish woman who believes the prophecy of a flood is madness. Noah appears more buffoon than hero, a henpecked husband who cannot hold his liquor. Noah is an important character in Southern author Roark Bradford's *Ol' Man Adam an' His Chillun*, Old Testament stories retold in the dialect of black slaves.

Filmmakers have been attracted to this colorful story, and one of the earliest biblical epics was *Noah's Ark*, released in 1929. The 1936 movie *The Green Pastures* had an all-black cast and featured Eddie Anderson as a good but comical Noah. The Noah story (with the drunken episode omitted) was the best part of the 1966 film *The Bible ... In the Beginning*, with Noah played by the film's director, John Huston (who also provided the voice of God and the narrator). A rather bad 1999 TV movie *Noah's Ark* played fast and loose with the Genesis story, introducing pirates (!) into the saga. French composer Camille Saint-Saens wrote an opera about the story, *Le Deluge (The Flood)*.

Noah's story is probably one of the most secularized stories from the Bible. The story itself is deeply spiritual since it shows how strongly God feels about human sin (enough to wipe out almost everyone!). For popular consumption, the story is packaged as a pleasant tale about a man parading the wild animals into the ark and riding out a long storm—a floating zoo, in other words. (It's no surprise that a chain of pet stores is called Noah's Ark.) The number of children's books about Noah's ark are countless, but like the paintings of the animals boarding the ark, many of them miss the story's spiritual message.

Since the Book of Genesis names the "mountains of Ararat" as the site where the ark settled, people have been hoping for centuries to find remnants of the ark. A mountain called Ararat is on the border of Turkey and Iran, and neither government has been cooperative in letting archaeologists explore the area. Since Genesis refers to "mountains" (plural), there is no certainty that the one mountain called Ararat today is the one on which the ark landed.

N

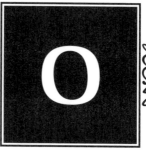

Old and New Testaments

The agreement archives

The Bibles used by Christians are in two sections, the first called the Old Testament, the second called the New Testament. The Old Testament is longer and covers a much greater period of time, from the creation of the world to the return of Jewish exiles from Babylon. It was also written over a long period of time, while the New Testament was probably written within one generation after the time of Jesus and the apostles. When Jews refer to "the Bible," they mean only the Old Testament. The New Testament consists of early Christian writings—the Gospels, Acts, epistles, and the Book of Revelation. Jews don't regard the New Testament as divinely inspired writings, but Christians regard both Old and New Testaments as divinely inspired by God—although they value the New Testament more highly because it is the more recent revelation of God's will. Christians don't believe they must abide by most of the ritual laws—such as the kosher food laws—in the Old Testament. However, some Christian groups choose to abide by the kosher laws, believing that "God's plan" is still valid.

What is a "testament" anyway? It can mean *covenant*—an agreement between two parties, in this case God and humankind. It can also mean a record of the dealings of God with humankind.

The Old Testament is written in Hebrew (with a few sections in Aramaic), the New Testament in Greek. There are thirty-nine books in the Old Testament, twenty-seven in the New Testament, or sixty-six in all.

Jewish worship services always include the reading of the Bible (Old Testament), and most Christian services include readings from the New Testament, sometimes the Old Testament as well. Muslims claim to honor God's revelation in the Bible, but they believe the Bible was somehow corrupted over the years, and where it disagrees with the Koran, Muslims accept the Koran. Muslims believe that Muhammad, the "seal of the prophets," had divine revelations that supersede the Bible. They believe that the Koran "corrects" the Bible in many places; for example, it teaches that Abraham's son Ishmael was Abraham's favorite son, not Isaac.

oil of anointing
No fossil fuels then

In biblical times, oil was used for *anointing*, or marking a person for some special purpose. Priests were anointed, and so were kings. Through the ages the custom of anointing a king's head or face at the time of coronation has continued. Olive oil, the common household oil of all the people, was used for anointing, but Exodus 30 makes it clear that the oil for anointing was a "heavenly blend," with fragrant herbs added to set it apart from ordinary oil. The anointing oil could be used for no other purpose.

Olivet
Agony hill

O

The Garden of Gethsemane (SEE PAGE 129) where Jesus was betrayed and arrested was probably on a ridge called Olivet, or the Mount of Olives. On the days Jesus preached and taught in Jerusalem, he and the disciples would spend the nights at the Mount, which was a favorite spot for people tired of the crowded city. Two of the Gospels name Gethsemane as the place of Jesus' agony before his arrest, but all four refer to the Mount of Olives, so Gethsemane was probably on the Mount. Long ago Christians built churches on the mountain, including one called the Church of the Agony. The groves of olive trees that gave the site its name were chopped down by the Roman emperor Titus when he was putting down a Jewish revolt. Composer Ludwig van Beethoven wrote an oratorio called *Christ on the Mount of Olives*, dealing with Jesus' agony over his coming arrest and crucifixion.

Olivet is also connected with the warning of Jesus to his disciples about things that would occur at the end of time. Jesus warned not to be misled by false Christs, or frightened by wars, earthquakes, and famines. He told them there would be persecution ahead, and that they should always be spiritually prepared for the end (Matthew 24-25, Luke 21). The speech is sometimes called the Olivet Discourse, or the Olivet Apocalypse. Christian beliefs about the end of time have been influenced greatly by the Olivet Apocalypse.

Olivet has been used as a name by many churches and Christian schools.

Palestine

Home base for the faith

The nation of Israel today occupies a space that has gone by many names in the past, including Canaan, Israel, Judah, and Judea. Naming the region *Palestina* was part of the Romans' attempt to secularize the area after the final Jewish revolt against Rome in the year 135. The old Jewish name for the province, Judea, was scuttled, with the Romans borrowing the name Palestina from those warlike inhabitants of early times, the Philistines. They couldn't have picked a name more repugnant to the Jews.

Israelites, Philistines, and many other peoples lived in the region long before the Arabs did, so Palestine hardly qualifies as an Arab or Muslim name for the region; although they often use it, they do not acknowledge the existence of Israel on their maps. In fact, the area was Christian for three centuries before the Muslims invaded. Between the time of the Romans and the twentieth century, the area continued to be called Palestine and was occupied by various Muslim empires, including the Ottoman Empire of Turkey. Briefly, during the Middle Ages, parts of it were under the control of the Christian Crusaders from Europe, who renamed it the kingdom of Jerusalem. Turkey lost control of the region following World War I, and it was governed by the British (and still called Palestine) until the nation of Israel was created in 1948. The daily news brings us constant reminders that the nation known as Israel is regarded by Muslims as Palestine, who think Jews have no business being there.

Palm Sunday
A bright beginning

Christians celebrate the Sunday one week before Easter as Palm Sunday, based on the Gospels' story of Jesus riding a donkey into Jerusalem and being welcomed by the people, who waved palm branches and greeted him as the Son of David (another name for the Messiah). They shouted to him "Hosanna! Blessed is he who comes in the name of the Lord!" (John 12:12-15). Actually, three of the Gospels refer just to "branches," but John's Gospel specifies they were "palm branches." Riding on a donkey was a sign of humility, and the disciples regarded it as the fulfillment of the prophecy of Zechariah: "Behold, your king is coming, sitting on a donkey's colt" (Zechariah 9:9). The event is called Jesus' "triumphal entry," since he was, for the time being, riding a wave of popularity. It is a key event in the life of Jesus, and most films or plays dealing with Jesus depict the Palm Sunday processional. In *Jesus Christ Superstar*, lyricist Tim Rice mildly spoofed the word "Hosanna" by having the crowd sing, "Ho-sanna, Hey-sanna."

Some churches display palm branches on Palm Sunday, then, the following year, burn the dried-out branches and use the ashes for marking people's foreheads in Ash Wednesday services. Ash Wednesday is the beginning of the season of Lent, which ends at Easter. In the Middle Ages, it was a custom in many areas to begin a worship service in one church, then walk to another church nearby, waving palm branches and re-enacting the entry of Jesus into Jerusalem.

Palm Sunday is considered the beginning of Holy Week (SEE PAGE 153).

parables
Like, they were like stories

Some of the most-quoted parts of the Bible are Jesus' parables. These were "simile stories," comparing one thing to another to show a spiritual truth. Many of them explain the "kingdom of God," with the parable beginning, "The kingdom of God is like …" Jesus would then compare it to something everyday and understandable: a farmer sowing seed, a treasure hidden in field, a grain of mustard seed, etc. Most of these parables were short, barely more than a sentence. Some were more involved, such as the stories of the Good Samaritan (Luke 10:29-37), the prodigal son (Luke 15:11-32), and the workers in the vineyard (Matthew 20:1-16). Some of the more famous parables are described below. The stories are simple and direct, but they also puzzled most of his listeners, and Jesus sometimes had to explain them to his own disciples. John's Gospel is distinctive for having no parables of Jesus.

the parable of the Good Samaritan
Love breaking barriers

Jesus' most famous parable has given the language a phrase, since we use "Good Samaritan" to refer to someone acting unselfishly. The parable was told after Jesus spoke the words, "Love your neighbor as yourself," and a Jewish teacher replied, "Who is my neighbor?" Jesus told a story in reply: A man on the road is beaten, robbed, and left for dead. Two "religious" people, first a priest and then a Levite, pass him by and do nothing. Then a Samaritan stops, binds up the man's wounds, and carries him to an inn, even leaving money with the innkeeper to provide for the man's care. The story hit the original listeners like a sledgehammer, since Jews despised Samaritans, regarding them as heathen lowlifes. When Jesus finished his story, he asked, "Which of these three do you think was a neighbor to the man?" The answer was obvious enough: "The one who showed mercy on him." Jesus replied, "Go and do likewise" (Luke 10:25-37). No greater story of love breaking down social barriers is found in all the world's literature. The brief parable has been preached on and quoted endlessly, and of all Jesus' parables, it has appealed most to artists, who usually depict the Samaritan lifting the wounded traveler onto his own horse.

P

the parable of Lazarus and the rich man
Rich and burning

There are two men named Lazarus in the New Testament, the best-known being the man Jesus brought back to life. The other is a character in a parable—in fact, the only character that Jesus actually names. In the story, found in Luke 16:19-31, a wealthy man lives in luxury while a poor beggar name Lazarus sits outside his gates. The tables turn when both men die, and the rich man goes to hell while Lazarus goes to heaven—called "Abraham's bosom" because in heaven one was supposed to be able to meet the great patriarchs of old time. The rich man is tormented in the fire and asks for Lazarus just to touch his tongue with a drop of water to ease the pain. Abraham reminds him that during his earthly life he received good things while Lazarus suffered; now Lazarus is being comforted. Then the rich man asks if Lazarus would warn his family about hell, but Abraham tells him they have the Law and prophets to guide them, and they would be unlikely to believe in someone raised from the dead—an obvious reference to Jesus' coming death and resurrection. Jesus was needling the Jewish religious leaders with this parable, pointing out that "nobodies" like Lazarus had a better chance of being saved than people who were satisfied with their earthly lives—a dramatizing of his saying that "the last shall be first and the first shall be last."

the parable of the Pharisee and tax collector
Oneself on a pedestal

Jesus called people to be righteous, but *self*-righteous was another matter altogether. He spoke against hypocrisy and self-congratulation, seen clearly in his parable of two men praying in the temple (Luke 18:10-14). One is a Pharisee, whose prayer is, "God, I thank you that I am not like other men"—in other words, the real praise is for himself, not God. He even counts off the types of terrible sinners that he is *not* like—including tax collectors. By contrast, the other man praying is a tax collector, painfully aware of his sins. His prayer is, "God, be merciful to me, a sinner." At the end of the story, Jesus explained that it was the tax collector, not the Pharisee, who was in a right relationship with God. "For everyone who exalts himself will be abased, and he who humbles himself will be exalted" (Luke 18:14).

"God, be merciful to me, a sinner" is often called the "sinner's prayer." In times past, someone on the verge of death might utter the words in the hope that God would view it as a last-minute conversion. It is still a common prayer in the Eastern Orthodox churches.

the parable of the prodigal son
The ultimate Dad story

This parable rivals the parable of the Good Samaritan for best-known and most-quoted of all Jesus' stories. In the oft-told tale, found in Luke 15:11-32, the son of a wealthy father asks for his share of the family inheritance, then squanders it on riotous living, till he ends up tending a pig farm (for a Jew, a truly horrible fate). He comes to his senses and runs home repentant and shamed to dear Dad, who accepts him joyfully, ordering the servants to hold a feast for the son who was lost. Preachers have pointed out that the story ought to be called "the forgiving father," since the real point of it is God's mercy, not the wastefulness (prodigality) of the son.

In the parable, the father orders his servants to "kill the fatted calf" for the welcome-home feast. The phrase "kill the fatted calf" has been used to mean a party or feast with no expense spared.

Painters often depict this scene with the ragged son kneeling at his father's feet, while servants bring in

The Prodigal Son
LUKE. CHAPTER 15, VERSES 20-24.

fresh clothing and lead in the "fatted calf" for the party. Bartolome Murillo's painting in Washington's National Gallery is probably the best known, along with Rembrandt's *Return of the Prodigal Son*.

Rather surprisingly, this very short story has served as the basis for two full-length films, one made in the 1920s titled *The Wanderer*, and a technicolor extravaganza from the 1950s titled *The Prodigal*, starring glamour queen Lana Turner as a pagan priestess who leads the title character into "riotous living" before he comes to his senses. The popular play and movie *Godspell* is based on the Gospel of Matthew, but includes an acting out of the parable of the prodigal son (which is in Luke, not Matthew), probably because audiences in the 1970s needed assurance that the "generation gap" could be bridged. English composer Benjamin Britten wrote an opera *The Prodigal Son*.

the parable of the sheep and goats
Split the different

Jesus taught that at the Last Judgment, lots of people were in for surprises. People who thought themselves righteous would find themselves condemned, and vice versa. In this parable (Matthew 25:31-46), a shepherd divides his flocks, putting sheep on one side, goats on the other. The sheep are the righteous ones, and the shepherd (Jesus himself, that is) thanks them for showing him kindness and hospitality. The sheep are surprised: When did we ever do that for you? The shepherd tells them that when "you did it to one of the least of these my brethren, you did it to me." In other words, when you neglect your fellow man's needs, you neglect God. For the goats, the situation is reversed. They are condemned for neglecting others: "Depart from me, you cursed, into the everlasting fire prepared for the devil and his angels. ... inasmuch as you did not do it to one of the least of these, you did not do it to me."

Did Jesus intend the "everlasting fire" to be taken literally? Christians have been debating that for ages. "Everlasting fire" does at least tell us that showing kindness is something to be taken seriously.

This "separation parable" had its effect on artists, particularly when depicting the Last Judgment, with the blessed on one side and the hell-bound on the other. Michelangelo's dramatic *Last Judgment* in the Vatican owes much to this parable.

the parable of the sower
Sprouting the truth

The Gospels say that Jesus' parables were often misunderstood, even by his own disciples. For the parable of the sower, Jesus explains it fully. As the story goes, a farmer sows seed in a field, some of the seed falling on fertile soil, some on rocky soil, some among thorns, some along the path. The seed, Jesus said, is the word of God. The seed on the path is eaten by the birds—meaning, it never has a chance to take root at all. The seed on rocky soil sprouts but withers away—that is, people receive the word but it doesn't take root. The seed that fell among the thorns manages to grow, but the weeds choke it out—people's worldly focus prevent the word from growing. But the seed on good soil thrives and produces a hundredfold crop (Mark 4:1-9).

the parable of the unjust judge
Persistence pays off

This could be subtitled "the parable of the whining widow." In this story, a judge "who did not fear God nor regard man" meets his match in a widow who begs for justice in her case. He turns a deaf ear to her, but her persistence finally wears him down and he gives the woman her day in court. Jesus told the story as an illustration of what God is like: If a corrupt judge can be worn down by human persistence, then certainly a merciful, caring God will listen to people's prayers (Luke 18:1-8).

the parable of the wheat and tares
Global weed control

The Bible is very clear about one thing: We don't see things the way God does. In fact, we can't even tell which people are really good and which aren't. That is the main point of Jesus' parable of the wheat and the tares. A farmer plants wheat in a field, but by night his enemy sows tares (weeds). The two grow together in the field, and it isn't until the harvest that the wheat is harvested, while the tares are bound up and burned (Matthew 13:24-30). The parable is one of several dealing with the Last Judgment, where God separates the good from the wicked, and (in case you hadn't noticed), the bad ones end up burned. The "enemy" in the parable is Satan, of course.

The word "tares" is from the King James Version and probably referred to some thorny weed, the bane of all farmers and gardeners. Most newer translations have "weeds."

paradise

As good as it gets

The word "paradise" occurs only three times in the Bible, all three meaning "heaven." The first time it occurs Jesus was agonizing on the cross. One of the two thieves crucified with him was repentant for his crimes and asked Jesus to be taken into his "kingdom." Jesus replied with, "Truly, I say to you, today you will be with me in Paradise" (Luke 23:43). The apostle Paul told of a man who was "caught up to paradise and heard inexpressible things" (2 Corinthians 12:4). People have always believed Paul referred to himself, and that he was caught up in a vision of heaven. Appropriately, the last mention of paradise is in the Bible's last book, Revelation: "To him who overcomes, I will give the right to eat from the tree of life, which is in the paradise of God" (Revelation 2:7).

The word comes from the Greek *paradeisos*, meaning "park," or a well-tended place of lush greenery. When the Old Testament was translated from Hebrew into Greek, the word *paradeisos* was used many times, notably in referring to the Garden of Eden in Genesis. From the way Jesus, Paul, and the author of Revelation used the word, it has come to mean not just any beautiful park but the ultimate beautiful place, heaven. The word has become a familiar one in English, both to refer to heaven or to any beautiful place.

Passion

No, not that kind …

Thanks to the Mel Gibson film *The Passion of the Christ*, the world became reacquainted with the theological meaning of "Passion." The word, based on Latin, simply means "suffering," so depictions of the Passion—art, music, plays, or films— show Jesus' arrest, trial, and crucifixion. The "happy ending" of the Passion is Jesus' resurrection, of course.

Passion Plays are dramas showing these events, and they have been staged since the Middle Ages. The most famous Passion Play, still being produced, is at the German town of Oberamergau, where a lavish production has been staged every ten years since the 1600s. Around 1895, the first depiction of a biblical subject on film was a very brief French film titled *La Passion de Jesus Christ*, and several other early films had *Passion* in their titles. The choice of subject makes sense, since Christians believe that Jesus' crucifixion and resurrection are the most important events in the Bible—and in the history of the world, for that matter.

Composers have written choral works presenting the Passion, and the great J. S. Bach wrote two masterpieces, *The Passion According to St. Matthew* and *The Passion According to St. John*. Like the Passion plays, most of the musical Passions were written to be performed during Holy Week, the week between Palm Sunday and Easter.

The word has made its way into gardening, with the passionflower a flowering vine that (so some people say) has blossoms resembling a man on a cross. A Catholic monastic order founded in 1720 calls itself the Passionists.

Passover

Festival for those on the move

This was the first and most important of Jewish holy days. It's rooted in the Book of Exodus, where God sends ten terrible plagues on the Egyptians to make them free the Hebrew slaves. The last plague is the death of all the firstborn in the land. Moses instructs the Hebrews to mark their doorposts with lamb's blood so the Lord's death angel will pass over their homes in the night. The first Passover, also called the Feast of Unleavened Bread, is described in detail in Exodus 12. Because the Hebrews would depart Egypt so suddenly, God told them to make bread without leavening (yeast), since leavened bread takes longer to prepare.

Surprisingly, for a holy day so filled with meaning and memories, later generations neglected the day. Centuries after Moses, King Josiah reinstituted the Passover celebration (2 Kings 23:21-23). The Jews have observed it faithfully ever since. It is held over seven or eight days, and on

The Origin of the Paschal Lamb
EXODUS. CHAPTER 12, VERSES 1, 3-8, 11-14.

the first night of Passover a ritual meal called the Seder is prepared, while the story from Exodus 12 is recounted. The traditional unleavened bread, matzoh, is eaten.

At the time of Jesus, devout Jews tried to be in Jerusalem during the Passover season, since the Lord's temple was there. Jesus' arrest and crucifixion was during Passover, which is why the Jewish Passover and the Christian Easter occur around the same time on the calendar. Jesus' famous Last Supper with his disciples was a Passover meal. Since the Passover festival celebrated freedom from oppression and tyranny, the Romans who ruled the Jews kept a close watch on Jerusalem at Passover time, fearing a Jewish revolt. This situation is one of the reasons Pilate and the Jewish priests feared Jesus as a potential troublemaker. John's Gospel mentions that there was the custom of the Roman governor releasing a Jewish prisoner every year at Passover. Ironically, the crowd shouted for the release not of Jesus, but of Barabbas, a political revolutionary.

The early Christians regarded Jesus as the "Lamb of God" and the "Passover Lamb" (2 Corinthians 5:7), which is why the celebration of Passover died out among Christians, who began celebrating those events they regarded as more important than the Passover: the crucifixion and resurrection of Jesus.

patriarchs
Father figures

In discussing the Bible, the word "patriarchs" has several meanings. Basically it means "important ancestors." The word itself is Greek and means "rule of the fathers." The most important ancestor for the Jews was Abraham (SEE PAGE 7), who was told by God to leave his idol-worshipping home in Ur and settle in Canaan, where God would make him the father of a great nation. Abraham finally (at the age of one hundred) fathered Isaac, who fathered Jacob, who was given the name Israel by God, and who had twelve sons, the ancestors of the "twelve tribes of Israel." "The patriarchs" usually means Abraham, Isaac, Jacob, and Jacob's twelve sons, since all Jews could trace their ancestry back to these men. It was to these men that God gave the promise of the land of Canaan, a promise that still irks the Muslim inhabitants of that region.

The Bible sometimes uses "patriarch" more loosely. Acts 2:29 refers to "the patriarch David," even though David lived centuries after the original patriarchs.

In Jewish and Christian tradition, "patriarchs" can also refer to the ancestors of the human race—Adam, Methuselah, and Noah.

The patriarchs are found in much Christian artwork, since they represent God's ancient covenant with Israel, which was (spiritually) passed on to Christians.

Paul, Saul

From chief persecutor to world evangelist

Next to Jesus, the most important person in the New Testament is the apostle Paul, whose dramatic story is told in The Book of Acts, and who authored the epistles from Romans to Philemon—a huge chunk of the New Testament. He is first mentioned by his original Hebrew name, Saul, in Acts 7, where he approves of the stoning of the first Christian martyr, Stephen. A devout Jew, Saul saw the Jewish Christians as heretics and blasphemers, and he had many of them arrested. But while en route to the city of Damascus, he had a life-changing encounter. He was confronted by a vision of the risen Jesus, who asked him why he was persecuting Christians. Saul quickly changed from persecutor to believer, and the Jews regarded him as a dangerous traitor. Acts 13-28 tells of his missionary journeys through the eastern part of the Roman Empire, where he made many converts but also had foes, with his life in danger numerous times. His companion on his early travels was the apostle Barnabas, then later Silas. Another of his possible traveling companions was Luke, the author of Acts. When Acts ends, Paul is under house arrest in Rome, witnessing to the faith. Tradition says he was released, then made good on his vow to carry the faith all the way to Spain—the western edge of the empire. Tradition also says that Paul was later beheaded during the persecution of Christians by the vile emperor Nero, possibly because he had converted one of Nero's concubines to Christianity. Most of the key events in Paul's story are covered elsewhere in this book.

Paul's Arrival in Rome
ACTS. CHAPTER 28, VERSES 16, 30, 31.

P

Thanks to Paul's letters and the Book of Acts, we know the man extremely well—in fact, probably better than any man in the ancient world. He was extremely devout, passionate, loving, but not afraid of confrontation when he knew he was right. He grew up as a pious Jew, studied under rabbis in Jerusalem, and was also a Roman citizen, a fact that was useful as he traveled spreading the faith (and on at least one occasion, it saved his life). He had been a Pharisee, one of the Jews who were very strict about following the Law of Moses. Paul was no hypocrite, as many of the Pharisees were, for he did try to practice what he preached. Believing in Christ gave him an inner satisfaction he had not found when trying to live by the Law. In three of his epistles, he opens by calling himself a "slave" of Jesus Christ—a slavery that he welcomed, since it freed him from the Law.

As the author of a large part of the New Testament, Paul is regarded as Christianity's first theologian. His epistles were written to groups of Christians in various cities, mostly as Paul's responses to questions about belief and morals. His longest letter, the Letter to the Romans, is also the best summary of Christian belief, and one of the most-quoted and most-studied parts of the New Testament. Paul was eloquent at times, and his famous "love chapter" (1 Corinthians 13) is a beautifully phrased description of what true love is; it is often read at weddings. Equally eloquent is the "resurrection chapter" (1 Corinthians 15), which gives a stirring description of the future state of people of faith. (Quotes from this chapter were set to beautiful music in George Frideric Handel's *Messiah*.) His description of the "whole armor of God" in Ephesians 6 is extremely inspiring. Paul's two letters to the Thessalonians are probably the oldest documents in the New Testament, written around the year 51.

Paul regarded himself as "apostle to the Gentiles," appointed by God to spread Christianity to non-Jews. Although raised according to the Jewish law, he believed Christianity set people free from legalism, and that anyone, Jew or Gentile, could find salvation by believing in Jesus. This idea led to frequent trouble with the Jewish leaders, who saw him as a dangerous traitor. They were correct in seeing him as a threat to their religion, for thanks to Paul and his followers, Christians would become more numerous than Jews.

The apostle must have been a physically tough character, because he survived five scourgings, a stoning, a shipwreck, more than one stay in prison, an earthquake, the bite of a venomous snake, and numerous attempts on his life. Some readers have noted that his real-life adventures are as colorful as those of the fictional hero of Homer's *Odyssey*.

In our time, Paul's reputation has suffered because of Political Correctness, for he condemned homosexuality and told Christian wives to be submissive to their husbands. Novelist Gore Vidal wrote a scandalous novel, *Live from Golgotha: The Gospel According to Gore Vidal*, in which Paul himself was a homosexual. In the film *The Last Temptation of Christ*, Paul was depicted as judgmental and intolerant (not to mention violent—he kills Lazarus). The falsehood that Jesus was loving and merciful, while Paul was intolerant and unkind, has been around for centuries, but Acts and Paul's letters prove he was not that type of man at all.

Throughout history, Jews did not have a high opinion of Paul. They believe he was not the faithful Jew he claimed to be, but was much more influenced by the Greek mystery religions and pagan philosophies than by the Old Testament. Some of them also doubt whether he actually wrote most of the New Testament letters that are attributed to him.

In art, Paul is often depicted holding a sword, since he spoke of "the sword of the Spirit, which is the word of God" (Ephesians 6:17). His beheading was probably done by the sword also. (A convent in Spain claims to possess the actual sword that beheaded Paul.) His other symbol is an open book, a reminder that he wrote much of the New Testament. Many of the key events in his story have been depicted in art, especially his conversion on the road to Damascus. For no particular reason, he is often shown as short and bald. Rembrandt's *The Apostle Paul* in Washington's National Gallery captures some of Paul's depth and intensity. He has appeared as a character in numerous works of fiction, notably the best-selling novels *Great Lion of God* by Taylor Caldwell and *The Apostle* by Sholem Asch. Country music legend Johnny Cash published a novel about Paul, *Man in White*. Colorful as Paul's story is, he has not been featured in many films, though two TV movies, *A.D.* and *Peter and Paul*, dealt with his saga, and he is a minor character in the book and movie *Quo Vadis*. German composer Felix Mendelssohn wrote the famous oratorio *Paulus* (sometimes called *St. Paul*), which included Paul's persecution of the Christians, then his dramatic conversion and his travels with Barnabas.

Catholics observe January 25 as the feast of Paul's conversion. Numerous cities, churches, and schools are named for him, including the capital city of Minnesota and the beautiful Baroque cathedral in London. The Society of St. Paul is an order of Catholic monks active in media. Because Peter and Paul were both prominent in the Book of Acts, and because both were associated with the growth of Christianity in Rome, Catholic and Orthodox Christians observe June 29 as the joint

P

feast day of Paul and Peter. Many churches are named for both apostles, including the National Cathedral in Washington and Westminster Abbey in London.

Regarding his names: Many Jews, especially those who lived among Gentiles, had two names, a Hebrew birth name and a second name used among Gentiles. His family and his Jewish acquaintances would have called him by his birth name Saul, while others knew him as Paul. Eight popes have taken the name Paul (six Pauls, two John Pauls).

peace
As good as it gets …

The word we translate as "peace" in our Bibles was *shalom* in Hebrew and *eirene* in Greek. Neither word meant "peace" as an absence of war. The word was richer than that, meaning something like "security and contentment" or "wholeness." Both Jews and Christians used it as a greeting—"Peace be with you"—wishing the person well when meeting them or leaving them.

Jesus himself said "Peace be with you" many times, and also used the farewell, "Go in peace." Jesus told his disciples that in this troubled world they could still find peace, for he had "overcome the world" (John 16:33). The apostle Paul spoke of "the peace of God, which surpasses all understanding" (Philippians 4:7). All of Paul's letters open with the greeting "Grace and peace to you." The two epistles of Peter open with "grace and peace be multiplied to you." Several times the New Testament refers to God as the "God of peace." Jesus is honored in Christian tradition as the "Prince of Peace," based on the prophecy of Isaiah 9:6. "Prince of Peace" is a fairly common name for churches.

In the 1970s, many Christians rediscovered the Hebrew word *Shalom*, using it as a greeting and incorporating it into many songs and sermons.

Pentecost
Day of wind and fire

Pentecost is the only holy day that Christians and Jews have in common. Also called the Feast of Weeks, it is described in Leviticus 23 and was connected with the annual barley harvest. By the time of the New Testament, the Jews celebrated it as the time God gave the law to Moses on Mount Sinai.

For Christians it has an entirely new meaning. In the Book of Acts, Jesus' disciples gathered in Jerusalem on the day of Pentecost, and the Holy Spirit descended on them, enabling them to speak in other languages. From that point on, the disciples spread the faith with great power and energy. In time, Christians celebrated Pentecost as the day when the Holy Spirit was given to believers. Sometimes Pentecost is referred to as the "birthday of the church."

According to Acts 2, Jesus' disciples were in one room when they heard the sound "like a mighty rushing wind," then "tongues of fire" appeared over each man, "and they were all filled with the Holy Spirit." This scene has been depicted by many artists, who apparently liked the challenge of showing the "tongues of fire."

The New Testament speaks of certain "gifts" of the Holy Spirit, such as being able to work miracles, prophesy, and speak in unknown languages. It also speaks of a time when believers would be "baptized with the Holy Spirit and with fire." In the twentieth century, many Christians felt that worship services had become dry and boring, and they believed that if Christians really felt the power of the Spirit, they would be more lively and emotional, and would possess some of the gifts of the Spirit. These Christians used the name

The Descent of the Holy Ghost
ACTS. CHAPTER 2, VERSES 1-4.

"Pentecostal," and in the late twentieth century, Pentecostal churches experienced huge growth. One of the Pentecostal denominations, the Assemblies of God, is the fastest-growing denomination in the world.

In England, Pentecost has always been called Whitsunday ("White Sunday") from the tradition that newly baptized people wear white robes from Easter through Pentecost.

The "rushing mighty wind" and "tongues of fire" have sometimes been expressed musically, as in composer Richard Wagner's *Love Feast of the Apostles*, a work he wrote for a 1,200-voice male choir, and also in Edward Elgar's oratorio *The Kingdom*.

Persia

Pre-Iran land

One of the great empires of ancient times was centered in the area we now call Iran. Persia stretched as far east as India and as far west as Greece. It came very near to conquering the Greeks at one point. It conquered the empire of Babylon, and took over the area of Israel from the Babylonians, including the Jewish exiles living in Babylon. The Jews found the Persians more humane and tolerant than the Babylonians had been. The Persians worshipped one god only, whom they called the "wise lord," so perhaps they felt a kinship with the Jews, who were also monotheists. (They shared the Jews hostility toward making images of their god.) It was the Persian ruler Cyrus who allowed the Jewish exiles in Babylon to return to their homeland and rebuild their temple, a story told in the books of Ezra and Nehemiah. Nehemiah was in fact a servant in the household of King Artaxerxes.

The Book of Daniel begins in Babylon and relates the conquest of Babylon by the Persians. Daniel becomes a trusted aid of the Persian king, Darius, but is thrown into a den of lions when he will not treat Darius like a god (Daniel 6).

The Book of Esther is set entirely in the Persian capital city of Susa. Esther, a Jewish orphan girl, becomes the wife of King Xerxes (called Ahasuerus in the Bible) and manages to foil a plot to exterminate all the Jews in the Persian Empire.

The Magi—or "wise men"—who visited the newborn Jesus were probably from Persia, where the Magi served as a kind of priesthood for the Zoroastrian religion. They also dabbled in astrology, which explains why the star that arose over Bethlehem when Jesus was born intrigued them.

The Persian ruler Cyrus, who reigned until 529 B.C. is mentioned in 2 Chronicles, Ezra, Isaiah, and Daniel—always favorably. In fact, Isaiah 45:1 even calls him the Lord's "anointed one." It is rare in the Bible for any foreign ruler to be described in such glowing terms, but after the suffering under the Babylonians, the Jews must have found Cyrus a welcome change. He even allowed the Jews the treasures the Babylonians had plundered from the temple in Jerusalem. This may sound "tolerant" and "inclusive," but in fact, it was the way the Persians did politics: Letting the conquered people keep their own religions and customs made rebellion less likely.

Historians think that the Persians were probably the first people to practice crucifixion. The Persian emperor was referred to by the title "king of kings," a term that was picked up by the Jews and, in the New Testament, applied to Jesus Christ.

In communicating with their vast empire, the Persians used the Aramaic language, which the Jews were still using at the time of Jesus. The Persians were conquered by the Greek wonder boy Alexander the Great, who spread the Greek language and culture over the entire region. In the New Testament period, the region was known as the Parthian Empire, and Christianity was spread there very early, with Christians experiencing much less persecution than they did in the Roman Empire. After the Roman emperor Constantine became a Christian in 312, the Parthians changed their tune and began persecuting Christians—apparently on the theory that any religion the Romans liked must be bad.

Peter
The rocky fisherman

He was born Simon, and the name Peter ("rock") was bestowed on him by Jesus. He was a fisherman, as was his brother Andrew, who introduced him to Jesus. He was present at Jesus' first miracle, turning the water into wine. He was the only disciple that we know was married since the Bible tells us that Jesus healed his mother-in-law of a fever (Mark 1:30).

The name Peter (or *Cephas*, in Aramaic) was given when he acknowledged that Jesus was "the Christ, the son of the living God" (Matthew 16:18). Jesus replied, "You are Peter, and on this rock I will build my church ... and I will give you the keys of the kingdom of heaven." Catholics interpret this passage to mean that Peter was to be the first pope, and that all his successor popes would have the "keys of the kingdom." Other Christians interpret it differently, saying that the "rock" was not Peter himself, but his statement that Jesus was "the Christ, the son of the living God."

Whether or not Peter was to be the head of the Christian church, it is true that he is mentioned more in the Gospels than any other disciple, and seemed to be the spokesman for the other eleven. He belong to an inner circle of Jesus' disciples, the brothers James and John being the other members of that circle. The three were present with Jesus at his dazzling Transfiguration (SEE PAGE 367), where Peter, a rather impulsive

P

character, suggested building shelters for Jesus, Moses, and Elijah. When Jesus walked on the water, Peter tried to walk to him, but lost faith and sank. At the Last Supper, Peter claimed he would die for Jesus, who predicted that before the rooster crowed the next morning, Peter would deny him three times—which proved to be true (Matthew 26:69-75). He was with Jesus in Gethsemane at the time of his arrest, and in the scuffle he cut off the ear of one man, whom Jesus healed. Peter and another disciple went to Jesus' empty tomb. After the resurrection of Jesus, his master told him three times to "Feed my sheep"—which Catholics also take to mean that Peter was to be head of the Christian church. From such passages as these, Catholics give him the title "Prince of the Apostles." In the cupola in St. Peter's Basilica in Rome, the Latin words of Matthew 16:18 ("Thou art Peter ...") are seen in six-foot-tall gold letters.

In the Book of Acts, Peter does indeed seem to be chief among the twelve apostles, and Acts 2 has him preaching on the day of Pentecost. He and John healed a crippled man, fulfilling Jesus' prophecy that the disciples would perform miracles. He was imprisoned by Herod but miraculously delivered by an angel. Later he had a vision of a sheet filled with "unclean" (non-kosher) animals, which symbolized the non-Jews in need of the preaching of the Gospel. Peter went to the home of the Roman soldier Cornelius and converted his household.

Two epistles in the New Testament are attributed to Peter. The first epistle claims to be written from "Babylon," which was probably a code name for Rome. Tradition says that Peter went to Rome and headed the large group of Christians there, but that he was martyred under the vile emperor Nero. Supposedly he was crucified upside down, after claiming he was not worthy to die in the same manner of his master Jesus. The enormous St. Peter's Basilica in the Vatican claims to have his bones, an assumption that has been around since Roman emperor Constantine built a church on the site. Tradition says that he fled Rome when persecution of Christians began, but on his way from the city, he met Jesus and asked him, "Where are you going, Lord?" Jesus replied, "To Rome, to be crucified again, since you desert my people." Hearing this, Peter returned to Rome and died as a martyr. Peter probably appears in more Christian artwork than any other person besides Jesus and Mary. Although he is a highly honored figure, the scene of his denial of Jesus has been painted countless times, and rightly so, since it is an emotional moment, particularly since the Gospels say he "wept bitterly" after he had denied Jesus the third time. His denial is a testimony to human weakness—Jesus' most devoted disciple denied knowledge of him. Most films about the arrest and crucifixion of Jesus include Peter's denial.

Peter came to be depicted in art as an older man, often bald or balding, gray, stoutly built. Perhaps artists figured that as the leader of the apostles, Peter had to be the oldest, the most paternal in appearance. He is often shown holding two large keys and sometimes, as a reminder of his human weakness, with a rooster. In films about Jesus, he is often shown as the most outspoken of the apostles. He was the main character in the novel and film *The Big Fisherman*, and featured in the TV movie *Peter and Paul*. The popular novel *Quo Vadis* (and the three film versions of it) features his upside-down crucifixion. He is a featured soloist in Edward Elgar's two oratorios about the early church, *The Apostles* and *The Kingdom*.

Thanks to the passage in which Jesus says that Peter has the "keys of the kingdom of heaven," people have often imagined Peter as standing at the gate of heaven, a kind of celestial gatekeeper admitting people (or turning them away). Who could count all the jokes that begin, "A guy died, and when he got to heaven, St Peter said …"?

Countless churches have been named for Peter, the most famous being the chief church of Catholicism, St. Peter's Basilica. Peter has been a common name among Catholics, although it has never been taken by any pope, probably because it would seem presumptuous for a pope to bear the same name as the first one. In most Christian countries, some form of his name has been a common one for boys—Peter, Pierre, Pedro, Pietro, Peder, etc.

Catholics and Orthodox Christians celebrate June 29 as the Feast of Sts. Peter and Paul. Catholics also celebrate February 22 as the Feast of the Chair of Peter the Apostle—meaning, they honor Peter as the first pope on that day. Since Peter was a fisherman, each pope has an official "fisherman's ring" engraved with his name and a figure of Peter. A popular Morris West novel about a modern pope was titled *The Shoes of the Fisherman*.

The species of fish called the John Dory has also been called "St. Peter's fish" because the dark spot on the body reminded fishermen of the fish Peter caught with a coin in its mouth (Matthew 17:27).

Pharisees

Rule fixation

The Pharisees saw themselves as the Jews who took God and his Laws most seriously. Yet Jesus spoke harshly against them on several occasions, calling them "hypocrites" who would "strain out a gnat and swallow a camel"—so devoted to rules that they neglected loving one's neighbor and loving God. The many rules about eating and drinking, what was proper behavior on the Sabbath, and other humdrum matters were things the Pharisees delighted in. Jesus told his disciples that they had to be *more* righteous than the Pharisees—not about keeping the law, but in loving more (Matthew 5:20). Matthew 23 contains the "seven woes" that Jesus pronounced against the Pharisees, including this one: "Woe to you, teachers of the law and Pharisees, you hypocrites! You are like whitewashed tombs, which look beautiful on the outside but on the inside are full of dead men's bones and everything unclean." He also scolded them for not practicing what they preached (Matthew 23:3). They criticized Jesus for hobnobbing with tax collectors and other sinners (Matthew 9:11) and accused Jesus of having power to exorcise demons because he was in league with Satan (Matthew 9:34). Luke's Gospel mentions that the Pharisees loved money (Luke 16:14) and also contains the famous parable of the self-righteous Pharisee praying in the temple (SEE PAGE 268). On one occasion John the Baptist called the Pharisees a "generation of vipers" (Matthew 3:7).

Still, on occasion Jesus dined with Pharisees (Luke 14) and some Pharisees warned Jesus that Herod wished to kill him (Luke 13:31). John's Gospel tells of the Pharisee named Nicodemus, who came to Jesus and learned about the need to be "born again" (John 3). Even so, the Pharisees connived with the priests to bring about Jesus' crucifixion.

As it happened, the apostle Paul had been a Pharisee, although he actually practiced what he preached. He turned from persecutor of Christians to the greatest Christian missionary of all time. Several of his letters in the New Testament show how he had turned his back on the legalism of the Pharisees.

The word Pharisee means something like "separated ones"—people striving to be holy, that is. Because Jesus so often spoke of them as self-righteous hypocrites, the word Pharisee continues to carry that meaning.

Philistines
The uncut version

For many centuries, the area of Israel and the surrounding region was called Palestine. The name came from the Philistines, a people who settled on the coast and generally made life difficult for the other nations there, especially Israel. The Book of Judges shows the Israelites fighting them off, with the judge Samson their greatest menace. Israel grew so weary of these warlike people that they begged the judge Samuel to give them a king who would unite them and help them fight. Their first king was Saul, who died in battle with the Philistines. The second king, David, had more luck fighting off these oppressors, and by the end of his reign, they had left Israel in peace.

Historically, we don't know much about the Philistines except what the Bible tells us. They were notorious for not circumcising their males, and the Israelites sometimes referred to them (with contempt) as "the uncircumcised." (David killed two hundred Philistines in battle and brought their foreskins to Saul as a "bride price" for marrying Saul's daughter in 1 Samuel 18:25-27.) They were skilled in metalworking, which the Israelites were not, so the Israelites had to go to them for farming tools (1 Samuel 13). They worshipped a god named Dagon, and in the Book of Judges, Samson kills many of the Philistines (and himself) by dislodging two pillars in a temple of Dagon. (Samson had been married to a Philistine woman, and had been made a captive by the wiles of another Philistine woman, Delilah.) Later the Philistines captured Israel's most sacred object, the ark of the covenant, but while they had it in their custody, it kept causing the statue of Dagon to fall on its face, breaking off its head and hands, so they returned it to Israel (1 Samuel 5). Later, the Philistines menaced Israel with the giant Goliath (SEE PAGE 134), who, to everyone's great surprise, was killed by one stone fired from the sling of the boy David.

The Philistines were centered in five cities—Gaza, Ashkelon, Gath, Ashdod, and Ekron. Their kings, or lords, had the title *saren*.

The name "Philistine" took on a new meaning in the 1600s, when Germany university students began referring to the uneducated as "Philistines." In the 1800s, English author Matthew Arnold also used the term to refer to crude, uncultured people, and it is still sometimes used today.

Pilate
The world's most mentioned Roman

At the time of Jesus' arrest and crucifixion, Pontius Pilate was the Roman Empire's prefect (governor) in the province of Judea. Pilate, like most Romans, despised the

Jews and their religion, which is evident in Jesus' trial, where Pilate considers the whole matter a "Jewish thing," a religious question that should be no concern of his. He did not consider Jesus a political threat to Rome and would have released him had the Jews not insisted that Jesus intended to set himself up as "king of the Jews." Pilate was amazed at Jesus' passivity during the trial, and probably appalled that the Jews begged for the release of Barabbas, a political revolutionary who really *was* a threat to Rome. Pilate gave in to the Jews' pleas but literally washed his hands of responsibility for Jesus' death (Matthew 27:19-24).

The Gospels have been accused of sugarcoating Pilate, especially since ancient historians—such as the Jewish writer Josephus—describe Pilate as cruel and snobbish, going out of his way to rile the Jews. But then again, the Gospels may be correct in depicting Pilate as sympathetic to Jesus: His compassion to the innocent, nonpolitical carpenter from Galilee may have been a deliberate attempt to irk the Jewish authorities and their supporters—and in that he succeeded. Still, Mark's Gospel notes that Pilate was "wishing to satisfy the crowd" when he released Barabbas and ordered Jesus crucified (Mark 15:15).

One of the Gospels records an interesting moment in Jesus' trial before Pilate. Jesus said to him, "Everyone who is of the truth hears my voice." Pilate's famous (and cynical reply) was "What is truth?" (John 18:38). The famous essay "Of Truth" by English author Francis Bacon begins with the words, " 'What is truth?' said jesting Pilate, and would not stay for an answer." Thanks to Bacon, the phrase "jesting Pilate" entered the language, suggesting a person of power with no fixed beliefs or moral center. (In other words, a typical politician, which is what Pilate was.)

The Christian confession known as the Apostles' Creed states that Jesus "suffered under Pontius Pilate," and considering how often the creed has been repeated over the centuries, Pilate may be the most-mentioned Roman who ever lived, despite the fact that we know little about him before or after the trial of Jesus. He was recalled to Rome in the year 37, and one old tradition said he was executed by emperor Nero. In early Christian legend, both he and his wife became Christians themselves, and in some areas Christians even honored them as saints. In some other legends, his failure to save Jesus is punished by many misfortunes, until he finally commits suicide.

Thanks to his crucial role in Jesus' life, he has appeared in millions of artworks, plays, and novels. In most films he is portrayed somewhat sympathetically, an honest official trying to deal fairly with Jesus, and not willing (at first, anyway) to let the Jewish priests bully him into executing an innocent man. The Pilate of the 2004

Mel Gibson film *Passion of the Christ* is typical of these "good" Pilates, who seem to embody Roman justice at its best. In other films, such as *The Last Temptation of Christ* and the 1999 TV movie *Jesus*, Pilate is more cynical and flippant, not caring whether Jesus dies or not. Maybe the Pilate of *Jesus Christ Superstar*—cynical, but also aware of Jesus' innocence—is closest to the real Pilate

Pilate's wife is mentioned in Matthew's Gospel (Matthew 27:19) as sending a message to Pilate while he was trying Jesus. The message told him, "Have nothing to do with that righteous man, for I have suffered much because of him today in a dream." The wife is unnamed in the Bible, but tradition calls her Claudia, or Procula, or Claudia Procula. Because she told Pilate to leave Jesus alone, Christian tradition viewed her as saintly, and she was played very sympathetically in *Passion of the Christ*.

The Trial of Christ
MATTHEW. CHAPTER 26, VERSES 63-66.

Here's an odd little tidbit: The Punch and Judy puppet shows of England, featuring the clownish character Punch and his wife Judy, may have their origin in the names Pontius and Judas. In the Middle Ages, dramas about Jesus' arrest and trial always featured the characters Pontius Pilate and Judas Iscariot. At times these serious plays degenerated into slapstick comedy (which church leaders frowned on), with Pilate often speaking in a funny, squeaky voice (the voice that Punch always uses in the puppet shows, that is). As the plays became sillier and less religious, the names morphed into Punch and Judy (overlooking the fact that Judas was male, not female), and the origins in religious drama were completely forgotten.

pilgrims
Just passing through, thanks …

The first Christians saw their life in this world as temporary, since their minds were fixed on eternity. Hebrews 11 recalls saints of the past and says they were "strangers and pilgrims on the earth," and 1 Peter 2 also refers to Christians as "strangers and pilgrims." The English folks who settled the colony of Plymouth, Massachusetts, in 1620 are known as the Pilgrims, although the name wasn't actually used until 1820, when statesman Daniel Webster gave a speech at a bicentennial festival and spoke of the "Pilgrim Fathers."

Potiphar and his wife
The desperate housewife syndrome

Potiphar was one of the Egyptian pharaoh's officials, and Genesis 39 tells that he bought young Joseph, who had been sold into slavery by his jealous brothers. Joseph proved so competent that Potiphar made him overseer of his whole household. Things went well until Potiphar's randy wife tried to seduce the handsome young Joseph. He resisted, and the wife, after many tries, became the furious woman scorned. She accused Joseph of trying to seduce her, and Potiphar had Joseph thrown in prison (Genesis 39).

Potiphar's wife is unnamed in Genesis, but in Muslim tradition her name is Zuleika. Because of the incident involving her, Joseph is considered as a role model of integrity and self-control. In the many films dealing with Joseph in Egypt, the incident with her is always included. It is also included in the popular stage musical *Joseph and the Amazing Technicolor Dreamcoat*, where Mrs. Potiphar has only one line: "Come and lie with me." In a PBS production of *Dreamcoat*, she was played by actress Joan Collins.

prayer shawls
Fringe benefits

Many Jewish men wear the prayer shawl, or *tallit*, which is made of white silk or wool, with stripes at the ends and tassels or fringes at the four corners. Generally a boy can begin wearing the *tallit* after the time of his bar mitzvah. The shawls are described in Numbers 15:38-39 and Deuteronomy 22:12, which says the tassels are there as reminders of God's commandments (though exactly why the tassels remind them of commandments is not stated). We know Jesus wore the *tallit* at times, because Matthew 9 records the healing of an ailing woman who touched the fringe of Jesus' *tallit*. However, Jesus spoke out against people whose long fringes were meant to give them the appearance of a spirituality they did not possess (Matthew 23:5).

the Presentation
Infant messiah

The Jewish law mandated dedicating one's firstborn son to God, and if possible going to the temple in Jerusalem to present the child "to the Lord." Luke 2 states that Joseph and Mary did so with the infant Jesus, and at that time an old man named Simeon praised God because he had been promised to see the Messiah before he died. He also said some rather mysterious words to Mary: "A sword will pierce your own soul also," which the early Christians took to be a prophecy of Mary seeing Jesus crucified. Simeon's song of praise to God is named after its first words in Latin, *Nunc Dimittis,* and has been recited and set to music many times (Luke 2:25-34). Luke's Gospel also states that an elderly woman named Anna, called "a prophetess," saw the infant Jesus and praised God.

Catholics and Eastern Orthodox Christians celebrate this event on February 2 as the Feast of the Presentation of Our Lord in the Temple. In earlier times it was also called Candlemas Day, from an old practice of church candles being blessed on that day. The TV mini-series *Jesus of Nazareth* was one of the few films to depict this episode in Jesus' life.

priests
God's middlemen

In the earliest chapters of the Bible, there were no priests. Any person could make an offering to God, as Cain and Abel did, and Noah. The idea developed that there should be a "go-between" person, to make sacrifices to God on behalf of someone else. The first priest mentioned in the Bible is Melchizedek (SEE PAGE 240). Israel itself had no priest until the time following the Exodus from Egypt,

P

when Aaron, Moses' brother, became Israel's first high priest (SEE PAGE 3). His clothing and other accoutrements are described in Exodus 28-29 and Leviticus 8. As high priest, he offered sacrifices on behalf of all the people and confessed their sins to God, restoring a right relationship between them and God. Only the high priest could enter the Holy of Holies and sprinkle blood on the ark of the covenant. Israel's priests traced their descent from Aaron, but many of them were greedy and corrupt, including Aaron's own two sons.

From the time of Moses until the time of Solomon, the priests performed their activities in the tabernacle, or tent of meeting (SEE PAGE 354). Solomon built the beautiful temple in Jerusalem, and the priests performed their duties there. Some priests were noble characters, but as the Gospels make clear, in Jesus' time most of them were corrupt, greedy bureaucrats, and the high priest Caiaphas condemned Jesus to death as a blasphemer. In Jesus' famous parable of the Good Samaritan, a priest is depicted as lacking compassion. Within forty years of Jesus' crucifixion, the Romans destroyed the temple and the Jewish priesthood was completely done away with. There are no priests in the Jewish religion now.

The Letter to the Hebrews in the New Testament says that Christians have one priest—Jesus, in heaven, who is not only the final sacrifice ("the Lamb of God") but also the priest who brings God and man together. The old system of priests and sacrifices was no longer necessary.

Christian ministers are not called "priests" in the New Testament, which uses the words "bishops," "elders," and "deacons." The Christian belief in the "priesthood of all believers" is based on several passages in the New Testament, such as 1 Peter 2:9: "You are a chosen people, a royal priesthood, a holy nation, a people belonging to God." The Book of Revelation several times refers to believers as "priests of God."

Priscilla and Aquila
Husband-and-wife act

Christianity was open to the gifts and leadership of women, and one of the most prominent of these is Priscilla, who, with her husband Aquila, was a close friend of the apostle Paul. They were both tentmakers by trade, as was Paul, and they seemed to have traveled around the Roman Empire, spreading the new faith wherever they went. We know they were in Rome for awhile, and in the city of

Ephesus a Christian fellowship met in their home. Paul states that at one point "they laid down their necks for me" (Romans 16:3-4), but some later versions have "risked their necks." When mentioned in the New Testament, Priscilla's name usually comes first. Tradition says they both died as martyrs. The Catholic Church observes July 8 as their feast day.

prodigal son
(SEE *parable of the prodigal son*)

the Promised Land
Real land, or heaven?

The person who received the promise was Abraham, the ancestor of the Israelites. Genesis 12 relates that God called Abraham to leave his pagan home in Ur and move to Canaan, a land that God promised would belong to him and his descendants. Canaan roughly corresponds to the nation of Israel today. Abraham and his descendants were not there for long, for his grandson Jacob brought the whole family to Egypt during a famine, and they lived there for generations, eventually becoming slaves until Moses led them out. By the time the Israelites arrived back in Canaan, the land was inhabited by people who weren't impressed that the Israelites had been "promised" the land by God. The Books of Joshua and Judges tell of the wars fought by the Israelites against the natives. Centuries later, Assyrians and Babylonians conquered the region and deported many of the Israelites, but many of them resettled there, and even the ones living far away had an affection for "the promised land." A Jewish revolt in the year 70 led the Romans to destroy the Jews' temple and secularize the area. It was later conquered by the Muslims, who held it until World War I. The nation of Israel, formed in 1948, allowed the region to become the "promised land" once again, not without serious conflict with Muslims who lived in the area. In the late 1800s, many of the Russian Jews who immigrated to the U.S. referred to America as the Promised Land.

As with the name Canaan (which applies to the same region), Christians have interpreted "promised land" very differently, taking it to mean heaven, not any

P

place on earth. "Promised land" occurs frequently in Christian hymns and other writings. In the 1990s, a TV drama series was titled *Promised Land*.

prophets
Quoting God

Throughout the Bible, some people are privileged to hear the voice of God directly. But mostly God's word came through the people called prophets. They weren't really predictors, although they did do some forecasting. Primarily they were God's mouthpieces, speaking on God's behalf, as if God had given them his message and commanded them to share it. A prophet wasn't "his own man," he was the humble spokesman for the Lord. Most often his role was to remind people they were sinning and to warn them of dire consequences if they did not stop. The prophet believed the words he uttered were in some sense God's own words, as seen in Jeremiah 1:9, where God tells Jeremiah, "I have put my words in your mouth."

There were *false* prophets, since anyone wanting attention can say, "God spoke to me and told me to ..." The Old Testament law mandated that false prophets had to be put to death (Deuteronomy 13). Even so, there were plenty of them around, and kings often had court prophets who functioned as "yes-men," saying that God approved of whatever the king did.

The Jews divided the Old Testament into the Law (the first five books, also called the Torah and the books of Moses) and the Prophets. The books of Joshua through 2 Kings are called the Former Prophets. The Latter Prophets are the last

The Test of Baal's Prophets
I Kings. Chapter 18, Verses 36-40.

books in the Old Testament—three called the Major Prophets (Isaiah, Jeremiah, Ezekiel) and twelve others called the Minor Prophets—because their books are so much shorter. In Jewish tradition, the Minor Prophets—also called "the Twelve"—fill one scroll altogether. Some of the most inspiring and touching passages in the Bible are found in the writings of the Latter Prophets, especially Isaiah, who is quoted frequently in the New Testament. On the other hand, some of the prophets' writings are literally "ancient history," dealing with political quarrels that don't have much meaning for people today.

Of all the prophets in the Old Testament, the mostly highly regarded was Elijah (SEE PAGE 106), the fiery prophet who staged a famous showdown with the prophets of Baal. As centuries passed, Elijah became the symbol of all the prophets in the Bible. The last book in the Old Testament contains a prophecy by the prophet Malachi that God would send an Elijah-like prophet before the Day of Judgment. The early Christians believed that John the Baptist, Jesus' relative, was that prophet, and so did Jesus himself (Matthew 11:13-14).

In the period between the Old and New Testaments, there were no prophets. For several centuries, people relied on the Law to guide them in life, and no man was recognized as a true prophet sent from God. The Christians, as already stated, believed John the Baptist was a prophet, and the Book of Acts shows that there were other prophets among the first generation of Christians (Acts 13:1, 15:32, 1 Corinthians 12:28). Jesus himself was considered a prophet by many people, but in one sense he was very different: While the Old Testament prophets began their speeches with "Thus says the Lord," Jesus spoke on his own authority, with "I say to you …" Jesus' enemies viewed this as arrogance.

In the New Testament, you often encounter the word "fulfill." The early Christians looked at events in the life of Jesus and his apostles and regarded those events as "fulfilling" the words of the prophets—meaning that the words had come to be in real life. One outstanding example was the Virgin Mary's conception of Jesus, which Matthew's Gospel says is a fulfillment of the words of Isaiah 7:14: "Behold, a virgin shall conceive and bear a son, and shall call his name Immanuel." When Jesus entered Jerusalem, riding on a donkey, people saw it as a fulfillment of the words of the prophet Zechariah: "Your king is coming to you, humble, mounted on a donkey." Christians have tended to "spiritualize" the writings of the prophets—that is, when the prophets spoke of Jerusalem and Israel being restored, with peace and security and prosperity for everyone, Christians took this to refer not to this world, but to heaven.

The Hebrew word for "prophet" was *nabi*. In the late 1800s a group of French artists called themselves *Les Nabis*, the prophets, although there was nothing religious about their artwork.

proselytes and God-fearers
The difference was surgical

In the ancient world, most people believed in many gods (polytheism), but there was always a handful who believed in only one God (monotheism), and that he was very different from the unpredictable, fornicating gods of most cultures. The Jews were widely mocked for worshipping one invisible God, but their God was attractive because he was moral and just. Also, the Jews' morality, especially their commitment to family life, was attractive to people who wanted to live a good life. In some cases, these people lived more ethical lives than the Jews themselves because they *chose* the Jewish moral code instead of being born into it.

People who were attracted to the Jewish religion fell into two categories: proselytes and God-fearers. Both groups tried to live by the Laws of Moses, as the Jews did. Essentially the difference was a surgical one: men who wanted to become proselytes—full-fledged members of the Jewish community—had to be circumcised. Those not willing to go quite that far were considered God-fearers. Incidentally, Greeks and Romans who prayed to the Jews' god often used the name *Iao*—the Greeks' version of the Hebrew name for God, *Yahweh*. Some Greeks and Romans didn't see *Iao* as the only god, but as one among many.

In the New Testament we see several people, mostly Roman soldiers, who were either God-fearers or proselytes. One of these was the Roman centurion Cornelius, described as "righteous and God-fearing," who became a Christian after hearing the faith presented by the apostle Peter (Acts 10-11). Cornelius was one of many proselytes and God-fearers who later embraced Christianity. In Acts 13, Paul preaches in a synagogue to "men of Israel and you who fear God"—meaning the synagogue had both Jews and God-fearers. Many God-fearers converted because they saw the new faith in Christ as being the fulfillment of the Jewish religion that had attracted them in the first place.

Proverbs
Read 'em and keep

Of all the books in the Bible, Proverbs is most-read by people who aren't Jews or Christians—or any religion at all. Many of the sayings contained in the book are plain commonsense advice that makes life a little easier. Still, the book is religious, as seen in the saying, "Trust in the Lord with all your heart, and lean not on your own understanding" (Proverbs 3:5) and "A man's ways are before the eyes of the Lord, and he ponders all his paths" (Proverbs 5:21).

The book opens with the statement that the sayings are those of Solomon, the wise king of Israel. However, some parts of the book claim to be by a certain Agur and a king named Lemuel. Neither of these was an Israelite, so the book draws on the wisdom of folks who were not among the "chosen people," Israel.

Many of the sayings are quoted often: *Like a dog that returns to his vomit is a fool who repeats his folly. Let not your heart envy sinners, but continue in the fear of the Lord all the day. Many a man proclaims his steadfast love, but a faithful man who can find? Better to be of lowly spirit with the poor than to divide the spoil with the proud. There is a way that seems right to a man, but the end thereof is the way of death. A soft answer turns away wrath, but a harsh word stirs up anger. The cheerful of heart has a continual feast. Whoever spares the rod hates his son. Whoever walks with the wise becomes wise. Hatred stirs up strife, but love covers all offenses. A slack hand causes poverty, but the hand of the diligent makes rich.*

One interesting aspect of Proverbs is that it warns against the loose woman (Proverbs 5, 6:20-35) and heaps praise upon the "excellent wife" who manages the home with love and wisdom (Proverbs 31:10-31).

Psalms

Pssst, the P is silent

Psalms is the longest book in the Bible, and the one quoted most often in the New Testament. The book's Hebrew title is *Tehillim*, meaning "songs of praise," but that isn't quite accurate, because Psalms is a book of many moods, which is why it has been so widely read for so long. The 150 Psalms are poems or songs covering every facet of spirituality—praise, despair, hope, pleading, joy, even revenge against one's enemies. Martin Luther, leader of the Protestant Reformation in the 1500s, called Psalms "the Bible in miniature." They were written over a period of centuries, seventy-three of them said to be written by King David, others by Solomon, Moses, and other famous men. The Bible's longest chapter is Psalm 119, which has 176 verses and is a long praise of the Law of Moses. Some of the psalms are "songs of ascents," sung by Jewish pilgrims visiting the temple in Jerusalem. The "imprecatory" psalms are ones calling on God to punish one's tormentors. (Christians are uncomfortable with some of these, since they seem mean-spirited and vindictive.) Psalm 23 is the famous "shepherd psalm," beginning "The Lord is my shepherd." Psalm 51 is David's heartfelt prayer of confessing his sins. This is one of the "penitential Psalms," seven touching poems baring one's soul (and sins) to God and pleading for mercy. When Jesus was tempted by Satan, he quoted from Psalms. Psalm 22 is a deep cry of despair, and its first verse, "My God, my God, why have you forsaken me?" was spoken by Jesus on the cross, as was "Into your hand I commit my spirit" (Psalm 31:5).

The Jews loved the Psalms, and most devout Jews knew the book by heart (and also knew the melodies used for singing the Psalms). Since the early Christians were all Jews, they retained their affection for the book, often seeing things in it that seemed to apply to the life of Jesus. The Psalms were read aloud, sung, or chanted in Christian worship services, and even today every worship service in Catholic, Orthodox, and Episcopal churches includes a reading (or chanting) from Psalms. Most of them have been set to music. In the Middle Ages, the custom was antiphonal singing of the Psalms—two halves of the choir singing alternate verses. In fact, for many centuries the only hymns sung in churches were the Psalms. In the 1500s, many poets wrote rhymed versions of the Psalms, and many Christian hymns (including "Joy to the World") are revisions of the words from Psalms. Since they were part of the Bible, the Psalms were believed to be divinely inspired, while other songs and poems were only "hymns of human composure." Nahum Tate, England's poet laureate, wrote some metrical Psalms that were used for many years. It wasn't until the 1700s that churches began adding the "human" hymns to their worship service. Many of the Psalms are featured in George Frederic Handel's *The Occasional Oratorio* and in Igor Stravinsky's *Symphony of Psalms*. Composer Heinrich Schutz wrote his fine *Psalms of David* (1619) for the Lutheran churches of Germany.

The Psalms are also known as the Psalter, and some people owned luxuriously bound and illustrated copies of the Psalter. Most people believe the first printed book was the Bible, printed by Johann Gutenberg around 1456, but we now know that a book containing just the Psalms was printed first. One of the earliest books printed in the American colonies was the *Bay Psalm Book*, a

Psalter printed in 1640 in Massachusetts. Throughout the centuries, literary critics (even ones who weren't religious) have stated that the Psalms are some of the finest poetry ever written.

purgatory
Cleaning up for heaven

In Catholic teaching, when a person dies he goes to heaven, hell, or purgatory. As its name suggest, purgatory is a place of purging, or cleansing. The person in purgatory is destined for heaven, but requires a time of moral and spiritual "make-over" before entering the presence of God. In the 1500s, Protestants cast this belief aside, saying it was not clearly taught in the Bible. In the Apocrypha, 2 Maccabees 12:4 speaks of "praying for the dead," which Catholics take to mean praying for the people in purgatory. Protestants don't accept the Apocrypha as authoritative—in fact, one of the key reasons they tossed the Apocrypha aside was that the belief in purgatory was based on it. However, some Protestants, such as the great Christian writer C. S. Lewis, have suggested that purgatory might be real since the idea of spiritual cleansing before entering heaven has a certain logic to it.

All Souls Day, observed by Catholics on November 2, was instituted as a day to pray for the souls in purgatory.

P

the queen of Sheba

Just how friendly was she with Solomon?

Israel's King Solomon gained fame for his wisdom, and also for maintaining a splendid court. In 1 Kings 10, he is visited by the queen of Sheba, who arrived in Jerusalem with a caravan of spices, gold, and gems. The queen tests his wisdom and is in awe. According to 2 Chronicles 9:3, "there was no more spirit in her"—that is, Solomon was breathtaking. She sings the praises not only of Solomon but of his God. Was there really such a place as Sheba? The Bible scholars believe Sheba was probably an area in south Arabia, noted for its spices and other luxury items.

Jesus referred to the queen's visit to behold the wise king, noting that his own people ignored one who was greater than Solomon (that is, Jesus himself).

Down to the twentieth century, the emperors of Ethiopia claimed to be descendants of Solomon and the queen of Sheba. The Bible itself does not give us her name, but in legend she is sometimes called Belkis, sometimes Makeba. (The Koran calls her Balkis.) Considering how many wives and concubines Solomon had, it isn't too far-fetched to believe that he and the queen produced a child together. Whether the rulers of Ethiopia are descended from that child is another matter. Legend has it that the queen (whom the Ethiopians call Makeda) bore a son, Menelik, who at age twenty-two journeyed to Jerusalem to learn the Hebrew Scriptures, visit his wise father, and carry the true faith back to his homeland. In Muslim legends, the queen was the daughter of *jinn* (spirits), not of a human couple.

Solomon and the queen are a favorite subject for artists, who love depicting this fateful meeting of two very rich rulers. George Frideric Handel, in his oratorio *Solo-*

mon, included the queen's visit (naming her Nicaule, for some reason, and having her sing of arriving "from Arabia's spicy shores"). Italian composer Ottorino Respighi wrote an instrumental piece called *Belkis, Queen of Sheba.* The queen's encounter with Solomon was the basis of several movies, most memorably Cecil B. DeMille's *Solomon and Sheba,* starring Yul Brynner (with a headful of hair!) and Italian beauty Gina Lollabrigida. Several other films have been made about this exotic queen and her luxury-laden caravan. English poet Robert Browning's 1883 poem "Solomon and Balkis," is a witty conversation between Solomon and the queen of Sheba, in which they pretend to be talking of deep subjects but in reality are flirting with each other. French composer Charles Gounod wrote an opera about the queen, as did Hungarian composer Karl Goldmark.

Q

R

Rachel and Leah

Sneaky Jacob's comeuppance

It's always a pleasure to read a story where a tricky character gets tricked himself. This is true in the case of Jacob, the son of Isaac and Rebecca, who tricked his twin brother Esau out of his inheritance. Esau plotted to kill him as soon as Isaac died, so Jacob fled to live with his mother's brother, Laban. At the first sight of his beautiful cousin, Rachel, Jacob fell madly in love—so much so he kissed her and wept at the first meeting. His uncle Laban welcomed him warmly, and Jacob agreed to work for him for seven years in order to marry Rachel. Jacob got a surprise on the morning after his wedding night: The woman in his bed was not Rachel, but her homely older sister, Leah. The wily Laban then informed Jacob it was their custom to marry off the older sister first. We can assume Jacob was annoyed at

Jacob and Rachel at the Well
GENESIS. CHAPTER 29, VERSES 1-12.

being hoodwinked, but Laban relented and allowed him to marry Rachel too—if he agreed to work for Laban another seven years (Genesis 29). The additional seven years "seemed to him but a short while, so great was the love he bore her."

Leah, the unloved wife, got some compensation: She had children by Jacob while Rachel did not. In fact, she had four sons, including Judah, who was the ancestor of David and, centuries later, Jesus. Rachel gave Jacob her maid as a concubine, so that in some sense the maid's children would be hers. The maid had two sons by Jacob. Leah had stopped bearing, so she gave her maid to Jacob, who bore him two sons. One of the sons found some mandrake roots, which were thought to cause fertility, and the two sisters fought over the mandrakes. Leah got them and had two more sons by Jacob, and also Jacob's only daughter, Dinah. Finally, at long last, Rachel had a child, Joseph, who was his father's pet, since he was the son of the beloved Rachel. Years later Rachel had one more son, Benjamin, but she died shortly after his birth. The entry on Joseph (SEE PAGE 196) tells more about the sibling rival among these half-brothers.

After serving his uncle for twenty years, Jacob packed up his goods and his large family and went back to Canaan in a camel caravan, but Laban wouldn't have it, since so much of his wealth was now in Jacob's hands. Rachel had even made off with her father's household idols, and Laban pursued Jacob. The two tricksters finally made an agreement, at a place called Mizpah, with these words: "The Lord watch between thee and me while we are apart, one from another" (Genesis 31:49). This is known as the "Mizpah benediction" and has often been used by Christians when they are saying a farewell to each other. The original meaning of the words wasn't as spiritual: Jacob and Laban were reminding each other that they were both untrustworthy sneaks, but that God was watching their every move.

The name Rachel has been popular among Christians and Jews since it sounds pretty and the Rachel of the Bible is physically beautiful. There have been far fewer children named Leah.

Rahab
Harlot with the heart of gold

Literature and movies have made the "whore with a heart of gold" a stock character, and one of the earliest in world literature is the prostitute Rahab in the Book of Joshua. She and her family lived in the old Canaanite city of Jericho, which was about to fall (literally) to the Israelites under the leadership of Joshua. He sent spies into Jericho, and Rahab hid them on her roof, then sent the pursuers on a wild goose chase and helped the spies escape through a window. For her help, they agreed to spare her when they conquered the city.

Surprisingly, she appears in Matthew 1 as among the ancestors of Jesus, and she is mentioned in both the Letter to the Hebrews and the Letter of James as an example of faith.

Incidentally, linguists who study ancient languages think it's possible that when the Hebrew text refers to her as a "prostitute," it might actually mean "innkeeper."

Rapture
Rising and shining for all to see

The early Christians spoke of death as "falling asleep"—just a temporary condition, for they would be "awakened" in a dramatic way when Jesus returned to earth. In 1 Thessalonians, the apostle Paul wrote that Jesus would descend from heaven, that the "trumpet of God" would sound, "and the dead in Christ will rise first," then the Christians still alive on earth would be "caught up together with them in the clouds to meet the Lord in the air." (1 Thessalonians 4:16-17). This meeting in the skies is known as the Rapture.

Reconstructionism
The "Bible only" policy

For two thousand years, Christians have been trying to get "back to the Bible"—or back to the New Testament anyway. Many churches and denominations have been established because Christians looked at their own church and didn't see any resemblance to the Christianity described in the New Testament. The Churches of Christ, which began in the U.S. in 1832, describe themselves as "Reconstructionists," trying to create churches with the same beliefs and practices as the New Testament Christians. Their rule of thumb is, if you can't find it in the New Testament, don't do it. For this reason the Churches of Christ do not use musical instruments in their worship services, because the New Testament does not mention them (not counting the Book of Revelation, which says there are harps in heaven). The Churches of Christ have hymn singing, but no accompaniment. Oddly, some of these churches have organs or pianos, which can be used for weddings or funerals, but not at worship.

the Red Sea

A famous site, with an incorrect name

Here is a case where the King James Version of the Bible is simply wrong. Moses and the Israelites did *not* cross the Red Sea, the large body of water that lies between Egypt and Arabia (Exodus 14). In the Hebrew Old Testament, they cross the *yam suph*, the "reed sea" or "marshy sea." We aren't sure where the *yam suph* is, but it was probably narrower and shallower than the actual Red Sea. The scholars' best guess is that it was a place today called Lake Timsah, which is fresh water, not salt sea. It is not as large as the Red Sea, but God parting the waters of it is still a mighty impressive miracle, one that the Israelites remembered for centuries as a sign that God looked after them.

Incidentally, the parting of the waters wasn't quite as immediate as it appears in movies about Moses. Exodus 14:21 says that God "drove the sea back by a strong east wind all night and made the sea dry land, and the waters were divided."

the Reformation

Open book policy

A bookstore today may carry dozens of different Bibles in English. That would have shocked our ancestors 500 years ago, because the church authorities did not allow translations into the languages people actually spoke. The only legal Bible was in Latin, a dead language used only by scholars. Beginning with Martin Luther in the early 1500s, Protestants began translating the Bible into the people's languages, basing them not on the Latin Bible but on the original Hebrew and Greek texts. The first and most important English translator was William Tyndale, who translated the New Testament and much of the Old Testament before he was burned at the stake as a heretic. A major part of the beloved King James Version was a fine-tuning of Tyndale's translation.

The new translations were widely circulated thanks to the printing press, and the more books were printed, the more people learned to read. In fact, having the Bible in their own languages was the motivation for many people to learn to read.

R

Catholics eventually allowed the Bible to be translated into the people's languages—but the translations had to be made from the Latin Bible, not the original Greek and Hebrew. It wasn't until the twentieth century that Catholics could get "back to the basics" and translate from the originals.

resurrection
Basic Beliefs 101

The key event in the New Testament is the resurrection of Jesus from the grave. The first Christians believed in this wholeheartedly, and also believed that his resurrection was a kind of "preview" of what would happen to them in the future. In all four Gospels, Jesus is crucified on a Friday and raised to life on a Sunday, which is why Christians have made the first day of the week their day of worship. In fact, the first Christians referred to Sunday as "the Lord's day" (Revelation 1:10). Easter (SEE PAGE 100) is the annual celebration of Jesus' resurrection, and until the twentieth century, Christians placed much more emphasis on Easter than on Christmas.

The heart of the message the apostles spread far and wide was that God raised Jesus, and the apostles were the witnesses, having seen him and talked with afterward (Acts 2:32). The resurrection, they taught, was God proving that Jesus was right—an innocent executed by human cruelty, but brought back to life by divine power. Almost every Christian creed written states that Jesus was raised to life again. The resurrection is the "great divide"—millions of people worldwide

The Resurrection of Christ
MATTHEW. CHAPTER 28, VERSES 2-4.

admire Jesus as a moral teacher but don't believe in the resurrection. Since the very beginning, skeptics have said that Jesus' apostles stole his body from the tomb and spread the rumor that he had been resurrected.

The Bible doesn't give many particulars about how the resurrection took place. Matthew's Gospel says there was an earthquake, and an angel rolled away the large stone in front of Jesus' tomb.

But how Jesus' body emerged from the tomb is a mystery. The Gospels give the impression that Jesus' risen body was similar to his earthly body—it still had the wounds from the crucifixion (John 20:24-28)—but it was also different in some way, since some of his followers did not recognize him (Luke 24:36-37). This mystery is why the resurrection itself has not been a common subject for artists. In the Middle Ages, though, some painters produced *Imago Pietatis*, an image of Christ standing upright in his tomb. In some paintings the risen Jesus is surrounded by a *mandorla*, an almond-shaped gold halo. The final scene in the film 2004 *The Passion of the Christ* briefly shows Jesus' graveclothes "deflating," and a few seconds later the living Jesus stands up and walks out of the tomb, a rare case of a film depicting the miracle. One reason such films as *Jesus Christ Superstar, The Last Temptation of Christ*, and *The Passover Plot* arouse such controversy is that they show the crucifixion but not the resurrection—in other words, they omit the one event that Christians have always said was the most important of all.

In 1 Corinthians 15, the apostle Paul explains that "believing in Jesus" is pointless if Jesus died and stayed buried. This is in the famous "resurrection" chapter, explaining that after the resurrection, people will have "spiritual bodies" (an oxymoron, but he was trying to describe the indescribable). Some of the verses from the resurrection chapter were set to stirring music by George Frideric Handel in his *Messiah*.

Jerusalem has the Church of the Holy Sepulchre (also called the Church of the Resurrection), though no one is certain whether this was the actual tomb of Jesus.

Reuben
A good name for bumpkins

Reuben was the firstborn of Jacob's twelve sons, but not the favorite, as Jacob favored his two youngest sons by Rachel, Joseph and Benjamin. Reuben and the other sons were especially jealous of Joseph, plotting to kill him, but Reuben had enough compassion to suggest leaving Joseph in a pit in the wilderness, with Reuben secretly planning to rescue him later. When Reuben returned to the pit, he found the other brothers had sold Joseph as a slave (Genesis 37).

As the firstborn son, Reuben should have had the largest inheritance, but Jacob withheld it, referring to Reuben as "unstable as water" and one who "would not excel" (Genesis 49:3-4). As one of Jacob's twelve sons, Reuben was ancestor of one of the twelve tribes of Israel, but the tribe was relatively unimportant.

Sometime in the late 1800s or early 1900s, the name Reuben came to be thought of as a "hick" name, which resulted in bumpkins being referred to as "rubes." Many rural folks named their children for Bible characters, even if those characters weren't always important or admirable, and Reuben was probably among those names.

Revelation / Apocalypse
666, and other mysteries

The Book of Revelation is the last book of the Bible, and appropriately so, since its main subject is the end of the world—and the beginning of a new one, which is good news for the saints and bad news for the sinners. It is sometimes known as the Apocalypse, from the Greek word *apokalypsis*, meaning "revelation." Its author was a man named John, possibly John the apostle of Jesus, but probably someone else, since John was a common name. It was written on the bleak, stony Greek island of Patmos where (tradition says) John had been exiled by the Christian-hating Roman emperor Domitian (who persecuted anyone that would not refer to him as "Master and God," as the early Christians would not).

The book almost didn't make it into the Bible. There were literally dozens of books calling themselves the "Revelation of" some important person, usually one of the twelve apostles or one of the Old Testament notables. Some Christians thought its images of persecuted Christians finally seeing the downfall of the evil earthly powers was comforting, while others thought its many episodes involving dragons, angels, a "beast" with the number 666, four horsemen, a "great whore," bowls of wrath poured out on the earth, and other symbols to be too puzzling to benefit many readers. It was finally accepted as divinely inspired writing, but the people who had doubts about it were right: Readers have indulged in all sorts of weird interpretations of its meaning. Regrettably, a number of looney (and occasionally dangerous) people claim to have been inspired by the book, including Charles Manson, leader of the band of stoned-out youth who committed some atrocious murders in 1969. (Manson also claimed to be inspired by the Beatles' *White Album*, so his taste in "inspiration" was wide.)

Revelation needn't be puzzling (or dangerous). The first three chapters are actually the words of Jesus (delivered to John, that is) addressed to seven Christian communities in Asia (the area we now call Turkey). Jesus scolds them for their failings but offers encouragement. Beginning with chapter 4, angels, dragons, and other symbols appear, and things get mysterious. But the basic message of the book is simple: Saints will endure horrible persecution at the hands of earthly powers, but in the end God will triumph, and the persecuted will live forever in the new Jerusalem of heaven. In fact, Christians throughout centuries have taken comfort from the book, and always will, as long as there is religious persecution in the world.

People have spilled a lot of ink speculating about who the "beast" with the 666 is (SEE PAGE 342). Readers also wonder: Was John writing about the end of time, or about persecutions in his own day, or a recurring pattern of persecutions by evil empires—or perhaps all of the above? How does Revelation square with other prophecies in the Bible? And how does it square with Jesus' own statement in the Gospels that no person can predict the day or hour of the Last Judgment? The book states that it is revealing things that will "soon" happen (Revelation 1:1) and that "the time is near" (Revelation 1:3)—but did John mean a matter of days, months, centuries? Or was "soon" another way of telling all readers to "get prepared, for evil times are coming, but all will be well in the end"?

There isn't space to answer those questions here, but we can look at some elements that have made their way into popular culture. The book is full of often-quoted passages, including Jesus saying, "Behold, I stand at the door and knock. If anyone hears my voice and opens the door, I will come in" (Revelation 3:20-21)—very comforting words, and the inspiration for familiar religious artwork showing Jesus knocking at a door. Another comforting passage: "God will wipe away every tear from their eyes" (Revelation 7:17). Another: "Blessed are the dead who die in the Lord" (Revelation 14:13). Chapter 3 scolds the Christians of the city of Laodicean for being "lukewarm" in their faith—which is how the word "Laodicean" entered the language to refer to anyone whose faith is shallow. This passage contains the famous verse, "because you are lukewarm, and neither hot nor cold, I will spit you out of my mouth" (3:16). The book speaks of seven angels opening seven seals—hence the title of a classic Swedish film, *The Seventh Seal*. Chapter 8 speaks of the saints wearing white robes—the source of the image of people in heaven wearing white robes. Depicting Satan in the form of a red dragon is the root of the popular image of Satan as red and horned. The book refers several times to Babylon—not the

R

literal city, but a symbol of any evil power. Chapter 16 speaks of a final decisive battle at a site called Armageddon, which has come to refer to any dramatic battle. Chapter 20 tells of the destruction of Satan and all wicked people in a lake of fire and brimstone—the source of our familiar image of hell. Chapter 21-22 close the book with a breathtaking description of heaven, with its gold streets, gates made of pearl, and other images we know well.

Full of vivid images, the book has inspired many artworks, notable German artist Albrecht Durer's book *Apocalypse*, with classic engravings (some very hor-

The Seventh Seal
REVELATION. CHAPTER 8, VERSES 6-7.

rifying) of the book's episodes, most famously the "four horsemen of the Apocalypse" in chapter 6, and also the archangel Michael triumphing over Satan. The number 666 inspired the movie *The Omen* and its two sequels (and remake). All "end of time" books and movies are in some way based on Revelation. In fact, the opening camera shot of the movie *End of Days* scans the original Greek text of Revelation. In 2005 a TV mini-series dealing with

the end times was titled *Revelations* (note the S). English novelist D. H. Lawrence's last work was a book about Revelation, called *Apocalypse*. Probably the most famous use of the title was in the film *Apocalypse Now*, though the film had nothing to do with the end of time.

An interesting bit of trivia: The rock group Genesis's debut album released in 1969 was *From Genesis to Revelation*.

By the way, the Book of Revelation, at the very end of the Bible, ends with an appropriate word: *Amen*.

revivals
Firing up the faith

Revivals and evangelism are similar, except that evangelism is directed at people who aren't Christians, while revivals are directed at Christians to rekindle their faith. In practice, any preaching service is both revival and evangelism since the listeners may include Christians and non-Christians. The crowds who gather together to hear Billy Graham, for example, probably include more Christians than non-believers, and the Christians who are there expect their own faith to be deepened.

Revivals have taken place in many times and places, such as the Great Awakening in the U.S. in the early 1700s. Many religious denominations began as revival movements, such as the Methodists in the 1700s. As the "revived" churches become less enthusiastic over time, new groups split off, seeking a more vital religious experience. You might even say that Christianity began as a revival movement within the Jewish religion. Even further back in time, Israel's prophets called the people to remember the God they worshipped and to begin acting like holy people. The story of the religious revival under King Josiah is described in 2 Kings 22-23.

Many revival preachers like to refer to revivals as "times of refreshing," based on a sermon in Acts 3 by the apostle Peter: "Repent, and turn again, that your sins may be blotted out, that times of refreshing may come from the presence of the Lord."

the rich young man
Golden boy with too much gold

One of the Bible's most quoted verses about materialism is Jesus' statement that "it is easier for a camel to go through the eye of a needle than for a rich person to enter the kingdom of God (Matthew 19:24)." That statement followed his encounter with an unnamed young man who asked him how to obtain eternal life. Jesus reminded him of the moral commandments, and he replied that he had always kept them. He must have made an impression, for the Bible says that Jesus looked at him "and loved him." He told the young man, "You lack one thing: go, sell all that you have and give to the poor, and you will have treasure in heaven." The young man "went away sorrowful, for he had great possessions" (Mark 10:17-22).

Did Jesus mean that every person would need to give away everything in order to enter heaven? A few people have thought so, including the famous Francis of Assisi, a wealthy playboy who literally gave everything he had to the poor, including his last stitch of clothing. The usual interpretation of the story is that Jesus discerned that this particular young man appeared to be a spiritual seeker but

R

was too devoted to his wealth to enter heaven. This encounter has been depicted often in art, with Jesus' simple garb contrasting with the finery of the young man, who is often shown walking away with a sorrowful look.

righteous remnant
Moral minority

From the time of Noah, the Bible suggests that the human race has been terribly sinful, but there has always been a righteous minority that God wishes to preserve. Thus Noah and his family were saved from the global flood. Later, the nation of Israel was supposed to be God's holy, righteous people, but the nation as a whole was never very righteous. Israel's prophets saw this clearly and spoke of a "remnant" that would be preserved by God. Isaiah mentions the righteous remnant dozens of times, as do most of the other prophets. Zephaniah predicted a time when "the remnant of Israel shall not do unrighteousness, and speak no lies nor shall a deceitful tongue be found in their mouth: for they shall feed and lie down, and no one shall make them afraid" (Zephaniah 3:13). In the New Testament, the first Christians saw themselves as the righteous remnant that God would preserve in heaven forever.

Romans (epistle)
Faith at the empire's hub

The apostle Paul traveled the Roman Empire spreading Christianity, and it was his goal to take the faith to Rome itself. Even before he arrived, there was a thriving Christian community, and Paul's longest and most important letter was sent there. The Letter to the Romans is the closest that the New Testament comes to a systematic statement of Christian belief. Paul began by saying that both Jews and non-Jews had strayed from the right path, but God provided salvation for all through Christ. Faith is what matters. Adam's sin was a symbol of every person's sin, but faith in Christ could save any person from sin. People led by God's Spirit are adopted as his true children. Paul told the people to present their bodies "as a living sacrifice, holy and acceptable to God" and not to be "conformed to this world, but transformed by the renewing of your minds" (Romans 12:1-2). He reiterated Jesus' teachings about loving one's enemies, and advised, "do not be overcome by evil, but overcome evil with good" (Romans 12:21). In closing the letter, Paul did a "shout out" to people he knew in the Roman church, a common practice in most of his letters, as was his encouragement to "greet one another with a holy kiss."

Romans has had a huge (and controversial) effect on relationships between Christians and government, due to chapter 13, which begins with Paul urging Christians to obey earthly governments, because "the powers that be are ordained of God." Paul doesn't try to convince Christians that our governments all good (he lived in the Roman Empire, and knew better), but he states that all governments are put on earth to restrain evil, so in a sense all political authorities are God's servants. Throughout the centuries, many Christian leaders have followed this advice. Just one example: In the 1920s, Tikhon, head of the Russian Orthodox Church, told Russian Orthodox Christians to subject themselves to the new Communist government, fulfilling the words of Romans 13—although the Communists were blatantly atheistic and wished to exterminate Christianity. However, in another place in the New Testament, two of the apostles who have been arrested state that, "We must obey God rather than men" (Acts 5:29). Not long after Paul wrote Romans 13, the Roman Empire began persecuting Christians, telling them to deny their faith or be tortured and killed—many chose martyrdom. Christians have always lived the tension between Romans 13 (obey the government and be good citizens) and Acts 5 (at certain times it is right to disobey). The general trend has been this: Obey the government, but not to the point of denying your faith.

The Letter to the Romans is one of the most-read and most-quoted parts of the New Testament. The Protestant Reformation of the 1500s really began when Martin Luther in Germany studied the letter closely and decided that the Christianity Paul taught was nothing like the legalistic, ritualistic religion of the Catholic Church in Europe. In the 1700s in England, John Wesley studied the letter and launched the Methodist revival. English poet Samuel Taylor Coleridge called Romans "the most profound book ever written." In a sense the letter is a poke in the eye of "religion" because it says that genuine faith could transform any person and allow him into the family of God; faith isn't a matter of rituals and rules (legalism), nor is it a license to be selfish and immoral.

R

Rome

Iron empire

Somehow, through a combination of luck, ambition, and efficiency, the city of Rome came to govern an empire that controlled a huge part of Europe, North Africa, and the area we call the Middle East, Israel included. The Romans conquered Jerusalem in 63 B.C. In the time of Jesus and the apostles, the area that had been called Israel made up three Roman provinces: Judea, Samaria, and Galilee. A handful of puppet kings (like Herod the Great) technically held power, but only with the permission of Rome. The Romans ruled the area not from Jerusalem, the Jews' chief city, but from the coastal city of Caesarea (a very revealing name, as you might guess). The Roman governor, with the title *prefect*, usually went to Jerusalem with his soldiers during the Jewish religious festivals, in case an anti-Roman revolt began. This is why the Roman prefect Pilate was in Jerusalem at the time of the Passover, when Jesus was arrested.

The Romans' own language was Latin, but over much of their empire Greek was the common language. A Latin-speaking governor like Pontius Pilate probably used Greek to communicate with the Jews, whose own language was Aramaic. The Romans had a reputation for loving efficiency and luxury. They also thought of themselves as fair-minded and just, which they were—at times. They did not find it easy to govern the Jews, who resented any foreign power taxing them and stationing soldiers in their midst. As a benefit, the Romans helped keep the peace among these unruly people. They were proud of their building projects, including an aqueduct to bring water to Jerusalem. But building projects must be paid for, and the Jews resented the taxes and tolls. Of all the foreign powers that had dominated them, Jews hated the Romans the most. Whenever the Romans imposed a new tax, a Jewish revolt was almost guaranteed. The Romans always beat the rebels, of course, but that only increased the Jews' hatred.

In terms of religion, the Jews and Romans could not see eye to eye. Rome worshipped many gods and goddesses, though the more intelligent Romans did not take the old gods seriously. They found the Jews' God—an invisible one, and with only one temple in the world—hard to comprehend. They certainly could not grasp the Jews' obsession with not making statues of God. And yet many Romans found themselves attracted to the Jews' religion since it taught that God was moral and just, and they admired the Jews' emphasis on family life and monogamy. Romans who tried to follow the Jewish law closely were known as God-fearers (SEE PAGE 294). Men who converted fully to Judaism had to be circumcised—but to most Romans, circumcision was a ridiculous practice.

Religiously, the empire was a crazy quilt, with beliefs, superstitions, and rituals from all over. Officially the empire paid lip service to the old Roman gods (Jupiter, Juno, Mars, etc.) but few people really believed in them, seeking their emotional and spiritual satisfaction elsewhere. Gods and mythical figures from one part of the empire were worshipped a thousand miles away, such as the Egyptian Isis and the Greek Orpheus. Despite (or maybe because of) the empire's notorious immorality, many people sought a religion that would give them assurances of salvation and also moral guidance in the present world, and this yearning was the door through which Christianity entered.

In one sense, the Romans had a lot of control over the Jewish religion: They kept the high priest's official robes in the Roman fortress of Antonia, releasing them only for the official holy days of the Jews. Since they would only release them to a priest they approved of, the Romans essentially controlled who would be high priest. The priest would kowtow to Rome—a situation that most Jews resented since it meant the highest religious official was a Roman puppet.

Still, the Romans were lenient with the Jews in some ways. Jews were exempted from the empire's military draft. Jews were not required to acknowledge the emperor as divine but could get by with just praying for him. In deference to the Jews' feelings about sex and nakedness, Romans did not crucify Jewish men nude—although they made all other victims suffer that indignity. The Romans did not invent crucifixion, but they were the most notorious practitioners of it. For some reason, Jews often referred to Rome by the code name "Edom," the old name of one of Israel's hostile neighbor nations.

In the New Testament, some Romans look pretty good. Pontius Pilate (SEE PAGE 285) gave in to the priests' demand to crucify Jesus, but he tried to give Jesus a fair trial. Jesus encountered a few soldiers and spoke well of some who had faith (Matthew 8:5-13). A soldier at the crucifixion of Jesus says, "Truly, this was the Son of God." On the other hand, three of the Gospels record the soldiers' cruel mockery of Jesus at his trial. (Luke's Gospel, the most favorable to the Romans, fails to mention Jesus being mocked by the soldiers.) In

R

Acts, a devout soldier named Cornelius practices the Jewish religion, then becomes a Christian (Acts 10). In the later chapters of Acts, Paul (who was a Roman citizen) found himself generally well treated by Roman soldiers, who protected him from mob violence. Acts even mentions one centurion, Julius, by name.

The Book of Acts ends with Paul able to witness to his faith in Rome, as he had wished. Regrettably, tradition says that Paul and other apostles, including Peter, were martyred during the persecutions of Emperor Nero. The Book of Revelation was written when Rome was persecuting its Christians. John, its author, had been exiled to the bleak island of Patmos by the Emperor Domitian. It was considered risky to write anything critical of Rome, so in Revelation the old name "Babylon" is a code name for Rome—and for any political power persecuting people of faith. Still, every historian admits that the Roman roads and ships made it fairly safe to travel—a condition called the *Pax Romana*, Roman peace—and Christianity spread throughout the empire. Paul's Letter to the Romans confirms that there was a Christian community in the capital of the empire very early on, and that it grew, even during the times of persecution.

Jesus was born during the reign of the emperor Augustus, as Luke's Gospel records (Luke 2:1). At the time of Jesus' ministry and his crucifixion, the emperor was Tiberius (Luke 3:1)—a "dirty old man," if the contemporary records are trustworthy, but a reasonably good emperor. The next emperor was the mad Caligula, not mentioned in the Bible, though the Jews remembered him because he had planned to set up a statue of himself in their temple. Acts mentions the next emperor, Claudius, who expelled all the Jews from Rome (Acts 18:2). When Paul "appealed to Caesar" for his trial, that Caesar, or emperor, was the vile Nero, who would become the first imperial persecutor of Christians, making them scapegoats for the great fire in Rome.

A note about the name "Caesar": the Roman emperor usually bore the title Caesar before his name—Caesar Augustus, for example. It was normal not to use the emperor's name in conversation but simply to refer to him as "Caesar," just as we might today say "the president." The reigning Caesar's image was usually stamped on Roman coins, as seen in the incident where Jesus' enemies asked him if it was right to pay taxes to Caesar. Jesus asked to see a coin, and asked whose image was on it: "'Caesar's,' they replied. Then he said to them, 'Render unto Caesar what is Caesar's, and to God what is God's'" (Matthew 22:21).

The Romans destroyed the Jews' temple in the year 70, after tiring of putting down Jewish revolts. The temple was never rebuilt, and the priesthood died out completely. The Jews' religion became centered in their synagogues.

After the New Testament period ended, some of the Roman emperors persecuted Christians to stamp out the new religion. Eventually the new faith conquered Rome, for in 312 the emperor Constantine declared himself a Christian, ended all persecution, and made Christianity the favored religion of the empire. He also put an end to crucifixion.

Ruth

Short, sweet, and touching

The very short Book of Ruth is a real gem, four chapters about love and loyalty following the rather brutal Book of Judges. In fact, Ruth follows Judges because it is set "in the days when the judges ruled" (Ruth 1:1). A man from Bethlehem faces a famine, so he goes to live in the nation of Moab, taking his wife and two sons. The sons marry Moabite women, then all three men die, leaving three widows. The widow Naomi decides to return to Israel. One daughter-in-law, Orpah, chooses to stay in Moab, but the other daughter-in-law, Ruth, asks to go with Naomi, using some very tender words: "Ruth said, 'Entreat me not to leave thee, or to return from following after thee: for whither thou goest, I will go; and where thou lodgest, I will lodge: thy people shall be my people, and thy God my God'" (Ruth 1:16). The rest of the book is concerned with Ruth and Naomi eking out a living, just this side of starvation, until the rich landowner Boaz, impressed with Ruth's loyalty and goodness, marries her. The "punch-line" of the story is that the son of Ruth and Boaz, named Obed, is the father of Jesse, the father of Israel's favorite king, David.

Israel always had problems with the surrounding nations, and the Moabites, like the others, worshipped false gods. In fact, their main god, Chemosh, was

Ruth Travels With Naomi to Bethlehem
THE BOOK OF RUTH. CHAPTER 1, VERSE 11-19.

offered children as sacrifices. The Book of Ruth seems to suggest that even the great king David had a "pagan" ancestor, although one who had converted to Israel's religion. The book was directed at Jews who saw foreigners as beyond the reach of God's love. In the New Testament, Matthew's genealogy of Jesus specifically names Ruth among the ancestors.

Jews read the Book of Ruth in its entirety every year at the Feast of Pentecost. Ruth's moving words to Naomi, quoted above, are sometimes read in wedding ceremonies.

Ruth is a simple but beautiful story, one that has appealed to artists, who like to show Ruth gleaning wheat in the fields. In the masterpiece *Summer (Ruth and Boaz)* by Nicholas Poussin (1664, the Louvre) Ruth kneels before Boaz, who is richly dressed. Other gleaners are in the background. An even more famous painting is Jean Francois Millet's 1953 *The Gleaners*, also known as *Ruth and Boaz*. The book was made into a film, *The Story of Ruth*, released in 1960, in the heyday of biblical epics. The film managed to stretch the four brief chapters of the book into two hours by focusing on Ruth's childhood in Moab, with its ritual sacrificing of children. As a foreigner she faces hostility in Israel (which is not mentioned in the book, but highly probable). Composer Cesar Franck wrote an 1846 oratorio, *Ruth*, and Russian composer Mikhail Ippolitov-Ivanov wrote an opera about her.

Ruth is one of three books of the Bible named for a woman, the others being Esther and Judith. Ruth is a common name for both Jewish and Christian girls.

Sabbath

No work except holy business

Genesis 1 says that God made all things in six days, then "rested" on the seventh. In Exodus 20, one of the Ten Commandments that God gave to Moses mandates resting on the seventh day, meaning no work at all, since the day is holy, to be devoted to God. In ancient times, non-Jews mocked the Jews for this practice, which they saw as wasteful. Non-Jews had their own "days off," usually some kind of religious festival, but refusing to work one day out of seven seemed foolish. In 169 B.C., an invading army captured Jerusalem because the Jewish men would not fight on the Sabbath. After that, the Jews wisely decided that fighting in self-defense was permitted on the Sabbath.

Of course, the Jews themselves weren't always strict about keeping the Sabbath, as the prophets pointed out (Jeremiah 17:19-27, Isaiah 56:2-7). By the time of Jesus, strict Jews like the Pharisees were very fussy about keeping the Sabbath, so much so that they criticized Jesus for healing a man on the day (they saw the healing as a form of work). Jesus told them that God had made the Sabbath for man, not man for the Sabbath (Mark 2:27). As a faithful Jew, Jesus attended synagogue services on the Sabbath.

Since the first Christians were Jews, they continued to abide by the Sabbath rule. Christians who were not Jews felt no obligation to do so, and in time it became a practice to meet for worship on the first day of the week, called "the Lord's day," since Jesus was raised from the dead on the first day. In time, Jews and Christians parted company, with the Jews regarding Saturday, the seventh day, as holy, and Christians regarding Sunday, the first day, as holy. In 321, the Roman emperor Constantine, who had become a Christian, proclaimed that all business would cease on Sunday, setting a precedent that would stand for centuries.

Many Christians believed it was important to apply the Old Testament's Sabbath rules to Sunday, and they would not work on Sunday; some would not even engage in recreation, devoting the entire day to attending church, studying the Bible, etc. Most Christians today are comfortable attending church in the morning and spending the rest of the day in rest and relaxation. (The Chick-Fil-A fast food chain is closed on Sunday, thanks to its founder's belief in honoring Sunday as a day of worship, not work.) The Christian movement to make Sunday a day focused on religion is called Sabbatarianism.

Throughout history, some Christian groups have believed they were obligated to rest and worship on Saturday; the most notable of these groups is the Seventh-day Adventists.

Incidentally, the Jews' Sabbath technically begins at sunset on Friday and ends at sunset on Saturday. Some synagogues have services on Friday nights, others on Saturday mornings.

In Jewish legend, Sambation was the name of the "Sabbath river" that flowed six days a week and ceased to flow every Sabbath.

sacrifice
Giving to be given to

Almost every religion involves some form of sacrifice, giving up something valuable to God (or gods), either to be pardoned for sin or to receive benefit, or both. Most religions have had some kind of priest (SEE PAGE 289), who presented the sacrifice to the god. However, other sacrifices were "do-it-yourself," as in the Book of Genesis, which mentions the sacrifices of Cain and Abel, Noah, and Abraham, with no priest involved. After Moses led the Hebrew slaves out of Egypt, God delivered his laws to Moses, including detailed rituals about what could be sacrificed and for what reason. God also installed Aaron, Moses' brother, as the first high priest of Israel. The Book of Leviticus gives the rules for the various sacrifices—burnt offerings, grain offerings, sin offerings, peace offerings, guilt offerings, etc. The Israelites sacrificed oxen, sheep, goats, and pigeons, and also wine, oil, and grain.

No one actually thought that God consumed the items, of course (although other cultures *did* believe that). By giving up something, the person acknowledged their sins and repented of them. With the sacrifice done properly, you were back in a right relationship with God. (The rules also required restitution—that is, if you harmed someone or their property, you were required to pay for the damages, and you could not just make a sacrifice and forget about it.) At the root of it, sacrifice is a "pre-emptive strike"—you did wrong, so you're giving up something you value, in a way punishing yourself so that God won't punish you.

Sacrificing animals strikes most of us as rather cruel, although it was actually no crueler than butchering animals for their meat, and some of Israel's sacrificial animals were eaten, not just killed and discarded. What is genuinely cruel is human sacrifice, practiced around the globe in various times and places. The prophets of Israel were horrified that some of their people participated in the worship of the pagan gods Moloch and Chemosh, worship that involved the sacrifice of children. The early Christians were accused of human sacrifice and cannibalism because they spoke of eating the flesh and drinking the blood of Jesus—but they were referring to the bread and wine used in Holy Communion, of course.

The Old Testament prophets saw nothing wrong with Israel's system of sacrifices, but they perceived that people could go through the motions of religion without any change on the inside. The prophet Hosea heard God saying, "I desire steadfast love and not sacrifice, the knowledge of God rather than burnt offerings" (Hosea 6:6). Another prophet, Amos, pictured God turning away from people's sacrifices because the people did not practice justice and virtue in their lives (Amos 5:21). Jesus proclaimed that loving God and loving one's neighbor were more important than sacrifices (Mark 12:33).

The early Christians saw Jesus as the greatest sacrifice of all, the perfectly innocent man beaten, mocked, and crucified, taking the punishment that guilty humankind deserved. Jesus was the "Lamb of God," an innocent sacrifice that God himself provided to mankind. The Letter to the Hebrews explains that Jesus is not only the ultimate sacrifice, but is also the ultimate priest, the "go-between" who presents the sacrifice (himself) to God so that God and man can have fellowship. Roman Catholics see their worship service (the mass) as a re-enactment of Jesus' sacrifice, and the Lord's Supper is intended to remind Christians that Jesus sacrificed himself for them. Some Christians occasionally practice fasting, which is a form of sacrifice, as is "giving up something for Lent." The apostle Paul told

S

Christians to offer themselves as "living sacrifices" to God (Romans 12:1).

The Jewish temple was destroyed by the Romans in the year 70, ending forever the Jews' priesthood and system of sacrifices.

Sadducees
Lots of cash, no future

In the time of Jesus, most Jews believed in an afterlife. However, the most powerful, influential, and wealthy of them did not. These were the Sadducees, the aristocrats who dominated the priesthood and the ruling council, the Sanhedrin (SEE PAGE 328). They did not believe in an afterlife, nor in angels. In short, they were very "of this world." Jesus had harsh things to say about the Pharisees (SEE PAGE 283) and the Sadducees, and he warned his disciples to guard against the teachings of either party (Matthew 16:6). Both groups disliked him, but the Sadducees regarded him as a troublemaker who might irritate the Romans to the point where they would eliminate the priesthood and all its wealth. Some Sadducees presented Jesus with a silly question about marriage in the afterlife, which was meant sarcastically, since they did not believe in afterlife (Matthew 22).

In the Book of Acts, the apostle Paul was on trial before the Sanhedrin. When he announced that he was on trial because of his belief in the resurrection of the dead, the Sanhedrin divided, since the Pharisees believed in the resurrection and the Sadducees did not.

After the Romans destroyed the temple and did away with the priesthood in the year 70, the party of the Sadducees ceased to exist.

saints
Salt of the earth, and heaven too

The word refers, loosely, to any virtuous person. In the New Testament, it is interchangeable with the word "Christians"—for example, Paul's Letter to the Ephesians is addressed to "the saints who are in Ephesus." Since the Bible teaches that all people, even the best ones, sin occasionally, saints aren't expected to be perfect, but they do have to strive to be holy. In a world filled with immorality, the saints are God's "righteous remnant," what you might call the "moral minority." The New Testament letters constantly remind Christians to remember their divine call and act like holy people.

Centuries ago, "saint" took on another meaning: a person who had died and gone to heaven. As time passed, churches had official lists of such people. Most of the great figures of the New Testament—Jesus' apostles, Paul, Mary Magdalene, Jesus' mother Mary, and others—were regarded as saints in heaven, so people would speak of St. Paul, St. Peter, St. John, etc. The Catholic and Orthodox churches observe special feast days throughout the year to celebrate saints of the Bible and later times. The Orthodox churches also have saints days devoted to some of the great figures of the Old Testament—the prophets, Moses, Job, and others. Catholics don't observe these days, since technically all Catholic saints have to be Christians—and the Old Testament heroes lived before Christianity. Celebrating saints on certain days was intended to remind people to imitate their good behavior. In art, saints were often depicted with haloes to set them apart from the non-saints in the pictures. Christian artists borrowed the halo from Roman art, which showed the emperor with a halo around his head.

Honoring of saints had a huge effect on the naming of children—Christians often named their offspring after important saints, especially those of the New Testament. As early as the year 250, one Christian writer noted that the two most common names given to boys in his region were Peter and Paul.

Jesus himself, by the way, was never thought of as "St. Jesus." As the Son of God, and therefore sinless, he is thought of as Lord and Savior. He is in a category all by himself.

Salome

That famous dancer, unveiled

Salome is probably one of the best-known women of the Bible, even though the Bible itself doesn't tell us her name. She is simply called "the daughter of Herodias," and it was her mother's hatred for the great wilderness prophet John the Baptist that led to John's beheading by the Jewish ruler Herod. Mark 6:14-29 tells that Herod's wife Herodias had earlier been married to Herod's brother, Philip. She divorced Philip and married Herod, violating Jewish law. John spoke boldly against this, and Herod threw John in prison, though he hesitated to execute John because the public believed John to be God's prophet. Herodias despised John and found a way to bring about his execution: Her daughter by her first marriage fasci-

nated Herod with her dancing. Herod offered her anything she wished. But at her mother's urging, the girl asked for the head of John the Baptist on a platter. Herod reluctantly granted the wish, then later wondered if Jesus was actually John the Baptist brought back from the dead.

This young woman is not named in the Bible itself. We know it was Salome from the writings of the Jewish histo-rian Josephus. According to legend, her

The Beheading of John the Baptist
MARK. CHAPTER 6, VERSES 22-28.

famous dance before Herod was the "Dance of the Seven Veils," in which (we assume) she gradually removed each veil in the manner of a striptease.

Salome and John proved irresistible to artists throughout the centuries, and almost any art museum will have a painting with a title like *Herodias's Daughter with the Head of John the Baptist*. Italian master Guido Reni (1575-1642) painted a fine depiction of the scene, now found at the Art Institute of Chicago. Botticelli's 1488 *Salome with the Head of John the Baptist* in the Uffizi Gallery, Florence, shows a blonde pale Salome carrying the platter as if she is rushing food to a table. Caravaggio's painting of the same title, c. 1607, in London's National Gallery, shows the executioner holding John's head by the hair, depositing it on the platter held by Salome. Massimo Stanzione's *Beheading of John the Baptist*, c. 1634, in the Prado, actually shows a bearded John kneeling in prayer as the executioner raises his sword, with Salome and Herodias watching in the background.

In Jules Massenet's opera *Herodiade*, John is in love with Salome, who pleads for his life, then stabs herself after Herod has John beheaded. The witty Irish play-wright Oscar Wilde (1854-1900), who gave the world such comedy classics as *The Importance of Being Earnest*, also wrote a tragic play, *Salome*. Wilde's play served as the basis for Richard Strauss' opera of the same title. In both the play and opera, Salome kisses the dead mouth of John the Baptist (his head on the platter, that is), and for this perverse kiss, Herod orders her execution. The opera was highly controversial when it was first staged in 1905. Some modern productions of the opera actually have Salome stripping down to nothing in her famous dance.

Thanks more to Wilde's play and Strauss's opera than to the New Testament, Salome has been the subject of several films, notably a silent one with vamp Theda Bara, and a gaudy 1953 Technicolor extravaganza with Rita Hayworth (an oddity in which Salome becomes religious and tries to *save* John). In fact, there have been more films about Salome than about any other New Testament character except Jesus himself. The 1950 movie classic *Sunset Boulevard* ends with the delusional silent film star Norma Desmond believing she is playing the role of Salome in a film. ("I'm ready for my close-up, Mr. DeMille.")

German author Herman Sudermann (1857-1928) wrote the play *The Fires of St. John* on the same theme, as did French author Gustave Flaubert (1821-1880), who penned *Herodias, the Story of Salome*. Because of the wicked associations of the name, it was often used by authors for sinful female characters, like the evil stepmother in Eudora Welty's comic novel *The Robber Bridegroom*.

For the record, Salome was a common name for women in New Testament days, and the mother of the disciples James and John was one (Mark 15:40-41). One possible reason the dancing daughter of Herodias was unnamed in the Gospels was that the writers didn't want to get her confused with the *good* Salome, mother of two of Jesus' disciples.

the Samaritans
Half-blood folks

The only thing most people know about Samaritans is that there was a "good" one in a famous parable of Jesus. Most Jews at that time hated the Samaritans and didn't expect any of them to be good. The Samaritans' story goes back to 722 B.C., when Israel was conquered by the brutal Assyrians. They killed or deported most of the Israelites and settled the region with foreigners. These intermarried with the remaining Israelites, producing "half-breeds" (2 Kings 17:33) who worshipped Israel's God but also worshipped foreign gods. These people came to be called Samaritans, after Israel's old capital, Samaria.

South of that area, the Jews had been conquered by the Babylonians, sent into exile, then later allowed to return and rebuild Jerusalem's temple and walls. The

Samaritans felt that since they worshipped the same God, they should play a role in the new temple, but the Jews wanted no part of them. Eventually the Samaritans constructed their own temple and evolved their own religious practices. A Jewish ruler destroyed the Samaritans' temple in 128 B.C., ensuring that the two groups would never come together. The Jews denied the Samaritans' claim to have Israelite blood.

By the time of Jesus, Samaritans and Jews had several centuries of enmity. The region Jesus lived in was divided into three provinces, Galilee in the north, Samaria in the center, Judea in the south. Jews passing from Galilee to Judea detested the people of Samaria so much they often avoided passing through Samaria. Jews could hardly say the word "Samaritan" without spitting, so Jesus'

Jesus and the Woman of Samaria
JOHN. CHAPTER 4, VERSES 24-26.

parable about a Samaritan showing love and compassion to a wounded Jew hit his original listeners harder than it hits us today. The wicked Herod, who ordered the beheading of John the Baptist, was half-Samaritan by blood, one more reason for the Jews to despise him.

John's Gospel tells of Jesus talking at a well with a Samaritan woman, telling her that the Samaritan form of worship and the Jews' form of worship are both being surpassed by a higher form of worship (John 4:4-42). The fact that he engaged in conversation with a Samaritan shows he did not share the Jews' prejudice toward them. The unnamed Samaritan woman—often referred to as "the woman at the well"—is sometimes regarded as the first missionary, since she spread the news of Jesus to her people. John's Gospel mentions that the woman had had several husbands and was now living with a man out of wedlock, so in Christian tradition, she is remembered as a "woman with a past" whose life is changed by her encounter with Jesus.

In the Book of Acts, the new faith is preached to the Samaritans, showing that the first Christians had overcome their prejudices.

The Samaritan religion survives in the nation of Jordan, a few hundred people who still celebrate Passover on Mount Gerizim, the site of their former temple.

Samson

Gotta be the hair …

Here's one Old Testament character whose name is still familiar. No wonder, since he is a muscleman whose story involves violence, lust, betrayal, and revenge. The Samson saga is found told in Judges 13—16. Samson was one of Israel's "judges"—not a judge in our modern sense, but more like a military leader or "liberator." Samson is born to a woman who had been barren, and an angel tells his parents to dedicate the child to God. He was a Nazirite, meaning he did not cut his hair, drink alcohol, or have contact with anything dead. In spite of being dedicated to God, Samson does some questionable acts. Instead of choosing an Israelite wife, he picks a Philistine woman. On the way to meet her, he rips apart a lion with his bare hands and, much later, finds that bees have made a honeycomb in the carcass. At his wedding feast he poses the Philistines a riddle: "Out of the eater came something to eat, and out of the strong came something sweet." (The answer: honey from a lion.) The Philistines persuade Samson's bride to wheedle the answer out of him, which she does with a formidable weapon: whining. Samson is so angry when the Philistines reveal the answer that he strikes down thirty men. Later

he burns the Philistines' fields by tying torches to foxes' tails. He accomplishes other wonders, like killing a horde of Philistines with the jawbone of an ass, and carrying off the enormous gates of the Philistine city of Gaza.

But the best-known part of his story involves the infamous Delilah. The Philistines use her to find out the secret of Samson's strength. She inquires several times, each time Samson lying to her. Finally he tells the truth: If his long

Samson's Vengeance and Death
JUDGES. CHAPTER 16, VERSES 23-30.

locks are shaved (breaking his Nazirite vow), his strength is gone. Asleep in Delilah's lap, Samson gets his first haircut, and his strength departs. The Philistines bind him, blind him, and force him to work as a slave turning a millstone.

The Philistines overlook one detail: When the hair grows back, his strength returns, unknown to the Philistines. They drag him to the temple of their god Dagon for "entertainment." As his last act, Samson pushes apart the main pillars of the temple, literally bringing the house down. He himself is killed but, as Judges 16:30 puts it, he killed many more when he died than while he lived.

While this story doesn't have much spiritual depth (Samson isn't exactly a saint), it has proved irresistible to artists, writers, and composers. One of the world's greatest poets, John Milton, wrote one of his finest poems, *Samson Agonistes*, telling of what happened to Samson after being captured and blinded. Milton himself was blind, so he sympathized with Samson, who changes from a violent man of action to a man utterly dependent on God. George Frideric Handel wrote an oratorio about Samson, taking some of his libretto from Milton's poem. But more important in music is Camille Saint-Saens' opera *Samson and Delilah*, which shocked people when it premiered in 1877 because at that time no one wrote operas on biblical subjects. Cecil B. DeMille's 1949 color epic *Samson and Delilah* was the first in a wave of popular, lushly produced movies based (loosely) on the Bible. It ended, of course, with the spectacular destruction of the temple. In the 1950s and 1960s, some cheaply made Italian movies—the "sword and sandal" genre—were built around a he-man named Samson, though he bore no resemblance to the man in the Book of Judges.

Artists have been fascinated by the Hebrew strongman, and there are numerous paintings and sculptures of beefy Samson (often nude) killing the lion, slaying men with the jawbone of an ass, or carrying off the gates of Gaza. *The Blinding of Samson* (1636) by Rembrandt shows the brawny Samson with several men trying to subdue him. One Philistine is about to gouge out his eyes with a long spear. All the men but Samson wear armor of the 1600s. In the background, a giggling Delilah holds Samson's locks in one hand, shears in the other. In *The Triumph of Samson* by Guido Reni (1612) a muscular but very slender Samson raises his jawbone weapon as he stands with the fallen Philistines around him. He is nude but draped. *Samson and Delilah* by Peter Paul Rubens (1609) shows muscled Samson, with his head laying in the lap of the buxom, blonde Delilah, while a man shears his locks. In the background, the Philistine men are watching. Samson with his head in Delilah's lap is one of the most popular Old Testament subjects in art.

Because Samson died along with the many Philistines he killed, the phrase "Samson's crown" refers to a great achievement that cost the life of the person who did it.

Samuel

The transition team

Samuel is one of several examples in the Bible of a child born at last to a childless woman, making her dedicate him to God in gratitude. Samuel's mother Hannah gave him to the keeping of the priest Eli. While still a child he heard the Lord's voice calling to him at night, to which he answered, "Here I am, Lord" (1 Samuel 3). Eli's sons were so corrupt and greedy that God passed over them and gave the chief authority in Israel to Samuel. He became a respected leader of Israel, its judge, prophet, and priest, but the Israelites demanded a king to lead them more effectively—or more accurately, "to be like other nations." In 1 Samuel 8, the prophet told them what oppression a king would bring upon them. Samuel followed God's will and anointed the tall, brave, handsome Saul as Israel's first king. Regrettably, Saul was bold but impulsive, and Samuel learned that God had another man, the shepherd boy David, in line as the next king. Samuel anointed David (keeping it a secret from Saul, of course), who soon proved himself by killing the giant Goliath. Samuel wept for the disappointing Saul. For a time he had to hide David from Saul's wrath. After Samuel's death, he and Saul met once more, in very strange circumstances: Saul had a sorceress bring up Samuel's

ghost from the underworld to advise him. The ghost predicted defeat and death for the king, which occurred the next day (1 Samuel 28). (See page 379 for more about the witch of Endor and this "séance.")

Samuel, so tradition says, is the author of the two books that bear his name, although it is unlikely. He is a respected figure in Jewish and Christian tradition, and in many art-works, novels, plays, and films dealing

The Word of the Lord to Samuel
I Samuel. Chapter 3, Verses 8-13.

S

with Saul and David. He is the "kingmaker" in Israel, and the "transition man" between the time of the judges and the time of the kings ruling Israel. The Letter to the Hebrews in the New Testament includes Samuel in its "Faith Hall of Fame" (Hebrews 11). The Eastern Orthodox churches celebrate August 20 as the Feast of the Prophet Samuel.

With the Protestant Reformation in the 1500s, Samuel became a popular name for male children, especially when, like Samuel's own mother Hannah, a woman had a child after much waiting and prayer. It became the most common name among the Protestants in France, and in the colonial period was also common in America.

Samuel has been a character in the films dealing with Saul and David, notably the 1985 *King David*.

Sanhedrin
Grumpy old men

In the time of Jesus, the Jewish governing body in Judea was known as the Sanhedrin (or "council" in some Bibles). Judea was a province of Rome, but the Sanhedrin had its own military force and could decide religious disputes that were not Rome's concern. It was essentially a group of respected old men, including the high priest. "Respected" doesn't mean "wise" or "good," as the Gospels show, since the Sanhedrin accused Jesus of blasphemy and handed him over to Pilate, the Roman governor, for execution. One member of the council, Joseph of Arimathea, is described as being a decent man and a secret admirer of Jesus. All four Gospels show that Pilate considered Jesus innocent and saw no reason to crucify him, but the council pressured him, making it clear that if he freed Jesus, he was not "Caesar's friend"—and every Roman bureaucrat had to appear to be "Caesar's friend." Pilate ordered the crucifixion since the Sanhedrin had no authority to execute.

Jesus predicted that his disciples would be persecuted, just as he was. The council threw Peter and John in jail for preaching that Jesus had been resurrected (Acts 4). Acts 5 shows one member of the Sanhedrin, a rabbi named Gamaliel, urging moderation toward the Christians, but the council still had Peter and John flogged. The council accused the Christian follower Stephen of blasphemy, and he was stoned to death, without the Roman governor's approval—an illegal act, but one that created the first Christian martyr (Acts 7).

The apostle Paul found himself on trial before the Sanhedrin, and the council would have had him killed had he not been in Roman custody.

In the many books and films about Jesus' trial and crucifixion, the Sanhedrin is depicted as tradition-bound old men lacking in compassion.

After the Romans destroyed the Jews' temple in the year 70, the Sanhedrin ceased to have any political authority. It morphed into a more spiritual body that tried to keep the Jews' religion alive as a moral force while making no attempt to revolt against Rome.

Sarah
Beautiful but barren

Sarah was the beautiful wife of the patriarch Abraham, who had been promised by God that he would be the father of a great nation. Nature wasn't cooperating, because poor Sarah could not conceive a child. Sarah let Abraham conceive a child with her maid, Hagar, who became so uppity toward her barren mistress that Abraham finally sent Hagar away. Hagar returned and submitted to Sarah, then gave birth to the son Ishmael. Abraham received three divine visitors who prophesied that when they returned in a year, Sarah (aged ninety—well past child-bearing age) would have borne a son. The prophecy caused Sarah to laugh, but it proved true, for she gave birth to Isaac, who would be the ancestors of the Hebrews. (Her laughter is the source of Isaac's name, since Isaac means "laughter.") A few years later, Ishmael mocked his half-brother Isaac, and Abraham banished Hagar and Ishmael to the wilderness. Sarah's story is told in Genesis 11-23.

Sarah is remembered by Jews and Christians not as a role model but as the mother of God's chosen people. Her name has been popular in both religions and in the culture at large. In 1 Peter 3:6, Peter told Christian wives they were "daughters of Sarah" if they were submissive to their husbands.

S

Saul
First (but not best) king

In the days before Israel had a king, the nation was (in theory) a *theocracy*—ruled by no one but God himself. The judge-prophet Samuel tried to discourage the people from having a king, but they "wanted to be like other nations." He gave

Saul is Rejected as King
I SAMUEL. CHAPTER 15, VERSES 22-31.

in and, guided by God, anointed the tall, handsome Saul as king. According to 1 Samuel 9:2, "There was not a man among the people of Israel more handsome than he." Saul never really got to enjoy being king, since he had to play the role of commander in chief of the military, not monarch enjoying the life of a palace. The handsome new king's chronic problem was constant war with the Philistines. The poor man also battled what we would today call depression (called "an evil spirit" in the Bible), experiencing deep gloom, soothed somewhat by his servant David's harp-playing. David had killed the giant Goliath with only a stone, gaining in popularity. People were fascinated with the young David, saying "Saul has slain his thousands, and David his tens of thousands"—not quite true, but a sign to Saul that his public appeal was slipping. Much of the book of 1 Samuel is the story of the jealous Saul alternately loving and trying to destroy the loyal David. (David had opportunities to kill Saul but would not do so.) Saul detested anyone who took David's side, almost killing his own son Jonathan for doing so. He ordered the massacre of the priest Ahimelech's family for siding with David. Samuel learned that God had rejected Saul as king and intended David to replace him. Saul learned from the ghost of the dead Samuel that he would die in battle with the Philistines the following day, and David would become king. (SEE PAGE 379 for more about the "séance" with the witch of Endor.) Seeing the battle going against him, Saul committed suicide. David lamented the loss of the king and the king's son, his beloved friend Jonathan.

Saul's sad and colorful story has enchanted artists and writers through the ages. He is depicted as the man with many abilities—and many flaws. Most people sympathize with his being edged out by the more popular and younger David, even though David goes out of his way to remain loyal to the king. Saul did not tax the people or conscript the men into his army, so despite Samuel's warnings, Saul was not an oppressor.

Guercino's 1646 painting *Saul Attacking David* in Rome shows a crowned, armor-clad Saul about to hurl his spear at the fleeing David, who carries his harp. *Saul and David*, by Rembrandt, 1660, in The Hague shows a richly dressed, melancholy Saul, who holds a spear and wears a turban topped with a crown. The very Jewish looking David plucks a harp, absorbed in his music. George Frideric Handel wrote an oratorio about Saul, containing the famous "Dead March." Danish composer Carl Nielsen wrote an opera, *Saul and David* (1902). English poet Robert Browning's long poem "Saul," published in 1855, is the meditation of the young harpist David, called in to sooth the mind of the tormented king. Poet Laurence Housman wrote *The Kingmaker*, a play about the dealings of Samuel, Saul, and David. James Barrie, author of the famous play *Peter Pan*, also wrote the play *The Boy David* (1936). As in Peter Pan, it celebrates the innocence of the boy David, but it is also sympathetic to the adult Saul, who was once a boy like David. In movies dealing with David, Saul is usually an important character. In the 1960 movie *David and Goliath*, Orson Welles played Saul and was billed above the two actors playing the title characters. In the 1949 Cecil B. DeMille film *Samson and Delilah*, Saul as a boy is a kind of servant to the strongman Samson—not probable, given the chronology, but since Samson and Saul both fought the Philistines in their lifetimes, the movie has us believe that Samson "passed the torch" to the boy before he died.

In the New Testament, there is another Saul (Saul of Tarsus), better known by the name Paul, the apostle.

Savior

Rescuing the heart

In the Old Testament, God is referred to many times as Savior, especially in the Book of Psalms, where the phrase "my Rock and my Savior" is applied to God. The Israelites saw God as their only reliable deliverer from the world's calamities.

People have been referring to Jesus as Savior for centuries, but, oddly enough, the word is rarely used in the Gospels. The angel announcing the birth of Jesus said that he would "save people from their sins," and the angel who appeared to the shepherds in Bethlehem announced "a Savior, who is Christ the Lord (Luke 2:11)." In the ancient world, Savior (in Greek, *Soter*) meant a deliverer from worldly ills—sickness, war, accidents, etc. Earthly rulers and military heroes were sometimes called *Soter*. Jesus cured diseases and saved people from demon possession, but primarily he was a spiritual Savior. The Christians saw Jesus as the Lamb of

God, the innocent man suffering in place of the guilty. Paul uses "Savior" many times in his epistles, and it has become one of the most familiar titles for Jesus, often in the phrase "Our Lord and Savior." Theologians use the word *soteriology* to refer to the study of salvation.

In Christian hymns, the title Savior may be applied to either God or Christ.

scribes / teachers of the law
Bring on the lawyer jokes …

Depending on which Bible version you use, the word might be "scribes" or "teachers of the law" or even "lawyers." In New Testament times, these were experts in the Laws of Moses (Exodus through Deuteronomy), with the duty of applying those Laws to life situations. Studying the Laws closely, they made nitpicking into an art form, something Jesus condemned them for, since they put "sticking to the Laws" above real love for God and one's fellow man. Jesus lumped them in with the Pharisees (SEE PAGE 283) and condemned both for being self-righteous and hypocritical. He accused them of burdening people with so many rules that no one could bear them all (Matthew 23:4). The New Testament's emphasis on Christian freedom is a reaction to the fussiness and self-righteousness of the scribes and Pharisees, who had turned the personal God-man relationship into something cold and legalistic.

The Jewish ruling council called the Sanhedrin was made up of scribes of both the Pharisee and Sadducee parties.

Scripture songs
Words from Word

One of the innovations of the 1980s was churches' use of "Scripture songs," portions of the Bible set to music. For centuries, Christians sang Psalms and also portions of the New Testament that seemed poetic, such as the angels' announcement to the shepherds ("Glory to God in the highest, peace on earth, good will toward men"). Beginning in the 1700s, Isaac Watts, Charles Wesley, John Newton, and others began writing hymns (often based on the Bible) that rhymed, and these became the standard hymns for most churches until the 1980s, when a younger generation found the old hymns and the way they were usually sung to be boring. Scripture songs rely more on the rhythm of the music than on the rhyming of words. With many churches encouraging hand clapping and body swaying, the new songs are anything but boring.

Second Coming
Dramatic entrance

The early Christians firmly believed that Jesus, who had ascended into heaven, would one day return to earth in a dramatic way, bringing the present age to an end and judging everyone for their deeds. In Matthew's Gospel, Jesus told his followers that there would be a great tribulation, followed by signs in the heavens (the sun and moon darkening), then Christ himself would appear "on the clouds of heaven with power and great glory" (Matthew 24:29-31). The oldest writings in the New Testament, Paul's two letters to the Thessalonians, were written to give Christians assurance about the Lord's return to earth. The first Christians expected it to happen in their own lifetimes. It hasn't happened yet, but later generations have not given up hope. The message of these predictions is still valid: Be ready at any time, and live a life you won't be ashamed of.

The event is known as the Second Coming—the First Coming is Jesus' birth as an infant in Bethlehem, an event that went largely unnoticed except by the shepherds and wise men. Most Christian creeds include mention of the Second Coming. The famous Apostles' Creed states that Jesus ascended into heaven, and "from thence he shall come to judge the quick and the dead." The Athanasian Creed is more specific, adding that at Jesus' Second Coming "all men shall rise again with their bodies and shall give account for their own works." The Nicene Creed states that Jesus "shall come again with glory, to judge both the quick and the dead, whose kingdom shall have no end." ("Quick" here means "living," by the way.)

Over the years, various people have claimed to predict the time of the Second Coming, and some denominations had their origins in such people. For example, the Seventh-day Adventists began as followers of William Miller, an American who set the date as sometime between March 21, 1843 and March 21, 1844.

S

As a general rule, liberal Christians don't expect the Second Coming to take place, or at least not in the way described in the New Testament. Many conservative Christians still devote a lot of time to speculation of when the Second Coming will occur.

One of the most quoted poems of modern times is "The Second Coming" by W. B. Yeats. The poem is not about Christ but is a kind of prophecy of horrors of the modern age. It contains the famous line, "The best lack all conviction, while the worst / Are full of passionate intensity."

Several figures of legend are said to be forced to wander the world until the Second Coming, such as the Wandering Jew and the Flying Dutchman. The same fate is, legend says, that of all the gypsies on earth.

Sennacherib

Assyrians versus angel

Sennacherib was a king of the mighty and brutal Assyrian empire. His armies captured several of the cities of Judah and threatened to capture Jerusalem itself. Judah's king Hezekiah panicked, then prayed, and he was assured by the prophet Isaiah that God himself would deliver them from the Assyrians. In answer to the king's prayer, the Lord's angel struck down the Assyrian troops—185,000 of them. Sennacherib departed for his homeland, and while he was worshipping in the temple of his god Nisroch, two of his sons murdered him (2 Kings 19).

The story of miraculous deliverance from a mighty army was told lyrically in Lord Byron's famous poem "The Destruction of Sennacherib," which tells how the Assyrian troops "melted like snow in the glance of the Lord."

seraphim

A drop-dead vision

Chapter 6 of the Book of Isaiah is probably the most-read passage in all the book of the Prophets. In it, Isaiah tells of the occasion when God called him to be a prophet. He was in the temple in Jerusalem when he experienced seraphim (plural) singing praise to God, their hymn beginning "Holy, holy, holy is the Lord

Almighty." Isaiah believed he saw the long train of God's robe filling the temple. This experience of power and holiness led him to cry out, "Woe is me! for I am undone." He was suddenly aware he was "a man of unclean lips," dwelling among other unclean people. One of the seraphim used tongs to take a live coal from the altar and touched it to his lips, purifying them. When God asked, "Whom shall I send?" Isaiah replied, "Here am I, send me!" (Isaiah 6:8)

What were these seraphim (or seraphs)? The Hebrew word means (we think) "burning ones." As Isaiah described them, each had six wings, two covering the face, two covering the feet, and two for flying.

This is all the Bible says about seraphim. They are remembered because Isaiah's vision has been read and discussed so often. The popular Christian hymn "Holy, Holy, Holy" is based on the seraphim's words. In Jewish and Christian tradition, they were regarded as the highest order of angels since they attended the very throne of God. (The Angel Records Company named one of its labels Seraphim, with the ad line, "Angels of the highest order.") Like the cherubim, they are regarded not as angels that appear on earth to aid humans, but as attendants in the heavenly court.

the Sermon on the Mount
The good life in a nutshell

Probably the most quoted words of Jesus are from Matthew's Gospel, chapters 5-7, usually called the Sermon on the Mount. This famous speech has been quoted over the centuries since it sums up what Jesus taught about living a

moral life. It begins with the Beatitudes: "Blessed are they who ... " Jesus refers to the Old Testament Law and then urges his listeners to aim for a higher standard of behavior, such as forgiving their enemies and not seeking vengeance. These follow a formula: "You have heard it said ... But I say to you ... (The passage about "turning the other cheek" is here.) The Lord's Prayer, certainly the most quoted

The Sermon on the Mount
MATTHEW. CHAPTER 5, VERSES 1-12.

prayer among Christians is here, as is the famous passage about "seek, and ye shall find." Every word has been quoted, preached about in countless sermons, turned into songs, etc. These simple words about living a moral life are direct that even children can grasp the meaning immediately. Jesus probably knew that the hard part about the Sermon on the Mount was not understanding the words, but putting them into practice.

seven words of Christ on the cross
Things to etch into the memory

Because there are four Gospels in the Bible, there are four different versions of Jesus' arrest and crucifixion. The four are similar, of course, but the details differ. In each of them, Jesus speaks while hanging on the cross, and his utterances from all four Gospels total seven in all, generally known as the "seven words of Christ on the cross." Matthew's and Mark's Gospels have only one, the Hebrew words "Eloi, Eloi, lema sabachthani" which is the first verse of Psalm 22, in English, "My God, my God, why have you forsaken me?" In Luke's Gospel, Jesus says "Father, forgive them, for they know not what they do." Then when one of the thieves crucified beside him says to Jesus, "Jesus, remember me when you come into your kingdom," Jesus replies, "Truly I say to you, today you will be with me in Paradise." John's Gospel has Jesus speaking to his mother, who is there at the cross with the unnamed "disciple who Jesus loved." Jesus says to her, "Woman, behold your son," then, to the disciple, "Behold your mother." He is entrusting his mother to the custody of the disciple. Then Jesus says, "I thirst," and the soldiers daub his mouth with a sponge dipped in sour wine. Finally, he says, "It is finished"—or, more correctly, "It is accomplished."

Since Christians regard Jesus' crucifixion as extremely important, these words spoken on the cross are important also. By crying out, "My God, my God, why have you forsaken me?" and "I thirst," Jesus proves that he is fully human. By saying, "Father, forgive them," he is showing how merciful he is. When he says, "It is finished," Christians believe he is saying that his mission on earth is completed. Entire sermons and even books have been built around the "seven words." Joseph Haydn, Heinrich Schutz, and many other composers have written choral works titled *The Seven Last Words of Christ on the Cross*. Most plays and movies depicting the crucifixion use some or all seven of the utterances.

sheep and goats, parable of
(See the parable of the sheep and goats)

the Shepherd of Israel / Good Shepherd
A necessity for straying folks

One of the most quoted of the 150 Psalms is Psalm 23, known as the "Shepherd Psalm." Supposedly it was written by David, the king of Israel, who had been a shepherd in his youth. It begins with "The Lord is my shepherd," and describes the Lord's protection and gifts, ending with "surely goodness and mercy shall follow me all the days of my life, and I will dwell in the house of the Lord forever." It has been recited and set to music countless times, and in calligraphy or needlework, has graced the walls of many a devout home.

The Bible refers many times to God as the Shepherd of Israel, and Jesus was also known as the Good Shepherd "who lays down his life for his sheep." There are so many references in the Bible to God as Shepherd and his people as sheep that translators have quite a task making the Bible clear to cultures with no understanding of sheep and shepherds. Good Shepherd is a fairly common name for churches. The term *pastor* for a church's minister is actually the Latin word for shepherd.

Simon of Cyrene
Crossing the color barrier

The Gospels state that when Jesus bore his cross to the place of execution, the Roman soldiers compelled a man named Simon of Cyrene to help carry it. We can assume that Jesus must have been so weakened by his scourging that he was unable to bear the cross himself. The Romans could have grabbed any passerby and forced him to the task, so probably Simon looked solid enough for the job. Mark's Gospel mentions that Simon was "the father of Alexander and Rufus"—making it likely these two men were among the early Christians. Possibly Simon was also.

Cyrene was a city on the northern coast of Africa, so Simon has sometimes been show in art and film as a black-skinned man—even though the people of Cyrene would not have been black-skinned. The 1965 film *The Greatest Story Ever Told* featured black actor Sidney Poitier in the small role of Simon. In the 2004 *The Passion of the Christ*, Simon was lightskinned but had more screen time, showing emotion as he changed in a few minutes from being angry at being forced to carry a stranger's cross to showing deep compassion for the suffering Jesus.

One interesting legend connected with Simon: He was an egg merchant, and he found on Easter morning that the eggs he brought to sell had all turned beautiful colors.

Simon the sorcerer
Day trader in spirituality

The Book of Acts strongly disapproves of any kind of magic or occult activity, as the whole Bible does. However, one magician mentioned in Acts was Simon the sorcerer, also called Simon Magus. He lived in Samaria and had amazed the people with his magical powers (whether they were faked or were the power of Satan is not stated). Simon listened to the preaching of Philip the evangelist and was baptized as a Christian. Later, when he saw that some of the apostles could pass on the power of the Holy Spirit to others, he offered money if they would give him the same power. The apostle Peter scolded him for thinking that a gift of God could be bought. Simon asked Peter to pray for him.

That is the last mention of Simon, so we don't know if he became a sincere believer or went back to his old magic routines. His attempt to buy the Spirit is the root of our word *simony*, the purchasing of a church position for money. (Simony was common in periods when bishops and other high-ranking church officials had a lot of power and wealth.)

Many legends have sprung up about the later career of Simon, who is regarded as the source of a hundred heresies and cults. The Christian writer Irenaeus credits Simon with being the founder of Gnosticism, a serious rival to Christianity for several centuries. Some stories say he traveled to Rome and tried to lead Christians astray, but was opposed by Peter. Supposedly his mistress was a woman named Helen, a former prostitute. The two asked people to worship them, but unlike the Christians, they taught an "anything goes" morality. Some said that the Romans set up a monument to "Simon the Holy God." Supposedly Simon was buried alive after promising he would arise the third day after his death.

Simon is a character in the novel and film *The Silver Chalice*.

sin
Whatever you call it, it ain't good

In the twenty-first century, we are more likely to talk about "unacceptable behavior" than about "sin." In the Bible, sin also included evil thoughts as well as evil deeds. Also, sin (singular) can refer not only to an individual act, but to the whole human inclination to do bad things.

Sin started early—at the very beginning, in fact, since Adam and Eve allowed the serpent to tempt them to eat the forbidden fruits so they could "be like gods." In effect, they disobeyed God by aspiring to be gods themselves, and as a result, they are thrown out of Eden and into a hostile world. The first child born, Cain, murders his own brother, so within two generations human beings are already guilty of disobeying God, and having too much pride, jealousy, and violence. Even people who think the story is a myth see a basic truth in it: All human beings are Adam and Eve, because we all prefer our own way (often self-destructive) to God's way. Theologians call this evil inclination *original sin*—"original" as in "from the beginning."

It's worth noting that Adam, Eve, and Cain were all guilty of trying to evade responsibility for their sins. When God asked Adam why he had eaten the forbidden fruit, Adam claimed "the woman that you gave me" tempted him—shifting the blame to both Eve and God. Eve was equally evasive: It was the fault of the serpent that tempted her. When God asked Cain where his brother was, Cain's famous reply was, "Am I my brother's keeper?" The basic human evasions—"Who? Me?" and "It wasn't my fault!"—go back to the very beginning.

In Genesis 6, God sees that the whole earth is corrupt, "for all flesh had corrupted their way on the earth," so God destroys all human life except Noah and his family. But this "fresh start" doesn't put an end to sin. Psalm 14 laments that "all have turned away from God, all have become corrupt. There is none who

S

are righteous, no, not one." The Book of Judges describes the horrible situation that results when "every man did what was right in his own eyes." The apostle Paul summed it up neatly: "All have sinned and come short of the glory of God" (Romans 3:23).

In the Gospels, "sinners" was sometimes used to refer to Jews who weren't observing the Jewish laws. Some of Jesus' critics sneered at him and the disciples for mingling with "sinners" (Matthew 9:10-13). The critics assumed that Jesus should have been like other religious Jews, avoiding non-Jews and "sinners" like the plague.

Jesus broadened the idea of sin: Evil acts were sinful, but so were evil thoughts. He told his listeners that adultery was a sin, but so was "lusting in one's heart." Murder was a sin, but so was hating someone, or calling him or her cruel names. Jesus knew there were people who appeared to be squeaky clean on the outside but who were vicious and immoral on the inside.

People who haven't read the Bible have the impression that it condemns only "vice sins" like smoking, drinking, and sexual sins. It's true that the Bible does have a strict sexual code, but it also has a lot to say against dishonest business dealings, greed, bribery (what we would call "white collar crime"), oppressing the poor and charging interest, and also "neighborhood sins" like slander, gossip, and stirring up trouble. One of the Ten Commandments even condemns coveting, or being envious of what someone else has—an "internal sin" that would go undetected except by God. The Bible makes it clear that plenty of "respectable" people are good at concealing their sinful deeds and thoughts. Jesus said that the two most important commandments were to love God and love one's neighbor—which involves more than abstaining from alcohol, tobacco, and extra-marital sex. (For the record, the Bible says nothing about tobacco, since tobacco wasn't used in ancient times. And it does not tell people to abstain from alcohol either!) The Old Testament prophets saw any abuse of human power as sin, and they spoke out not just against the tyrants in foreign countries, but their own kings and priests. The Law is full of gems like, "You shall not follow the crowd in doing evil" (Exodus 23:2) and "You shall open wide your hand to your brother, to the need and to the poor in your land" (Deuteronomy 15:11).

In the Old Testament, a system of sacrifices and restitution existed so that people could make peace with their fellow man and with God. The New Testament regarded Jesus as the ultimate sacrifice, the sinless man suffering in place of sinful human beings. People were "off the hook" because someone else had taken the punishment they deserved. The proper response to this show of divine mercy was to live a better life.

Catholic tradition refers to the "Seven Deadly Sins." There is no actual list of these in the Bible, but all are sins that the Bible condemns. The seven are: pride, envy, lust, anger, gluttony, greed, and sloth. Pride is always first on the list because it is mankind's first sin—wanting to be gods, as Adam and Eve did.

In many works of literature, sin is personified as a person, most famously in John Milton's epic poem *Paradise Lost*, where Sin is the daughter of Satan, and the two of them incestuously bring forth Death. This wicked threesome was intended as a kind of "anti-Trinity," the evil counterpart to the Holy Trinity—Father, Son, and Holy Spirit.

Sinai and Horeb
Whatever the name, it's sacred

Mount Sinai in Egypt was the site of one of the most famous divine-human encounters of all time, where Moses meets God face to face: "Mount Sinai was completely covered in smoke, because the Lord descended upon it in fire. ... and the whole mountain quaked greatly ... Then the Lord came down upon Mount Sinai, on the top of the mountain. ... And the Lord called Moses to the top" (Exodus 19:18, 20). God gave Moses the laws found in Exodus, Leviticus, and part of Numbers.

The Old Testament is confusing since it uses two names for the mountain: Sinai and Horeb. Perhaps the site had two different names. Exodus 3 names Horeb as the place where God appeared to Moses in the burning bush and told him he would lead the Hebrew slaves out of Egypt.

Centuries later, Sinai/Horeb was the site of another notable divine-human encounter. The prophet Elijah had fled there to escape from wicked Queen Jezebel, who had pledged to kill him (1 Kings 19). While on the mountain, Elijah experienced an earthquake, a mighty wind, and a fire—then the voice of God, experienced as "a still, small voice." God reminded the despairing Elijah that there were still good people in Israel, that he was not alone.

These dramatic events made Sinai a sacred place, but since it was far from Israel, the Jews did not travel there for a pilgrimage. Christians did, however. In

S

the period when Egypt was Christianized, a monastery was built at the base of the rocky, 7,000-foot Jebel Musa ("Mount of Moses"), which Arabs believe is Mount Sinai. When director Cecil B. DeMille filmed *The Ten Commandments*, he shot the film's Sinai scenes at Jebel Musa. The oldest Greek text of the New Testament, called the Codex Sinaiticus, was kept for centuries at the monastery there. It dates from around the year 350.

Sinai is the name of a famous hospital in the U.S.

666

Adding up to Antichrist

This famous—or infamous—number is mentioned in Revelation 13, which describes a "beast, coming up out of the earth … Let him who has understanding calculate the number of the beast, for it is the number of a man: His number is 666." Just who is this man/beast? People have been speculating about that since Revelation was written. Early Christians thought it applied to the Roman emperor Nero, who persecuted Christians. In fact, any persecutor has been connected with the number. The "beast" might not even be an individual, but a nation or government that does horrible things. People have assumed it was the number of the Antichrist. In the Bible, seven is a "good" number, while six is "bad," since it falls short of seven—so it denotes incompleteness.

People whose names have six letters each have been accused of being the Antichrist—to name two recent high-profile examples, one U.S. president (Ronald Wilson Reagan) and a media mogul (Robert Edward Turner, more commonly called Ted). But clever (and usually misguided) people have found ingenious ways of twisting almost anyone's name so that it somehow "adds up" to 666. Practically every famous person who ever lived, especially political leaders, has been accused of being the evil 666 person—Roman emperor Nero, Napoleon Bonaparte, Adolf Hitler, to name just three.

People throughout history have enjoyed speculating about who or what the 666 beast is. The number got a lot of publicity due to the 1976 movie *The Omen*, which featured the 666 in its ads. In the movie, the Antichrist actually has a 666 birthmark on his scalp—which is pretty darn silly. (The 2006 remake premiered on June 6—that is, 6-6-06.) The number has also made its way into comedy, such as in the 1989 film *The Burbs*, where it is the house number of the sinister family next door.

snake handling
Flirting with venom

Handling of venomous snakes is practiced by a few Christian groups who take literally Jesus' words in Mark 16:17-18, where he said that true believers could handle snakes and drink poison and not be harmed. The vast majority of Christians do not take the words literally, while snake handlers consider it the sign of deep faith in God to trust in his protection. Snake handling has been practiced off and on throughout Christian history, but in America it began in 1909 when a Pentecostal pastor in Tennessee handled venomous snakes and urged his congregation to do so. The denomination he was part of booted him out, and most other Pentecostal churches forbade their members to practice it. Snake handlers have sometimes been bitten and even died. Interestingly, in defense of religious freedom the American Civil Liberties Union has defended snake handlers—or, more precisely, voiced its disapproval of laws against snake handling. Snake handling is often mocked as a "backwoods" practice, with most of the snake handlers living in the Appalachian highlands.

Snake handling isn't just a practice of a few Christians here and there. It is practiced in several religions, and in the time of Jesus was done by the Maenads, the wine-drunk, frenzied followers of the god Dionysus.

Sodom and Gomorrah
That wicked, wicked pair

These famously wicked cities were two of the five "cities of the plain" in the Book of Genesis. The patriarch Abraham's nephew Lot went to live in Sodom, but Sodom and Gomorrah were so immoral that God told Abraham he planned to destroy both cities. Abraham asked God if he would destroy them if as few as ten decent people could be found there, and God said he would not—but apparently there weren't ten, so God chose to destroy the cities, although he sent two angels (in the form of male "visitors") to rescue Lot and his family before the destruction came. At night the men of Sodom surrounded Lot's house and demanded he send out the two visitors so the men could have sex with them—which is why *sodomy* refers to homosexuality. The visitors struck the men of the town with blindness, then told Lot and his family to flee the city and not look back. Lot's wife did look back and was turned into a "pillar of salt." God destroyed the cities with fire and brimstone (Genesis 19), brimstone an old word for sulfur.

The story might be pure legend, but archaeologists speculate that Sodom and Gomorrah might have been destroyed by a volcano—hence the fire and brimstone raining down—and may now be beneath the waters of the Dead Sea. In fact, a mountain near the Dead Sea is still called Mount Sodom.

Throughout the Bible, Sodom and Gomorrah are used as examples of extremely wicked places. In the New Testament, 2 Peter speaks of the "sensual conduct of the wicked in Sodom" and the "lawless deeds" that led to the city's destruction (2 Peter 2:7-8). Christians living in the cities of the immoral Roman Empire regarded themselves like Lot, trying to live decent lives in indecent surroundings. When archaeologists dug into Pompeii, the Italian city destroyed by volcano in the year 79, they found that someone—probably a Christian—had scratched the words SODOMA GOMORRA into a wall.

French novelist Marcel Proust titled one of his novels *Sodom et Gomorrhe*, and some of its characters are homosexuals. (Oddly, the English translation is titled *Cities of the Plain*.) A handful of films have been made about the story, one of the best being the 1966 epic *The Bible ... In the Beginning*. A rather bad 1963 film titled *Sodom and Gomorrah* makes it appear that the cities were wicked because of slavery, with not even a hint of homosexual practices. French author Jean Giraudoux wrote a play about the two doomed cities. For centuries, laws prohibiting homosexuality have been called "sodomy laws." The Italian Renaissance painter Giovanni Bazzi apparently took pride in his nickname, Sodoma, and art historians know him by that name.

Solomon
Wealthy, wise, and womanizing

Solomon was one of the greatest kings of Israel, in some ways outshining his famous father, King David. David managed to unite the twelve tribes of Israel into a cohesive nation, and Solomon expanded the borders of the country, kept things peaceful, and made a deep impression on his contemporaries by building a magnificent palace for himself and, more importantly, a temple for the Lord in Jerusalem. Solomon's story is found in 1 Kings 1-11 and 2 Chronicles 1-10. He was the son of David's favorite wife, Bathsheba, and David designated Solomon as the heir, but Solomon had to fend off an attempt by his older brother Adonijah

Solomon's Judgement
I Kings. Chapter 3, Verses 17-28.

to seize the throne. Once Solomon was secure on the throne, he prayed to God for wisdom above all else, and because of the prayer, God promised him not only wisdom but also riches and honor—on the condition that Solomon would follow the Lord always, which, eventually, he did not do. But for many years the country was safe and secure, and Solomon launched his massive building projects. The temple is described in loving detail in 1 Kings 6 and 7, and chapter 8 tells of the sacred ark of the covenant being brought in with great ceremony, followed by an eight-day feast for all the people.

In 1 Kings 10, Solomon is visited by the queen of Sheba, and he deeply impressed the exotic woman. Many legends have grown up around the visit, most of them claiming that the king and queen produced a child between them. (See page 298 for more about the queen and her visit.)

Solomon's legendary wisdom is illustrated in the famous story of two prostitutes, who both claim that a certain child is theirs. When the case is brought to Solomon, he calls for a swordsman to divide the child in half. Naturally, the woman who is really the child's mother gives up her claim, as Solomon knew she would (1 Kings 3:16-28). Solomon had "knowledge beyond measure and breadth of mind like the sand on the seashore," and he was an expert in plants and animals (1 Kings 4:29-34). He also wrote three thousand proverbs and more than a thousand songs.

Solomon had two weaknesses during his reign. One was that his extensive building projects required conscripting men into labor, which no one liked. One of his labor foremen, Jeroboam, learned from a prophet that after Solomon's death, the kingdom would split in two, and that Jeroboam and his descendants would rule over ten of the tribes of Israel. This happened as predicted.

S

Solomon's other weakness was women—*lots* of women. His father David managed to get by with seven wives and three concubines, but Solomon had "seven hundred wives of royal birth, and three hundred concubines." (Translation: he had a large harem, ten times larger than David's.) Since many of these women were foreigners, Solomon built temples to their gods, something God had specifically told him not to do. "And the Lord was angry with Solomon" and said to him, "Surely I will tear the kingdom from you"—though in fact the kingdom would be divided during the reign of Solomon's tactless son, Rehoboam, who alienated the ten northern tribes so much that the broke away to form a separate kingdom.

Because he was so famously wise, Solomon is reputed to be the author of Proverbs, Ecclesiastes, and two of the Psalms. And, logically, because of his experience with women, the rather erotic Song of Solomon is also reputed to be his work. The Book of Wisdom in the Apocrypha is also attributed to him. Whether he wrote any of these books is doubtful, but at least the authors may have considered him as their inspiration.

In the New Testament, Jesus admired the "lilies of the field" and told his disciples that "even Solomon in all his glory" was not more splendid than the wildflowers (Matthew 6:28-29). The Jews spoke very highly of Solomon, admiring his wisdom and wealth and generally forgetting that his wives had led him to worship false gods. Solomon has been a common name for Jewish boys, much less common among Christians. It is a common name among Muslims in the Arab form Suleiman. Throughout history, many kings have been referred to as Solomons if they had a reputation for wisdom. King James I of England encouraged his court to refer to him as the "English Solomon." The adjective "solomonic" is applied to anyone with great wisdom.

Solomon has fascinated artists and authors, particularly the episode of the queen of Sheba and the judgment concerning the divided child. Since Solomon's court was so luxurious, artists have enjoyed depicting the king on his ivory throne, with gold everywhere. Several films have been made about Solomon, most of them revolving around the queen of Sheba.

In some Jewish legends, Solomon has a magic ring with four gems that tells him all he wishes to know and also gives him power over the spirits. In Muslim legends, Solomon (Suleiman) has a green silk magic carpet that carries his court wherever he wishes to go. Muslims also believe that Solomon used *jinn* (benevolent spirits) to complete the temple. They claim he made a pilgrimage to their city of Mecca, sheltered from the sun by a canopy of birds. In the Koran, Suleiman is regarded as a prophet.

Several flowering plants are named for the king, including Solomon's plume, Solomon's lily, and a variety named Solomon's seal.

Son of God

Just like his Father ...

The early Christians believed that Jesus of Nazareth was the Son of God—not in the general sense that all human beings are children of God, but in a special way (which is why we capitalize Son in the English Bible). He almost never referred to himself as Son of God, but he did speak of God as his Father, using the intimate name *Abba*—something Jews at that time did not do.

Two of the Gospels (Matthew and Luke) tell the story of the Virgin Mary miraculously conceiving Jesus through the power of God. This is known as the "virgin birth," although the miracle is not referred to except in Mathew and Luke. When people saw Jesus' miracles and heard his teaching, he seemed to be God walking among them in human form. Jesus was condemned to death by the Jewish authorities because when they asked him, "Are you the Son of God?" he replied, "You have said so"—not exactly a "yes," but enough to have them condemn him as a blasphemer, since Jews could not conceive of God having a son (Matthew 26:63-33). Contrary to what many people think, Jesus was not condemned for claiming to be the Messiah, but for claiming to be the Son of God.

The ancient Greeks and Romans had plenty of myths about gods and goddesses fornicating with human beings and producing divine-human hybrids. (Hercules and Achilles were some of the most famous.) Any of these could be referred to as a "son of a god" or "son of the gods," and so could anyone who had a reputation for working miracles. But the early Christians didn't see Jesus as just another wonder-worker. He was *the* Son of God, in a special unique relationship with the Father, obeying God totally and representing him on earth.

A classic statement on Jesus as the Son of God is found in the opening of the Letter to the Hebrews, which states that God in the past spoke through his prophets, but now has been revealed through his Son, the "heir of all things." The Son is the "radiance of the glory of God and the exact imprint of his nature."

S

Son of Man

And maybe more than human ...

In the Old Testament, the expression "son of man" is another way of saying "a man" or "a human being" or even "John Doe." In the Book of Ezekiel, God addresses the prophet ninety-two times as "son of man," although some modern versions have "mortal man"—whatever expression is used, it means the awesome God is addressing a mere human being.

Strangely enough, in the New Testament, "Son of Man" was the title that Jesus used to refer to himself. The Son of God deliberately chose to identify with ordinary human beings, the John and Jane Does of the world. But he may have had a second meaning in the phrase, one rooted in the Book of Daniel, where Daniel sees a "Son of Man" in a heavenly vision. At the time Jesus lived, many Jews believed this "Son of Man" mentioned in Daniel was a divine figure who would appear on earth to judge people. When Jesus was arrested and brought before the high priest, the priest asked, "Are you the Christ, the Son of the Blessed?" Jesus answered, "I am, and you will see the Son of Man seated at the right hand of Power, and coming with the clouds of heaven" (Mark 14:60-62). This reply led to Jesus being condemned as a blasphemer.

Jesus never referred to himself as Son of God or as Messiah (Christ). More than eighty times he referred to himself as Son of Man (in fact, in many instances it appears he used "Son of Man" simply as a substitute for "I"). Oddly, the early Christians almost never used it to refer to him.

Song of Solomon

Love bustin' out all over

Anyone who thinks the Bible is anti-sex or anti-body should read the Song of Solomon, also known as Song of Songs, or Canticles. The short book is a series of love poem, some spoken by a man, some by a woman, both of them expressing intense love, including physical attraction. The first line spoken by the woman sets the pattern: "Let him kiss me with the kisses of his mouth, for your love is better than wine." The man's words are equally vivid: "Your hair is like a flock of goats leaping down the slopes of Gilead. Your teeth are like a flock of shorn ewes. ... Your lips are like a scarlet thread. ... Your two breasts are like two fawns." More than once the two people use the expression "I am sick with love." The two people are deeply in love and crave each other. At times the poetry rises to the sublime: "Many waters cannot quench love, neither can floods drown it."

Did Solomon actually write the book? We don't know for certain. According to 1 Kings, he had literally hundreds of wives and concubines, so he knew something about the attractions of women. Whether he focused his attention on one is not known. At any rate, the book opens with "The Song of Songs, which is Solomon's," so he is traditionally given credit as author, although "which is Solomon's" might mean the book is dedicated to him. We know that he had a reputation as a poet-songster (1 Kings 4:32).

Why is the book in the Bible? Some Jews and Christians say it is simply a poem about human love, letting us know that physical attraction and intense passion are not bad things. The Jews long ago decided it had a deeper meaning, a spiritual one. The man in the poem is really God, the woman is really Israel. Some Jewish interpreters "decoded" every verse of the book, explaining that all the sensuous images weren't meant to be taken literally. As Christianity spread, and Christians accepted the Old Testament as their own, they said the man in the poem was indeed God, but the woman represented the church (all Christians, that is). The book, incidentally, does not mention the name of God at all, so to find any spiritual meaning in it, you must interpret it allegorically. Apparently a lot of theologians did, because in the Middle Ages, there were more Christian commentaries written about the Song of Solomon than any other Old Testament book.

On the assumption that the book expresses God's love for Israel (and vice versa), Jews read the book aloud in their synagogues on the day of Passover, the holy day celebrating God's liberation of the Jews from slavery in Egypt—the supreme expression of his love, that is. The Passover holiday is in the spring, and the book gives several indications that it is spring, when the flowers (and passions) are in bloom.

With its many mentions of plant, birds, animals, and geography, the book has been a gold mine of titles for plays and novels—such as *The Little Foxes* (Song of Solomon 2:15), *The Voice of the Turtle* (turtle-dove, that is, Song of Solomon 2:12)—and has even been the source of names for garden plants—rose of Sharon, lily of the valley (Song of Solomon 2:1).

sower, parable of

(See the parable of the sower)

star of David / magen David

Shield of the faithful

The most familiar symbol of the Jewish religion is the "star of David," also called by its Hebrew name *magen David*, meaning "shield of David." The six-pointed star consisting of two interlocking triangles appears on the flag of Israel today and has been used as a Jewish symbol for centuries, but it's doubtful it went all the way back to King David himself. Jews of a mystical mindset have often read meanings into the star's six points. And like any religious symbol, it has often been misused by those who dabble in magic.

Stephen

Martyrdom 101

The first Christian martyr was a certain Stephen, whose story is told in Acts 6 and 7. Stephen was "full of faith and the Holy Spirit" and worked miracles among

The Stoning of Stephen
ACTS. CHAPTER 7, VERSES 55-59.

the people, but the Jews' high priest had him arrested as a blasphemer and heretic for preaching that Jesus was the Messiah. Stephen defended himself in an eloquent speech found in Acts 7, a speech which is a summary of how the Jews had persecuted God's true prophets. His opponents were so riled up by his speech that they plugged up their ears, dragged him out of Jerusalem, and stoned him to death. Before he died, he said, "Lord Jesus, receive my spirit" and "Lord, do not hold this sin against them"—words recalling those of the dying Jesus, who said, "Father, forgive them, for they know not what they do" and "Father, into your hands I commit my spirit." After Stephen's death a persecution of Christians began. One person present at the stoning was Saul, who approved of the deed. Later Saul would become a Christian himself, using the name Paul.

Catholic and Orthodox Christians refer to Stephen as the "proto-martyr" (first martyr). Catholics celebrate him on December 26, Orthodox on December 27. Because he was stoned to death, Stephen has been considered the patron saint of stonemasons. The old phrase "fed with St. Stephen's bread" meant martyrdom, especially by stoning. Stephen's dying words, "Lord Jesus, receive my spirit" have been remembered by many Christians over the centuries, and often uttered as a dying person's last words. Stephen's martyrdom is an episode in Felix Mendelssohn's oratorio *St. Paul*.

stigmata
Marked for glory

Over the centuries, many Christians have claimed to receive the stigmata, meaning that their bodies showed the same wounds as those of Christ on the cross: the hands, the feet, and the side. (*Stigma* is the Greek word for "mark" or "brand," *stigamata* being the plural form.) The well-loved medieval saint Francis of Assisi supposedly had the stigmata, along with many other saints honored by the Catholic Church. The one mention of stigmata in the Bible is in the apostle Paul's statement that "I bear on my body the marks [stigmata] of Jesus" (Galatians 6:17). Paul was undoubtedly referring to the wounds he received while spreading the gospel of Jesus. Since he was stoned, beaten, and otherwise abused, we can assume he had quite a few marks on his body.

stoning
Rock executions

Among the Jews, stoning was the usual form of execution. The Old Testament laws prescribed stoning for murder, blasphemy, idol worship, breaking the Sabbath, adultery (all of these being acts prohibited by the Ten Commandments), witchcraft, and human sacrifice. The rule was that the two witnesses required for conviction would be the first to throw stones at the offender. The laws commanded "the entire assembly" to participate in the execution. The executions were not only very public, but also made the participants realize that if they broke the laws, they too could end up suffering the same fate. The laws use the phrase, "you must purge the evil from among you" as rationale for the death penalty.

Sadly, the people were sometimes eager to stone saints, not just sinners. Moses and Aaron came near to being stoned when the people rebelled against their authority (Numbers 14:10). Jesus referred to Jerusalem as the city that stoned the prophets (Matthew 23:27), which was ironic, since the city was the Jews' religious center, and should have welcomed God's prophets. In fact, since Jesus himself was condemned by the Jewish authorities as a blasphemer, he could have been stoned, but they turned him over to the Romans for execution. Earlier in his ministry, he had almost been stoned on two occasions (John 8:59, 10:31-33). In the Book of Acts, the saintly Stephen gave an eloquent defense of his Christian beliefs, which so offended the Jews that they stoned him, making him the first Christian martyr (Acts 7). The apostle Paul was stoned and left for dead, but amazingly recovered (Acts 14:19-20). The 1962 film *Barabbas* depicts a Christian woman being stoned.

Stoning was spoofed in the 1979 film *Life of Brian*, which depicted meddlesome, bored people thoroughly enjoying the stoning (which might not be far from reality). The famous short story "The Lottery" by Shirley Jackson tells of a town where one unfortunate person is stoned each year.

synagogues
Temple surrogate

Israel's worship was focused on the temple in Jerusalem, but the destruction of the temple by the Babylonians in 586 B.C. changed that. With the people sent into exile and scattered abroad, they developed the synagogue as a place to meet and pray and to read and discuss their sacred writings. They kept the scrolls of the writings in a chest called the ark. Even after the temple was rebuilt, Jews continued to meet in their synagogues each Sabbath; they tried to visit the temple if possible on major holy days like Passover. (The seats in the synagogues always faced in the direction of Jerusalem, by the way.) As a child and young man, Jesus attended the synagogue in his hometown of Nazareth. Traveling with his disciples to various towns, he usually visited synagogues (Mark 1:39). The apostles did the same, and as Christianity spread, some Jews in the synagogues rejoiced and accepted it; most did not. Worship services of the early Christians were modeled on the meetings in synagogues.

The temple was destroyed by the Romans in the year 70, and from that point on there has been no attempt to rebuild it; for all Jews worldwide, the synagogue is the center of their religious lives.

S

tabernacle

Temple for people on the move

Before the Jews had a temple for God, they had a large tent, called the tabernacle. It was used during their years of moving from slavery in Egypt to their new home in Canaan. The tabernacle was a "portable temple." Its description is found in Exodus 26-27 and 35-38, where its dimensions are given, including the type of cloth, wood, and altars used. The innermost part of the tent was the Holy of Holies (SEE PAGE 151), an area off-limits to everyone except Israel's high priest. The ministers of the tabernacle were from the tribe of Levi, the tribe of Moses and Aaron.

David, who made Jerusalem the capital of Israel when he was king, wanted to build a temple for God, but that task fell to his son Solomon. Once the temple was built, there was no need for the tabernacle, of course.

The word tabernacle got a new lease on life in the 1800s, when evangelists in the U.S. and elsewhere conducted religious revivals in large tents they called tabernacles. The word had a double meaning—not only was the tabernacle a large tent, but also, as in Exodus, the place where one "met God." Some churches have chosen to call themselves tabernacles for the same reason. In Catholic churches, the name tabernacle is given to the ornate box or small vault that holds the consecrated bread used in the Eucharist.

Another tent mentioned in Exodus was the "tent of meeting," which Moses would enter to seek God's guidance. God's presence was shown by a cloud descending on the tent (Exodus 33:7-11).

tax collectors
Yes, even back then …

Taxation is almost as old as human civilization, and the tax collector has never been a popular person. In the time of Jesus, tax collectors were especially hated because they worked for the Roman government, which Jews saw as a foreign oppressor. Many were dishonest, lining their own pockets with what they skimmed off from the taxes. Their fellow Jews despised them, but on several occasions Jesus socialized with them, including the famous incident of Zacchaeus (SEE PAGE 387), who experienced a true change of heart after Jesus dined in his house (Luke 19). Jesus also called a tax collector, Matthew, to be one of his twelve disciples, which must have irked the other eleven at first. (Matthew is the patron saint of tax collectors.) Jesus' enemies were scandalized that Jesus hobnobbed with such sinners as tax collectors. Jesus told these self-righteous people that "the tax collectors and the prostitutes are entering the kingdom of God ahead of you" (Matthew 21:31). One of Jesus' best-known parables concerns a self-righteous Pharisee praying in the temple, looking down on a tax collector praying nearby (Luke 18:13).

Incidentally, the King James Version uses "publican" instead of "tax collector." (For more on the parable of the Pharisee and the tax collector, SEE PAGE 268.)

tefillin
Boxing the Word

The small leather boxes that some Jewish men wear on their foreheads and left arms are called phylacteries, or *tefillin*. They contain passages from the Old Testament law and are a literal obedience to the commands in Exodus 13:9 and Deuteronomy 6:8 to wear the Law as "a sign upon your hand and as a memorial between your eyes." Jesus condemned the wearing of them, saying that they were worn by hypocrites hoping to impress others with their devoutness (Matthew 23:5). Today, most liberal Jews do not take the Exodus 13 and Deuteronomy 6 commands literally, and thus do not wear the *tefillin*.

temple

A home for a God who is everywhere

A temple is a building dedicated to a god—or the god's house, you might say. The Jews had one temple to their God, the one in Jerusalem. Most of the pagan gods had many temples dedicated to them, always with a statue or other image of the god. The Ten Commandments prohibited the Jews from making an image of God, so their one temple in Jerusalem had no image of him, something that pagans found puzzling.

When the Israelite slaves were led out of Egypt by Moses, God gave Moses instructions on how to construct a portable temple called the tabernacle, or tent of meeting (SEE PAGE 354). Once they were settled in Canaan, the tabernacle was moved from one location to another. King David wanted to build a temple for God, but God told him that the task would fall to David's son Solomon. The details about the building of Solomon's magnificent temple are found in 1 Kings 6-7. The tabernacle furnishings were moved from the tabernacle into the new temple, and at a dedication ceremony, God sent down fire (perhaps meaning lightning) to indicate his presence. Regrettably, Solomon's fine record as king was marred because he built temples to other gods to

Solomon Builds the Temple
I KINGS. CHAPTER 6, VERSES 11-14.

please his many foreign wives. When the kingdom split in two after Solomon's death, the king of the northern tribes, Jeroboam, built shrines at Dan and Bethel so his people wouldn't be tempted to visit the temple in Jerusalem in the south.

Throughout 1 and 2 Kings, the gold and other valuables of the temple were removed at times to appease foreign invaders. In fact, during the reign of Solomon's son Rehoboam, the Egyptians invaded the land and made off with all the gold items Solomon had made for the temple. The worst blow came in 586 B.C. when the Babylonian king Nebuchadnezzar looted and destroyed the temple and deported most of the people. The Jews were without a temple for many years until the Persian king Cyrus conquered the Babylonians and allowed the Jews to return to Jerusalem to rebuild their temple. The story of the rebuilding is found in the Book of Nehemiah. The Jew in charge of the rebuilding was named Zerubbabel, and the new temple was called the Second Temple, the earlier one under Solomon being known as the First Temple.

Centuries later, the Second Temple was renovated by King Herod, who was trying to placate his Jewish subjects. The Jews were pleased at the magnificence of the temple, but they still hated Herod and never liked to admit that the project was really a Third Temple, more magnificent than the first two. It was still called the Second Temple, which thoroughly irked Herod. It was this temple that Jesus visited on several occasions: his dedication as an infant; his visit at the age of twelve; and during the last week of his life, when he drove out the moneychangers who plied their trade in the temple courts.

As a devout Jew, Jesus had an affection for the temple, of course, calling it his "Father's house," but he also predicted a time when not one stone of it would be left standing on another. That prophecy was fulfilled in the year 70, when a Jewish revolt against the power of Rome provoked the Romans to destroy the temple, leaving only one wall of it standing, the Western Wall, or Wailing Wall, that is still seen in Jerusalem. The Romans built a temple to the god Jupiter on the former site of the Jewish temple. The city was declared off-limits to Jews for many years, and there was never any attempt to build another temple. The Jews' religious life became centered around their local synagogues. While the destruction of the temple seemed like a tragedy, it also had the effect of making both Judaism and Christianity into universal religions, not tied to any one locality. It had the effect of "de-Judaizing" Christianity, since Jewish Christians no longer felt any tie to Jerusalem or its temple. In the New Testament, the apostle Paul stated that the Lord "dwells not in temples made with hands," for God is anywhere and everywhere (Acts 17:24). Interestingly, many Jewish synagogues and Christian churches still choose to call themselves "temples."

Living in exile in Babylon, the prophet Ezekiel had a vision of the restored temple of the Lord—not a real temple on earth, but a kind of heavenly vision of a temple that would exist in a city called "The Lord Is There." The closing chapters of Ezekiel describe the city and temple in great detail.

temptation of Jesus
Field-testing the Messiah

The Gospels record that after Jesus' baptism in the Jordan River, the Holy Spirit led him into the wilderness for forty days. At the baptism, Jesus had heard God's voice saying, "This is my beloved Son." Once in the wilderness, Satan offered him three temptations, each one beginning, "If you are the Son of God …" The first was to turn stones into bread—an interesting temptation, since Jesus had been fasting for forty days. But his reply to Satan was a quote from Deuteronomy: "Man shall not live by bread alone." Christians interpret this as Satan tempting Jesus to be a wonder-worker, and to use his power selfishly. In the second temptation, Satan

The Temptation in the Wilderness
MATTHEW. CHAPTER 4, VERSES 1-11.

took Jesus to the pinnacle of the temple in Jerusalem and told him to throw himself down—on the assumption that God would not let his Son be injured. Jesus again quoted the Old Testament: "You shall not put God to the test." In the third temptation, Satan "showed him all the kingdoms of the world in a moment," saying he would give Jesus power over them—if Jesus would worship him. Again Jesus answered with the Old Testament: "You shall worship

the Lord your God, and him only shall you serve." This wasn't the last time Jesus would face Satan, for Satan "departed from him until an opportune time." The temptation story is recorded in Matthew 4 and Luke 4.

One of the most overlooked aspects of the story is that Satan himself quotes the Old Testament to Jesus—which should serve as a warning that quoting the Bible can be done with a sinister purpose. This part of the temptation story is the root of William Shakespeare's line in *The Merchant of Venice*, "The devil can cite Scripture for his purpose."

One of the great works of literature is John Milton's 1671 epic poem *Paradise Regained*, which adds detail to this face-off between Jesus and the tempter. Milton had published *Paradise Lost*, telling of how Adam and Eve faced temptation and failed the test. In *Paradise Regained*, Jesus faces temptation, but passes the test, proving he is worthy to be mankind's Messiah. In a sense Jesus was a "new Adam" who "undoes" the harm of the old Adam.

The temptation has been featured in many artworks, some showing Satan as a monster with horns, others showing him more humanlike. In films he is usually shown as human but somehow sinister. The controversial 1988 film *The Last Temptation of Christ* had Satan taking the form of a woman, a lion, and a cobra. The truth is that the New Testament has no interest in what Satan looked like.

The season of Lent is observed by many Christians as the forty days preceding Easter. The number forty was based on the number of days Jesus fasted at the time of the temptation.

the Ten Commandments
Better than the movie …

The Ten Commandments are found in Exodus 20 and Deuteronomy 5, and according to Exodus, God's finger wrote them in stone for Moses. This was done at Mount Sinai, three months after thousands of Hebrew ex-slaves left Egypt. With the people camped out at the base of the mountain, God gave hundreds of other laws to Moses, but the Ten were special, a distillation of how to treat God and one's fellow man. In a slightly condensed form, the Commandments are: 1) worship no other gods but God, 2) make no idols, 3) don't take God's name in vain, 4) observe the Sabbath, 5) honor your parents, 6) don't murder, 7) don't commit adultery, 8) don't steal, 9) don't bear false witness, and 10) don't covet what others have. Later laws given to Moses prescribed the death penalty (by stoning) for breaking Commandments 1-4, 6, and 7.

The ten divide into what scholars call the "two tables": the first five com-

Moses Receives God's Holy Commandments
Exodus. Chapter 20, Verses 1-5, 7-10, 12-17; Chapter 31, Verse 18.

mands have to do with respect for authority (God and parents), the last five have to do with respecting one's neighbor. Regarding the Sixth Commandment: Older Bible translations have "kill," but the Hebrew word actually means "murder"—something people ought to be aware of when they discuss issues like capital punishment or war. (The Old Testament does not prohibit all killing—in fact, it provides for the death penalty for many crimes.) Regarding the Third Commandment: People think that "taking God's name in vain" means swearing, but it actually means more than that, since it prohibits any misuse of God's name (such as when a person says "God wants us to do so-and-so"). The Tenth Commandment is interesting because it prohibits not an act but an attitude. Coveting is an "inner sin," one we might commit without anyone knowing, except for God. The commandment is a reminder that while outward behavior is important, God knows the heart also.

The most distinctive of the Commandments is the prohibition of idols or "graven images." This set the Hebrews apart from almost every culture that existed, for most peoples have made statues or pictures of the gods they believed in. For the Hebrews, God was an invisible spirit, one that could not be "localized" in a manmade object. It was a law the Hebrews broke constantly—in fact, they broke it by making the golden calf idol while Moses was on the mountain receiving the command against idols. But in one sense, Israel did keep the commandment because although the people worshipped images of other gods, they never actually made a statue of God (Yahweh).

The original stone tablets God wrote upon had a short life: Moses broke them when he came down from Sinai and saw the Israelites in a wild orgy around the golden calf idol (SEE PAGE 131). Another set was written in stone and eventually carried in the ark of the covenant. One of the most famous statues of all time is the *Moses* by Michelangelo, showing the bearded man holding the stone tablets in his arm. The statue, like many old artworks, shows Moses with horns on his head—the result of a mistranslation of the Latin Bible, which speaks of Moses' radiant face after being near God. A Latin translation mistake had Moses "horned" instead of "radiant." While the Commandments were originally in Hebrew, Philippe de Champaigne's painting *Moses with the Ten Commandments* (1648) has the laws in French.

One of the best-loved films ever made is titled *The Ten Commandments*, the 1956 epic with Charlton Heston as Moses. It was a remake of a 1923 silent film, and both versions were directed by Cecil B. DeMille. A 2006 TV movie had the same title, although, in fact, all three would have been more aptly titled *The Story of Moses*.

After the Protestant Reformation in the 1500s, many Protestant churches had the commandments painted or carved into the church walls. While Christians have always believed Jesus' words that the greatest commandments were to love God and love one's neighbor, the Ten Commandments are still valuable moral guidance.

The Ten Commandments have been big news in recent years, with courts debating whether posting the Commandments on public property is a violation of church-state separation.

The Ten Commandments are often known as the *Decalogue*, from the Greek for "ten words."

the ten plagues on Egypt
Special effects, courtesy of God

After God called Moses to lead the Hebrew slaves from Egypt, he assured him the hardhearted Pharaoh would never willingly let the slaves go, but God promised to do "wonders" that would change Pharaoh's mind. The "wonders" were the ten horrible plagues that defiled the Egyptians but left the Hebrews untouched. The first was the turning of the Nile River waters to blood, which made the water undrinkable and created a mass of stinking, dead fish—and was also a slap at Egyptian religion, since they worshipped the Nile as a god named Apis. The second plague followed the first one: frogs left the waters and became a nuisance on land. The third was gnats, the fourth flies, the fifth a disease causing the death of livestock, the sixth boils (happening after Moses scattered some dust into the air), the seventh hail (nor just normal crop-destroying hail, but hail "that ran like fire upon the ground"), the eighth locusts (damaging whatever plants the hail hadn't), and the ninth three days of pitch darkness ("darkness that could be felt").

Pharaoh was continually urged by his counselors to free the slaves so the horrible plagues on the Egyptians would end, but he continued to "harden his heart." The tenth plague convinced him: all the firstborn children died, including Pharaoh's own son (who would presumably have been the next Pharaoh, had

T

he lived). As instructed by God, Moses had the Hebrews mark their doorposts with lamb's blood so the death angel would pass over their houses, visiting only the Egyptians. (This is the source of the festival of Passover; SEE PAGE 273.) The ancient people revered the firstborn child, especially a son, and this final plague broke the will of Pharaoh, and he freed the slaves—only to change his mind afterward, pursuing them to the Red Sea, where his troops were drowned. The accounts of the plagues are in Exodus 7-12.

Skeptics have wondered if there was a "natural" explanation for the plagues. Certainly there are cases of red mineral deposits staining the Nile waters red, and this contaminant in the river would lead to the frogs exiting the waters. People of faith have insisted that even if all the plagues were "coincidences," the timing of them close together was the work of God. One interesting theory about the final plague, the death of the firstborn: The Egyptians might have been so desperate after enduring their first nine plagues that they themselves sacrificed their own firstborn, in the hopes of appeasing the Hebrew God, or of changing Pharaoh's mind, or both.

The plagues have been a favorite subject for artists. They are spectacularly depicted on film, with the 1956 epic *The Ten Commandments* creating a Hollywood version of the plagues, especially the Nile waters turning into blood, the fiery hail, and the sinister death angel passing through the streets.

Thomas
The original skeptic

The expression "doubting Thomas" is based on the story of one of Jesus' twelve disciples who would not believe Jesus had been raised from the dead. According to John 20, Thomas claimed he would not believe Jesus was alive until he saw the wounds from the crucifixion himself. Jesus appeared and, indeed, his resurrected body did have the wounds from his ordeal, leading Thomas to exclaim, "My Lord and my God." In Christian tradition, Thomas is not so much the doubter as he is the first person to acknowledge that Jesus was divine.

The Bible tells us little else about the disciple Thomas except that he also had the name Didymus, meaning "twin." Tradition says that he carried the gospel to faraway India. Supposedly he was martyred and buried near the city of Madras. A very old Christian community in India has the name Mar Thoma (meaning "Lord Thomas"), but it's possible this group took its name from a later evangelist named Thomas. A more reliable tradition says he took the gospel to Parthia (today Iran). The Catholic Church bestowed the title Apostle to India on Thomas in 1972. The Feast of St. Thomas is observed on July 3. Thomas's name has been a common one for male children in all Christian countries.

A so-called Gospel of Thomas has attracted some attention in recent years, being one of many gospels that did not make it into the Bible. Most of these gospels (all with the name of an apostle attached to them) were written by Gnostics, whose religion was a serious rival to Christianity for several centuries.

The shrub *Bauhinia tomentosa* of Asia is called the "St. Thomas tree" because the red spots on the flowers represented the blood Thomas shed when he was martyred in India.

Tigris and Euphrates Rivers
Iraqi waters

These are known today as the main rivers of Iraq. The two are also the first bodies of water mentioned in the Bible, near Eden, or man's original dwelling place (Genesis 2:14). The mighty Assyrian and Babylonian empires were centered in the area of the two rivers, which the Greeks called *Mesopotamia*, meaning "between the rivers." Nineveh, capital of Assyria, was situated on the Tigris, and Babylon, capital of Babylonia, on the Euphrates.

Timothy and Titus
Mentored by the great man himself

Three of the epistles (letters) in the New Testament are from the apostle Paul to two of his protégés, Timothy and Titus. These were men younger than Paul, and both were leaders of Christian groups, so Paul's letters to them are often called the Pastoral Epistles, since Paul gave them good advice on how to be faithful pastors. Paul was fond of them both since he addresses them as "my true child in the faith" and "my beloved child." Timothy was head of the Christians in Ephesus, while

Titus was head of the group on the Greek island of Crete. In 2 Timothy 3:16, Paul refers to the Bible as "God-breathed," meaning that God inspired its writers in a special way. Catholics observe January 26 as the Feast of Timothy and Titus.

In his scandalous novel *Live from Golgotha*, Gore Vidal depicted a homosexual relationship between Paul and Timothy.

tithing

That ten-percent thing

The old word *tithe* means "tenth," and tithing refers to the Old Testament practice of giving one tenth of one's goods or income to God. Of course, the goods didn't actually go to God himself, but to help the poor, and to support the priests and Levites who were the Lord's ministers. Religious Jews took the tithe very seriously, and Jesus referred to some who were so fussy about tithing that they even gave a tenth of their kitchen herbs and spices to the Lord. (Jesus also noted that you could be fussy about tithing and still not be a very good or moral person.)

The early Christians disagreed about whether the tithe was necessary for them. They agreed that helping the poor was a good thing, but the New Testament doesn't actually say that giving ten percent was essential. As Christianity spread through Europe and became the established religion, tithing was mandated for everyone, like it or not. In countries like the U.S. with no established church, many churches emphasize tithing, saying it is good even if it isn't actually necessary. Many Christians choose to tithe, or even to go beyond it, although they disagree about whether the tenth they should give to the church is "gross" or "net" income—i.e., before or after the IRS and state governments take their part. In many churches people place their weekly tithes in the plates or baskets passed during the Sunday worship; some people mail their tithes, or even have them deducted from their bank accounts or credit cards. Many Christians believe that anything beyond the ten-percent is an *offering*, not a tithe—the difference is that the tithe is *owed* to God, while the offering is freely *given*. Some Christians even believe that if the tithe is not given to the church, God will somehow "deduct" it from the person's assets by bringing some financial burden on them. They base this belief on Malachi 3, which states that not tithing is a way of "robbing" God.

Many churches have a "Stewardship Sunday" each year, in which the minister preaches the importance of tithing.

The tithe in the old days was in goods—a tenth of your livestock and farm produce, for example. But today it is almost always in money, used to pay the pastor and other church employees, maintain the building, and (hopefully) engage in charitable work.

One of the surprising things about Christianity is that tithing is more likely to be done by lower- or middle-income people than by the wealthy. In fact, the denominations with the highest rates of tithing are made up of people fairly low on the economic ladder.

tongues / glossolalia
Speaking of God …

In the New Testament, "tongues" had the meaning of "languages." Some of the early Christians had the ability to speak in "unknown tongues"—either real languages they had never learned, or a kind of "heavenly language" known only to them and God. In Acts 2, the Holy Spirit gives the twelve apostles power to speak to people in their own languages, which amazes the people of Jerusalem. Some Christian missionaries have claimed they had the power to speak in languages they had not been taught.

When Christians talk about "speaking in tongues" (also called *glossolalia*), they are usually referring to the "heavenly language" in which the person speaks/prays in sounds that seem like babbling to anyone listening. People who have done it claim that the words/sounds "bubble up" from inside them, a kind of filling with ecstasy that can't be kept quiet. (For purposes of comparison, think of how people shout, whistle, and hoot at concerts and sports events. A person who had never attended such an event might think the nonsensical sound was rather silly, but the fans certainly don't.) The apostle Paul "spoke in tongues" and listed it among the "spiritual gifts" that Christians have. But he was aware that speaking in tongues was a divisive issue among Christians, with some of them lording it over others who did not have the "gift." Also, he feared that newcomers to the Christian group might think the Christians were out of their minds when speaking in tongues (1 Corinthians

T

14). He gave his approval to speaking in tongues, but urged people not to disrupt worship services with it.

In the early 1900s, people in some conservative churches began speaking in tongues, the beginning of what is called the Pentecostal movement (based on Acts 2, which tells of the apostles speaking in tongues). Pentecostal churches emphasize tongues and other "gifts of the Spirit." In the 1960s, many people in mainline churches began speaking in tongues, which caused great controversy in some churches, with people even claiming that speaking in tongues was the work of the devil.

Torah, Pentateuch, Books of Moses
Five alive

The first five books of the Bible, Genesis through Deuteronomy, are called the books of Moses, since he is the main character, and also (so tradition says) their author. (We can assume Moses did not write the end of Deuteronomy, which reports his own death.) The five books are also called by the Hebrew name *Torah*. People generally translate this as "law" but it really means "instruction." The books are intended as God's rules to live by. At the risk of confusing things further, the five are also known by another name, *Pentateuch*, which is Greek for "five tools." Jews regard them as the first and most sacred part of their Bible. They were accepted as divinely inspired before the two other groups of books, the Prophets and the Writings. The Torah (or Pentateuch) records the creation of the world; the calling of Abraham to be the ancestor of a "chosen people," later called the Israelites; the exodus of the slaves in Egypt, led to Canaan by Moses; and the delivery to them of God's holy laws for living. Some of the most interesting and famous stories in the Bible are contained in the Torah: Adam and Eve, Cain and Abel, the tower of Babel, Noah and the flood, the sagas of Abraham, Jacob, and Joseph, the plagues of Egypt, and the years of the Israelites trekking through the wilderness to Canaan.

In the time of Jesus, most of the Jewish priests and aristocrats belonged to a group called the Sadducees, which believed that only the Torah was divinely inspired. The Pharisees, on the other hand, also accepted the Prophets and the Writings as inspired. This created some arguments since the Sadducees claimed the Torah did not teach any belief in an afterlife. In a famous episode in the Book of Acts, the apostle Paul started a near-riot by pitting the two groups against each other: "Then Paul, knowing that some of them were Sadducees and the others Pharisees, called out in the Sanhedrin, 'My brothers, I am a Pharisee, the son of a Pharisee. I stand on trial because of my hope in the resurrection of the dead.' When he said this, a dispute broke out between the Pharisees and the Sadducees, and the assembly was divided. The Sadducees say that there is no resurrection, and that there are neither angels nor spirits, but the Pharisees acknowledge them all" (Acts 23:6-8, NIV).

The huge body of Jewish writings known as the Talmud is the Jews' attempt to apply the laws in the Torah. Though the Torah is full of rules, they don't cover every life situation in detail. The Talmud is the attempt of devout Jews to see that all of life is ordered by the Torah—business transactions, ceremonies for holy days, marriages and divorce, legal procedures, and other issues. The Talmud wasn't completed until a few centuries after the time of Jesus, but the New Testament shows how the most devout Jews (the Pharisees) were already formulating the thousands of rules that would make up the Talmud, and Jesus scolded these people who would "strain out a gnat but swallow a camel" (Matthew 23:24).

Transfiguration
They saw dead people …

One of the most interesting (and puzzling) episodes in the story of Jesus is known as the Transfiguration. Jesus took his three closest disciples—Peter, James, and John—to a mountain, where his face and clothes became white and shining, and the long-dead Moses and Elijah were seen talking with him. (To the Jews of those days, Moses symbolized the Old Testament law, while Elijah symbolized Israel's prophets.) The impulsive disciple Peter was so impressed with what he saw that he suggested building "three booths" at the site to commemorate the event, which is recorded in three of the Gospels (Matthew 17:1-13, Mark 9:1-13, Luke 9:27-36). A cloud overshadowed Jesus, Moses, and Elijah, and God's voice said, "This is my beloved Son, with whom I am well pleased. Listen to him."

What exactly did the event mean? One obvious meaning is that the saints of the past—like Moses and Elijah—were not dead, but were alive with God in

T

The Transfiguration of Christ
MATTHEW. CHAPTER 17, VERSES 1-8.

heaven. The radiance of Jesus' face and garments is usually taken to mean that he was divine. The Transfiguration was a brief glimpse at the "real" Jesus, who was a human but also divine, with God's voice confirming that Jesus was indeed the Son of God.

The Catholic and Orthodox churches celebrate August 6 as the Feast of the Transfiguration, and many local churches have the name Church of the Transfiguration. The Transfiguration supposedly occurred on Mount Tabor, which is also a common name for churches. In the Middle Ages, Eastern Orthodox monks pursued a form of meditation in the hope of seeing the "uncreated light" that the disciples saw at the Transfiguration. The event has been a favorite subject for artists through the centuries, probably the most famous rendition being Raphael's 1520 painting in the Vatican, showing Jesus, Elijah, and Moses literally floating in the air with the three apostles below them. Fra Angelico's 1441 fresco in Florence conveys the dazzling white spoken of in the Gospels, with the rest of the scene bathed in gold. The painters of icons in the Eastern Orthodox churches have been especially fond of the subject, partly because the Orthodox are very devoted to Elijah. French composer Olivier Messiaen wrote a choral work titled *The Transfiguration of Our Lord Jesus Christ*.

The actual Greek word used in the Gospels for the event is one we are all familiar with—*metamorphosis*.

the Trinity
A mind-boggling divine three

Christians believe there is one God, but that that he somehow exists as three "persons"—Father, Son, and Holy Spirit. This is known as the Trinity. Jews and Muslims do not accept the name or the description since they see the Trinity as three gods, and they cannot accept the idea that the one God has a "son." Christian theologians have spilled lots of ink trying to explain just how God can be "one in three, and three in one," but in the final analysis, they admit it is a great mystery, for who can fully grasp what God is like? Books with titles like *On the Trinity* could fill a huge warehouse, but a human author can never quite describe the nature of God in words. Saying that God exists in three "persons" or "essences" doesn't quite convey the mystery.

At least the concept of Father and Son is fairly easy to grasp. Jesus prayed to God and addressed him as father, and the first Christians believed that Jesus of Nazareth was also the Son of God—fully human, but in some way fully divine also. The Bible indicates that even before Jesus of Nazareth was born, the Son of God existed—from all eternity, in fact (John 1:1-5, Philippians 2:5-8). The apostle Thomas referred to the risen Jesus as "my Lord and my God." In the New Testament, Jesus is seen as the Son of God, yet also, mysteriously, he *is* God.

The Holy Spirit (explained in more detail on PAGE 152) is harder to grasp, though the Bible depicts him (the Spirit is always *he*, not *it*) as the divine power personified in some way. The New Testament teaches that each Christian has the Spirit dwelling within them, and that the Spirit gives each believer a "spiritual gift," an ability that should be used to benefit the whole fellowship.

There are only a few passages in the Bible that mention Father, Son, and Spirit together. One notable incident is Jesus' baptism, where the Spirit descends on Jesus (the Son) in the form of a dove, and from heaven God the Father says he is "well pleased" with his Son. One of the most common subjects in religious paintings is the baptism of Jesus, with the dove (Spirit) over his head, and white-bearded male figure (the Father) looking down from heaven. (Sometimes the Father is not represented by a human figure but by rays of light.) At the end of Matthew's Gospel, the risen Jesus tells his disciples to spread the Gospel to all nations, and to baptize converts "in the name of the Father, the Son, and the Holy Spirit"—a formula that has been used in most Christian baptisms throughout history (Matthew 28:19). There is also the "Trinity blessing" at the end of 2 Corinthians: "The grace of the Lord Jesus Christ, the love of God, and the fellowship of the Holy Spirit be with you all." Many pastors use this formula to conclude worship services.

The actual word Trinity is not found in the Bible. Around the year 200, the Latin theologian Tertullian coined the word *trinitas* in trying to describe God. Many Christian hymns praise the Trinity, generally in three verses, one verse each for the Father, Son, and Holy Spirit.

T

Christians can find "previews" of the Trinity in the Old Testament. The patriarch Abraham was visited by three "men" who are also referred to as "the Lord," and Christians see this as a visit of the Trinity to Abraham, long before the Son took earthly form as Jesus. Artists, especially those in the Eastern Orthodox churches, have painted pictures of Abraham and this "Old Testament Trinity."

Trinity is a popular name for churches and religious schools everywhere, and there are even some cities named Trinity, plus the island of Trinidad in the Caribbean. Roman Catholics celebrate the Sunday after Pentecost as Trinity Sunday.

the twelve disciples
Apostles in training

Jesus had numerous followers in his lifetime, including a group called the Seventy. But his closest followers were a band of twelve, probably chosen because Israel was composed of twelve tribes, and there were twelve books of the prophets in the Old Testament—twelve was a sort of "sacred" number for the Jews. In Matthew's Gospel, the disciples are Simon (also called Peter), Andrew his brother, James the son of Zebedee, John his brother, Philip, Bartholomew, Thomas, Matthew the tax collector, James the son of Alphaeus, Thaddaeus, Simon the Zealot, and Judas Iscariot, who betrayed him (Matthew 10:2-4). Lists are also found in Luke 6 and Mark 3. Of the twelve, the first four (Peter, Andrew, James, and John) were fisherman. Matthew was a tax collector, which must have made for interesting conversations with Simon the Zealot, since the Zealots hated people who collaborated with the Romans, and that included tax collectors.

Although the twelve disciples have always been held in high regard in Christian tradition, the Gospels and Acts don't tell us much about them. Peter, James, and John were an "inner circle" especially close to Jesus, and these three are active in the Gospels and Acts (James being the first one to die for his faith, as Acts tells us). Judas, of course, is remembered as the traitor, and Acts 1 tells how the disciples, after the ascension of Jesus into heaven, replaced him with a man named Matthias, keeping the number at twelve. Thomas and Philip say a few words in John's Gospel, but otherwise we know little about the group. Because they were attached so closely to Jesus, numerous legends have grown to fill in the gaps, with each disciple traveling to distant lands and being martyred, sometimes in horrible ways. In this book you'll find separate entries for the more important disciples (Peter, James, John, Matthew, Judas, and Thomas).

While the disciples have been honored as Jesus' companions and witnesses to his resurrection, the Gospels make it clear they were not superhuman, and Jesus often scolded them for their selfishness and foolishness. Only one, John, was actually present at the cross, while the others remained in hiding. It was Mary Magdalene, not one of the twelve disciples, who first saw the risen Jesus.

A word about the difference between "disciples" and "apostles": a disciple is a learner, so while Jesus was on earth, his twelve close followers were in a pupil-teacher relationship with him. After his ascension, they were known as apostles, meaning "ambassadors," speaking on his behalf. The Gospels use both terms, but more often "disciples." The Book of Acts almost always uses "apostles." Acts also extends the term to include others besides the original twelve. In fact, the most famous apostle of all is Paul, who was not one of the original band and persecuted Christians until his dramatic conversion experience.

Incidentally, the early Christians referred to themselves as "disciples" more often than they used the word "Christian" (SEE PAGE 70).

the twelve tribes of Israel
Jacob and Sons, Inc.

Every Israelite traced his ancestry back to one of the twelve sons of the patriarch Jacob, who also bore the name Israel (Hebrew for "struggles with God") after his famous wrestling match with the Lord (SEE PAGE 166). Jacob's twelve sons were the children of his two wives and two concubines. In order of birth, the sons were Reuben, Simeon, Levi, Judah, Issachar, Zebulun, Gad, Asher, Dan, Naphtali, Joseph, and Benjamin. Jacob's personal favorites among the sons were the last two, since they were sons of his beloved wife Rachel. The descendants of each son were called a "tribe."

The Book of Joshua describes how the Israelites, formerly slaves in Egypt, settled in the land of Canaan and divided up the land among the twelve tribes. Maps of the Old Testament period show the boundaries of the tribes, but two sons are not there: Joseph and Levi. The Levites were the priestly tribe (Moses and Aaron were Levites), so they served as priests throughout Israel and had a few cities allotted to

T

them. Joseph, the son who was sold into slavery in Egypt and became the pharaoh's right-hand man, had two sons, Ephraim and Manasseh, so instead of finding Joseph on the tribal map, you'll find the two "half-tribes" of Ephraim and Manasseh. Giving the Levites no area and Joseph's sons two areas, it adds up to twelve tribal regions.

In the Book of Judges, each tribe handles its own affairs. The twelve are not really a nation, just a loose confederation. They were not truly united until Israel got its first king, Saul.

Over time, some of the tribal areas simply disappeared by being absorbed into the hostile nations nearby. Simeon, for example, disappeared very early in Israel's history. The tribe that eventually was most important was Judah, the tribe David was from, and also the area containing Jerusalem. Jesus was a descendant of Judah.

Israel divided into two kingdoms—Israel and Judah—after the death of Solomon. Israel was composed of the ten northern tribes, and these were conquered and deported by the Assyrians in the year 722 B.C. Because they were scattered abroad and no longer formed a political unit, they are referred to as the "lost tribes of Israel." (SEE PAGE 221 for more about the lost tribes.)

Jesus chose twelve disciples to be his close followers, and some people think this symbolized he was starting a "new Israel," based on spiritual beliefs and not genealogy. In the New Testament, some important characters' tribal descent is mentioned—for example, Paul was from the tribe of Benjamin, and Barnabas was from the tribe of Levi. But among the early Christians, the tribal connections ceased to matter.

the two thieves
Last-minute choices

In some images of Jesus' crucifixion, you see three crosses, not just one. Jesus was crucified, the Gospels say, between two thieves, although Bible scholars tell us the word for "thieves" could also indicate revolutionaries—in other words, they were being crucified for acting against the Roman government, not just plain robbery. In Luke's Gospel, one of the thieves has the energy to mock Jesus, saying, "If you are the Christ, save yourself and us." (It could have been mockery, but it could have been a last-minute cry for help, or both.) The other thief was more compassionate, reminding the first one that the two of them were being punished fairly, while Jesus was innocent. He said to Jesus, "Lord, remember me when you come into your kingdom." Jesus famously replied, "Today you will be with me in Paradise" (Luke 23:39-24).

Preachers throughout the centuries have made the most of this story, since it sends the message that it is never too late to repent and be saved. On the other hand, people who delay their conversions would often point out to their friends and preachers that they might as well wait to the point of death, since, after all, the thief on the cross was saved at the last moment.

The thieves are not named in the Bible, but for some reason tradition has called them Dismas (the one Jesus promised Paradise) and Gestas (the other one, who presumably went elsewhere). In novels and films, the two are usually called by these names. In Mel Gibson's film *The Passion of the Christ*, the scene on the cross is made more horrifying by a raven that flies down to peck at the eye of the unrepentant thief.

T

the unpardonable sin
Ultimate choices in words

The Bible never actually uses the words "unpardonable sin," but Jesus did speak of blasphemy against the Holy Spirit as unforgivable (Mark 3:22-30). Christians have debated for centuries over what it meant to blaspheme against the Spirit. In fact, Jesus' meaning was clear: He had been accused by his enemies of being in league with Satan, who, they said, gave him the power to cast demons out of people. Jesus was referring to the sin of calling God's work the work of Satan. This sin was what the prophet Isaiah had in mind when he said, "Woe to those who call evil good, and good evil" (Isaiah 5:20).

"Unpardonable sin" is part of our language, and it is not used to refer to the sin Jesus described. More often, people use it in a joking way, as in, "She wore white after Labor Day, and that is the unpardonable sin."

unjust judge, parable of
(See the parable of the unjust judge)

Visitation

Mother bonding

Luke's Gospel records two amazing pregnancies: that of the aged Elizabeth, mother of John the Baptist, and Mary, mother of Jesus. Both births were foretold by the angel Gabriel. In the case of Elizabeth, the father was her elderly husband Zechariah. In the case of Mary, the father was God. Luke 1:39-45 states that Mary went to visit Elizabeth for three months, and on her arrival, Elizabeth's baby "leaped in her womb." Elizabeth said to Mary, "Blessed art thou among women, and blessed is the fruit of thy womb." The event is known as the Visitation and is celebrated each year on May 31 by Roman Catholics. It has been depicted in many works of art, though the only film to depict the visitation was the TV miniseries *Jesus of Nazareth*.

water from the rock
Dry and nearly stoned

When Moses led the Hebrew slaves from Egypt, God provided food in the wilderness by sending the miracle food called manna (SEE PAGE 229). Lack of water was also a problem in this area that was basically a desert, and on two occasions God worked a miracle by having water gush forth from a rock. The first incident was soon after the parting of the Red Sea. The people proved their ingratitude to Moses by threatening to stone him for bringing them into the dry wilderness, but God told Moses to strike a rock and water would gush out (Exodus 17). Several years later, still in the wilderness, the people complained again about no water, and the Lord provided—except in this instance, he told Moses not to strike a rock, but merely to speak to it, telling it to send forth water. Moses struck the rock instead of speaking to it, and though the water came forth, God was angry that Moses had not obeyed his direct order to speak to the rock. Moses' punishment was severe: After all the years of leading the people from Egypt toward Canaan, he would never enter Canaan himself (Numbers 20:2-13). The story bothers many readers, since it makes God seem nitpicky and unkind to the man who had been so faithful.

water into wine
So much for tee-totalers …

According to John's Gospel, Jesus' first miracle was performed at a wedding in the town of Cana when the hosts ran out of wine. Jesus turned six large jars of water into wine—not just ordinary wine, but wine so good that someone said to the groom, "You have saved the best till now." And, says John, Jesus thus "manifested His glory, and His disciples believed in Him" (John 2:1-11). Like all of Jesus' miracles, this was not a divine power "showing off" but a man of compassion using his power to fill a human need.

The Marriage Feast in Cana
John. Chapter 2, Verses 1-11.

Countless art museums have paintings with titles like *The Miracle at Cana*, often showing the wedding guests looking surprised to see red wine being dipped from jars that they thought contained water. The famous miracle is featured in most movies about Jesus.

wheat and tares, parable of
(See the parable of wheat and tares)

wise men / Magi
But not kings, and not necessarily three

It is hard to imagine the Christmas story without the wise men. According to Matthew's Gospel, the wise men (he uses the word "magi") journeyed from the east and asked the Jewish king, Herod, "Where is he who has been born King of the Jews? For we have seen his star in the east and have come to worship Him." This wasn't good news for the paranoid Herod, who considered himself the king of the Jews. Herod's counselors told him the Christ (or Messiah) would be born in Bethlehem. The wise men journey to Bethlehem, find Jesus' family, and present the baby with gold, frankincense, and myrrh. A dream warns them to return to their country without reporting back to Herod. As residents of the Persian Empire, which was a rival to Rome, their presence would have rattled Herod, who always kowtowed to Rome.

W

How many wise men were there? The Bible doesn't say. The tradition of three developed because the Gospel mentions three gifts. We have no idea how many there were. In some early traditions, there were as many as twelve. There is no basis for the tradition that the wise men were three kings. Nor does the Bible mention their names, which tradition calls Caspar, Melchior, and Balthasar. Still, the idea of three kings visiting the newborn king of the Jews caught people's imagination, and it's hard to imagine Christmas without the song "We Three Kings of Orient Are." Christians may have recalled the words of the prophet Isaiah, "Nations shall come to your light, and kings to the brightness of your rising," in a chapter which later says those kings "shall bring gold and frankincense" (Isaiah 60:3, 6). (Incidentally, Myrrh is the name of a Christian music company today.)

Matthew's Gospel refers to them as *magi*, which means they practiced astrology and other magic arts. (Some modern translations have "astrologers" instead of "wise men" or "magi.") Since they came from "the east," their homeland was probably Persia or Arabia. In all likelihood they came from Persia, where they were priests of the very old Zoroastrian religion, which worshiped one god.

They have intrigued artists, who delight in depicting them in exotic robes and crowns. The earliest paintings show them in Persian garb, which was probably correct. Later, artists tried to be "multi-cultural," showing the three with various skin tones and costumes to indicate that people of different races and backgrounds were drawn to the infant Jesus (though, in fact, they probably came from the same nation). More often, artists have shown them as fair-skinned and as thoroughly European-looking as the artists themselves were. In German artist Albrecht Durer's 1504 version, he made himself one of the Magi. And thanks to Nativity scenes, they

The Star in the East Shines on the Infant Jesus
MATTHEW. CHAPTER 2, VERSES 9-12.

are among the most-pictured of Bible characters. No art museum is without one or more paintings titled *Adoration of the Magi* or *Adoration of the Kings*. They have been portrayed in several movies dealing with Jesus' birth, and in *Ben-Hur*, one of them is a powerful influence on the main character. Gian Carlo Menotti's opera *Amahl and the Night Visitors* has the magi as characters. The TV special *The Little Drummer Boy* follows tradition and depicts the three men as kings. One of the most-read short stories of all time is O. Henry's "The Gift of the Magi," which despite its title has nothing to do with the magi of the Bible.

Numerous towns in Iran and Iraq claim to have the birthplace—or tombs—or homes—of the magi. When Marco Polo trekked through the region in the Middle Ages, he was shown the reputed tomb of the magi. Helena, mother of the Roman emperor Constantine, supposedly found their tombs and sent their relics to Constantinople. At some point the relics made their way to Milan, Italy, which was plundered by German emperor Frederick Barbarosa, who sent the relics to Cologne, where they became the foundation of the magnificent cathedral there. The bones were placed in a magnificent gold casket encrusted with jewels, which has been on view for 800 years. For many centuries, Cologne was called the "City of the Three Kings."

The Christian holiday called Epiphany, January 6, celebrates the visit of the Magi. (Epiphany means "manifestation" or "being revealed." The holiday celebrates Jesus revealed to the Gentiles, the non-Jews.) In the past, Epiphany was sometimes called the Feast of the Three Holy Kings. In many countries gifts are exchanged on Epiphany instead of on Christmas, in remembrance of the gifts of the Magi. The following of the star toward Bethlehem is, of course, the source of the custom of having a star atop the Christmas tree.

the witch of Endor

Bringing up an old friend

Occult activity, including the "channeling" of spirits, occurred in Biblical times. Israel's law prohibited any kind of occult activity, and 1 Samuel 28:3 relates that Saul, Israel's first king, had expelled the mediums and occultists from the land. But, ironically, before a fateful battle with the Philistines, Saul consults a medium (called "witch" in older translations) in the village of Endor. Saul assures her she will not be punished, and at his request she calls up the spirit of his dead mentor, Samuel. The spirit, not pleased, asks Saul, "Why have you disturbed me by bringing me up?" Poor Saul explains that he wants Samuel's advice, since God appears to have abandoned him. Samuel states that the kingdom will be handed over to Saul's rival, David, and "tomorrow you and

W

your sons will be with me"—that is, dead. As Samuel predicted, Saul and his sons die the following day.

The encounter is interesting in that the "witch" seems surprised that the spirit of Samuel actually appeared. We can assume that she was (like most such people) a fake, and that for some mysterious reason God actually did allow Samuel's ghost to appear to Saul. At any rate, Saul, the witch, and the ghost proved to be an interesting subject for artists over the centuries, who seemed to delight in showing the shock on the face of the witch.

Regarding the name "Endor": Do you recall that in the popular TV sitcom "Bewitched," the main character's mother was named "Endora"? Coincidence?

witchcraft and magic
Zero tolerance policy

For the Jews and Christians of the Bible, there was no distinction between "white" and "black" magic. All magic was bad, as was what we today call "channeling" of departed people's souls. Egyptian Pharaohs had court magicians, and apparently they had some spiritual powers (or at least were good fakers), but the people of Israel were told to avoid magic and the occult, and to execute those who practiced it (Leviticus 22:18, Deuteronomy 18:10). Rather sadly, those laws have been put into effect from time to time by Christians, notoriously at the witch trials in Salem, Massachusetts. Some of Israel's kings dabbled in witchcraft and consulted magicians, and God's prophets condemned this heartily (Jeremiah 27:9). The most famous encounter with a so-called witch was Saul's visit to the witch of Endor (SEE PAGE 379).

In the New Testament period, witchcraft and the occult were widely practiced throughout the Roman Empire. A magician named Simon became (supposedly) a Christian, then tried to buy spiritual power from the apostles (Acts 8), and another sorcerer named Elymas was an opponent of the apostle Paul (Acts 13). Some of the Christian converts were people who had dabbled in the occult, and on one occasion they made a bonfire of the books of magic they had used (Acts 19:19). The Book of Revelation includes sorcerers and occultists as being among those who will be destroyed in the lake of fire and brimstone (Revelation 21:8, 22:15).

Remember that for the Jews and Christians, God was in control of human destiny, and they believed it was wrong to use spells or rituals or contact with spirits to get through life. Also worth noting, the ancient Romans were notoriously superstitious, and on occasion the emperor would expel all the magicians from Rome—or at least those thought to practice *harmful* magic. Christians did and do condemn witchcraft and the occult, making no distinction between "white" and "black" magic. Some Christians are even leery of stories (such as the popular Harry Potter novels) that present magic in a favorable light, and some Christians will not allow their children to celebrate Halloween since it has associations with witchcraft. Muslims have been even stricter regarding witchcraft than Christians and Jews, and in our own century, Saudi Arabia has announced its plan to "terminate" those dabbling in the occult.

Interestingly, the Bible condemns the occult but doesn't actually link it with the power of Satan. As Christianity spread, there was a kind of spiritual backlash, with sorcerers and occultists claiming a connection with Satan, the opponent of the Christians' God.

the woman caught in adultery
A story of mercy—and a forgotten punchline

This story, found in John 8:3-12, is often quoted because it seems to show how "tolerant" and "nonjudgmental" Jesus was. As the story goes, Jesus' enemies, the scribes and the Pharisees, try to trap him in a moral dilemma to make him appear "soft on sin." They bring to him a woman caught in the act of adultery (meaning, not just gossip, but caught with the other man). The Law of Moses mandated stoning her to death. They wanted to know what Jesus would do to her. To everyone's frustration, Jesus "wrote on the ground with his finger, as though he did not hear." Then he spoke the words that give this story its "toler-

Jesus and the Sinner
LUKE. CHAPTER 7, VERSES 44-50.

W

ant" tone: "He who is without sin among you, let him throw a stone at her first." The accusers depart, leaving Jesus and the woman alone. He says to her, "Woman, where are they? Has no one condemned you?" She replies, "No one, Lord." But Jesus isn't "soft on sin." He says to her, "Go, and sin no more." She is forgiven—but not free to commit the same sin again.

Even with Jesus' words, "Go, and sin no more," the story shows his deep compassion. Rembrandt's painting *The Woman Taken in Adultery* (1644, National Gallery, London) is interesting because Jesus appears taller than anyone else in the image, as if Rembrandt was showing his moral superiority.

The Bible does not tell us the woman's name. In many film versions of the story, the woman is Mary Magdalene, who becomes a follower of Jesus. This isn't the case in the Bible. Whatever she is called, the story seems to appeal to modern filmmakers, since it appears in practically every film about Jesus. In D. W. Griffith's 1916 silent classic *Intolerance*, the film does not include the line, "Go, and sin no more." Griffith, a notorious adulterer himself, apparently didn't think the woman's sin was serious. In Cecil B. DeMille's 1927 *The King of Kings*, the words that Jesus writes on the ground are the sins of the people who are about to stone the woman. When each of them sees his own sin written in the sand, he drops his stone and walks away, looking guilty.

women

Helpers, or something higher?

By today's standards, almost everything written in the ancient world was "sexist," with men playing a much more important role than women. According to Genesis, man was created first, then woman to be his "helpmeet." Throughout the Bible a person is often referred to by the father's name, as in "John, son of Zebedee" or "Dinah, daughter of Jacob," and the mother is seldom named. On the other hand, the Old Testament commanded people to honor both their parents, and striking one's mother or father was a capital crime. The Book of Job mentions the name of Job's daughters, but not his sons, which is surprising. The Book of Proverb's final chapter is a hymn praising the good wife and mother. Three books of the Old Testament are named for their main characters (Ruth, Esther, and Judith), though it's not known if women wrote any of the books of the Bible. In the Book of Judges, the judge Deborah occupied a position of leadership.

The New Testament seems more gender-inclusive than the Old Testament. Jesus seems to have had a high opinion of women, and there were several women who took care of the needs (not sexual ones) of Jesus and the disciples. Jesus was close friends with Martha and Mary, and also their brother Lazarus. The first person to see the risen Jesus was Mary Magdalene. The apostle Paul's good friend Priscilla was praised by him highly, and he also praised Phoebe as a woman of faith. In the past fifty years, however, Paul has been criticized for his statements that women should not hold leadership roles in the churches (1 Corinthians 11 and 14). Some churches prohibit women from being ordained ministers, based on Paul's words, although all churches allow women to teach and serve in other positions. (In fact, in practically any church there are lots more women than men.) However, Paul's most memorable statement about women was that among the Christians, there was no discriminating between men and women, free people and slaves, Jew and non-Jew, "for all are one in Christ Jesus" (Galatians 3:28). He told wives to submit to their husbands, but also commanded husbands to love their wives as much as they loved themselves, and not to be harsh with them (Colossians 3:18-19). He also stated that "woman is not independent of man, nor man of woman" (1 Corinthians 11:11).

In the centuries following the time of the Bible, one of the most honored figures among Christians has been Jesus' mother Mary, although Protestant Christians don't revere her the way that Catholics and Eastern Orthodox do.

God himself is always "he" in the Bible, and is thought of as male, especially since he is "Father." But God also commanded people never to make images of him, so in Israel there were no statues or pictures showing him as a man. Most of the pagan people thought of their gods as man-shaped, and usually the highest god was a fertility figure (often shown complete with the sexual organs). In the Old Testament, God is spoken of as the husband of Israel, but the meaning is spiritual: God wants Israel to worship him alone, not the immoral gods of the pagans. God is thought of as male, but never as a man. Many Christian artworks depict God in human shape, most familiarly as the brawny, white-bearded figure reaching out to touch Adam in Michelangelo's famous painting. However, other artists are unwilling to show God; instead of a human figure, he is shown as a kind of radiant glow.

the Word

Just call him "Logos"

When you see Word with a capital W, it refers to Jesus Christ, who is identified in John's Gospel as the Word of God, who existed with God from all eternity, and in some mysterious way *was* God. The "Word" is a translation of the Greek word *logos*. John is the only New Testament author to use the word. It was a good choice, because it had meanings that appealed to both Jews and non-Jews. The Jews were familiar with the "word of the Lord," God's voice that brought the world into existence and was spoken to the people through the prophets. For Greeks and other non-Jews, the Word (*logos*) was a kind of intermediary between man and God (or gods). Both groups would have understood *logos* to mean a revelation of the divine will. The early Christians believed that Jesus was the Word living on earth as a human being, and that he was the latest (and final) way of God revealing himself to humankind. John used the term *logos* as a kind of "hook" to make the story of Jesus appealing to both Jews and non-Jews.

For Christians, Word has another meaning: the Bible is the "Word of God."

Yahweh / Jehovah
Just say "Lord"

"God" is not really God's name in the Bible. His actual name, which he revealed to Moses in the burning bush, is "Yahweh," which means something like "causes to be." It's impossible to translate, although "Supreme Being" wouldn't be a bad translation. Throughout the Old Testament, the original Hebrew sometimes refers to God as God (the word *Elohim,* or just *El*) or as Yahweh. As time passed, people had such reverence for the name Yahweh that they thought it was too holy to pronounce out loud. When they read aloud, they substituted the Hebrew word *Adonai* (meaning "Lord" or "Master") for Yahweh. When the Old Testament was translated from Hebrew into Greek, the translators used the Greek word *Kurios* ("Lord") for Yahweh. Translations into other languages did the same, using that language's word for "Lord" instead of using Yahweh.

In English Bibles, you'll notice that the word "Lord" is sometimes spelled normally and sometimes "LORD." When you see "LORD," you know that it's a translation of Yahweh, whereas "Lord" could refer to God or to a human being. One English translation, the Jerusalem Bible, actually uses the word "Yahweh" in the Old Testament, but almost all other English Bibles use "LORD." When you open the Jerusalem Bible to Psalm 23 and read "Yahweh is my shepherd," it doesn't sound quite right, since we are so accustomed to "LORD."

What about the name "Jehovah" for God? Believe it or not, it's a slightly altered form of Yahweh—in old days a "J" was usually pronounced like "Y," and "v" and "w" were practically interchangeable. A few older translations still use "Jehovah." The name remains familiar because it is used, of course, by the Jehovah's Witnesses. It was introduced into English Bibles around 1530 by scholar William Tyndale, the first man to translate the Hebrew Old Testament into English.

In biblical times, Greeks and Romans who were attracted to the Jews' religion sometimes prayed to God by the name *Iao*—their approximation to the Hebrew name Yahweh.

Z

Zacchaeus

Tax collector comes up short

Here's an appealing story: a crooked tax collector encounters Jesus, his life changes, and he pays back all the money he gouged from people. The story is found in Luke 19. Jesus is passing through the ancient town of Jericho, and the local tax collector, named Zacchaeus, is so short he can't see Jesus for the crowd. He shimmies up a sycamore tree. To his great surprise, Jesus addressed him: "Zacchaeus, make haste and come down, for I must stay at your house." Although the locals mutter about Jesus socializing with a tax collector (they were hated then as much as now), Zacchaeus himself was so moved by Jesus' compassion that he claimed he would pay back all the money he had taken dishonestly.

Zacchaeus is not an important character in the Bible, but the story is a memorable one, and generations of children have learned the song that begins, "Zacchaeus was a wee little man, a wee little man was he." It is one of those "small" stories that makes the Bible interesting and thoroughly human.

Zealots

Freedom fighters—or scroungy radicals?

A Zealot is someone zealous for a cause. In the New Testament period, it referred to Jews who were zealous for self-rule, meaning they wanted to boot out their Roman overlords. Most Jews grumbled about Roman oppression, but they accepted it. The Zealots did not, and many of them resorted to violence, killing and robbing Romans whenever possible, often hiding out in the hills and coming out periodically to wage guerrilla warfare. In a revolt that occurred during Jesus' boyhood, a Roman general crucified thousands of Zealot rebels. The crucifixions only increased the people's sympathy with the Zealots. The Zealot cry of "No king but God" was something many Jews found appealing.

Like any violent group, the Zealots attracted idealists, along with some men who just enjoyed violence and robbery in the name of "the Cause." At least one of Jesus' disciples, Simon, was a Zealot (Luke 6:15), though we don't know if he was violent himself or just a sympathizer. It is highly possible that Judas Iscariot, the disciple who betrayed Jesus, was a Zealot, and that he betrayed his master because he had hoped Jesus would lead a rebellion against Rome.

In many movies and novels, the Zealots are depicted as violent freedom fighters, whose way of revolution is contrasted with the peaceful way of Jesus—political change versus a change of the heart. Barabbas, the murderer who was released at the time of Jesus' trial, was in all likelihood a Zealot, and in many movies he is portrayed as Jesus' opposite in every way. Both the 1961 film *King of Kings* and the 1977 TV mini-series *Jesus of Nazareth* featured Barabbas and the Zealots as prominent characters. The audience was not expected to like them. In the 1998 film *The Last Temptation of Christ*, the Zealots are portrayed more sympathetically.

Thanks to the Zealots' violence, the Romans destroyed the temple in Jerusalem in the year 70.

Zechariah
The Holy Week prophet

The Old Testament prophet Zechariah is remembered by Christians because several of his prophecies seem to be fulfilled in the life of Jesus, particularly during the events of Holy Week, the dramatic week before Jesus' resurrection. Zechariah prophesied that Jerusalem would receive a king "humbled and mounted on a donkey" (Zechariah 9:9), and indeed Jesus entered the city of Jerusalem riding a donkey. Zechariah also spoke of the weighing out of thirty pieces of silver (Zechariah 11:12-13), the "blood money" that the priests paid Judas Iscariot to betray

Jesus. Zechariah's words, "Strike the shepherd, and the sheep shall be scattered" (Zechariah 13:7) was seen as a prophecy of Jesus' arrests, when all his disciples fled in fright.

Zechariah is one of the few books of the Old Testament that mentions Satan, who is described as "the accuser" (Zechariah 3:2).

Zeus and Hermes
Case of mistaken divinity

Zeus was the chief god of the Greeks, and Hermes was his messenger. The two are mentioned briefly in the Book of Acts, when the missionaries Paul and Barnabas heal a crippled man. The people were naturally impressed with this miracle and began shouting, "The gods have come down to us in human form!" The local priest wanted to sacrifice bulls to the two gods, but Paul insisted that he and Barnabas were only human. Paul was the speaker, so the people believed he was Hermes, while Barnabas was Zeus. Nicolaes Berchem's 1650 painting *Paul and Barnabas at Lystra* shows the bizarre scene of the priest of Zeus about to sacrifice a bull to the two apostles, who have healed a man. The two are protesting this act of reverence. The episode is featured in Felix Mendelssohn's great oratorio *St. Paul*.

Zion
Holy hill

Zion was a hill in Jerusalem, belonging to the Jebusites. David captured it from them, and it became known as the City of David (2 Samuel 5:7). He had the ark of the covenant brought there, which gave the hill a sacred quality. As time passed, the name Zion came to stand for the site of the Lord's temple, even though technically the temple was on Mount Moriah (SEE PAGE 247). Then in time, Zion came to mean Jerusalem, and after the capture of Jerusalem by the Babylonians, the Jewish exiles used Zion to refer to their homeland in Israel. Several of the Psalms show the affection the Jewish exiles had for the name: "I have installed my King on Zion, my holy hill" (Psalm 2:6, NIV). "From Zion, perfect in beauty, God shines forth" (Psalm 50:2). "Great is the Lord in Zion; he is exalted over all the nations"

Z

(Psalm 99:2). Then, one of the most quoted of all the Psalms: "By the rivers of Babylon we sat and wept when we remembered Zion" (Psalm 137:1). In fact, the name Zion occurs much more often in the Psalms than the name Jerusalem does. These and other Psalms that refer to Zion show that the name had come to mean something more than just one hill or even one city. The name Zion had come to symbolize the presence of God. Jews had come to think of themselves as "sons and daughters of Zion."

It's no surprise that when Jews everywhere sought to establish a Jewish nation in Palestine, the movement would be called Zionism. This dated from the 1890s, but the name Zionism still refers to Jews who want to maintain the state of Israel.

In the New Testament, the early Christians looked at Zion differently: It referred not to a spot on earth, but to heaven, the believers' real homeland: "But you have come to Mount Zion, to the heavenly Jerusalem, the city of the living God. You have come to thousands upon thousands of angels in joyful assembly" (Hebrews 12:22). The Bible's last book, Revelation, speaks of Mount Zion, but it is clearly referring to something spiritual, not a locale on the face of the earth: "Then I looked, and there before me was the Lamb, standing on Mount Zion, and with him 144,000 who had his name and his Father's name written on their foreheads" (Revelation 14:1).

The Bible is full of names difficult to pronounce, but Zion is short and easy to say, and both Jews and Christians have used the name in thousands of hymns and poems. Practically every town in America has at least one or more churches named Zion or Mount Zion, and there are several cities named Zion, not to mention Zion National Park in Utah.

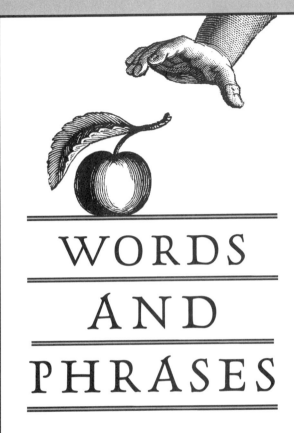

WORDS
AND
PHRASES

Adam's apple

We don't know exactly what fruit Adam and Eve ate that got them into such trouble, though we generally call it an apple. Legend says that when Adam ate the forbidden fruit (Genesis 3), a piece of it stuck in his throat forever. The legend does provide an amusing explanation for why men (more so than women) have a bulge in the center of the throat (the Adam's apple).

Akeldama

In the Gospels, the traitor Judas is so grief-stricken after Jesus' arrest that he gives the Jewish priests back the thirty pieces of silver they paid him to lead them to Jesus. The priests consider this "tainted money," so instead of putting it back into the temple treasury, they use it to buy a field to use as a cemetery for foreigners. (In the version of the story in Acts, Judas himself buys the field then dies in it.) The field was called Akeldama, meaning "field of blood." People have used the name to refer to any site associated with bloodshed, such as the locale of a bloody battle.

anathema

If something is anathema to you, you really despise it. It's a Greek word used several times in the New Testament, generally translated "accursed" (Romans 9:3, 1 Corinthians 16:22, Galatians 1:9). As Christianity spread, religious councils would meet to decide if certain ideas or teachings were to be banned or anathematized.

apple of the eye

The "apple of the eye" in the Old Testament it is a translation of Hebrew words that mean, literally, "the eye's pupil." Figuratively, it refers to a person who is highly valued. Deuteronomy 32:10 says that God guarded Israel "as the apple of his eye." Psalm 17:8 asks God to "keep me as the apple of your eye; hide me under the shadow of your wings." In Proverbs 7:2, God commands people to "keep my commandments, and live; and my law as the apple of thine eye."

Armageddon

You might have the vague feeling that this refers to some frightening battle at the end of time, which is correct. The word is from Revelation 16:16, which speaks of kings gathering together for the "battle of the great day of God Almighty. ... And they gathered them together to the place called in Hebrew, Armageddon." There literally is a place called Har-Megiddo, but Revelation is probably referring to a spiritual battle, not a literal one. Running in 1912 for president as the Progressive Party candidate, Theodore Roosevelt announced, "We stand at Armageddon, and we battle for the Lord." He was not the first or last politician to rally his supporters by using this very "loaded" biblical word. A 1998 film about an asteroid about to collide with the earth was titled *Armageddon*.

at ease in Zion

The Old Testament prophet Amos spoke out boldly against people who were lukewarm or lazy about their religion, especially the idle rich "who lie on beds of ivory" (Amos 6:4). Zion was the site of the Lord's temple, and Amos coined the phrase "Woe to them that are at ease in Zion!" (Amos 6:1). Throughout the long history of Christianity, people who wanted a spiritual reformation would preach about the dangers of being "at ease in Zion."

behemoth / leviathan

Something large and formidable is often called a behemoth or a leviathan. Behemoth is a water beast described in Job 40:15-24. The passage may be referring to a hippopotamus, or perhaps to a purely mythical monster. Leviathan is mentioned in Job 41:1, Psalm 74:14, and Psalm 104:26. It is a fearsome water creature, possibly a whale or crocodile, or, again, a mythical water monster. English philosopher Thomas Hobbes gave the title *Leviathan* to his book on politics, the title referring to an all-powerful government.

biblical span

What was the average life span among the ancient Israelites? Psalm 90:10 suggests it was "three-score years and ten"—meaning, seventy. ("Score" was an old term for "twenty.") The same verse mentions that some manage to live on to "four-score," but not very enjoyably. Whether the Psalm was accurate or not, the phrase "three-score and ten" passed into English as meaning living out to a reasonably good age, and the phrase "the biblical span" meant the same thing. While seventy is now lower than the average life span in the U.S. and Europe, people in centuries past considered themselves lucky if they lived "three-score and ten."

blind leading the blind

In Matthew 15:14 Jesus says, "If the blind leads the blind, both will fall into a ditch." He was referring to false teachers who lead people astray. Pieter Bruegel the Elder's painting *The Parable of the Blind Leading the Blind* (1568, in the Galleria Nazionale, Naples) is both funny and sad in its image of six blind men literally stumbling over each other.

bricks without straw

In the story of Moses and the Exodus from Egypt, Moses demands that Pharaoh let the Israelite slaves go free. Instead of giving in, Pharaoh increased the work load: They had to make bricks without straw, which was a necessary component (Exodus 5). The phrase "bricks without straw" has come to refer to any task that is nearly impossible.

brother's keeper

The first human child born into the world set a bad precedent: Cain, first son of Adam and Eve, killed the second son, his brother Abel. According to Genesis 4:9, "the Lord said to Cain, 'Where is Abel your brother?' And he said, 'I do not know. Am I my brother's keeper?'" The phrase entered the language to indicate someone avoiding responsibility for the welfare of others.

Can a leopard change his spots?

It was the prophet Jeremiah (Jeremiah 13:23) who raised the questions, "Can the Ethiopian change his skin, or the leopard his spots?" The obvious answer to both questions is "No way!" His point was that people who are accustomed to behaving badly aren't likely to change.

clay feet

In Daniel 2, Daniel interprets the puzzling dream of the Babylonian king Nebuchadnezzar. In the dream, a statue of a man is composed of various metals—gold head, silver chest, bronze mid-section, iron legs—and feet of clay mingled with iron. "Feet of clay" has come to mean a personal flaw that isn't readily apparent. A huge metal statue with clay feet isn't destined to stand for very long.

Come now, let us reason together

You hear this phrase occasionally in political speeches. Originally it was spoken by God to the prophet Isaiah: "Come now, let us reason together, says the Lord; though your sins be like scarlet, they shall be white as snow" (Isaiah 1:18).

crystal clear

This commonly used phrase originated in the King James Version of Revelation 22:1: "And he showed me a pure river of water of life, clear as crystal, proceeding out of the throne of God and of the Lamb."

den of thieves

One of the most dramatic scenes in the Bible is when Jesus makes a whip out of cords and drives the moneychangers out of the temple court, telling them, "My house shall be called a house of prayer, but you have made it a den of thieves" (Matthew 21:13). "Den of thieves" has passed into common use to refer to any group of unscrupulous people.

driving like Jehu

Jehu was the man who exterminated the wicked family of King Ahab and helped stamp out Baal worship in Israel (2 Kings 10). The name Jehu came to refer to any fast and furious driver, based on 2 Kings 9:20: "the driving is like the driving of Jehu … for he driveth furiously"

drop in the bucket

The prophet Isaiah is the source of this phrase. Like the other prophets, he had a low opinion of oppressive empires, and believed that God did also. "The nations are as a drop in a bucket, and are counted as dust on the balance" (Isaiah 40:15).

each man under his own vine and fig tree

This lovely phrase has long been used to express peace and security and is found in several places, notably Micah 4:4, Zechariah 3:10, 1 Kings 4:25, 2 Kings 18:31, and Jeremiah 5:17. In the past, it was used often in everyday speech. For example, George Washington wrote a friend that he intended to "sit under his own vine and fig tree" after retiring from the military.

eat, drink, and be merry

This familiar phrase is found in Jesus' "parable of the rich fool," a cautionary tale about being too attached to one's possessions. The rich fool said to himself, "You have many goods laid up for many years; take your ease; eat, drink, and be merry." But then God said to him, "You fool! This very night your soul will be required of you; then whose will those things be which you have provided?" (Luke 12:13-21). In other words, the Bible does not look kindly on people whose only goal in life is to "eat, drink, and be merry."

eye for an eye

Here's the direct quote from the Old Testament: "If any man causes disfigurement of his neighbor, as he has done so shall it be done to him—fracture for fracture, eye for eye, tooth for tooth; as he has caused disfigurement of a man, so shall it be done to him" (Leviticus 24:19-20).

In the New Testament, Jesus taught a higher morality: "You have heard that it was said, 'An eye for an eye and a tooth for a tooth.' But I tell you not to resist an evil person. But whoever slaps you on you right cheek, turn the other to him also" (Matthew 5:38-39).

Jesus' teaching seems better than the Old Testament ethic, but in fact, the law in Leviticus was rooted in fairness. "Eye for eye, tooth for tooth" imposed a *limit*. It meant "tit for tat"—but no more. Typically human beings want to go beyond just getting even—two teeth for one, or both eyes for one. So the "eye for eye" law was progressive for its times.

faith to move mountains

If you think every word of the Bible was meant to be taken literally, consider these words of Jesus: "If you have faith as small as a mustard seed, you can say to this mountain, 'Move from here to there' and it will move. Nothing will be impossible for you" (Matthew 17:20). Clearly he meant that faith can do truly amazing things.

fat of the land

In Genesis 45:18, Joseph, right-hand man of the Egyptian pharaoh, tells his eleven brothers, "I will give you the best of the land of Egypt and you will eat of the fat of the land"—not a bad gift for the brothers who had sold him as a slave years earlier.

flesh and blood

Five times the New Testament uses the Greek words *sarx kai haima*—literally, "flesh and blood." We use "flesh and blood" to refer to family ("she is my own flesh and blood"), but the Bible never uses it this way. Instead, it's a way of saying "human nature" or more precisely "human nature with its tendency to do the wrong thing." Paul used it this way in 1 Corinthians 15:50: "Now this I say, brethren, that flesh and blood cannot inherit the kingdom of God; neither doth corruption inherit incorruption." But Paul also observed that there were more powerful things in the world than human nature: "We wrestle not against flesh and blood, but against principalities, against powers, against the rulers of the darkness of this world, against spiritual wickedness in high places" (Ephesians 6:12).

fleshpots

Here's a word that has taken on a radically different meaning from the one in the Bible. The Old Testament records that the Israelites, led out of slavery in Egypt by Moses, grumbled during their years in the wilderness, complaining that at least back in Egypt they had "fleshpots"—meaning, literally, pots with meat to eat

(Exodus 16). In other words, they preferred being slaves and having meat to eat, rather than to be free and wandering through a dry wilderness.

Over time, "fleshpots" took on a different meaning: a place of sensual (that is, sexual) enjoyment.

fly in the ointment

This phrase refers to something detestable ruining something valuable. The phrase comes from Ecclesiastes 10:1: "Dead flies putrefy the perfumer's ointment and cause it to give off a foul odor."

forbidden fruit

Adam and Eve had a perfect home in the Garden of Eden, a beautiful place with no problems and few rules—in fact, only one rule that God imposed: "Of the tree of the knowledge of good and evil you shall not eat, for in the day that you eat of it you shall surely die" (Genesis 2:17). The fruit of that one tree was the "forbidden fruit." The wily serpent tempted Eve (who then tempted Adam) into eating the fruit by telling Eve a lie: "You shall not surely die, for God knows that in the day you eat of it your eyes will be opened and you will be like God, knowing good and evil" (Genesis 3:4-5). The couple did not die, but God banished them from Eden for their disobedience.

We often speak of the forbidden fruit being an apple, but in fact we have no idea what it really was. Perhaps it was something that grew only in Eden.

fruit of the womb

Were you aware that the Fruit of the Loom underwear brand actually borrowed its name (sort of) from the Bible? In the Old and New Testaments, the expression "fruit of the womb" meant "children." "Lo, children are a heritage of the Lord: and the fruit of the womb is his reward" (Psalm 127:3) "And she spake out with a loud voice, and said, Blessed art thou among women, and blessed is the fruit of thy womb" (Luke 1:42). With a slight change of letters, "fruit of the womb" easily morphed into "fruit of the loom."

gird up one's loins

In ancient times, before the days of trousers, a man setting out to run or do vigorous work (including fighting) would take his belt (probably a piece of rope) and bind up the lower hems of his cloak so they wouldn't encumber him. This was "girding up the loins," and figuratively it meant to prepare oneself for action.

In the Book of Job, God, speaking out of a whirlwind, challenges Job: "Gird up now thy loins like a man; for I will demand of thee, and answer thou me" (Job 38:3). The apostle Peter used the term in a figurative sense: "Wherefore gird up the loins of your mind, be sober" (1 Peter 1:13).

go the extra mile

Jesus taught a very high level of compassion and generosity: "Whoever compels you to go one mile, go with him two. Give to him who asks you, and from him who wants to borrow from you do not turn away" (Matthew 5:41-42). Our phrases "going the extra mile" or "the second mile" are rooted in this moral command.

God save the king

The English national anthem is "God Save the King" (or "Queen," depending on who is ruling at the time). The phrase occurs numerous times in the Old Testament (1 Samuel 10:24, 2 Samuel 16:16, 1 Kings 1:25, 2 Kings 11:12, and many others). But in fact, "God save the king" isn't an accurate translation. The Hebrew means, "Let the king live," and does not mention God. Modern versions are more accurate with, "Long live the king."

grapes of wrath

John Steinbeck took the title of his novel *The Grapes of Wrath* from Julia Ward Howe's "Battle Hymn of the Republic," which says that God is "trampling out the vintage where the grapes of wrath are stored." Howe was familiar with the Bible, and she mixed phrases from the Book of Revelation, such as "the wine of the wrath of God" (Revelation 14:10) and "the winepress of the fierceness and wrath of Almighty God" (Revelation 19:15).

handwriting on the wall

One of the Bible's most intriguing stories is found in Daniel 5, which tells of a feast given by the Babylonian ruler Belshazzar. The king is drinking from vessels plundered from the Jewish temple at Jerusalem. During the feast, a strange disembodied hand appears and writes four mysterious words on the palace wall: MENE, MENE, TEKEL, PARSIN. Belshazzar is so terrified that "his knees knocked against each other." The faithful Jew Daniel appears and interprets the message, which is bad news: The words mean that God has brought the Babylonian empire to an end and given it over to the Medes and Persians. That very night Belshazzar, king of Babylon, is killed, and Darius the Mede takes over the kingdom.

This story of a blasphemous pagan king receiving a mysterious message of his own doom has inspired countless works of art. The great Rembrandt's painting *Belshazzar's Feast* in London's National Gallery is only one of many. English composer William Walton based his 1931 oratorio *Belshazzar's Feast* on the story.

We still use the phrase "handwriting on the wall," and, yes, it is based on this story. It would probably be more appropriate if we wrote it as "hand writing on the wall."

For some reason there is a tradition that Belshazzar is one of the four kings found in a deck of playing cards.

heart's desire

Writing to the Christians in Rome, the apostle Paul said, "Brethren, my heart's desire and prayer to God for Israel is, that they might be saved" (Romans 10:1). He borrowed the phrase "heart's desire" from the Psalms. "The wicked boasts of his heart's desire, and blesses the covetous, whom the Lord abhors" (Psalm 10:3).

"You have given him his heart's desire, and have not withholden the request of his lips" (Psalm 21:2)

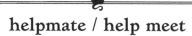

helpmate / help meet

At the time the King James Version was published (1611), the word "meet" had a meaning it no longer has: It was an adjective meaning "suitable" or "appropriate." In Genesis 2, God saw that it was not good for Adam to be alone, so he chose to make "a help meet for him." As time passed, people forgot the old meaning of "meet" and assumed the intended word was "helpmate," and people still occasionally use "helpmate" to refer to a spouse. In contemporary versions of Genesis 2, the phrase used is "a help fit for him" or something similar.

hocus-pocus

Magicians use this meaningless phrase in their acts as "the magic words" that cause something to change. In fact, hocus-pocus comes from the words of Jesus at the Last Supper, when he took the bread and gave it to his disciples with the words, "This is my body." Those words became a standard part of the Christian communion service, and when translated into Latin, it came out as *Hoc est corpus meum*. Since the Catholic Church teaches that those words actually change the Communion bread into the body of Jesus, people believed the words *Hoc est corpus meum* were "magic words." In time, *Hoc est corpus meum* morphed into "hocus-pocus."

holier than thou

In our day, nothing is considered worse than someone having a "holier than thou" attitude. According to the Bible, God doesn't like that self-righteous attitude either: "I have spread out my hands all the day unto a rebellious people, which walketh in a way that was not good, after their own thoughts; a people that provoketh me to anger continually to my face; … that say, 'Stand by thyself, come not near to me; for I am holier than thou'" (Isaiah 65:2-5).

holocaust

This word refers to Nazi Germany's attempt to exterminate all Jews. But the original word has been around much longer. It referred to a sacrifice in which the whole animal, not just parts, are consumed by fire (Leviticus 1). The Greek word *holokaustos* means, not surprisingly, "burnt whole." It is regrettable that a word with a religious meaning came to be applied to something so horrible as genocide.

How are the mighty fallen!

David, the bosom friend of Jonathan and friend-enemy of King Saul, uttered a famous lament when both Jonathan and Saul died after battle with the Philistines: "The beauty of Israel is slain upon thy high places ... How are the mighty fallen, and the weapons of war perished!" (2 Samuel 1:19, 27). David was sincere in his grief, but people today often use "how are the mighty fallen" snidely, happy that someone in a high position has lost it.

jeremiad

Jeremiah lamented so much over his nation's sins that he was called the "weeping prophet." He is considered the author of the brief Book of Lamentations, his sad reflection on the city of Jerusalem, devastated by the Babylonians. A long, tearful lament is thus called a jeremiad.

Job's comforters

In the Book of Job, the title character endures all kinds of calamities. His three closet friends try to comfort him but, in fact, they insist that he must have done something truly awful to deserve these disasters. The expression "Job's comforters" refers to people who claim they are offering consolation when, in fact, they are "blaming the victim."

jubilee

Our words *jubilee* and *jubilation* (meaning "joyous festivity") are rooted in Leviticus 25, in which the Israelites are commanded to set aside every fiftieth year as the jubilee year. During the jubilee year, people who had sold themselves into slavery were to be freed, and ancestral properties that were pawned were returned to the families of the original owners. Oddly, there is no evidence in the Bible that the Israelites ever observed the jubilee year. However, the word came to refer to any fiftieth anniversary—or any special anniversary. In 1617, Protestants observed the Reformation Jubilee, celebrating the hundredth anniversary of the Reformation. Roman Catholics have observed several jubilee years, the last one being 2000.

judas-colored

On the assumption (which is not based on the Bible) that Judas Iscariot had red hair, "judas-colored" is a term applied to red hair.

judas duck

Duck decoys used to be called "judas ducks," since their purpose was to "betray" live ducks into landing where hunters should shoot them more easily.

judas goat

Meat-packers know what this is: an old goat can be trained to get a flock of sheep to follow him—to the slaughter-house, that is. Since he is leading them to their death, he is a "judas goat."

judas window, judas hole

Since Judas Iscariot sneaked around and arranged with the authorities to betray Jesus, his name has been connected with all forms of sneakery and stealth. In prisons, a "judas window" or "judas hole" is a small opening through which guards can spy on what prisoners are doing.

keeping the faith

The apostle Paul, expecting to die soon, wrote to his young friend and protégé Timothy, "I have fought the good fight, I have finished the race, I have kept the faith" (2 Timothy 4:7). "Fight the good fight" has also passed into common usage.

kingdom come

This phrase came to mean "heaven" or "the afterlife." It comes from the Lord's Prayer (Matthew 6:10), where Jesus prays, "Thy kingdom come, thy will be done on earth as it is in heaven."

"know," in the biblical sense

When someone talks about " 'knowing' someone, in the biblical sense," they are referring to having sexual relations. The phrase is usually uttered in a snicker-snicker nudge-nudge manner. Maybe a few people know the words are rooted in Genesis 4:1, which relates that sometime after Adam and Eve were expelled from the garden of Eden, "Adam knew Eve his wife, and she conceived and bore Cain." The Hebrew word translated "knew" means (obviously) something more than mere acquaintanceship. It means knowing someone deeply and personal—and could (if the context indicates it, as it does here) also be a polite say of saying "had sexual relations with."

labor of love

Ever done something and called it a "labor of love"? The phrase is rooted in the Bible. "Remembering without ceasing your work of faith, and labor of love" (1 Thessalonians 1:3). "God is not unrighteous to forget your work and labor of love" (Hebrews 6:10).

lamb to the slaughter

God's chosen servant is described by the prophet Isaiah as one who "was led as a lamb to the slaughter, and as a sheep before her shearers is silent, so he opened not his mouth" (Isaiah 53:7). Christians have interpreted this as a prophecy of Christ, who accepted his horrible fate without protest. In time, "lamb to the slaughter" came to refer to any innocent victim.

land o' Goshen!

In Exodus, Goshen was the region of Egypt where the Israelite slaves lived. Why exactly "land o' Goshen" came to express surprise or amazement is anyone's guess.

land of milk and honey

The phrase means "a rich, fertile land" or even "a nice place to live." It is used many times in the Old Testament to refer to Canaan, the land God promised the Israelites after they left their slavery in Egypt.

land of Nod

We often use "the land of Nod" to refer to going to sleep. In the Bible, Nod was an actual locale. "And Cain went out from the presence of the Lord, and dwelt in the land of Nod, on the east of Eden" (Genesis 4:16). In fact, the Hebrew word *Nod* means, "wandering." Perhaps Nod simply meant "land of wandering" and was not a specific location.

Laodiceans

The Book of Revelation begins with messages from Christ to seven churches, praising their good deeds and scolding them for their bad ones. One church was in Laodicea, a wealthy city where even the Christians were smug and self-satisfied. In Revelation 3:14-22, Jesus tells the Laodiceans that they are "lukewarm," neither hot nor cold, and because of their blasé attitude, "I will spew you out of my mouth." The threat is followed by some consolation: "As many as I love, I rebuke and chasten. Therefore be zealous and repent." The name "laodicean" has come to refer to someone who is lukewarm about religion, not taking it very seriously. More broadly, it applies to someone who is smug and self-satisfied about life in general.

laws of the Medes and the Persians

This phrase is used several times in the Book of Daniel, and has passed into the language as a symbol of old and irrevocable (and perhaps stupid) rules. The exact phrase in Daniel is "the law of the Medes and Persians, which altereth not" (Daniel 6:8, 12, 15). The same chapter has the Persian king's counselors saying to him, "Know, O king, that the law of the Medes and Persians is, that no decree nor statute which the king establisheth may be changed." In other words, the king didn't even have the freedom to alter his own decrees, which seems rather silly.

laying out the fleece

Is it ever right to test God? Apparently it is, on occasion. In Judges 6, the valiant soldier Gideon puts God to this test: he lays a fleece on his threshing floor and asks God if, overnight, he can wet the fleece with dew and leave the ground dry. The next morning, the fleece is saturated but the ground is dry. Gideon asks for the same miracle—in reverse, this time. The next morning the fleece is dry but the ground is wet. "Laying out the fleece" has come to mean any kind of testing of God—or a person.

lazaretto

In ancient times, the skin disease leprosy was taken seriously. Lepers lived a sad life, separated from their fellow man and forced to call out "Unclean!" if they approached people. A house or colony for lepers was called a lazaretto or lazar house after the character Lazarus in one of Jesus' parables. Luke 16:19-31 describes Lazarus as a beggar "full of sores," which the dogs licked.

left hand doesn't know what the right hand is doing

We use this phrase often to refer to an organization or group that is so large or uncommunicative that one part doesn't know what the other is doing. Here are the actual words of Jesus, from his famous Sermon on the Mount: "When you give to the needy, do not let your left hand know what your right hand is doing, so that your giving may be secret. Your Father who sees in secret will reward you" (Matthew 6:3-4). Jesus was saying to do good deeds not to get praise from other people, but because it pleases God. Or, to put it another way, do good things out of habit, giving so little thought to who's watching that your left hand isn't even aware of what your right hand just did. Jesus criticized "religious" people who did acts of kindness not because they loved people or loved God, but because they enjoyed having the reputation of being a saint.

little wine for the stomach

This is a semi-humorous way of asking someone, "Would you like some wine?" But in fact the words are from the New Testament, where the apostle Paul advised his young protégé Timothy to "no longer drink only water, but use a little wine for your stomach's sake and your frequent infirmities" (1 Timothy 5:23). Apparently, Paul was offering a bit of fatherly medical advice.

lusting in one's heart

In 1976, presidential candidate Jimmy Carter said in an interview that although he had never committed adultery, he had "lusted in his heart"—a quaint phrase that caught journalists off guard. To Bible readers, the phrase was familiar enough: In his famous Sermon on the Mount, Jesus warned people that not only was actual adultery wrong, but so was "lusting in one's heart."

maudlin

Believe it or not, this word (which means overly dramatic or sentimental) is rooted in the name of Mary Magdalene. (In fact, the English pronounce "Magdalene" as "maudlin.") In artworks, Mary Magdalene is often depicted as weeping over her past sins. Her tearful expression impressed some people as overdone emotionally, so "maudlin" came to mean just that.

Since people believed Mary Magdalene was a reformed prostitute, a "maudlin home" was a home where former prostitutes resided and tried to clean up their lives.

meek as Moses

This was a common expression before the twentieth century, and it was based on the Old Testament's description of Moses: "Now the man Moses was very meek, above all the men which were upon the face of the earth" (Numbers 12:3). It's a surprising description (and certainly doesn't fit the way Charlton Heston played Moses in *The Ten Commandments*), but it's reassuring to know that one of the greatest men in human history, someone who had literally seen God face to face, could be described as "meek."

mess of pottage

Genesis 25 tells the story of the tricky Jacob and his brother Esau. Jacob is cooking stew, and when Esau returns from hunting, he is famished and wants to eat. Jacob gives him some, but at a great price: Esau's birthright (his inheritance as the oldest son). The King James Version refers to the stew as a "mess of pottage," and the phrase entered the language as referring to any kind of fool's bargain. In the New Testament, the Letter to the Hebrews refers to Esau as an example of sensuality and materialism since he sold his birthright for some pottage.

Methuselah

In the Book of Genesis, the earliest human beings had long, long lives. Adam lived to be 930, but Methuselah, grandfather of Noah, holds the record at 969 years. Hence our expression "old as Methuselah." One overlooked item: If the lifespans and chronology reported in Genesis 5 and 6 are correct, Methuselah did not die of old age—he died (along with almost everyone else on earth) in the great flood. The human lifespan shrank dramatically after the flood. Genesis 6:3 states that God decreed that man's years would be 120. Centuries later, it was shortened to (as the King James Version puts it) "three score and ten"—seventy, that is (Psalm 90:10), not so different from the average lifespan today.

Science fiction writer Robert Heinlein's 1958 novel *Methuselah's Children* deals with a genetically engineered family of people who live incredibly long lives. George Bernard Shaw's cycle of five plays titled *Back to Methuselah* spans the time from the Garden of Eden to the year 31,920.

money is the root of all evil

Most people have no idea this phrase is from the Bible—although it isn't, precisely. The actual words that Paul wrote were, "the love of money is a root of all kinds of evil" (1 Timothy 6:10). Note that money itself is not evil, but *loving* it is. Also, money is not the root of *all evil*, but the root of *all kinds of evil*.

my cup runneth over

The famous "Shepherd Psalm," Psalm 23, is a song in praise of God's care and protection. It contains this phrase, indicating that God will provide more than what we need. It pops up in speech now and then, oftentimes with the word "cup" referring to an article of women's undergarments. The popular musical *I Do! I Do!* includes a song, "My Cup Runneth Over with Love," which used to be popular at weddings and anniversary parties.

O ye of little faith

In his famous Sermon on the Mount, Jesus told his listeners that they needn't worry about their daily needs, for God would provide for them. He concluded this pronouncement with the scolding phrase, "O ye of little faith." The phrase is still used as a lighthearted slap at someone who is skeptical or cynical.

onanism

You don't hear this word much any more, but it used to refer to masturbation. The name is based on Genesis 38, which tells of the man Onan who "spilled out his seed on the ground" (Genesis 38:8-9). Onan's brother had died, leaving a widow, and according to the custom of the time, Onan was to impregnate his brother's widow, giving her a child that was legally the child of his deceased brother. Genesis doesn't actually refer to masturbation but to what we would call *coitus interruptus*. Apparently Onan's neglect of his family duty so displeased God that God killed him.

patience of Job

If you read the Book of Job, the title character appears to be a very tough man who could endure major calamities without losing faith in God. He had fortitude and perseverance, and saying he had "patience" doesn't quite do him justice. In the King James Version of the Bible, the Letter of James reminds suffering people of the "patience of Job" (James 5:11). Modern versions of the Bible are correct in using "endurance" or "perseverance" instead of the mild "patience."

patter

If you were raised Catholic, you might know that the Lord's Prayer is sometimes called the *Pater Noster*, Latin for "Our Father," the words that begin the prayer. Since people often repeated the Lord's Prayer without giving it much thought, the word "patter" came to refer to something repeated mindlessly.

peterman and peterboat

The Gospels state that Jesus' disciple Peter was a fisherman, so in times past a fisherman was called a "peterman," and a fishing boat was called a "peterboat."

Pharaoh's serpents

Ever heard this used to refer to fireworks? In times past, fireworks reminded people of the story of Moses at the court of Pharaoh, miraculously transforming his staff into a servant, then reversing the process, with Pharaoh's court magicians duplicated this amazing feat (Exodus 7). People with vivid imaginations (and some knowledge of the Bible) must have thought the sticks lying on the ground, then "coming to life" when lit, were like the staff of Moses turning into a hissing snake.

the powers that be

Should people resist an evil government or obey it passively? The Bible has words that seem to support either side. Paul, in a much-quoted verse, leaned toward obedience: "Let every soul be subject unto the higher powers. For there is no power but of God: the powers that be are ordained of God" (Romans 13:1). Paul used "the power that be" to refer to the civil authorities. Generally the New Testament agrees with Paul in urging obedience, but there is another side: When some of the apostles were arrested for spreading the gospel, their reply was: "We ought to obey God rather than men" (Acts 5:29).

A short-lived TV sitcom with a political setting had the title *The Powers That Be*, and several books dealing with politics (especially in relation to religion) have borne the title.

practice what you preach

Jesus condemned the hypocritical Pharisees and scribes, and he told his disciples, "Practice and observe whatever they tell you, but not what they do, for they preach but they do not practice" (Matthew 23:3).

pride goeth before a fall

Here's a case of a Bible verse getting "compressed" into an easy-to-remember saying. The actual words of Proverbs 16:18 are "Pride goeth before destruction, and a haughty spirit before a fall."

raising Cain

In a more polite age, people didn't like to use the phrase "raising hell," so for a substitute they used the name of someone they assumed was in hell, namely, Cain, the son of Adam and Eve, who murdered his brother Abel (Genesis 4). In the New Testament, 1 John 3:12 speaks of Cain as being "from that wicked one" (meaning Satan), and the name Cain was almost a synonym for Satan. "Raising Cain" came to be a polite way of saying "raising hell" or "raising the devil."

reap what we sow

As people become more familiar with Eastern religions, they may think that "reap what you sow" is rooted in the Eastern idea of karma. But in fact the phrase is from the words of Paul in the New Testament: "Do not be deceived, God is not mocked; for whatever a man sows, that he will also reap" (Galatians 6:7).

respecter of persons

For us, respecting others is a good thing, but in the older versions of the Bible, "respect" had the meaning of showing favoritism or partiality. Consider these verses: "These things also belong to the wise. It is not good to have respect of persons in judgment" (Proverbs 24:23). "Let the fear of the Lord be upon you; take heed and do it: for there is no iniquity with the Lord our God, nor respect of persons, nor taking of gifts" (2 Chronicles 19:7). "You masters, do the same things unto them, forbearing threatening: knowing that your Master also is in heaven; neither is there respect of persons with him" (Ephesians 6:9). When Paul said, "There is no respect of persons with God" (Romans 2:11), he meant that God shows no partiality but judges all people fairly.

In Acts 10:34, the apostle Peter, guided by a vision from God, went to home of Cornelius, a Roman soldier. "Then Peter opened his mouth, and said, Of a truth I perceive that God is no respecter of persons." Peter was making it clear that the faith was available to everyone, not just Jews, but to Romans, and anyone else.

risked their necks

At the end of his Letter to the Romans, the apostle Paul wrote, "Greet Priscilla and Aquila my helpers in Christ Jesus, who have for my life laid down their own necks" (Romans 16:3-5). Versions later than the King James have "risked their necks. This was a time when beheading was a common form of execution.

sabbatical

This comes from the word sabbath. In the Old Testament, the sabbath was a day of rest and worship. In the Book of Leviticus, God commands that every seventh year is a "sabbath year," letting the land lie fallow instead of being farmed (which, scientifically, is a good practice). Over time a "sabbatical" came to refer to taking time off from one's usual work in order to rest and recharge one's mental batteries.

St. Stephen's bread

Acts 7 records the death of the first Christian martyr, the saintly and eloquent Stephen, who was stoned to death. Stoning was a frequent punishment, and many of the early Christians were stoned (including the apostle Paul, though he survived). Since Stephen was the first martyr, people have used the phrase "fed with St. Stephen's bread" to refer to anyone who is martyred for the faith.

salt of the earth

You'll find this familiar phrase in Jesus' famous Sermon on the Mount (Matthew 5-7). Matthew 5:13 states, "You are the salt of the earth." Jesus was telling his followers that they were to serve as both a seasoning and a preservative in the world. If they were not doing this, they were useless.

In the ancient world, salt was a valuable commodity. Some people, including many Roman soldiers, were paid their wages in salt instead of money. Our word *salary* comes from the Latin word *salarium*, meaning "salt money." When Jesus referred to his followers as "salt," he wasn't referring to a cheap everyday item, but to something valuable and important.

scapegoat

We use the word so often in the figurative sense of "someone who takes the blame for another's wrongs" that it's easy to forget it originally referred to a real goat. Israel's high priest would lay his hands on a goat on the annual Day of Atonement. Laying hands on it was a symbol of transferring the nation's sins to it. It was then driven off into the wilderness. Another goat chosen for the Day of Atonement was sacrificed. The word "scapegoat" was coined by English translator William Tyndale in 1530, by the way.

scarlet woman

Revelation 17 refers to a vision of a "great prostitute" clad in scarlet and purple and riding on a scarlet monster. On the woman's forehead was a tattoo reading, "Babylon the great, mother of prostitutes." Throughout the Bible, prostitution often had a double meaning—not just a sexual sinner, but a person engaging in the worship of idols. The vision in Revelation 17 isn't referring to a literal woman, but to an earthly power or government, something as evil and oppressive as ancient Babylon was. The phrase "scarlet woman" came to refer to any woman of doubtful virtue.

seek and ye shall find

This familiar phrase is actually about prayer. In Jesus' famous Sermon the Mount, he said that God's children should bring their requests to God hopefully and expectantly. The actual words are, "Ask, and it will be given to you; seek, and you will find; knock, and it will be opened to you" (Matthew 7:7).

set your house in order

These words were, in times past, spoken to someone who was soon to die. The words are from 2 Kings 20, where the prophet Isaiah tells King Hezekiah to set his house in order, for he was about to die.

shibboleth

We use this word to refer to a custom or habit that a group uses to distinguish itself from another group, usually for purposes of snobbery. It's rooted in Judges 12, which says the word "shibboleth" was pronounced differently on the two sides of the Jordan River. The military leader Jephthah used the word as a test to determine if the speaker was friend or foe. ("Sibboleth" was the fatal pronunciation that led to execution.)

short-order slang

In the old days, short-order diners used colorful slang to refer to foods, many of them drawn from the Bible. "Noah's boy" meant ham (Noah had a son named Ham), "Adam's ale" was water (what else did Adam have to drink?), "Adam and Eve on a raft" meant two fried eggs on toast (your guess is as good as mine). A "Nebuchadnezzar" was a vegetarian customer, based on the description of Babylonian king Nebuchadnezzar losing his mind and eating grass in the fields like a wild animal (Daniel 4:33).

signs of the times

This phrase is used so often that hardly anyone recalls it comes from the Bible. Regarding the coming Day of Judgment, Jesus told his opponents, "you cannot interpret the signs of the times" (Matthew 16:3).

the skin of my teeth

We use it to mean "a close call" or "just barely," and the phrase comes from Job 19:20, in words spoken by poor Job himself: "My bone clings to my skin and to my flesh, and I have escaped by the skin of my teeth."

smite them hip and thigh

This phrase occurs just once in the Bible, appropriately enough in the saga of the Hebrew strongman Samson, who fought against the Hebrews' worst foe, the Philistines. Judges 15:8 tells how he "smote them hip and thigh" ("smote" being the past tense of "smite," meaning "strike" or "hit"). The phrase "smite them hip and thigh" made its way into the language, meaning "to give someone a real whipping." At the risk of being crude, "smite them hip and thigh" is basically the same as our modern "kick their a**." Human thought hasn't really changed all that much in three thousand years, has it?

spare the rod and spoil the child

The ancient Hebrews had a view of corporal punishment different from that of many modern parents. According to Proverbs 13:24, "He who spares his rod hates his son, but he who loves him disciplines him promptly." This bit of ancient wisdom passed into English as "spare the rod and spoil the child." Several other Proverbs offer similar warnings about the disastrous results of parents who are too lenient.

the spirit is willing

"The spirit is willing"—our intentions may be good—"but the flesh is weak." Matthew's Gospel describes Jesus' agony just before Judas betrays him to the Jewish authorities. While he is praying and agonizing, his disciples doze off instead of keeping watch for him. When he finds them asleep at their post, he says "Watch and pray, lest you enter into temptation. The spirit indeed is willing, but the flesh is weak" (Mark 14:38).

stiff-necked

In ancient times, rank was important, and so was showing proper respect. If someone was your superior, you bowed to him. In many places the Bible refers to people as being "stiff-necked," not willing to bow to the authority of God. "Stiff-necked" was another way of saying "proud" or "arrogant." "And the Lord said unto Moses, I have seen this people, and, behold, it is a stiffnecked people" (Exodus 32:9). When the saintly Stephen referred to the Jews of Jerusalem as "stiff-necked," they showed their anger by stoning him to death (Acts 7:51).

stormy petrels

If you've been on a cruise ship far out at sea, you may have seen the small, dark seabirds known as "stormy petrels" that hover just over the ocean surface, their tiny feet barely touching the water. Apparently this reminded people of the apostle Peter trying to walk on the water (Matthew 14:28-30). The name "petrel" is derived from Peter.

strait is the gate

In Matthew 7:14 in the King James Version, Jesus taught that "strait is the gate, and narrow is the way, which leadeth unto life." Note that the word is "strait," not "straight." "Strait" had the same meaning as "narrow"—Jesus was actually saying, "Narrow is the gate, and narrow is the way." Over time, people got confused about the words and began to use the expression "walk the straight and narrow path."

stumbling-block

We owe this term to the Bible, where it can mean a literal obstacle causing one to stumble, or, more often, something that causes a person to "fall" morally or spiritually. A literal stumbling-block was something placed in the path to cause a person to trip and fall into a pit or snare. Spiritually, it was anything that was a hindrance to living a moral life. Interestingly, the Greek word translated as "stumbling-block" was skandalon, also the source of our word "scandal."

suffer fools gladly

In 2 Corinthians 11:19, Paul scolded the wavering Christians in Corinth: "ye suffer fools gladly, seeing ye yourselves are wise." He was being sarcastic, of course. We use the phrase often today, with "he doesn't suffer fools gladly" meaning "he doesn't put up with a lot of nonsense."

sweating blood

This phrase comes from the Gospels' story of Jesus' agony in the Garden of Gethsemane. Aware that he was about to be arrested and executed, he prayed to God, and "being in agony, He prayed more earnestly. And His sweat became like great drops of blood falling down to the ground" (Luke 22:44).

talent

We use it so often to refer to human ability that we forget it was originally a unit of money—the *talanton*, worth about twenty days wages for a manual laborer. Jesus told a famous parable (Matthew 25:14-30) of people who use their talents (money) wisely (or don't). Over time the monetary meaning of "talent" was forgotten and it came to refer to a person's inner resources, not his economic ones.

tent-maker ministry

Acts 18:3 says that the apostle Paul was a tent-maker by trade. Apparently he still plied this trade even after he devoted himself to spreading the Gospel far and wide. Churches use the term "tent-maker ministry" to refer to pastors who have a full-time job outside of their church work, some of them getting paid little or nothing for being pastors. Many small churches in rural or inner-city areas cannot afford to pay their ministers much and so they rely on dedicated "tent-makers."

thorn in my side

Some people think this familiar phrase is from Paul's words about his "thorn in the flesh" (2 Corinthians 12:7), but in fact "thorns in your sides" is found in Numbers 33:55 and Judges 2:3, in both cases referring to the evil effects of the Canaanites on the people of Israel.

touch-me-not

There are several plants known as "touch-me-nots," so called because their ripe pods burst open and scatter seeds when touched. The name comes from John 20:17, when the resurrected Jesus says to Mary Magdalene, "Touch me not, for I have not yet ascended to the Father."

the voice of the turtle

We know whales can sing, but turtles? No, but turtle-doves do, and when the King James Version has "turtle," it usually means "turtle-doves." Hence the famous verse from Old Testament doesn't sound so silly: "The time of the singing of birds is come, and the voice of the turtle is heard in our land" (Song of Solomon 2:12).

weaker vessel

This phrase has been applied to women—many of whom did not like it. The phrase comes from 1 Peter 3, where the apostle gives this command to Christian husbands: "live with your wives in an understanding way, showing honor to the woman as the weaker vessel."

what God hath joined together

The old marriage rituals are still taking place, some using familiar words that go back to Jesus himself: "What therefore God hath joined together, let not man put asunder" (Mark 10:9). Jesus was expressing his belief that marriage should be permanent, and a zillion ministers performing the marriage service have spoken them optimistically.

when kings go out to battle

This phrase used to occur fairly often in English and American literature, referring to the spring season of the year. For soldiers, winter was a time for settling into camp, waiting for sunnier and warmer weather before going out to do battle. "It came to pass in the spring of the year, at the time when kings go out to battle" (2 Samuel 11:1).

the whole megillah

The Hebrew word *megillah* meant simply "scroll," which is what all the books of the Bible were written on. The modern expression "the whole megillah" meant you told an entire scroll—that is, a long, long story with all the details included.

wine bottles

In times past, extremely large wine containers bore the names of Old Testament characters—Jeroboam, Rehoboam, Methuselah, and Nebuchadnezzar. Who knows why? A jeroboam was, by the way, about 3.08 liters, a rehoboam 4.5 liters, a methuselah 6.15 liters, and the largest of all, the nebuchadnezzar 15 liters. Being ruler of the largest territory (Babylonia), the nebuchadnezzar had to be the largest.

In England, a jeroboam was the name for another kind of container altogether: a chamber pot.

wings of the wind

In the Bible, it is God himself who rides on the wings of the wind: "And he rode upon a cherub, and did fly: yea, he did fly upon the wings of the wind" (Psalm 18:10). "Who layeth the beams of his chambers in the waters: who maketh the clouds his chariot: who walketh upon the wings of the wind" (Psalm 104:3).

wit's end

Ever felt you were at your wit's end? The phrase is found in Psalm 107:27: "They reel to and fro, and stagger like a drunken man, and are at their wits' end."

Woe is me!

This familiar expression of despair comes from the vision of the prophet Isaiah, who was awestruck at encountering God in the temple: "'Woe is me, for I am undone! Because I am a man of unclean lips, and I dwell in the midst of a people of unclean lips, and my eyes have seen the King, the Lord of hosts'" (Isaiah 6:5). The prophets Jeremiah and Micah also used the phrase.

wolves in sheep's clothing

Jesus was the source of this phrase. "Beware of false prophets, who come to you in sheep's clothing, but inwardly they are ravenous wolves" (Matthew 7:15). He referred to religious teachers who appear good on the surface but are hypocrites.

Index of Illustrations